CIRCE

Acknowledgments

MY FIRST and greatest debt is to Lady Mairi Bury, the daughter of Lord and Lady Londonderry, who not only gave me access to the private letters between her parents, allowing me to use any that I chose in this book, but who gave unstintingly of her time and her memories without once seeking to influence in any way what I wrote. Her generous help made this book possible. I am also indebted to Lady Annabel Goldsmith, Lady Rayne, Mrs John Dugdale, D.C.V.O. and the late Mr Michael Stanley, grandchildren of Lord and Lady Londonderry, for their help and encouragement.

Most of the information in this book has come either from the Londonderry papers, or from personal interviews with those who knew Edith Londonderry well. Among those who were kind enough to talk or write to me, to answer my questions and look out letters and photographs, I would particularly like to thank Miss Barbara Cartland, Miss Lydia de Burgh, Lady Elliot of Harwood, the Hon. Lady Fairfax-Lucy, Miss Helen Hoare, Mr Neil Hughes-Onslow, Mrs Montgomery Hyde, Mr Robert Rhodes James, the late Lord Jessel, Mr H. J. (Jim) Joel, Mrs James Lees-Milne, the Earl and Countess of Longford, Mrs Gilbert McNeill-Moss, Lord Plunket, the Princess of Pless, Lady Elizabeth Scott, the Hon. Mrs Dennis Smyth, the Countess of Sutherland, Peggy Lady Wakehurst, Mrs Diana Barnato Walker, the Hon. Helen Ward and Mr Michael Ward Thomas.

I am enormously grateful to Mrs Sheila Lochhead for allowing me to use so many of the enchanting letters from her father Ramsay MacDonald to Lady Londonderry, and for her recollections of him.

My thanks are due to Lord Baldwin of Bewdley for permission to publish the letters from his grandparents, to the Hertfordshire Record Office and the executors of Lady Ravensdale for permission to publish letters from Lady Desborough to Lord Londonderry, to Lord Salisbury for permission to publish letters from his great-uncle Lord Quickswood, to Mrs Goldie and Mrs Barge for their permission to use the letter from Viscount Horne of Slamannan and to the Marquess of Londonderry for allowing me to use a long letter from Goering in his possession and to the Sutherland Trust for the photograph of Dunrobin facing page 168.

I must also thank the staff of the Public Records Office of Northern Ireland, which holds the bulk of the Londonderry papers, for their courtesy and helpfulness, and to its Director, Dr Anthony Malcolmson, for his knowledgeable assistance and interest. I am also indebted to Mrs Sue Flood, Senior Archivist of the Hertfordshire Record Office, which holds the Desborough correspondence, for her help and good nature in response to my many queries; and to the staff of the London Library for their customary helpfulness.

Other Londonderry papers are in the Durham County Council archives. Lady Londonderry's letters to Ramsay MacDonald can be found in the Public Records Office at Kew, which also holds his diaries and which states that any publication of their contents must be accompanied by the words 'these diaries are meant as notes to guide and revive memory as regards happenings; and must on no account be published as they are'.

To
ROBERT

EDITH CHAPLIN always thought of herself as a child of the Highlands. She belonged, she felt, to the wildness and beauty of these remote and empty hills, their legends, songs and customs, to these people in whom a streak of Celtic mysticism coexisted alongside a hard-headed practicality. For almost twenty years after her marriage, she continued to think of Dunrobin Castle, where she had spent most of her childhood, as home. It was only when she began to live at Mount Stewart, the Londonderry estate in County Down inherited by her husband when he succeeded to the marquessate, a place similarly touched by the imagery of past heroes, battles and Celtic lore, that her emotional centre of gravity shifted.

On her mother's side, Edith's ancestry was romantic enough to cause any small girl to identify with it. Her mother, Lady Florence Leveson-Gower, who died when Edith was only four years old, was a daughter of the third Duke of Sutherland, the largest landowner in Britain with estates in five counties that totalled almost 1,400,000 acres. Two of the biggest were in Shropshire and Staffordshire, but for sheer size they paled into insignificance beside his estate in Scotland: well over a million acres in the county of Sutherland (with a further 150,000 in Ross). His seat was Dunrobin Castle, perched above the sea on the remote and beautiful east coast. Gazing out of even its topmost window, Lady Florence, like some medieval Northern princess, knew that everything she could see belonged to her father. In the people around, the clan tradition that combined pride and independence with a feudal sense of hierarchy still survived, despite the savage clearances of the second Duke.

Though both were from the landowning classes, Edith's parents could hardly have been more dissimilar in background and tradition. Henry Chaplin, though his mother was a Scot, was the archetypal English foxhunting squire, robust, Tory, God-fearing, happiest out of doors and in the saddle – indeed, for most of his long life he was known as 'Squire' Chaplin. Born on 22 December 1840, he was the eldest of the five children of the Reverend Henry Chaplin, whose family had been Lincolnshire squires since 1658; his passion was sport and, in particular, foxhunting, which he regarded as pleasure, science, art and way of life rolled into one.

When Edith's father was young he hunted six days a week and would often ride one of his thoroughbred hacks forty miles to dinner and a ball after such a day. Nothing, from social life and short sight to increasing weight, straitened means and ministerial duties, was allowed to come between him and the sport he loved. As his girth increased, so did the size of his horses (mostly bought in Ireland to ensure good bone), and he would thunder down to the stiffest fences on one of these great 17-hand hunters. As a government minister, a special train would take him to where his stud groom and horses waited near the meet. No man was a better judge of a horse or hound and to the end of his life he would go anywhere in the country to look at a promising horse. He talked, wrote and thought horses constantly, doodling them on his order papers when an MP and, when he became a minister, leaving little sketches of them on the Cabinet table. Though an absentee father, he was a tender and affectionate one.

Edith was in many ways extremely like him. They shared the same vigour, high spirits and sheer *joie de vivre*, the same love of the outdoors, the same openness, generosity and magnanimity of spirit that not only forgave but was ready to admit fault. Both felt that money was their servant, but while Edith's tendency to extravagance was curbed by her anxiety not to displease the husband she adored and found its outlet largely in the giving of presents, Henry ran through three fortunes. 'All my life I have lived according to a very simple plan,' he once remarked. 'It is always to have what I like, when I like it, and as much of it as I like.' It was a philosophy he followed faithfully.

Perhaps the chief point Edith and her father had in common was the possession of a charismatic personality – what would later have been called 'star quality'. Both exuded an aura of splendour, a magnificence (at Oxford, Henry's nickname was Magnifico), a feeling that life was to be enjoyed, an allure that appealed to men and women alike, attracting, warming, even mesmerising. Henry's presence and manner made him as popular in drawing rooms as in the hunting field; when Edith came into a room, said one contemporary, you were instantly aware that here was *someone.*

Chaplin was but one of many Tory landlords who combined foxhunting with political duties. Yet by the time he married Lady Florence in 1876, he was a nationally known figure. His story was a romantic one, containing all the elements of drama designed to appeal to the Victorian imagination: youth, beauty, love, a scandal that flew straight across the rigid moral and sexual codes of the day, betrayal, aristocratic misbehaviour, a magnificent sporting victory and a morally satisfactory ending. If only for its effect on the youthful Edith, as she gradually learned the details of her father's past, it deserves to be told.

As a young man, Chaplin was tall, broad-shouldered and handsome, energetic and healthy from the hours he spent in the fresh air every day, with bright chestnut hair, a clear complexion and a firm jaw. His immaculate clothes were remarked upon in an age when dressing well was almost a profession, and he possessed a charming old-fashioned courtesy – when he encountered the Prince of Wales in the hunting field he would sweep his cap off until it touched his horse's flank, and in drawing rooms he would bow low over the hands of his hostesses. He liked only the best, in horses, hounds, food and wine, and admired only the most beautiful women.

At nineteen, by now an orphan and in his second term at Christ Church, he inherited the estates of his uncle Sir Charles Chaplin, Squire of Blankney. As well as Blankney, Tathwell and Metheringham, Temple Brewer and Little Caythorpe, he came into land in Hallington, Hougham, Maltby, Raithby and Scopwick – all in Lincolnshire, and covering about 23,000 acres altogether. Smaller acreages in Nottinghamshire and Yorkshire were soon sold.

Although he did not come into the rents from these until his majority, Henry Chaplin instantly began to live in the grand manner. At Oxford, he entertained, raced and hunted. He was also allowed to meet the Prince of Wales, almost exactly his own age but then diffident and subdued from his repressive upbringing, whom he befriended and dazzled. They formed a lifelong friendship. It was in Chaplin's company that the Prince saw his first fox killed, for hunting, as always, was Chaplin's priority: he kept four hunters in Oxford itself (a remarkable number even in those days) and had the use of eighteen others nearby. Finally the Dean, tired of castigating him for appearing in chapel with his hunting kit imperfectly hidden under his surplice, wrote to him: 'My dear Mr Chaplin, As far as I can gather you seem to regard Christ Church as a hunting box...'

Not surprisingly, Chaplin went down soon afterwards and settled in earnest to the business of enjoying life. By the time he was twenty-three he had bought the Burton country from Lord Henry Bentinck and added it to the Blankney, hunting that enormous country six days a week with four packs of hounds, two of which he hunted himself. He drove his four-in-hand to the races, stalked in Scotland in September and entertained constantly and generously. He was a popular and generous landlord, dropping rents when times were hard, and in return expecting only good galloping and clean fences. One day when hounds were held up by wire edging a drive, he was furious to discover that the house had actually been built as a hunting box, and exclaimed: 'There should be no wire anywhere about a hunting box, except on the champagne bottles – and that should be ready to come off at a moment's notice!'

When he came to London for the Season of 1863, he quickly became aware of one of that year's debutantes. This was Lady Florence Paget, youngest daughter of the second Marquess of Anglesey (she was the sixth child of the Marquess's second wife), acclaimed by common consent as the most beautiful debutante for many years. The moment she appeared she caused a sensation; even the Queen, to whom she was presented at St James's Palace, had remarked on her grace and carriage. The exquisiteness of her face and perfection of her tiny figure – she was as petite as she was beautiful – quickly ensured that she was known as The Pocket Venus. Almost at once she became, in the words of *Queen* magazine, 'the rage of the Park, the ballroom, the opera and the croquet lawn'.

She was much more than lovely, though. Warm, friendly and sympathetic – her 'dove-like eyes' were particularly admired – she was also excellent company. Although not rich, she had an unassailable position at the heart of aristocratic society. She was the granddaughter of 'Old One-Leg', Wellington's cavalry commander who as Earl of Uxbridge had had his right knee shattered in the Battle of Waterloo, undergone an amputation, and been created Marquess of Anglesey by the Prince Regent five days after the battle. All in all, she was one of the most desirable matches in the country; from Chaplin's point of view, everything about her, from her breeding to her finished perfection of appearance and manner, could have been designed to attract him.

It was soon clear that two of her admirers had drawn ahead of the field. One was Chaplin, the other a mutual friend, the Marquis of Hastings.

Harry Hastings, the fourth and last Marquis of Hastings, was a little younger than Chaplin (he was born in 1842) and a very different type.

Slim, dark and sensitive-looking – one contemporary description gives him 'the sad brown eyes of a spaniel' – with slender white hands, small feet and exquisite clothes, he had a slight air of foppishness. He had had a chaotic childhood, a broken education, and by the age of sixteen was an orphan. Insecure, pleasure-loving, emotionally deprived and weak-willed, he longed to be liked, and adored the flattery that seemed to promise this. His charm and gaiety, coupled with an underlying wistful-ness of manner, gave him a little-boy appeal which his moods of petu-lance enhanced rather than destroyed.

He and Chaplin had met at Christ Church (Hastings had been, briefly, at Eton; Chaplin at Harrow), where Hastings quickly became an invet-erate gambler, betting, as far as the racecourse was concerned, in huge sums and quite often apparently on anything that moved. When he won, he spent his winnings lavishly on the crowd of hangers-on that by now usually accompanied him. For where Chaplin, with his strong religious and High Tory background and close friendship with the Prince of Wales, was discreet in his choice of friends, Hastings was happy to entertain, or be entertained by, virtually anyone offering the adulatory companionship he craved. With his interest in gambling and low life, much of his time was spent at Limmers, a hotel in Conduit Street frequented by the racing fraternity (here, after a night on the town, his favourite breakfast was mackerel fried in gin, caviar on devilled toast, and an hors d'oeuvre called Fixed Bayonets, all washed down with claret cup). All in all, he was as different from the solid, equable, confident Chaplin as could be imagined.

Although Hastings was already a heavy drinker by the time he met Lady Florence, this had not yet affected his looks; and of the darker side of his life – the moneylenders, the disreputable racecourse associates, the rowdy and dissolute parties at dubious hotels like Long's or the Blue Post – she knew nothing.

Florence was clearly torn. From the point of view of a Victorian mamma, Chaplin, rich, generous, even-tempered, good-natured and chivalrously protective, was the better match; whereas stories of Hast-ings's wildness, gambling and bad behaviour were already circulating.

But Florence had not got a mother (hers had died when she was only two). Brought up by a father who adored her and older brothers who spoilt their enchanting small sister, she had grown up accustomed to masculine worship, to having her own way and to twisting men around her little finger. Besides, to any girl of spirit, confined in the iron corset of demure, missish behaviour deemed suitable for the Victorian young lady, Hastings's carefree recklessness, his aristocratic disregard for accepted standards and his unmistakable partiality for herself alone must have made him dangerously attractive. In addition, Chaplin still had not come up to scratch; by the end of 1863, at just twenty-three and still enjoying life as a bachelor, he went off big-game hunting in India and appeared to leave the field to Hastings.

But in May 1864 Chaplin returned to London again and quickly made up lost ground. By the end of the month, Lady Florence was watching the Derby with him from the royal box, at the invitation of his friend the Prince of Wales. Few girls would have asked for more. Lord Hastings rallied strongly, naming one of his fillies after her; it was to make its debut at Ascot that year – would she go with him? Yes, she would. Chaplin, cross and surprised that she preferred this to going in the royal party with him, was stung into the realisation that conclusive action was needed. A fortnight later, at a ball given by the Marquess and Marchioness of Abercorn for the Prince and Princess of Wales, he asked her to marry him. She accepted at once and the news was announced in *The Times* and *Morning Post* the next day, to a chorus of congratulations led by the Prince. The wedding was planned for August, two months ahead, and invitations were sent out straightaway.

Chaplin escorted his fiancée to balls and parties, to race meetings and out driving in his cabriolet along the Ladies' Mile from Apsley House to Kensington, a 'tiger', smart in his yellow and black striped waistcoat, standing up behind. Hastings, who had plunged back into even heavier gambling and into his old East End haunts, had been one of the first to congratulate them. His lost, pathetic air had its effect: Chaplin, a man to whom any idea of suspecting dishonourable conduct was foreign, several times asked him to join them at the opera, theatre, or private parties. He may even have thought that Hastings's youth – he was still only twenty-one – did not make him a serious contender for Florence's hand; after all, his rival had not taken the chance offered by his own eight-month absence.

One Friday evening in July, just after they had returned from a visit to Blankney where Florence had seen various improvements she had requested, all three went to Covent Garden, where Adelina Patti was appearing for the last time that season, in *Faust*. Chaplin had suggested to Florence that Hastings might like to join them. Hastings, moody and preoccupied, sat on the other side of an equally silent Florence.

The next morning, Saturday 16 July, Florence's wedding dress was delivered. She tried it on, calling her father to admire, then set off alone in his brougham at 10.00, giving the excuse for this unusual solitary expedition that she needed to do some last-minute shopping for her trousseau.

Arriving at Marshall and Snelgrove in Oxford Street, Florence entered by the side door and was met inside by either Hastings, his sister or his closest friend Freddy Granville (contemporary accounts differ). After a few words, the two of them left through the rear entrance of the store, beside which a closed cab was waiting. They were driven the short distance down Bond Street to St George's Church in Hanover Square, where a parson stood ready. By 12.00 Florence was married to Harry Hastings.

Immediately afterwards, at Captain Granville's lodgings in St James's Place, she sat down to write a long letter to Henry Chaplin; before the ink was dry, she and her bridegroom left for King's Cross where a special train had been ordered for them. At Loughborough, his four-horse travelling carriage waited to take them to his seat. Florence's own family coachman waited outside Marshall and Snelgrove for six hours before returning home.

It would be difficult to overestimate the size of the shock wave that ran through Victorian society. Lady Florence was castigated, publicly for her unkind and immoral behaviour, privately for her stupidity in picking the wrong man. Hastings was universally condemned as a cad. Henry Chaplin, shattered not only by the loss of his bride-to-be but by the dishonourable behaviour of the man he thought was a friend, turned for consolation to the sporting activities he loved, throwing himself into stalking, shooting and sporting tours. His friends rallied round; his sporting mentor and close friend Lord Henry Bentinck wrote: 'all your *friends*, and you have many ... look upon what has happened as a blessed deliverance'.

By the time Chaplin returned to London months of fresh air, strenuous exercise and semi-solitude, with only the laconic companionship of stalker, ghillie or sporting companion, had enabled him to conquer his distress and overcome any feelings of humiliation at such a public jilting. More to the point, he was no longer in love.

Florence Hastings had soon realised her mistake. She sent Chaplin pathetic little notes on the miniature writing paper with its blue or pink border and its disproportionately large monogram which was the fashion in the 1860s, folded into two-inch envelopes too small for the post. 'You don't know how awfully happy you have made me by speaking to me today,' ran the first. 'It was so good and kind of you and it is the first bit of sunshine I have had in my life for months.' Alas, to Chaplin the notes were so much paper. Though he remained fond of his former love, and frequently helped her with money, he had clearly put the whole episode, and his feelings, behind him. Indeed, much of the energy and passion he had formerly devoted to Florence and the plans for their life together was now focused on a new object: racing.

It was said of him in the year following Florence's elopement that he began 'to buy horses as though he were drunk and to back them as though he were mad'. Many people thought he wanted to revenge himself on Hastings, whose ambition was to win the Derby, but this was not so (for one thing, neither vengefulness nor malice were in his nature). Racing was simply a new distraction, another way of expressing his passion for horses. Fortunately, the miserable ending of his love affair did not affect his excellent judgement of these animals.

The feelings of the Marquis of Hastings for the man whose friendship he had betrayed had also undergone a change. The common human reaction of disliking, even fearing, those whom we have injured possessed him; with his tendency to extremes, he saw Chaplin as a rival still. Uneasily conscious that Chaplin was the better man and stood higher in public regard, Hastings longed not only to emulate but to surpass him. He accepted the mastership of the Quorn but hunted them so lazily and sloppily, sometimes only getting out of bed when hounds had already arrived at a meet ten miles away, that many of the field laughed at him; now, in this latest sport, he was equally determined to outdo Chaplin. His feelings were given a sharper edge when his great friend Captain Machell 'defected' – as Hastings saw it – to join Chaplin as trainer.

From then on, Hastings began to lay bets against Chaplin's horses whenever possible, often losing vast sums. By now, drink and the general dissipation of his life were taking their toll of his health just as his uncontrolled gambling was depleting his fortune.

On 17 June 1865, Hastings and Chaplin both went to the famous Middle Park Stud at Eltham, where an annual yearling sale was held on the last day of the Ascot meeting. It was a fashionable and crowded event, where the best of the future crop of racehorses was paraded before wealthy and knowledgeable judges of horseflesh. Here Chaplin, accompanied by his trainer, began to bid for Lot 27, a handsome dark chestnut with a white blaze on his forehead. The colt, notable for his placid temperament and his small size – he stood fractionally over 15.2 hands – was by Newminster out of Seclusion. Hastings, of course, instantly began to bid against Chaplin, running the price up until he finally left the colt to Chaplin at 1,000 guineas. On the way back in the coach, Chaplin and his party discussed what to call his new purchase. The name decided on was Hermit.

It was quickly evident that Hermit was worth every penny of his enormous price. His ability was apparent even as a yearling when, giving 35 lb, he beat a promising filly over four furlongs. And when Vauban and Marksman, the horses he had beaten as a two-year-old in 1866, came in first and third respectively in the Two Thousand Guineas the following year, Chaplin and his trainer Captain Machell knew they had a potential Derby winner.

For Chaplin, this meant more than glory: by now he was seriously embarrassed financially and, if Hermit won, the horse's stud fees would help to underwrite Chaplin's lavish way of life for another fifteen or twenty years. Hastings, mad with jealousy and by now almost destroyed financially, bet against Hermit wherever he could, and stood to lose £120,000 if Hermit won. Of this, £20,000 was a bet with Chaplin himself.

On Monday 13 May 1867, nine days before the Derby, when Hermit's jockey Custance was riding him during a serious pre-Derby trial, the horse suddenly gave a great cough, blood poured from his nostrils and he almost fell. After such a haemorrhage, scratching seemed the only option and Custance, then the top Derby jockey, was released to ride another mount. With the race only nine days away, all seemed lost.

But Machell had discovered that the bleeding, though severe, came from a broken vein in the horse's nose and not, as at first had been thought and feared, from his lungs. He went on working Hermit quietly, and always downhill. He took him to Epsom early, and on the Saturday before the Derby gave him six one-mile canters (if this had happened at Newmarket, word would have flashed round the racing world). He reported to Chaplin, who had also suffered injury – he was on crutches after a bad fall that had torn the cartilages of both knees – that he thought the horse had a chance.

Derby Day dawned icy cold. Earlier dry weather had produced hard going. Flurries of snow fell at intervals – once while the horses were walking round the paddock before the big race. All of them looked miserable and tucked up and Hermit, who even on a good day appeared listless at a slow pace, looked particularly wretched. To hide from the Ring that he might still be a prospect, and to prevent the odds against him shortening, he was walked round without a rug, his coat staring from the cold and his tail clenched down between his hind legs. It was only twenty minutes before the race that a jockey was found for him, a tall boy of twenty called Johnny Daley, only available because of his lack

9

of experience. Hermit's starting price was 1,000/15, and there were no takers. It appeared hardly worth running him.

But Chaplin knew better. Hermit had had a gallop over the Derby course the day before and his head groom Bloss, who looked after Hermit and had slept in his box every night for three months before the race, told him: 'He never went better in his life, Sir, and squandered them all as usual. He wouldn't have blown out a candle at the finish and what's more, I think he is certain to win the Derby after all.' Years afterwards, Chaplin wrote that he had told his friends 'that if, when they came into sight again at the top of the hill, Hermit was in the first three, where I had instructed my jockey to be, I thought he would certainly win. No one of course believed this, and they thought me a fool.' When he ran into Hastings on his way to the Stands, Chaplin warned him: 'I think Hermit still has a chance, Harry. You can easily cover your bet with me by taking the odds which they are offering now.' He himself waited until the horses were going down to the start then called the man he employed to place bets and instructed him to take all the long odds he could get.

It was in this atmosphere of tension that the race began. The snow cleared, Florence Hastings, pale-faced and listless in the furs that wrapped her against the chill, watched the horses of her husband and her former love go down to the post. There were eight false starts, and when the off finally took place the favourite, Vauban, leapt into the lead. But as they came round Tattenham Corner on concrete-hard ground there was Hermit going like an express train. In the final furlong he passed the favourite as if the latter were standing still, to beat Marksman by a head (Vauban was a bad third). Hastings, to his credit, was among the first to congratulate Chaplin, coming forward as Hermit was unsaddled and saying, 'A great horse. A truly great horse,' as he patted him.

Chaplin's triumph, like his popularity in the eyes of the general public, was complete. At twenty-six he owned a Derby winner, was fêted by the Prince of Wales and had somewhat avenged his jilting by this splendid victory. He had both behaved well and been seen to behave well. He compounded his triumph with magnanimity, sending word to Hastings to pay the £20,000 debt whenever he could manage this, instead of on the Monday after the race, as was then obligatory. Hastings replied, in a letter pathetic in its writer's consciousness of his humiliation: 'I can't tell you how much obliged I am for your kindness to me ... you may depend upon my *doing my utmost* to pay you as soon as possible, though you know as well as I do that however well off a man may be, to get

£120,000 in 24 hours is rather a hard job. I am just off to Paris, as I am sick of being pointed at as the man who has lost such a sum.'

But Hermit's Derby had finally swept Hastings over the brink. He had to sell his racehorses and give up the Quorn; and he sold his Scottish estates to the Marquis of Bute for £300,000. Even these drastic measures were not sufficient to clear the debts that had been mounting for years. By now, his system so abused that he had become a frail old man at the age of twenty-five, he had to be wheeled on to Newmarket Heath in a basket chair; the following year saw him almost completely in the hands of the moneylenders and booed at Ascot. He died that autumn and his last words were : 'Hermit's Derby broke my heart. But I did not show it, did I?'

After the race, Lady Hastings had also received a reassuring note from Chaplin. She replied to him, with a letter that could have come straight out of a Victorian morality tale. 'I could not help crying over your letter, tears of joy at first at the kindness of its tone, and then bitter, bitter tears of remorse at the thought of all I had caused you to suffer, and of the happiness that I know now was once so nearly in my grasp, and which I so recklessly threw away for a mere shadow. If what I am suffering now is a punishment for the way I treated you, it is indeed a hard one, and I feel at times it is more than I can bear. You don't know, you have no idea how miserable my life is, and for the future it will be nothing but one long regret.' In the event, within two years of her husband's death in 1868, she married another racing friend, Sir George Chetwynd.

Punch summed up popular feeling with the comment: 'Who after this year's Derby will dare to say racing is a sinful amusement? Think of the money carried off from a Rake by a Hermit for the benefit of a Chaplin!'

As for Hermit, like an actor who has heard applause for the first time, his Derby victory gave him a taste of the pleasures of popularity, and thenceforth he would always play up to an audience. If a visitor came to admire him while he was being exercised on the long rein, he would start to show off, standing up on his hind legs and prancing about, though his temperament remained as sweet as ever. 'He was always a dandy, vain as a peacock and every inch a gentleman,' said Edith later. When he died, on 29 April 1890, everyone at Blankney spoke as if the King had died. Blotting books and notecases, revered by the family as relics, were made from his glossy chestnut coat and one hoof was made into an inkpot, which Chaplin presented to the Prince of Wales. His skeleton was given to the Museum of the Royal College of Veterinary Surgeons, where it is still preserved.

II

WITHIN FIVE years of inheriting his uncle's estates and their
rent roll of over £30,000 a year, Henry Chaplin had mortgaged much of his land to secure loans of £95,000. His income
was, of course, augmented by the earnings of Hermit, who proved such
a successful sire that his initial stud fee of twenty guineas quickly rose
to 300, with the occasional nomination at 500 guineas. Hermit was Cham-
pion Sire for six successive seasons, between 1873 and 1897 his pro-
geny, including two Derby and two Oaks winners, won 846 races, worth
in all over £356,000.

Despite the extent of his borrowings, Chaplin continued to shoot, to
fish, to stalk, to race, to entertain his friends as generously as before,
disregarding endless warnings from his stewards. In 1868 he was returned
as Conservative Member of Parliament for Mid-Lincolnshire (later
known as the Sleaford Division), which increased his expenses – in those
days, MPs received no salary. When there was a series of bad harvests
in the 1870s, he reduced his tenants' rents. The profits from his wheat-
growing acres were further eroded by the cheap imported wheat now
flooding into the country. By 1874 his Lincolnshire estates were also
mortgaged, to the Marquess Conyngham and John Panbelow Haywood.

None of this did he allow to distress him, and the life of sport and
society continued unabated – though with one major change. He had
fallen in love with the woman who was to become his wife. Ironically,
her name too was Florence.

Lady Florence Leveson-Gower was the eldest daughter of the third
Duke of Sutherland and the sister of one of Chaplin's greatest friends,
the Duke's heir the Marquis of Stafford, always known as 'Strath' (one
of the family titles was Baron Strathnaver). Her mother, Duchess Anne
(née Mackenzie), was for many years Mistress of the Robes to Queen

Victoria, who created her Countess of Cromartie in her own right. Lady Florence was young and pretty, with blue eyes, golden hair and a superb complexion. She was also lively, intelligent, and – virtually a *sine qua non* for anyone contemplating marriage with Chaplin – loved riding, hunting and sport of all kinds.

Both of them wanted to keep their engagement to themselves for a while. Lady Florence did not want to announce it until after their friends had left London, which meant waiting until August; Chaplin, no doubt with memories of the earlier Lady Florence, concurred. But most of their circle knew something was in the wind and the Prince of Wales, always interested in the amorous affairs of his friends, tried unavailingly to extract their secret by volunteering to pay Chaplin a visit at Blankney – a signal honour – whenever he was married, 'which you know, my dear Harry, may happen to all of us sooner than we may expect!' On the 2nd of August, the Prince was able to write and congratulate his friend.

A week or two after their engagement, Chaplin had to tear himself away from his fiancée to take the cure at Homburg because his weight, always a problem, was increasing so fast (seven years later he was riding at eighteen stone). But to remind himself of Florence, he took her little dog Dot with him to Germany, as well as his own, Vic. Once back, he flung himself into plans for their marriage and sporting life together. The fact that he was by now mortgaged to the hilt, with annual interest charges of £11,425, did not deter him from dallying with buying or leasing the 40,000-acre deer forest of Coignafearn, in Inverness-shire. 'I have ordered you a little rifle, and I am going to have a spy-glass, a proper one, made for you as well, and I am going to teach you to shoot myself when I get to Dunrobin,' he wrote fondly to Lady Florence during their engagement, adding, 'I won't insist on your killing a beast – I think perhaps your heart is too tender for that – but you may kill a target as often as you please.'

He was particularly anxious to use his excellent eye for a horse in the pleasant task of buying a hunter or two for Lady Florence and spent some time trying to coax her to tell him what she weighed. Finally she admitted to ten stone. 'I thought it would have been 11 at the least,' he wrote back a trifle tactlessly. Armed with this knowledge he set off in pursuit of suitable animals, frequently staying with friends for a day's hunting so that he could see how a proposed purchase behaved in the hunting field.

One such visit was to Compton Verney, for a day with the Warwick-shire. 'The first time I saw him was when he came . . . to look at one of my father's horses called the Drone, that he thought likely to suit Lady Florence,' wrote Lord Willoughby de Broke. 'He was then in the very prime of life, and when he came down to breakfast in his red coat – as men did in those days – tall, fair, well-proportioned, the picture of health, he was indeed a handsome specimen of the Anglo-Saxon race.'

Chaplin and Lady Florence were married on 15 November 1876, at Trentham, in Staffordshire, one of the Sutherland houses. The hunters Chaplin had bought for Lady Florence were a great success and, extremely proud of his young bride, he basked in the delight of watching her go splendidly across his home country, in front of his friends. 'Everyone talks of your riding and performances out hunting in Lincolnshire.'

For both of them it was an idyllic marriage. For Chaplin, it was everything he had dreamed of after the souring débâcle nine years before. He adored his lively, happy young bride, treating her with the loving indulgence that characterised his relations with the women and children close to him ('There, darling ... admit that this neglected, stupid old frump sometimes does manage to arrange what his pretty, wilful, naughty, silly young child of a wife wants!').

For Lady Florence, the closeness between her husband and her brother meant that much of her time was spent in or near her beloved Dunrobin. Shortly after their marriage Chaplin had leased the shooting of Ben Hope, near Tongue, with his brother-in-law. The eldest Chaplin child, a son, Eric, was born in 1877. A little over a year later, on 3 December 1878, at Blankney, Florence gave birth to a daughter. The new baby was christened Edith Helen.

By 1880, Chaplin had the stalking over about 70,000 acres of Sutherland. It included Ben Armine (about twenty miles from Dunrobin), Loch Choire and Corrie-na-Fhearn, a further ten miles away. He also had a nineteen-year lease of Cleithbrie. The second Duke's wholesale Clearance policies had made the country emptier than ever and there was not even a bridle path within four miles of Loch Choire, where the only habitation was a shepherd's cottage. Here Chaplin intended to build a lodge; before doing so, he planned a smaller, rougher house from which to oversee the project and which could later be used by ghillies or servants. All the materials of which it was made – chiefly corrugated iron and wood – had to be brought first from Lairg station twenty-one miles along the road to Allt-na-Harra, then carried the twelve-mile journey across the shoulder of the mountain on ponies; to facilitate this, and for later use by the shooting parties, bridle paths were made from Ben Armine to Loch Choire and round the shores of the Loch.

In the General Election of 1880 the Conservatives were defeated but 'the Squire' was again returned unopposed as Member for Mid-Lincolnshire. That year there was another bad, wet harvest, and further rent reductions by the generous landlord, but the sporting round continued unabated, with its annual visit to Dunrobin. The children and Florence would spend two or three months there; Chaplin would pay a shorter visit because he insisted on first attending the St Leger meeting at Doncaster in early September and then, after a few concentrated weeks' stalking, going south for the cub-hunting at Blankney and the autumn meetings at Newmarket.

When Chaplin joined his family at Dunrobin in September 1881, Florence was over eight months pregnant with their third child. As usual, he was anxious for all the exercise he could get to counter his swelling girth, and soon set off for Ben Armine with his brother-in-law Strath. So much did he and his wife hate being separated during these few weeks at the Castle that she drove up behind her favourite pony, Dumps, to join her husband and brother at Sieber's Cross, a house halfway between Dunrobin and Ben Armine, arriving late in the afternoon. Their surprise was complete. As Chaplin wrote afterwards: 'We first heard the bells which Dumps wore on her collar, and then to our amazement she came full trot up the hill with Dumps and drove up to the door with her little face all wet from rain and bright as a little sunbeam. We passed a happy evening, we three together.'

After Florence returned to Dunrobin she developed a pain in her leg which she and everyone else believed was a strained sinew, possibly from her long drive, a diagnosis seemingly confirmed by the fact that the pain was better the following day, a Monday. But by Wednesday it had come back again; Chaplin, unaware of her mysterious ailment, was writing to her that although he had not got a stag he had lost half a stone. 'To my horror yesterday evening after Sieber's Cross I was back at 16.7; yesterday evening 16.4; tonight, with luck, I hope at least 16.3 will be reached.'

Lady Florence's condition worsened rapidly. She saw her doctor, who considered it so serious that on Thursday, a mere four days after their happy evening together, a note was dispatched to her husband at Ben Armine begging him to come back to Dunrobin immediately. But Chaplin was on the hill and did not get back to the lodge until dusk was falling. Travelling across twenty miles of pathless moorland in the dark was impossible; instead he sat down and wrote her a letter to be taken by a boy on a pony at first light. 'I wish I were with you now, for where ought I to be but by your side to comfort and cheer you, and please God, before many hours I will be . . . I hope and pray earnestly, my little one, you will be better when I see you.'

When he arrived some hours later, she seemed better, but Chaplin, worried, took her south to Blankney straightaway. Here, on the Saturday, her second daughter, Florence, was born. The birth was followed by convulsions from which Lady Florence never recovered. By now, she was clearly dying: on Sunday evening her breathing became shallow and rapid, and on the afternoon of Monday 10 October, as her distraught husband later wrote: 'My darling passed away, with her head resting on my shoulder and with the most beautiful expression on her face as she died.' Only five years after his marriage, the Squire was a widower.

Unless he had married again (he never did), there was little question of Chaplin having full charge of his own children. There was simply no place for them in their father's life on a day-to-day basis.

Quite apart from his local and parliamentary duties – and he was a conscientious landlord and MP – there were his sporting and social commitments. For men of his class and kind, much of the year was devoted to the pursuit of the fox or the killing of various kinds of game, as much ironclad social rituals as they were sport, and with which nothing, from childbirth to Christmas, was allowed to interfere. For a dedicated sportsman such as Chaplin there was shooting – first grouse, then partridge and pheasant – stalking and hunting from August the 12th until the following April, to be followed shortly thereafter by the London Season.

Here, as an eligible widower, Chaplin was much in demand; among his particular friends were the Duchess of Manchester (later to be Duchess of Devonshire), Lady Lonsdale (later Lady de Grey and later still the Marchioness of Ripon) and the Marchioness of Londonderry, mother of his future son-in-law. His good-natured generosity made him a great favourite. He would lend his women friends his carriages if required and place bets on their behalf, often winning them quite large sums and chivalrously 'forgetting' to tell them about their losses.

The children, then, were brought up largely by their mother's family – though their father often had them to stay at Blankney, since learning to ride and hunt was an integral part of their education. Most of their early years were spent in the capacious nurseries of Dunrobin, supposedly the oldest inhabited house in Britain, perched on the topmost of a series of terraces rising from a seashore covered in bright golden seaweed, the grey wastes of the sea in front and the mountains behind.

Their grandfather, the third Duke, a magnate who owned four stately homes, half a dozen other smaller houses, two yachts and had built his own private railway (it remained in the family until nationalisation in 1950), had taken as his second Duchess a woman who poisoned her husband's mind against his family and who certainly would not have welcomed three small grandchildren. Thus when Strath married in 1883 much of the responsibility for Eric, Edith and Florence fell on his wife, Millicent – known to the children as Aunt Millie.

Millicent was the daughter of Lord and Lady Rosslyn, and the half-sister of Daisy Brooke (later Lady Warwick), Edward VII's mistress. She was original, clever and cultured, able to speak both French and German fluently. She could recite long passages of Goethe and Schiller and when she was only twelve translated one of Gladstone's Midlothian speeches into German for her German relations – her aunt had married the German Ambassador.

Strath fell in love with Millicent when she was fourteen. They had met when her mother and her older sister Blanche, a beauty being trotted out for the thirty-year-old heir's inspection, were asked to stay at Dunrobin. Millicent, then a plain girl with a snub nose and crinkly hair, had been brought along too. One evening she sat next to Strath at dinner and, trying to make conversation, asked him if the portrait opposite them was a Romney. 'A Romney?' said Strath, impressed. 'How did a little girl like you find that out? Who told you?' 'No one,' replied Millicent. 'I just knew.'

From that moment, Strath's interest was irrevocably captured. The following Christmas, during a walk round the lake at Trentham, he asked her if she would like to marry him when she grew up. Millicent, hair in a pigtail against the wind – at fifteen she was not yet old enough to put it up – replied composedly that she would. They were married on her seventeenth birthday, 20 October 1884. Though he took charge of the servants, the household accounts and the general business of living, his young wife found herself in the daunting position of proxy mother to three young children while still little more than a child herself.

During the winters they all came south to one of the Sutherland estates, usually Trentham, where the Duke owned 12,744 acres. The kennels of the North Staffordshire hunt were there. Both Millicent and Strath adored hunting. Strath had been Master of the North Stafford since 1874; Millicent, who had six hunters, rode every day before breakfast and took family prayers clad in her riding habit. She also held a Bible meeting every week for the colliers employed at the Florence, her father-in-law's coal mine at nearby Longton which had been named after Edith's mother.

In London, the family lived at Stafford House (now Lancaster House) in the Mall, between Buckingham Palace and Clarence House. Stafford House had been built by George IV's younger brother the Duke of York and taken on a 99-year lease from the Crown by the first Duke of Sutherland. Such was its grandeur that Queen Victoria said to the second Duchess, her favourite Mistress of the Robes: 'I am returning from your palace to my house,' and the Shah of Persia, entertained there when visiting England, suggested to the Queen that it was too good for a subject and that she should have the Duke beheaded.

The children saw little of this magnificence. They lived a nursery life under the aegis of Nanny Webster, a strict but loving Scotswoman. Later, when Eric went to school, the little girls had a governess, Miss Harvey, who quickly became beloved by her charges. For Edith, whose only memory of her young mother was of seeing her long golden hair being brushed by her maid when brought in to say good morning to her, Miss Harvey filled a quasi-maternal role. She also inculcated in her charge a profound religious faith, together with High Church principles of worship, that endured throughout Edith's life. It was reinforced by the example of Aunt Millie, with her prayers, Bible meetings, and interest in theology.

Her aunt's influence can similarly be detected in other aspects of Edith's personality. By the time Millicent became Duchess she had formulated many of the opinions and attitudes that made her one of the original Souls, that band of aristocrats linked by a friendship of which the distinguishing marks were intelligence, culture, wit and sensibility. Millicent believed in the need for more equality between the sexes, had become deeply involved in charities and the welfare of her husband's workers, read copiously, and had also begun to write – poetry, a novel (published the year of Edith's wedding), short stories on the theme of love and even a play in blank verse that was put on at the Scala theatre.

Like any intelligent, idealistic adolescent, exposed to the deeply felt beliefs and interests of the woman who was the nearest thing she had to a mother, Edith unconsciously absorbed many of her aunt's ideals and attitudes, though these were tempered in her case with the sense of humour and self-ridicule she had inherited from her father. And, in the scintillating receptions Millicent inaugurated at Stafford House when she became Duchess, Edith surely learned much of what later made her the most consummate political hostess of her day.

The children were, of course, often visited by their father, who was a tender and affectionate, though mostly absent, parent, writing them frequent loving letters that exhorted them to be good and to ride well. He wrote to them from Monte Carlo and the Turf Club, from Welbeck Abbey and Wynyard Park and the other grand houses round the country where his weekends and sporting commitments took him – visits that held unquestioned precedence over any special dates on which his family might have legitimately expected his presence. 'Darling little Edie,' begins a note from Halton, Tring, dated 24 December 1888, 'This is to wish you a very happy and a very merry Xmas as I can't be with you. . . .'

Though he was never able to give his children a home again, his love for them was so evident that they, in turn, adored him. He would read to them from his favourite *Jorrocks*, tears of laughter streaming down his face, and he understood completely their deep-rooted longing for the closeness of family life. 'My Darling Child, I got your letter and Miss Harvey's when I returned from abroad last Monday,' he wrote to the fourteen-year-old Edith from the Carlton Club. 'I quite understand, you little Dear, all that you and the others think and feel about *Home*. . . .' All of them longed for his visits and approval; Edith, in particular, was fiercely determined to make him proud of her.

'Darling Daddy,' runs one of her letters, 'I hope we shall see you soon. We went out hunting on Monday. We had a splendid run. I got the brush and Eric was blooded.' She went on to describe what must have been a terrifying incident. They had been set a race by a groom and she had pulled up halfway at a gate to speak to Eric. '. . . He rushed by on his pony. I was riding a pony that reared and it was startled because it heard Eric but did not see him. I could not stop it. It rushed towards a tree and then I was stunned, Marks said, because the pony reared up and fell over backwards, but you must not be frightened. I did not hurt myself. I only bruised my eye and my side is a little stiff. I send my best love and kisses to you, darling Daddy. Your loving little child, Edie.' In spite of the hair-raising contents of this missive, her darling Daddy did not hesitate to correct it ('There are three little mistakes in Edie's letter. I have marked them each with red ink so that you may see them').

As a child Edith was high-spirited, active and irrepressible. Neither the conventions of the day nor the starched white dresses she wore even in Sutherland had a restraining effect. She would escape from Nanny Webster early in the morning to slip out and march behind the two pipers outside the Castle, accompanying them with a comb covered by a bit of paper as they played.

She rode the estate's Highland ponies astride when no disapproving adult was looking on, something no 'nice-minded' girl would have considered doing as it was thought not only unfeminine but likely to bring about sterility. The 'boneshaker' bicycles that appeared when she was ten or eleven were said to have the same effect. This belief prevailed in some quarters until well into the next century. Years later, when Edith was a young married woman, the Kaiser, in London after Edward VII's coronation, came to tea with her parents-in-law, Lord and Lady Londonderry, at Londonderry House. Although Edith invariably hunted riding side-saddle in the conventional manner, it was known that she rode astride when possible – including those occasions when she played in mixed polo matches before breakfast with her husband and his brother officers in the Blues. When she was led forward to be presented to the Kaiser, he wasted no time on small talk. 'I hear you ride like a man. Very wrong, you know. You'll never have children if you continue to do so!' 'Your Majesty,' replied Edith politely, but gazing steadily back at him, 'I already have two children – both in excellent health!'

Sometimes, as a child, she would go further and ride not only astride but bareback, wild gallops across the hills that gave her a sense of balance and a strength in her muscles that never left her.

Her childhood was passed in an age of formality, when a rigid code of dress and behaviour was as important as inner grace – even for a child, even in the wilds of Scotland. Adults changed their clothes endlessly: there were clothes for the morning, for riding, for croquet or for tennis (long full skirts), for shooting, for tea and for dinner. The woman who went on a visit had to count on at least four changes of clothes a day, most with numerous buttons and hooks down the back so that a maid was essential.

For the child Edith, appropriate dress for breakfast, a formal affair with the grown-ups in the salon, was a stiff, starched full-skirted white dress. Out riding, not yet old enough for the long tight habit that women wore even for a casual hour's hacking, she wore a long, full, circular skirt over a long, full, white starched petticoat and white starched and frilled cambric drawers. Whether riding Highland ponies or accompanying the guns on the hill, there were no concessions to practicality in female attire. Though a few women, chiefly those in an unassailable social position, shot or stalked – an unfeminine activity much disapproved of in royal circles – they did not dare flout convention by appearing other than in the regulation long tweed skirt; and when one brave spirit decided that, when stalking, decency demanded breeches, she was careful to keep her skirt on over the top of these immodest garments.

Chaplin devoted much of the time spent with his children to their sporting education. At Dunrobin he would teach them the intricacies of stalking, taking the ten-year-old Eric up to the lodge at Ben Armine with him. They would while away the twelve-mile drive from Dunrobin to Sieber's Cross by playing beggar-my-neighbour on a tartan rug spread over their knees before transferring to ponies for the last part of the journey. The Squire's bulk was still a problem; once, when in order to get within shot they had to crawl into view as unobtrusively as possible, his stalker hissed: 'Keep doon, Squire, keep doon. Ye're so splendidly built about the haunches that I'm afraid the deer will be seeing you.' Eric, who spent a lot of time with his grandfather's piper, already talked the same broad Scots.

At Blankney, the children spent much of their time on horseback, even, occasionally, being put on the back of the great Hermit and allowed to ride him round his box. Edith, at ten, used to drive a pair of Fetlar ponies in double harness. One was a beautiful little stallion, called Grouse, which she was forbidden to ride. But he was so quiet and well behaved that Edith, brought up of course in ignorance of the facts of life, took no notice of the ban as long as there were no grown-ups in sight. One day the inevitable happened: they passed a field wherein grazed a carthorse mare who happened to be in season. Grouse bolted headlong towards the mare; Florence, who was on his back at the time, flung herself off and was none the worse, and Eric explained to his sisters that the reason for Grouse's behaviour was that he was a 'father horse'. 'Like Hermit?' asked Edith. 'Yes,' said Eric, glad that no further explanations were required. 'Then I shall exercise him with Hermit in future,' said Edith.

Next day, out came Hermit, followed by the other Blankney stallions – Galopin, Bendigo and Friar's Balsam – and Grouse. The small pony, led by the short, plump rosy-cheeked child with her masses of blonde hair falling over her shoulders, went round and round after the thorough-breds until Grouse got bored.

Edith, who not only loved hunting for its own sake but longed to please her adored father, was a bold, almost foolhardy rider. Indeed, she often had little choice: her father's eye for a horse never took into account whether the good-looking ponies he chose for his children were difficult rides or not. He himself, with his experience, weight and superb hands, had no difficulty in controlling the 'hot' animals he preferred, but it was a different matter for a child. Fortunately, Edith was almost fearless and her only worry was how to evade the groom detailed to keep an eye on her so that she might keep up with her father. As he often got through a third as well as a second horse it was not an ambition she could achieve for more than a few fields, especially if they had not had a hunt and hounds were being taken home. Then, Chaplin would sometimes lead his house party home straight across country at full gallop, often for eight or nine miles (Princess Victoria and the future Queen Maud of Norway both received falls on one of these 'steeplechases').

In 1892, when Edith was thirteen, her grandfather died, to be succeeded by her uncle Strath. For the Chaplin children there was a little money. Though his second Duchess had attempted to prise everything possible away from the family, the Duke left each of his nieces the sum of £2,500 in trust, while Eric was left the Florence Colliery outright and the Florence and North Stafford Coal and Iron Company subject to the Duchess's life interest.

Then came two events that must have affected the adolescent Edith with a sudden, jolting sense of insecurity; and, perhaps, shaped her future need for one person as a lifelong partner to whom to cling, on whom to depend, without whom she would be lost.

Two years after her grandfather's death, there was a clash of temperaments between the new Duchess, Aunt Millie, and Edith's beloved Miss Harvey, which resulted in the departure of the governess. Both Edith and her sister were utterly miserable; Edith in particular showed signs of bitter distress, though it was to the younger Florence that their father wrote after this schoolroom tragedy: 'I longed to go off with you last night and take you on my knee and tell you all I thought and felt about you, little Darling!' To Edith he wrote a long and affectionate letter telling her of the new governess he was engaging.

The second and perhaps the more traumatic occurrence was the selling of Blankney at the beginning of 1897. The Squire's extravagances had finally brought him to the edge of ruin: he was virtually bankrupt, and his long-suffering creditors foreclosed. The last property remaining to him, the family home and estate, passed after two hundred years out of the Chaplin family.

This débâcle, on the eve of her debutante Season in London, must have given Edith a completely new perspective on her future. Though she lived with the Sutherlands, Blankney had always been *there*, with its rich acres, its stables, her father's generous, carefree and splendid way of life. Now, suddenly, no longer was there the comforting cushion of knowing that should the unthinkable happen and she fail to marry, she still had a home behind her. Her father wrote to her on 21 February 1897, in the midst of the removal from Blankney, to tell her he was sending her some of her mother's things, left undisturbed in her room at Blankney since her death.

'I have been through them all today,' he wrote, 'and with the exception of my letters to her, poor Darling – I think she must have kept them nearly all – and other letters I have burnt, I send them all to you and I should like them to be in your keeping. I will try to give you a rough list of what they are. There is the watch she wore herself and a head ornament of pink and white coral. These I should like you to have yourself. There is also her own Bible and many little Prayer Books and similar things, which you and Florrie will divide. . . .' Her father's letter also contained a true Chaplin bequest; among other things, he added, were 'her foxes' brushes, many of them killed after good runs in Staffordshire, some in Lincolnshire and one from Sandringham. I am afraid I have not made it very clear, but indeed, child, it is the saddest afternoon that I have passed for many days. It all comes back to me as if it was only yesterday, and for the moment I am quite unmanned.'

For his daughter, facing her first Season as a grown woman, in an era when marriage was not only the sole career open to women but its grandness or otherwise the criterion of success in that career, it was now more than ever important that she marry – and marry well.

23

III

EDITH CHAPLIN came out in 1897, the year of Queen Victoria's Diamond Jubilee. Never had Britain's power, wealth and prestige been greater, blazing in a final spurt of brilliance before their decline in the new century. In 1897 the struggles and miseries of the Crimea were a distant memory and the Empire on which the sun never set – one quarter of the land mass of the globe was coloured red – had convincingly demonstrated its loyalty. Its proconsuls were a governing class whose ideals were justice, service and the continuance of flourishing trade links with the motherland. At home, the country rode on the crest of a great wave of peace and prosperity. After the social upheavals of the Industrial Revolution, the massive new fortunes founded on coal, railways or building had acquired the respectable patina of old money. The Irish question was momentarily quiescent, the pound was solid gold, all over the Continent an Englishman's word was known to be as good as his bond and a Conservative government was in power again, its head a peer of the realm. The social order seemed immutable; the future, in so far as anyone scrutinised it, appeared to stretch out ahead as a broad golden path to a glittering horizon. In short – and particularly to those fortunate enough to be born into the upper classes – God was indisputably in his heaven and all was right with the world.

Victoria, whose grandchildren were by now on or comfortably close to most of the thrones of Europe, had also emerged from the shadows. The years of self-imposed seclusion following the Prince Consort's death, during which she had virtually withdrawn from public life, were over. Once more she was a popular and beloved queen, with the added aura of great age and wisdom.

She nevertheless continued to raise widowhood almost to a vocation, dressing in black and keeping her private rooms at Windsor as near as possible to how they were when Prince Albert died. The curtains, upholstery, mirrors, door mountings and panels were those chosen by Prince Albert in the early days of their marriage. The gold and crimson brocaded walls of her private sitting room were covered with the same pictures – 231 in all, hung from immediately below the deep cream and gold cornices to within four feet of the floor – as at the time of the Prince's death. But though, forty years on, much of her life was still devoted to the memory of her beloved departed, the Queen had begun to move about more freely outside the secluded environs of the Castle itself. In the spring of 1897 she had just returned from the Riviera where, as at Osborne and Balmoral, the rheumatism which plagued her at Windsor improved markedly and she enjoyed spurts of liveliness and energy.

That May, London saw more of her than it had for years. She had begun to appear, occasionally at first, at Drawing Rooms and, fine or wet, she drove out every afternoon; by now she was wearing spectacles for these jaunts. She covered surprising distances. On the day after Edith was presented, the Queen's horses, handsome and strong – the posting carriages she generally used were enormously heavy – took her at a brisk pace up Bond Street, along Portland Place, through Regent's Park and back by Hyde Park and Sloane Street. She bowed and smiled happily the whole way, while the enormous crowds waiting to see her cheered repeatedly.

Edith was presented at the fourth Drawing Room of the Season, on 13 May. That Tuesday morning, the sun shone brightly though the wind was icy. Nevertheless, from an early hour thousands of spectators congregated in the Mall and Birdcage Walk, with the crowd particularly dense outside the Palace. The royal standard whipping in the stiff breeze signified the Queen's presence, still rare enough to generate fascinated interest; to this was added the patriotic fervour of Jubilee year. The rumour that the Queen herself, instead of the Princess of Wales or Princess Christian, would preside over the Drawing Room made those attending determined to get to Court in good time to see her before her customary departure after half an hour or so. As early as eleven in the morning several carriages were hovering about the route, waiting until the police allowed them to take up the firstcomers' position at the top of Birdcage Walk.

Soon, to the delight of the spectators who peered in through the windows at the occupants, there were several hundred carriages, the grander peeresses arriving in the family's state coach. Among these was the Londonderry coach, conspicuous as always with its servants in yellow, blue and silver livery; within it sat Edith Chaplin's future mother-in-law, the Marchioness of Londonderry, splendid in white and pale green, with lilies of the valley embroidered on her dress in diamonds, pearls and green silk. On her haughty, beautiful head glittered the famous Londonderry diamond tiara.

The doors of the Palace opened at 2.00 p.m. No fewer than five duchesses were present, all bedecked in the family jewels. There were acres of white satin, purple velvet and silver tissue. The jewelled embroidery and glittering tinsel thread which was that Season's particular fashion gleamed against the red carpets, the gilt and the mauve irises in tall pots. It was, agreed everyone, *the* Drawing Room of the Season; some of the dresses cost as much as £300 and, adding a note of faintly risqué titillation, one woman was rumoured to be wearing a pair of white satin knickerbockers beneath her frock. The Queen, dressed in her usual black, sat on the little low chair she now found comfortable; beside her stood the Princess of Wales in ivory satin. Most of the company waited in the ballroom, with the overflow in the long corridor outside. The Sovereign, clearly in excellent humour, stayed until 4.00 (after which the Princess of Wales took her place), smiling reassuringly at each of the debutantes as they curtsied to her, leaning forward to plant a kiss on the cheek of those who were the daughters of peers and extending her hand to be kissed by the commoners, who removed their right gloves in mid-curtsey so as to place their own ungloved hands beneath hers.

In an effort to allay his daughter's nervousness at carrying through this ordeal successfully, Henry Chaplin, by now Minister of Agriculture, had written to her describing a contretemps at a previous Drawing Room at which the Queen was briefly present. 'I had to go to the Drawing-room yesterday as Minister in attendance, which I hated. But my virtue was rewarded by seeing a little old lady, just as she was going to make her obeisance to the Queen, turn turtle in the most delightful manner. I was just opposite her, about five or six yards off. Her feet slipped on part of her train or something. Down she came plump on her back. Her legs flew up into the air facing the Queen. She waved her little arms wildly; her coronet nearly fell off the back of her head, and whether the Queen or her Minister laughed most, I really can't tell. . . .'

In the event, Edith, presented by her father's sister, the Countess of Radnor, had no need to worry. Her curtsey was impeccable, her dress, in the prevailing tight-waisted and extremely *décolletée* fashion deemed suitable for debutantes, suited her tall, erect, full-bosomed figure to perfection. As *Vanity Fair* pointed out, 'No one was prettier than Mr Chaplin's daughter.'

It was easy to understand the magazine's comment. At eighteen, Edith, now 5 ft 8 in in her stockinged feet, had hazel eyes sparkling with life and mischief, hair that had darkened from its original yellow-blonde to a rich, bright golden bronze, and the wonderful skin inherited from both her parents. Slim and fit from a strenuous outdoor life, her natural *joie de vivre* was enhanced with glowing health. Her Scots nanny, her governess Miss Harvey and her Aunt Millicent had collectively seen to it that her deportment and manners were exquisite. Older people found her pretty and refined-looking; younger ones were drawn to her energy, warmth and capacity for making everything seem fun. She herself was determined to enjoy the Season, throwing herself into its pleasures with the same enthusiasm she showed for the delights of the hunting field or a day out with the guns.

There was plenty to enjoy. The mornings found her riding in the Park in the beautifully cut, tightly fitting habit in which many gentlemen thought the *fin-de-siècle* beauty looked her best. In the evenings there was a procession of elegant carriages, which always included a few barouches belonging to the grandest personages, for which 17-hand horses were required (finding a well-matched pair of such large animals was difficult). Some watched these spectacles on foot, congregating round Stanhope Gate where the riders and drivers entered and left the Park, or sat on green velvet chairs as a circle of friends gathered round them. Lord Castlereagh was one who rode in the Row in the summer while his sister, Edith's friend Lady Helen Stewart, often drove in the evening procession. Young marrieds, bachelors and girls chaperoned by their mothers patronised Prince's Skating Club.

First and foremost, with the advent of the new safety bicycle, there was the great cycling craze, with its exhilarating blend of fresh air, exercise and a freedom that had faintly illicit overtones. Invitations to the more dashing house parties would say 'Bring your bicycle', and fathers, mothers and debutante daughters would pedal round the gardens and grounds, along the terraces, through the shrubberies and across the lawns. Millicent became so passionate about cycling that everyone invited to stay at Trentham was asked to bring a bicycle – and, of course, a footman to clean it. On Sundays after church there was 'church parade', again at Stanhope Gate, where the fashionable congregated to see and be seen. And always, always there were the dances, often several on one night, where quadrilles and the occasional polka vied with Strauss waltzes

27

played by imported Viennese orchestras. In royal circles, reversing was taboo, so that sometimes giddiness was a real danger, and the embrace of a partner's arm afforded not simply a new and exciting way of dancing but a necessary support.

Two weeks after Edith's presentation she was invited to what afterwards became known as the ball of the century. The Duchess of Devonshire's ball was given to celebrate the Jubilee and, from the moment invitations were sent out on the last day of May until the day of the ball itself, 2 July, Society talked of little else. The Duchess had decreed that it was to be a costume ball: each of the 700 guests was to come as some pre-1815 historical or allegorical character. No expense was spared by those fortunate enough to be invited (those who were not invented some excuse to leave London). Hairdressers were brought over from Paris, fashionable women searched art galleries and museums for inspiration and authenticity, every dressmaker in London was engaged in sewing seed pearls on to satin or hooping brocade into panniers. At Devonshire House, the Duchess put even the servants into fancy dress for the evening.

On the night itself famous beauties shone. Lady Randolph Churchill came as the Empress Theodora, Lady Cynthia Graham as one of the two Queens of Sheba, and Edith's Aunt Millie as Charlotte Corday, while Louisa Devonshire herself was carried in on a palanquin as Queen of Egypt, surrounded by some of the most glamorous women of the day dressed as oriental slaves and carrying huge ostrich-feather fans. Among them was Margot Asquith, disguised as a snake charmer; her husband Herbert, a remarkably realistic Roundhead, sat next to Edith at supper. They must, Edith remarked later, have made a curious contrast: she was dressed simply in white as Elaine, the Lily Maid of Astolat, her hair hanging loose. 'I had an immense quantity, of a deep yellow colour, long enough to sit on. It got into Mr Asquith's way during dinner as well as my own!'

One of the most splendid was Lady Londonderry. Characteristically, she had chosen to come as one of the most imperious and magnificent of empresses, Maria Theresa of Austria. She wore white, with gold embroideries made in Ireland – the Londonderrys always tried to encourage the local County Down crafts of lacemaking and embroidery – and an imperial crown that was an exact copy of Maria Theresa's own, which she had had made from a number of her own necklaces and bracelets, broken up and reset for this one night. Fortunately there were still plenty more left to loop and pin about her. Pearl necklaces hung in profusion down the front of her dress, mingling with a magnificent rivière of diamonds; diamond clasps held her train at the shoulders, more diamonds were sewn on the front of her skirt, and a huge ruby blazed on her wrist.

As she and her attendant court came up the great circular marble staircase, there was a murmur of admiration. She literally dazzled, a figure so bejewelled, so regal in bearing, that she could have been a symbol of the power and wealth of the British aristocracy at this, its zenith.

By her side was her son, Charles, Viscount Castlereagh, dressed as the Emperor of Austria, in a white satin uniform glittering with stars. A few months older than Edith, he was just nineteen. Tall, slim and fair, with a spare, soldierly elegance – he was a cadet at Sandhurst, destined for the Household Cavalry – he combined a reserved, aristocratic courtesy with a sensuous, caressing glance. Even then, women found him irresistible.

Edith had met him once or twice. Her father knew the Londonderrys well, and often stayed with them at Wynyard Park, their huge house in Durham, to shoot; and she herself had come out with his sister, Lady Helen (always called 'Birdie' by her family and friends). But for the moment there were much more pressing things to think about, one of them being the coming-out ball to be given for her in the last week of the Season by her Aunt Millie.

By now, Millicent was at the height of her beauty. Once, when Winston Churchill and Edward Marsh stood at the door of a reception deciding how many ships the face of each woman present would launch, they awarded Millicent the maximum of 1,000 without hesitation. Tall – she was 5 ft 10 in – slim and graceful, with an entrancing smile and deep, velvety voice, she could not appear at any public function without receiving love letters. Some were signed and some anonymous, but all were so passionately written that at one point her husband censored her incoming correspondence. At Stafford House, by now both a social mecca and a focus for liberal and aristocratic causes, she would stand at the top of the staircase to receive her guests. Sometimes she would be dressed sumptuously and elaborately, with Marie Antoinette's diamond necklace sparkling round her white throat and a crown-shaped tiara on her red-gold hair; Vita Sackville West refers to 'Millie looking like a goddess, with a golden train halfway down the stairs. The charm of that woman!' Sometimes she would be in a simple, unadorned black or white dress with a single pearl strand round her neck. Often she held white, sweet-scented lilies, a practice which was not so much a pre-Raphaelite affectation as a typically graceful and romantic way of avoiding handshakes or kisses. For a niece of eighteen, such an aunt, a mere eleven years older, must have been overwhelming.

But at Edith's coming-out ball on Friday 19 July Millicent had done everything possible to ensure that her niece was the star. Even the flowers in Stafford House were pink and white to complement Edith's pink dress – huge baskets of orchids and malmaisons, with crimson carnations on the first-floor landing. About 1,500 invitations had been sent out. Most of the guests arrived about midnight, thronging the marble hall lit by flambeaux and lined with towering palm trees. There was such a crowd that many could not get upstairs in time for supper. Dancing was in the banqueting hall, a beautiful round white and gold room with a splendid floor, to a band hidden behind a screen covered with white roses. It was a warm night, and all the windows on the garden side were thrown up so that music floated out above the lawns. Supper was served at small round tables in the dining room. This, too, was almost smothered in flowers: pink sweet peas and malmaisons alternated on the tables, enormous baskets of pink and white orchids from the Trentham glasshouses stood round the room. At 12.30 the Princess of Wales was led in to her seat at the largest, central supper table by the Duke of Sutherland, the Prince followed with Millicent, and everyone processed in behind them. All the tables had place cards so that everyone knew where to go. The placement alone, for a party of this size, with all its complications of protocol and cross-currents of amatory intrigue, was proof of the organisational power needed by the successful aristocratic hostess, a lesson not lost on the observant Edith.

The party was a great success. After supper, the Prince and Princess of Wales danced a quadrille – their set consisted of their son the Duke of York (later George V), Prince and Princess Henry of Pless, Prince Francis of Teck, Princess Charles of Denmark, Duchess Millicent and Mrs Asquith – and stayed for one waltz. The Prince, like many others, sauntered through the gardens, poetically lit by Japanese lanterns; after smoking a cigarette in the marquee he returned to the house and most of the royal party left. The beauties of the evening were Lady Westmorland and Edith, 'sweet in pink', said one report, who was presented to all the royalties in turn by her aunt.

As ball followed ball – including one given by Lady Londonderry for Edith's friend Lady Helen Stewart – and dinner succeeded dinner, Edith grew in poise and confidence. By now she was recognised as one of the most beautiful debutantes of her year and, as her second Season approached, she could have taken her pick of the young men who flocked round her. One proposal came from Lord Derby, which Edith refused gently but firmly. Other requests for her hand came from men who mistook her overtures of friendship for flirtation – all her life her friends were men. Never having enjoyed the ease and intimacy of a mother–daughter relationship, although she got on with and liked other women, she never confided in any of them; conversely, her relationships with men, as with her father, were excellent.

Although Edith could ostensibly think of Stafford House and Dunrobin as home for as long as she wished, there was, nevertheless, a subtle pressure on her to marry. By now Millicent's life was not quite so whole-heartedly devoted to Strath as in earlier days. Her three children (a fourth had died in infancy) were growing up, good works and social causes were taking up much of her time and, even more to the point, she was listening more sympathetically to the many men who fell in love with her. One was Darcy Desmond Fitzgerald, an Irishman eight years younger than herself with whom she would, by the summer of 1900, be desperately in love. In short, the last thing Millicent wanted close at hand was an observant young woman fiercely loyal to her uncle Strath, given to asking awkward questions, and very little younger than herself. When, in the spring of 1899, Charley Castlereagh began to show a closer interest in his sister's friend, it was like an answer to a prayer.

IV

CHARLES STEWART Henry Vane-Tempest-Stewart, Viscount Castlereagh, eldest son of the Marquess of Londonderry, was a catch by any standards. A handsome young cavalry officer, he was brave, sporting, gay, charming, and the heir to great estates and position.

He came from a family of Anglo-Irish aristocrats – the marquessate was an Irish title – originally of Scottish extraction. The first Marquess of Londonderry was Robert Stewart.

The second, better known by his courtesy title of Viscount Castlereagh, was the famous Foreign Secretary who led the British delegation at the Congress of Vienna, at which the statesmen of Europe carved out the peace settlement following the downfall of Napoleon. He refused an English peerage so that he could remain in the House of Commons. Shortly after Castlereagh succeeded he committed suicide.

He was succeeded by his half-brother Charles Stewart, the third Marquess, who was granted an English peerage – the barony of Stewart – and thereafter the holder of the title sat in the House of Lords.

The third Marquess was the real founder of the colossal Londonderry fortune. He had been appointed Ambassador to Vienna by his brother Castlereagh and while there had met Lady Frances Anne Vane-Tempest, the greatest heiress of her generation, whom he married as his second wife in 1819. She had an income of £60,000 a year from her estates and collieries in the northeast of England. The third Marquess added to this wealth by sinking several successful new pits around Seaham and building a harbour there for the colliers which carried the coal to London and elsewhere. In recognition of what the Londonderrys owed to his wife's family, he took her surname of Vane-Tempest.

The fourth Marquess, Frederick (Charles Stewart's son by his first wife), sat in the House of Commons as MP for County Down for twenty-five years, until his succession. He too enlarged the family fortunes through marriage: his wife brought with her the Welsh estate of Plas Machynlleth in Merionethshire. When he died, childless, in 1872, he was succeeded by his half-brother Henry, Frances Anne's eldest son. Henry, whose sister married the Duke of Marlborough and was the mother of Lord Randolph Churchill (and grandmother of Winston Churchill), died in 1884. He was succeeded by his son Charles, the sixth Marquess, who restored the original family name of Stewart, adding it by royal licence in 1885 to the existing surname of Vane-Tempest.

In 1875 Charles, as Viscount Castlereagh, had married Lady Theresa Susey Helen Chetwynd Talbot. Born on 6 June 1856, she was the eldest daughter of the nineteenth Earl of Shrewsbury, the premier Earl of England. By the time their eldest son Charley (Edith Chaplin's future husband) was born on 13 May 1878, the Londonderrys were rich and influential even by the standards of the time, with a fortune based securely on coal rather than the vagaries of agriculture. Ten thousand miners worked in the Londonderry pits, Londonderry coal was shuttled busily by Londonderry colliers between Seaham Harbour and the Londonderry wharf on the Thames at Vauxhall. The income from the coal and the 50,000 Londonderry acres – almost half in County Down, 13,000 in Durham, and the rest scattered round Londonderry and Donegal in Ireland and Montgomery and Merioneth in Wales – brought in over £100,000 a year.

The family seat was Wynyard Park in County Durham. Built by James Wyatt, it had taken almost nineteen years to complete and, in February 1841, when almost finished, was totally destroyed by fire; up in the blaze went family portraits, furniture, records and treasures too. Wynyard was quickly rebuilt. Here the Londonderrys entertained those vast house parties that were such a feature of Victorian and Edwardian social life, sometimes for the races but more often for shooting. 'We had a most wonderfully good day's shooting here, about 2,600 rabbits and 408 pheasants,' wrote the Prince of Wales when staying at Wynyard in November 1890. 'It is the biggest rabbit day, I think, I have ever had. Herbert Bismarck* was out and although his gun went off occasionally when it was not intended, he did nobody any harm.' On his return home the Prince again mentions the formidable bag. 'In the two days shooting at

---

* Herbert Bismarck was the son of Prince Bismarck, who had been sent to England a few years before to get in touch with 'persons of prominence' and do what he could to allay their misgivings over German policy.

Wynyard we killed 7,843 head, out of which 5,817 were rabbits and 1,973 pheasants. Tomorrow I go to Waddesdon to shoot Baron Ferdinand's coverts, and on Friday go to Sandringham.'

In London there was Londonderry House, in Park Lane, originally built for the sixth Earl of Holdernesse and bought by the third Marquess and Frances Anne in 1822 as a suitably grand London establishment. Remodelled and refurbished (by Wyatt's son Benjamin Dean Wyatt) with £200,000 of Frances Anne's money, it became a huge and splendid private palace. Its vast high-ceilinged state rooms led one into another from the wide, pillared gallery above the magnificent square staircase. With their ornate plastered ceilings, enormous crystal chandeliers, gilding, portraits and walls hung with damask, they provided a perfect setting for the fashionably dressed crowds glittering with satins, jewels, stars, orders and decorations which so often filled them.

'Lunched at Londonderry House: a very brilliant affair; not fewer than 50 guests,' wrote John Morley in 1891, describing a luncheon given in honour of the German Emperor; '... the meal was sumptuous; the music not too loud; each table with a little mountain of roses, all pink here and deep rose there and so forth. Coffee and cigarettes in the fine gallery. We did not disperse until nearly four.' Of Kaiser Wilhelm he recorded: 'He is rather short; pale but sunburnt; carries himself well; walks into the room with the stride of the Prussian soldier; speaks with a good deal of intense and energetic gesture, like a Frenchman but staccato; his voice strong but pleasant; his eye bright, clear and full; mouth resolute; the cast of face grave, almost stern in repose, but as he sat between those two pretty women, the hostess and Lady Bland, he lighted up with gaiety and genial laugh; energy, rapidity, restlessness in every movement, from his short, quick inclinations of the head to the planting of the feet.'

And in Ireland there was Mount Stewart, handsome in grey stone, set in the low green hills of the Ards peninsular, facing southwest over the glistening silver waters of Strangford Lough. Here the Londonderrys normally spent Christmas, Easter and Whitsuntide (though in the Home Rule struggle of 1912–14 Theresa spent much more time in this 'villa by the sea', as she had earlier and rather dismissively called it). The shooting was excellent, particularly the woodcock, and there was wildfowling on the marshes which then existed at Downpatrick. There was also sailing on the Lough. Unlike her husband, Theresa loved sailing, and became an expert and fearless yachtswoman who would often sail her boat, *Red Rose*, to Portaferry at the end of the Lough and back. In March 1913 her diary records: 'Sailed every possible day. Cold weather but good breezes and sunshine.'

By all accounts Charley's father, the sixth Lord Londonderry, was simple, friendly and unaffected. Tall, slim and fair, with the slight reserve of manner that seems to have been a family characteristic since the days of the great Castlereagh, he had, said Sir Almeric Fitzroy (Clerk to the Privy Council from 1898) 'the manner of a grand seigneur'. It was impossible to mistake him for anything but an aristocrat – as Lady Fingall later remarked, 'he always did the right thing by instinct' – and indeed he himself was equally convinced of the semi-divine right of birth and position. *Vanity Fair* called him 'a good fellow, a pleasant companion and a very fine host who "does" his guests royally', though if they wanted to do full justice to the delicious food they had to eat quickly. Lord Londonderry, a sparing eater in contrast to the custom of the day, ate very fast: seldom did a meal, even one of the famous Londonderry House banquets, take longer than about half an hour. Quite often a guest who had spent too long talking to his neighbour or unwarily put his fork down would find his plate whipped away before he had finished by one of the footmen who stood behind almost every chair. Not that he was alone in this practice: in many great houses (Blenheim was another) dinner had to be eaten within the hour, well-trained servants smoothly serving and removing the eight or so courses usual at such a meal. But Londonderry was a generous host, especially to female guests; once, when one of his horses won a big race, he gave every lady in the house party a diamond brooch.

He also had a great sense of public duty, though this did not soften his views on the rights of the employer and property owner. When Lord Salisbury introduced the Workmen's Compensation for Accidents Bill, Lord Londonderry – supported by most of his fellow colliery-owners – thundered against it in the House of Lords, protesting that it was against Tory principles and that Lord Salisbury had deserted those principles for the sake of the alliance with the Liberal Unionists.

Theresa (always known as 'Nellie') Londonderry could hardly have been more different from her husband. She was a passionate woman of forceful nature, with a full-blooded, black-and-white approach to life. 'Happy, courageous and violent, with a mind which clung firmly to the obvious', Lady Cynthia Asquith described her a trifle superciliously; 'keen and vivid, but crude and impenitent'. She was proud, frank, courageous, materialistic, warm-hearted; she rode, she sailed, she took lovers, she relished every aspect of her position, performing her role as

Marchioness with gusto and professionalism. She knew what was expected of her and she gave it, using her personal splendour to dazzle and to solace: when a family on the estate at Wynyard was ill, she would dress up to the nines before visiting them, diamonds agleam, equipped with generous provisions and some of the medicine which she dispensed herself.

Theresa was worldly to her fingertips and unsurpassed as a hostess, partly because her own zest for life was infectious and partly because she was genuinely thoughtful and determined that her guests too should enjoy themselves. She was widely read, accustomed to the company of intelligent men, and a fluent and expressive writer, keeping notes and diaries and jotting down vivid descriptions of events that she thought memorable.

Colonel Repington, the military correspondent of *The Times*, described Theresa as 'one of the most striking and dominating feminine personalities of our time, terrifying to some, but endeared to her many friends by her notable and excellent qualities. She was ... clear-headed, witty and large-hearted, with unrivalled experience of men and things social and political, and with a most retentive memory and immense vivacity and *joie de vivre*.' She said of herself that she was a good friend and a bad enemy. 'When I love at all, I love passionately. But I like most people, and it is very few I hate.' She would always do her best to assist her friends, taking an intense interest in their love affairs and helping these along in any way allowed by discretion. If she was annoyed, there was no mistaking it – for one thing, she signed herself 'Theresa' instead of the usual 'Nellie'. George Wyndham, another of the Souls, once remarked nervously, 'I have just had a letter signed "Theresa" and am looking out for squalls.' But although fond of her women friends, she agreed vehemently with Lady Mary Wortley Montagu's comment that the only good thing about being a woman was that you could not marry one.

She was also ambitious, and determined to turn her husband's position in the Conservative Party and his special links with Irish politics to advantage. Soon the Londonderry House political receptions, at which she could influence, introduce, exert patronage and dazzle, grew famous. Rising politicians became her protégés: to be taken up by a woman of such wealth, beauty, sophistication and influence was a considerable advantage to a young MP. So great was the crush at some of these parties that the beautiful staircase had to be supported by scaffolding.

Physically, Theresa was an almost perfect specimen of Edwardian womanhood, of the type most admired by the Prince of Wales: imperious, full-bosomed and substantial. The day after she had sat on Sir Alan Lascelles' lap as they returned in a crowded launch from watching the final illuminations of the naval review at Portsmouth in 1911 (when she was in her fifties), he wrote in his diary: 'Next day my leg was a pulp of bruises; uneasy lies the knee that bears a Marchioness.' Most men, though, would have envied him. When the Shah of Persia came to England on a state visit in 1889 he was so impressed by Theresa's opulent, majestic looks, set off by the Londonderry diamonds, that he wanted to buy her.

Although the Shah did not succeed in winning Lady Londonderry, several other men did. She had in full measure the 'Talbot amorousness' – an inheritance she passed on to her son. Her first serious affair was with her brother-in-law Reginald, Lord Helmsley. However, she managed to keep this liaison quiet at the time, even though the son he fathered was named after her lover (the name Reginald had never before appeared in the Londonderry family tree).

Within ten years of her marriage she had embarked on a love affair that was to have much more serious consequences. It was with Henry Cust, cousin of Lord Brownlow, an immensely good-looking bachelor and the most notorious womaniser of his time (he was widely believed to be the father of Lady Diana Cooper), whose effect on women was legendary. He was twenty-two or twenty-three to Theresa's twenty-eight when their affair began in 1884.

Harry Cust was a man whose early promise was never fulfilled. At Eton he was so distinguished academically, his personality so outstanding, that he was tipped as a future prime minister – despite the fact that among his contemporaries there were Curzon and Balfour. Expecting to inherit his cousin's title and fortune (he never did), his great gifts were devoted not to a career but to dazzling society, in particular his fellow Souls. His conversation was marvellous: witty, moving and literary, throwing off classical allusions, puns, epigrams and tender compliments like a Catherine wheel. It was after such an evening at the dinner table that William Waldorf Astor crossed the room and offered him the editorship of his evening paper, the *Pall Mall Gazette*.

Under Cust's brilliant if *dégagé* editorship, the paper became fashionable and influential, though he brought about his own end by briskly refusing to print his proprietor's admittedly long-winded and boring contributions and, even worse, by his tone of mocking anti-Americanism. Astor's patience finally gave way and Cust was sacked at a week's notice.

His final headline was typical, a stylish classical pun: Qui Custodit Caveat (Who hates Cust, Let Him Beware).

Cust's real energies were reserved for the pursuit of women. He thought nothing of running several beautiful and well-born women at once – and, unfortunately, always kept their letters. When Theresa Londonderry fell in love with him he was already having a passionate affair with Lady de Grey (later Marchioness of Ripon), a woman of immense charm and elegance, so beautiful she could hush a ballroom, but neurotic and unstable.

Lady de Grey soon became suspicious that her lover was deceiving her. She managed to get into his home (perhaps he had given her a key) and found Theresa's letters – amorous to a degree and with mocking references to Lord Londonderry. Gladys de Grey took them away with her.

At first she contented herself with reading selected extracts aloud to her friends. Finally, though, she decided to eliminate her rival in the most painful way possible. She sent a footman to Londonderry House bearing the letters in a sealed package, with instructions that he was to place them in the hands of Lord Londonderry and no one else.

It was a shattering denouement. Lord Londonderry's misery and sense of betrayal were acute, aggravated by the bitter humiliation felt by anyone who lived by the strict Edwardian code of 'no scandal'. It was perfectly clear that if Gladys de Grey knew of his wife's love affair with Cust, so did many other people. He resolved the matter by not speaking to his wife except in public for many years. Whenever possible, he led his life apart from her, standing well to one side of her at the Londonderry House receptions and arriving in a different carriage at the opera or ball. In 1897, for instance, both had carriages at the Eton and Harrow match, and it was Theresa's son Charley who escorted her to the Duchess of Devonshire's ball.

So dramatic was this rift, and such an object lesson to the rest of Edwardian society on the terrible penalty of being found out that it became a legendary scandal, a story passed down through families. Many years later, Vita Sackville West made use of it in her novel *The Edwardians*.

But unlike Lady Roehampton, Theresa Londonderry was not exiled permanently to the country. Nor, contrary to accounts that later circulated, did she remain unforgiven for ever. By the spring of 1899 the Londonderrys were clearly reconciled. From that date his letters to her begin again, each starting 'My darling Nellie' and continuing in tones of the greatest affection. 'I cannot imagine how you could possibly think for one moment anything you could say or do could give me the slightest annoyance,' runs one. 'I am so sorry, dearest, that you could have thought so, for I should be so *dreadfully* miserable if I thought you did not care if I had a really bad fall or not. You know I will never care for anyone but *you.*'

Perhaps still more conclusively, between 1906 and 1913, in five separate codicils to his will, Lord Londonderry added to the already generous provision for Theresa further bequests, of £10,000, £20,000, £20,000, £10,000 and £20,000, to 'my dear wife'. He even seems to have forgiven the man who cuckolded him: there is a record in the Wynyard game book of a shoot that included Harry Cust just before the 1914 war.

Both Londonderrys were close friends of the Prince and Princess of Wales: their combination of blue blood, savoir-faire, sense of style and lavish expenditure on glittering entertainment was exactly designed to appeal to the Prince. Between 1890 and 1903 there were six royal visits to Wynyard, one to Macchynlleth and one to Mount Stewart, as well as parties and banquets given in the royal couple's honour at Londonderry House. When the Prince succeeded to the throne, Lord Londonderry carried the Sword of State at his coronation.

Theresa was a particular favourite (although there is no hint that she and the Prince were ever more than friends), someone who could be guaranteed always to amuse and charm him as a dinner partner, an inventive hostess and a woman whose beautiful clothes – velvet toques smothered in veiling, bunches of Parma violets, jewelled belts, finely tucked blouses – were admired by all her contemporaries. Sometimes, Edward would pay her a private visit, arriving in a small plain single brougham.

After their marriage, Theresa and her husband took Kirby Hall at Bedale, in Yorkshire, as their country house, and, in London, 76 Eaton Place. Here their first child, 'Birdie', Edith's friend Lady Helen Vane-Tempest-Stewart, was born on 8 September 1876.

Birdie was in many ways her father's favourite. Both he and she were musical and when she was young, they would spend Sunday evenings singing hymns at the piano together (secular music was of course forbidden on the Sabbath). In 1902 she married Lord Stavordale, eldest son of Lord Ilchester, whom he succeeded in 1905. As a wedding present her father gave her a superb diamond and emerald pendant; her grandmother, the Dowager Marchioness, presented her with the Antrim diamonds, part of Frances Anne's legacy of jewels.

Charley too was born at 76 Eaton Place, on 13 May 1878. In the same month his father, having unsuccessfully contested Durham in 1874 and Montgomery in 1877 in the Conservative interest, was elected as Member for County Down in a by-election, handsomely defeating his Liberal opponent. It was an era when aristocrats believed that on them lay not only the right but the obligation to govern. By and large those who owned the land – and in the 1880s almost three-quarters of it was shared out between the aristocracy and the landed gentry – expected to govern the country; the larger the estate, the greater the duty of its owner to maintain both his own and his country's material wealth. Eldest sons of peers with great estates went into the House of Commons as a matter of course before their succession sent them to the House of Lords. At the time of Lord Salisbury's administration of 1895 twenty-three eldest sons of peers, as well as numerous younger sons, brothers and cousins, were Members of Parliament. The sixth Marquess would in his turn expect this tradition to be continued by his eldest son.

Both Theresa and her husband were keen riders to hounds, and shortly after Charley's birth they acquired The Hall, a hunting box in the Cottesmore country, at Langham, near Oakham. Here Theresa's second son and last child, Charles Stewart Reginald, was born on 4 December 1879.

As a Tory, an Irishman and a grandee, Londonderry was a natural choice as Viceroy of Ireland for any Conservative prime minister. Equally important, he was a rich man: although the post carried an annual salary of £12,000 this was not nearly enough to cover the balls, receptions, banquets, levees and dinners expected from one who was the representative of the sovereign and *de facto* leader of Irish society. 'The wealthy avoid the office,' Disraeli had complained, 'and the paupers won't fit.'

Thus when Lord Salisbury became Prime Minister for the second time, on 25 July 1886, he wasted no time in offering the viceroyalty to the 34-year-old Marquess, who accepted it equally promptly. Within two days it was all settled, Lord Londonderry stipulating only that he did not wish to serve for longer than the statutory three years because of the needs of his growing family and his interests as a landlord and colliery-owner. Though both Londonderrys were unswerving Ulster Protestants, they had plenty of Catholic friends and neighbours near Mount Stewart, and Catholic visitors were scrupulously sent off in one of the family carriages to mass in Newtownards.

Londonderry was, in fact, the first Irishman to hold the office of Viceroy, a popular move somewhat counterbalanced in the eyes of the Nationalists by the fact that he was descended from Castlereagh, hated architect of the Act of Union (in 1800). When his term of office ended in 1889 he was given the Order of the Garter.

In such a household, the atmosphere was imbued with politics. Both Lord Londonderry and Theresa discussed them all the time, in particular the subject of the union between England and Ireland. Their young son, Charley, was brought up to dislike Liberals: when Gladstone, aged eighty-four, visited Londonderry House, the small boy's one thought was: 'Here is the arch-ruffian!' The only other Liberal leader allowed through the door was Sir William Harcourt, who happened to be a great friend of Theresa's.

Theresa was extremely keen that her son should take an interest in politics and talked to him constantly about political subjects. His father made him speak in public from the time he was twelve years old – a few words seconding a vote of thanks to the chairman of a meeting, for example. There were many such meetings which Lord Londonderry had to attend, and in the holidays he always made his reluctant son go with him.

Charley's formal education started at the Mortimer Vicarage School, in Berkshire. It was kept by the Reverend Charles Lovett Cameron, a brother of the famous explorer. 'Castlereagh has been a very good boy, getting along most happily in all ways. He certainly deserves credit for sustained industry,' wrote his headmaster that year and, in April 1890, after Charley had just won a prize, 'He was the most advanced boy of the division and, had it not been for mathematics, he would have gone up into the second class after Christmas.' His cricket was good and by September 1891 he was head boy.

At Eton, too, he did well (though mathematics were still a struggle), and by the age of seventeen had realised that all women, even mothers, adore compliments. One of his letters to 'My dearest Mother' reads '. . . I went into the shop Dreyfous yesterday and told them to send me some things to Londonderry Hse; the man (a Frenchman, I think) said to me, "You are not Lord Londonderry?" "No," I said. "Well," he said, "you are not Lady Londonderry's son?" "Yes," I said. "Oh, I never knew Lady Londonderry had a son as big as you, she is so pretty." So, you see, you have a great admirer there.'

In January 1896 he was admitted to the Register of Gentlemen Cadets of the Royal Military College, Sandhurst, as the first step towards becoming a cavalry officer.

Charley was, in fact, a natural cavalryman. He was not only, like his parents, passionate about riding and hunting, he was also an excellent

41

horseman. At Sandhurst he rode whenever possible with the Staff College Drag, won the riding prize and in the final examination (in June 1897) achieved the maximum possible marks, 200 out of 200, for riding. He also did well in the subjects of tactics and fortifications, ending up with a creditable total of 2,291 marks out of a possible 3,162. He was commissioned into the Royal Horse Guards on 8 September 1897 – the family regiment was the 2nd Life Guards, but by then the Blues had become extremely fashionable.

Now, young, handsome, rich, already with the elegance that was to be a lifelong distinguishing characteristic, he launched himself enthusiastically into a life where work was pleasure, where he and his dashing brother officers could play polo, hunt and race to their hearts' content. It was also his first real chance to meet women. He found them irresistible and they had difficulty resisting him.

Soon, reports of his success in this field began to cause his parents concern. They were already anxious that he should marry early for dynastic reasons; now, they became doubly so. He might be only twenty-one but it was time for him to settle down. Accordingly, the Londonderrys and their intimates arranged that the half-dozen or so girls who were each deemed suitable by birth, upbringing and family history to be Marchioness of Londonderry should be introduced to him. Among them was Edith Chaplin.

V

T HE INITIAL spark of interest between two attractive young people was quickly fanned, reinforced by the benevolent, insidious pressure of family approval. By the beginning of May 1899 they were corresponding, in carefully non-committal little notes that could have been read out at any public gathering without causing the slightest embarrassment – save, perhaps, for a certain immaturity. Her letters, always beginning 'Dear Lord Castlereagh' and ending 'Yours very sincerely, Edith H. Chaplin', were written in her rounded handwriting on four sides of pale-blue paper and sprinkled with exclamation marks as with a pepper pot ('Oh! That poem!! I'm furious!!!! It really is a beast!'). Though she is clearly delighted with every sign of interest on his part, she is equally clearly determined never to overstep the invisible line that separates the pursuer from the pursued.

His are equally brief, in a schoolboyish hand but with a purely adult note of teasing affection and a flirtatiousness that appears even in the formality then proper between two young single people of opposite sex ('The remarks in your letter were most certainly out of place but my forgiving nature has pardoned your offence').

By July, sentences indicating a deeper interest in 'My dear Miss Edie' ('Edie' was the name by which she was always known to family and close friends) mingle with the joking. 'Please write one line if you have a moment and tell me the news. I suppose you have been going like a two-year-old round every ballroom. I have had a card for the Sutherland exhibition. I wish I could come. I hope you are kept away from the supper rooms at the balls as really it does not look dignified to cannon against the doorposts as you go out and after a short time must become rather painful. Please write to me as I love hearing from you. Ever yours sincerely, Castlereagh.'

Though they met frequently at dinners and dances much of their courtship was by letter and note – the Victorian equivalent of the telephone call. Charley, now in the Blues, had regimental duties and both were frequently invited away to stay. Millicent, determined to do everything in her power to encourage the match, asked Charley to stay at Dunrobin and while he and Edith were out walking together on the 'near beat', Edith found a piece of white heather. It must have seemed an excellent omen to a girl by now certain that she had met the man she wanted to marry.

It was. Later that August, Edith and her father were asked to join the house party staying with the Londonderrys at Wynyard for the week-long celebrations there to mark Charley's coming-of-age. His twenty-first birthday had in fact taken place three months earlier, on 13 May, but Theresa Londonderry would never have dreamed of spending a precious week of the Season in Durham. The Chaplins had only been there a day or two when, after dinner on Monday 8 August, Charley suggested to Edith that they stroll on the long gravelled terrace outside the drawing room. There, in the jasmine-scented dusk, he proposed to her and was rapturously accepted. Their engagement was announced to the family and the rest of the house party at dinner the following evening.

Almost at once, it looked as if Edith might be going to lose her new fiancé. Next day, after the first of the presentations – from the schoolchildren on the estate – to mark Charley's coming-of-age, he took her out riding. They were cantering along the old racecourse when his horse bolted, tried to jump some strong, six-foot-high wire netting erected to keep foxes out of the pheasant-rearing pens, became entangled and crashed down, throwing Charley heavily on his head.

Edith stayed with her unconscious fiancé, ready to reassure and comfort him if he regained consciousness and hoping that his riderless horse would raise the alarm. It was 9.00 p.m. before he was carried back to the house, still unconscious. A specialist was summoned from Newcastle, bulletins were issued to the local press and a statement telegraphed to *The Times*. Fortunately, the doctors now grouped round his bedside said they thought there was no fracture of the skull but his concussion was considered to be so serious that all the birthday celebrations, including the ball planned for the following day to which 2,100 people had been invited, were immediately cancelled.

Charley made such an excellent recovery that the ball was in fact held a week later; again the special train bringing northern guests from Newcastle was booked, again supper was prepared in the statuary gallery, again the great dining room so admired by Lord Beaconsfield was arranged for dancing, though this time for fewer guests, as many had already left for the moors. Theresa, in white satin, was the belle of the ball – 'It seems ridiculous that she should have a son of 21,' remarked one guest; Edith, in white tulle and yellow roses, danced with her fiancé. Later, she stood by his side at the garden parties for the county and the officials of the Londonderry collieries, for the firework display that marked the finale and for the cyclists' church parade at Seaham on the Sunday after; and drove with him and the rest of the house party to Stockton Races.

Once they were engaged, their letters became more frequent; sometimes they are no more than a few lines proclaiming nothing except the desire to be in constant touch. 'Edie darling, I was delighted with your telegram. So glad you all arrived safely ... I have been told not to write letters but had to write you a line. Best love dearest, Your loving Charley.'

Edith, by now in Scotland for the autumn as usual, wrote more uninhibitedly, loving little notes full of descriptions of what they were doing – the shooting, the stalking, the dogs – interspersed with bursts of intense feeling. 'I do so wish you were here, darling, I do miss you so much.' 'I am longing to have you back and think about you all day.' 'If I didn't know how sane I was I should think I was dotty.' Only one cloud overshadowed their horizon: the steadily worsening illness of Charley's brother Reggie.

Lord Reginald Vane-Tempest-Stewart, youngest of Theresa's three children, the son fathered by her brother-in-law, was accepted and loved as a member of the family by Lord Londonderry. Reggie had been born with a painful hip disease and had to walk on crutches. He was so sickly that he was educated at home. His sweet, uncomplaining nature made him the chink in his fierce, proud mother's armour. She treated him with immense tenderness, teaching him how to use a camera – she was a keen amateur photographer – encouraging his interest in engineering, and letting him spend whole days indulging in his great passion, engine-driving. He would travel in the cabs of the locomotives that ran on the semi-private lines between Seaham, Sunderland and Wynyard, eat a picnic lunch with the drivers and stokers and return to Wynyard blissful and filthy. By the time he was fifteen he was driving the train single-handed from Wynyard to Seaham.

As Reggie got older his health deteriorated. He was found to have tuberculosis, and was sent first on a long sea voyage and then to spend a year in the Kimberley sanatorium in South Africa, after which he went to stay with Cecil Rhodes, a friend of Theresa's. When his terrible cough got worse, Theresa came out to fetch him. In May 1899 he was brought back, to Seaham Hall, where it was hoped that the sea air would benefit him.

By the time Edith and Charley became engaged, it was clear that Reggie was much worse. Their letters are spattered with references to his health; Charley's describe the faintings, the opium-taking (for pain relief) and the misery of fatigue suffered by his loved younger brother. 'I only saw Reggie for a moment before dinner last night and sat with him for about three quarters of an hour today,' he wrote on 1 September 1899. 'He gets weaker every day and now it is hardly possible to hear what he says.'

But as well as causing anxiety and wretchedness in his family, Reggie's worsening condition made it difficult to fix the date of the wedding. Should Edith and Charley settle an early date, when Reggie might still be alive? or should they postpone their wedding until 'afterwards'?

Occasionally he rallied, giving a false gleam of hope. 'I was so pleased to get your letter and to know that Reggie is so much better,' wrote Edith on 2 October. 'Pray God it may last, but it is almost too much to hope for.' Finally, the Londonderrys decided the wedding should be on 28 November.

Early on the morning of 9 October it became clear that Reggie was dying. Telegrams were sent to Charley, in Scotland, and to Lord Londonderry, but it was too late: Reggie died that day, his grandmother, mother and sister at his bedside. His funeral was four days later, in Old Seaham churchyard. Employees of the Londonderry Railway (many of whom had sat beside him in engine cabs) carried his coffin to a grave lined with ivy and flowers. His father, Lord Helmsley, was there.

Theresa was shattered, and for months afterwards was unable to hide her feelings. The loss of one son no doubt made her determined that the other should not risk his life: when the South African War broke out on 11 October both Londonderrys were determined to keep their surviving son at home – especially now that he was getting married.

For Charley, torn between his love for Edith and a longing to fight with his regiment, the issues were not so clear cut. 'Wynyard is d . . . d dull,' he wrote to Edith at the beginning of November. 'My parents keep crowing over my not going to Africa; there will be a row soon as I am hot-tempered by nature. I know I am a horrid beast to wish to have gone but it is the only ambition I have ever had.'

By now a positive fusillade of notes was being exchanged between them, all on the tiny sheets of writing paper bordered thickly with black of which all Victorian households kept a stock. These small missives are significant chiefly because they foreshadow not just the devotion to sport and its imperative routine but the endless separations that would be such a feature of their marriage. 'Have you got a stag yet? I am sure you would have shot that ten-pointer on Friday if you had taken the rifle,' writes Charley. 'Darling, it *will* be nice seeing you on Saturday. I do long to see you again,' replies Edith, going on to describe the beasts she did shoot and the hockey matches played in the evenings at Dunrobin to mop up surplus energy: '. . . six of ourselves and six of the servants. We got three goals to their two. It was great fun.'

They were married on Tuesday 28 November, at St Peter's, Eaton Square. The crowded church was decorated with palms and white flowers, its galleries packed with tenants and servants. The bride and her father arrived punctually at 2.00. In the portico she was presented with a bouquet of orange blossom and gardenias, tied with ribbons in the Brigade colours, by the Corporal Major of the Royal Horse Guards. She also carried a second bouquet, grown from the flowers Theresa had carried at her own wedding. The ten bridesmaids, in ivory satin dresses with pink velvet hats, carried armfuls of white lilies. Edith wore white satin, with old Brussels lace and a transparent silk mousseline train, orange blossom in her hair, and a tulle veil. Her only jewellery was a diamond crescent brooch given to her by Charley. Mourning had been put aside for the day but Theresa Londonderry was in half-mourning: a close-fitting Parma violet panne velvet dress that made the most of her sumptuous if slightly stocky figure.

There were presents galore, a diamond bow brooch sent by the Prince and Princess of Wales, a silver inkstand from Lord Salisbury, from Theresa some of the Londonderry family jewels, a magnificent tiara and necklace of diamonds and rubies. There was a fur cape from Millicent, which Edith wore over her white cloth going-away dress. All were faithfully reported in the press next day. The bridegroom's squadron provided a guard of honour, their cuirasses and accoutrements gleaming in the light. The bride and groom left in a shower of rice for a honeymoon at Lillieshall (a Sutherland estate in Shropshire). For Charley, there was a note of sadness: the Blues were leaving for the Cape next day and not being able to go with them was still a sore point. But for Edith, married, as she was frequently to tell him during the next half-century, to 'the most beautiful and attractive man I have ever seen in my life', all was happiness.

The young Castlereaghs began married life in an apartment in London-derry House. Although conveniently close to Knightsbridge Barracks, where the Blues were stationed, from Edith's point of view it had its drawbacks. She was at Theresa's beck and call, and her mother-in-law would summon Edith whenever she wished to know her son's movements – not always easy questions to answer. Though they did not have a house of their own in London they bought something that all of them – Edith, Charley and their respective parents – considered essential: a hunting box. This was Springfield, in Oakham, formerly the house of a well-to-do grocer.

To live without hunting would have been unthinkable. In any case the horse was central to the age, an economic and a military necessity. Though Britain had an unrivalled network of railways, all other methods of transport depended upon horses. In the country, farming was entirely based on heavy draught horses, the doctor made his rounds in a trap or on horseback, the archdeacon visited remote parishes in a carriage or on horseback (sometimes abandoning his flock if the hunt passed temptingly near), villagers relied on the local carrier to give them a lift into town or to buy their shopping for them and deliver it back for a fee. In the city, buses, cabs and trams as well as private carriages and delivery carts were horsedrawn.

In the Army, horses were equally essential. In the Boer War then being fought, the cavalry and mounted infantry skirmished and battled on the open veldt, the mounted Boer commandos swooped on the un-suspecting, all military supplies went up from the railhead by horse transport and all artillery was horse-drawn. To Charley, as a young cavalryman, a knowledge of every aspect of horsemanship, from feeding, exercise and stable care to the riding in which he excelled, would have been an essential military skill. And for him, as for Edith, the horse provided unparalleled sport.

More even than racing, foxhunting was an all-consuming passion among the aristocratic and the rich. Nothing was allowed to stand in its way, entertainments were arranged round it, and invitations for several days' hunting – with all the extra work involved in the influx of horses, grooms and saddlery as well as the usual ladies' maids and valets – rivalled those for the shooting weekend. 'Edith dear,' wrote Millicent's half-sister Daisy (now Lady Warwick), fourteen months after Edith's marriage, 'I am writing to ask if you and Lord Castlereagh will come to my hunting party on Saturday March 9th, spend the Sunday, and hunt Monday 11th with the Warwickshire, Tuesday 12th North Warwickshire, Wednesday 13th the Pytchley and Thursday 14th with the Warwickshire.' She added with a true sense of everyone's priorities, 'Then you could get back to Leicestershire for the Friday and Saturday if you wished for six days.'

The Castlereaghs hunted in the Shires with most of the famous packs. As they owned thirteen or fourteen horses, they could, if they wanted, hunt six days a week. In those days before cars, they returned home from distant meets on galloping ponies, leaving the long slow hack home on tired hunters to grooms. As both were such good riders, they were able to earn some of their hunting expenses by buying young horses, making them, and selling them on at a profit. Edith, in an elegant habit, with her superb hands and her courage across country, showed off a promising hunter to perfection. It was at Springfield, too, that her interest in gardening first began.

It was fortunate for Edith that she had such an all-absorbing interest as hunting, so frequently were she and Charley to be apart. Forty years later, Charley was to declare that he had never spent more than ten consecutive days in one place. These constant small separations, soon an integral part of their marriage, affected the development of Edith's character no less than the shape of her life. Left frequently on her own, she learned to rely on herself and to trust in her own judgement, an aptitude gratefully recognised by Charley when he was serving in France during the 1914-18 war; her nascent independence of mind and spirit flowered; she had perforce to establish her own circle of friends and her own interests. In many ways, these frequent separations were responsible for turning her into the powerful personality she later became, however in the early years of her marriage they were often difficult to bear.

Some of Charley's absences were at the demand of his parents. Within five weeks of their marriage 'the aged man', as Charley was wont to refer to his father, had had a crippling attack of gout and sent his son off to represent him at a function in Ireland. Occasionally, Edith's ill health prevented her from accompanying Charley back to London or down to Wynyard: she was plagued with sinus and antrum trouble all her life. Many more of their separations, however, were due to Charley's determination to comply with the immutable demands of the sporting calendar. Brought up by a father for whom these were imperative, Edith knew better than to question such priorities, but she felt them very much. For any young woman deeply in love and newly married, such separations would have been cruel; for Edith, there must have been an unsettling echo of the constant disappearances of her adored father during her childhood, adding an edge of insecurity to her wretchedness at being left alone.

All her letters breathe her longing for Charley's company. 'There are very good meets all week,' she writes temptingly. 'On Tuesday with the Cheshire, on Thursday with the Meynell and there is a Good Friday meet with the Cheshire. . . . I do long to see you again.' Even in London, there are countless little notes, sent round by hand from Londonderry House to Knightsbridge Barracks. 'Oh, it is rot, darling, not being able to see you when you're so close. I do hate it. Of course I shall wait in till you come tomorrow – what do you take me for? . . . I have been to the Palace, it is awfully good. The biograph is wonderful but I would just as soon have seen you turn out the guard this afternoon and made grimaces at you.'

Edith was very conscious of the glamorous figure her husband cut, especially in uniform. When Queen Victoria drove round London after the relief of Ladysmith on 28 February 1900, she had a subalterns' escort. Charley was detailed to command it, riding at the step of the Queen's carriage ('which will be a most uncomfortable long trot on a rough horse,' he complained. 'I do wish we could go at a slow canter instead'). Edith wrote to him admiringly: 'I wish I was going to see you doing Escort tonight. I am sure you swagger dreadfully! Almost as much as you do out hunting, I expect.'

Whether he did or not, his looks certainly made an impression on the Queen. At the end of the journey, after he had dismounted and escorted her from her carriage to the royal entrance of the Palace, the Queen turned round and, standing on the top step, her full skirts billowing round her, made him a graceful and dignified bow. Shortly afterwards, the Castlereaghs were summoned to dine and sleep the night at Windsor. The Queen liked to see the newly married children of her friends, and Edith's father Henry Chaplin, like the Londonderrys, was well known to Victoria: indeed, she had telegraphed to him from Balmoral for advice when her ponies there got pinkeye, just before Edith's wedding.

At Windsor, Edith and Charley found they were the only guests. Surrounded by the middle-aged to elderly members of the Household, they were the youngest members of the company by far. The Queen, by then nearing the end of her life, lame from rheumatism, sight failing, but as forceful a personality as ever, was pushed into the dining room in a wheelchair. The company sat round a small dining table in the dark, oak-lined room; the Queen, a rapid and copious eater, took little part in the conversation. The Household, chosen for their discretion, talked in hushed tones. After dinner, a circle was formed round her wheelchair and each person in turn called forward for five or ten minutes' conversation, bending down close to the royal face for questions and answers.

Edith was still slightly overwhelmed by her good fortune in marrying her dashing husband, the catch of the Season. She was conscious that in worldly terms he was everything to be desired, fascinated by his physical beauty and enthralled by a sexual expertise that had already caused a first, distant pang of jealousy. It is little wonder that with him she often seems to have assumed the faintly apologetic posture of the one who not only loves the most but does not want to irk the beloved.

'My own darling,' runs a typical letter, 'I am so sorry to bother you but I left the two darling photos of yourself you gave me yesterday in your room. Will you tell Neville to bring them with him. Also your mother has been asking when and where she can see you and wanting me to telephone to you, but I don't want to be a nuisance so I shan't. If you have a moment, you might telephone to someone here to say – you will do this, won't you, if you can. I hate to bother you but I told her I would. I loved seeing you yesterday but I expect I was awfully in the way.' There are little notes saying how she loved going out to dinner or the play with him, asking him to send a line to where she is lunching the next day to arrange a meeting, all showing – in a way incomprehensible to a modern husband or wife – her gratitude for every crumb of his company. 'I feel like a bird with only one wing when you are away.'

But the absences continued. One occurred when he was chosen to accompany Lord Wolseley, on a mission formally to announce the death of Queen Victoria and the accession of Edward VII, in various foreign capitals; in the course of five weeks they visited Vienna, Bucharest, Belgrade, Constantinople and Athens. Others were due to Charley's new job as Adjutant of his regiment. Again and again the demands of work, play and the numerous activities at which the Adjutant was supposed to be present meant that he put off seeing his wife. 'I am going to dine here, I am afraid, as there is a concert here and I shall have to see to it. It is a nuisance but I fear it can't be helped. I am playing in a match at Ranelagh at five o'clock.'

Edith, by now carrying her first child, knew only that no game of polo would have kept her away from Charley. She became depressed and worried by the amount of time he was spending away from her and her insecurities found vent sometimes in miserable and appealing letters, sometimes in spurts of anger. It was to be a recurring pattern – as were the reassurances that Charley invariably gave her. 'You precious old thing, you have made me so happy with your darling letter,' she wrote to him in May. 'I don't mean to worry you, really I don't. I think you imagine my face as I really didn't mean to look worried. I think it is unconscious and I will try hard not to any more.'

But she did. 'I feel such a beast for being so horrid last night,' she wrote in early June. 'But I couldn't help it, really I couldn't, although I knew it was very naughty. I felt so depressed all day and wanted you so much and then when I learned you had to go back I became naughtier' ('naughty' was Edith's euphemism for anger, weeping, or any behaviour that displeased her idolised husband).

'I feel I must have hurt you awfully so I shan't let you come and see me today unless I feel better which I don't at present, as I hate to depress you. You are such an angel. But I was quite good all night as I promised you I would. I don't know what is the matter but I should like to cut my throat when I get in these states. I only want you and I make you unhappy when you come, and I am such a beast that I feel as though you were going away for ages to Ascot. Darling, do forgive me. I know it's only because I have really been feeling very seedy and I will be all right when you come here, if you do, this afternoon. I am really the most selfish beast in the world and feel horrid when you are away. I know I am just a great bore but you do love me, don't you? You won't get this till late and I shall be quite good then. Bless you, darling.' She must not be depressed and unhappy and she must not cry, he replied. 'Please don't, as it is not good for you and you do make me so unhappy . . . darling, please don't be depressed or I shall give up being Adjutant. Bless you, my darling, ever your loving Charley.'

Because of her condition ('I am feeling wretchedly seedy') she did not go with him to Ascot, and neither of them would have expected him to stay away because of her. Ascot was exactly the sort of social occasion Charley liked best. He knew a lot about racing because his family had always bred and owned racehorses. Then there was the spectacle: beautiful horses and beautiful women, both in peak condition and looking their best, to be looked over and admired. While Edith stayed with friends at Cookham, he wrote to her of the goings-on. 'They are all telling foul stories and riddles. Here is one of the most presentable. What is the difference between a March hare and a beautiful woman? One is mad as a hatter of course, the other is had as a matter of course...'

Unfortunately, the latter part of the joke reflected Charley's own philosophy of life.

VI

EVEN BEFORE Edith and Charley's marriage the question of other
women had arisen. In the 'Marlborough House set' that revolved
around the Prince of Wales, while an unmarried girl had to have
a reputation whiter than snow, it was accepted that a married woman,
once she had dutifully presented her husband with one or preferably two
sons, might have discreet affairs. Lady Westmorland was one of the first
in the close-knit network of friends, relations and connections by marriage in which the Londonderrys moved to find herself attracted to their
goodlooking twenty-year-old son.

So obvious was Sybil Westmorland's penchant for the handsome
young cavalryman that there was gossip, which reached the Duke of
Sutherland a few weeks after his niece had become engaged to Charley.
Edith reassured him, and a month before her wedding wrote to Charley
from Dunrobin: 'I know Uncle Strath has written to you to Londonderry
House, for he told me so before he left this morning, darling. He quite
understands now but hopes you will come to Trentham, as he would
very much like to see you. But I assure you everything is all right. But
both father and Uncle Strath are very much annoyed with Sybil. Myself
I don't care because I know it is all nonsense and there is *no-one* like *you*,
is there? But I do think, under the circumstances, especially after having
talked with Uncle and Father, that it would be wiser if you didn't see
Sybil again just yet. ... people are so silly and say such unnecessary
things.'

Writing to him again three days later, still from Scotland, her letter
foreshadowed much of the future shape of their marriage – Charley's
frequent absences, the difficulties of communicating at long distance, his
unfaithfulnesses, their honesty with each other, and her own unqualified
loyalty and belief in him.

'Sybil is up here now, staying with Lady Rosslyn. Darling, you know I don't mind one little bit, I only tell you what I have been told as I promised you I would. You know I shan't say anything about it. I should so like to see you to talk to you. It is impossible to write. I don't know why people *must* talk but it appears that they have. It doesn't matter, does it, to either of us as I shall always tell you and I know you will tell me. I only write as I said I would.'

Now, only a few months after her marriage, she was to learn of something much more serious. Charley had not only had a full-blown affair with another woman, also older and married, he had had a child by her . . . born six weeks after he had married Edith.

This time, his relationship was with someone completely outside the circles in which he and Edith moved. Fannie Ward was a young American actress specialising in roles that chiefly demanded looks, style and allure. She was a beautiful dancer but acting was not her strong point. George Bernard Shaw once described her as 'a determined young lady with plenty of assurance, and gumption, enough to simulate the not very subtle emotions of her part plausibly enough; but she is hardly an artist'.

She first appeared on the London stage at the Gaiety Theatre in November 1884, as Eva Tudor, in *The Shop Girl*. George Edwardes, the owner of the Gaiety, was famous both for bringing the cancan to London and for his ability to pick the loveliest girls for his theatre. Fannie had just one line to speak, written for her by Edwardes himself. It was 'Watch for my wink!' The audience did; in fact, they could hardly take their eyes off her, especially in the principal boy's costume she wore in the second Act: it was said that the beauty of her mouth, often likened to a tiny rosebud, was only equalled by that of her legs.

Fannie Ward (born Fanny Ward Buchanan, in St Louis, Missouri) was petite, with pointed chin, wide-set eyes, a lively, bright-eyed gaze and a mass of dark auburn hair, a pretty doll of a girl and every man who saw her longed to pick her up and put her in his pocket. But her most striking attribute, especially as the years passed, was the youthfulness of her appearance. Later on in her career she was called the Eternal Flapper, and on her pale-blue writing paper were stamped the words Eternal Youth; when she was fifty she successfully played a girl of nineteen and when, at the age of fifty-six, she bobbed her great mass of hair, she looked like a girl in her twenties.

One reason for this extraordinary youthfulness may have been that right through the Edwardian age, when copious eating was the norm, she ate only when she was hungry – generally once a day. 'Avoid sugar, fats, white bread, use ice for your complexion and go to sleep lying on the right side' was one of her maxims. When she died at over eighty, on 27 January 1952, she still weighed only 7 st 2 lb. It was of Fannie that Anita Loos wrote in *Gentlemen Prefer Blondes*: 'When a girl is cute for 50 years it really gets to be history.'

After her London debut she was all the rage, invited wherever pretty young actresses were received socially. Among such places were the huge receptions given by the new 'diamond millionaires', the men who had made fortunes in the past thirty years from the discovery and opening-up of the rich South African diamond mines. One of these was Joseph Lewis, a friend and business colleague of the fabulous Barney Barnato. When 'Diamond Joe' met Fannie at a weekend house party just before the end of 1884, he fell for her straightaway.

For Fannie, it was an excellent match. Diamond Joe settled a huge sum of money on her and was happy for her to continue her stage career. Now, slung about with the marvellous jewels he bought her, she began to specialise in society-lady parts with an element of the titillating, appearing at Drury Lane in September 1895 as Mrs Cholmondely in *Cheer! Boys, Cheer!*, and as Marcella, in *A Night Out at the Vaudeville*, in 1897. Then came *Lord and Lady Algy* in 1898 and, in March 1899, *The Cuckoo*, a piece described by the *Era* as, though amusing, also suggestive 'in the opprobrious sense of the word. Many expressions of the club-room are used with a freedom that is scarcely permissible before a shirted audience.'

One member of this stiff-shirted audience was undoubtedly Charley. For somewhere between *Lord and Lady Algy* and *The Cuckoo*, Charley and the beautiful, diminutive, amusing actress had met. By then she was probably twenty-six or twenty-seven, but the date of her birth was always a well-kept secret. 'I have never known any professional who knows Fannie's correct age,' wrote the actress Geraldine Farrar. One report gives 22 June 1875, but 1872 is more generally accepted. Charley was twenty, just emerged into a London where rich and aristocratic young men regarded beautiful actresses and chorus girls as legitimate prey, before making the usual suitable marriages. Soon, Fannie had become Charley's mistress.

Just about the time of his first serious flicker of interest in Edith, in early May 1899, Fannie found herself pregnant. There is no evidence as to whether she told her lover immediately or, if she did, whether he confided in his father. The only thing certain is that within a month or two both Londonderrys had told their son it was time he got married.

Such a marriage would, of course, destroy any faint hope that Fannie might have of divorcing her own husband and marrying Charley. No doubt the Londonderrys also felt that a beautiful young bride of his own would curb Charley's dangerous tendency towards liaisons with the wives of others. Three months later, when Charley and Edith got engaged, one society columnist was writing: 'I hear that Lord and Lady Londonderry are delighted at Lord Castlereagh's engagement, as they wished him to marry. He is very young. . . .'

Fannie's child was born on 6 February 1900, at 48 Draycott Place, the house in Chelsea bought for her by Joe Lewis. The baby girl was christened Dorothy Mabel (she later changed the spelling of her first name to Dorothé), a blonde, blue-eyed little girl who was to grow up, as everyone later agreed, into 'a real Londonderry'. A few months later, Edith was walking in the Park with one of Charley's brother officers, who seemed to recognise a baby being pushed along in a pram by its nurse. With all the interest of one about to have a child herself, Edith asked him whose baby it was. The young man, embarrassed and apprehensive, refused to say. But her persistence soon elicited the truth.

Charley had apparently hoped to keep the whole affair from his young wife, no doubt terrified of the effect it would have on their relationship. It was natural, however, to confide in his parents. Lord Londonderry advised Charley that he must tell Edith the truth that evening. The next day, thinking that Charley had confessed, he spoke about the baby to Edith and quickly realised that she had known about it for some time.

It would have been enough to send many young women of twenty-two into a state of shock and misery. But Edith was no wilting Victorian flower. Her natural qualities of courage and loyalty came to the fore, banishing any anger she might have felt. She wrote to Charley expressing her complete forgiveness and understanding, saying that she longed only for his happiness, and chiding him for his lack of trust in the strength of her love.

'Darling, I can't go to Woolwich without sending you a short line as I have been thinking about you all the time, and I feel I must tell you that I know quite well *why* you were so unhappy yesterday. I meant to talk to you several days ago but as you never told me anything I wouldn't. I felt as you had never said anything to me you didn't wish to tell me so I wasn't going to ask. But now I wish I had told you I knew; I longed to tell you so last night. Darling, why do you never say anything to me? I have been *so* unhappy about you the last few days as I can't bear you to be unhappy like this. It is not for myself I mind at all, you know that, it is only of you I am thinking because I love you so much. Your Father has been up whilst I am writing and was under the impression that you and I had talked last night . . . I told him that I knew already but that of course I had said nothing. Darling, it makes me quite miserable to think that you should be so unhappy and you won't even tell me. You know I never say anything and I would do anything for you. Bless you darling, and don't be angry with me for writing. Your loving wife.'

Soon, though, the full impact of what she had learned began to make itself felt. The knowledge that someone else had already given her adored husband a child, had stood to him sexually in the same relationship that she did now – and had, perhaps, been loved by him – her views on the indissoluble sanctity of marriage, all resulted in her initial instinct to comfort and support Charley giving way to feelings of shock and distress. 'Although, darling, I am miserable without you, I'd sooner you didn't try and come and I shall hope to see you soon some time or other. I somehow feel now as if I had no right to see or speak to you,' she wrote pathetically a week later.

But in a month or two, both had put this reminder of Charley's past firmly behind them, thanks to Edith's natural good sense and Charley's fervent protestations. 'Oh, Edie my darling, I see by your note that you are most unhappy. . . . I will try and come to you at 11. Do for God's sake be in and don't judge too quickly, please don't. Oh darling, do trust me. I may have done wrong but I swear there is nothing in it. I can't write any more. Ever your loving *husband*.'

There were still storms, but chiefly for the old reason: Edith felt she did not get enough of Charley's time. By now the Blues were stationed at Windsor, there were the activities of the Season, and in addition Charley went to the Guards' Depot in Pirbright in July, to the School of Musketry at Hythe in August and to Inverness to shoot in September. She herself spent part of the summer at Hythe: pregnant women then customarily withdrew from society as their condition became more apparent, and in any case the Season's hectic round of balls, dinner parties and receptions would have been too much for someone suffering from the malaise of early pregnancy.

Living as the young Castlereaghs did in Londonderry House, Charley was to a considerable extent 'on call' to his parents. In July, still feeling neglected, Edith wrote from Hythe: 'I feel I have made you unhappy and myself miserable all because I have a filthy temper. I used not to get cross at things but now I always do. . . . I came up early on purpose to see you but as it is I might just as well have come up late. I haven't seen you to talk to and I did want to. I think that started my being cross. I do love you more than anything in the world, you know that, but I feel horrid at times. When I get stronger perhaps I shan't. Please forgive me, darling, I hate to make you unhappy. I wish we had dined here quietly by ourselves. I feel so unhappy and everything seems wrong but I do love you so much.'

But in September, in the calmer atmosphere of Wynyard, she writes enthusiastically to thank him for a 'lovely little rifle'. Unusual as a present to a woman even today, it reflects both Edith's comparatively convention-free upbringing and her sporting prowess. 'I have had such fun with it today. I got eight bunnies. It is a ripper. You can't miss with it – at least, one oughtn't to.'

Having no home of her own, Edith was anxious to have her child in the house she knew best. Dunrobin, so far away, was naturally out of the question but by the end of November she was installed in Stafford House, with a room for Charley next to hers. Even the imminence of his first child was not allowed to interrupt his sporting calendar: after one shoot in Berkhamsted he went on to another in Staffordshire, at Keele Hall. But Edith's early training in male priorities held firm. 'I do miss you awfully, especially now, but I don't want you to come back till the shoot is over, and you know that, as I really feel fit and well and I am sure you would hate being here. You are such an old angel.' Next day's note – 'I am very well really so you mustn't fuss about me. I am a real beast to keep wanting you back' – continues the pattern of apologetic longing so steadily becoming a feature of their marriage.

On 6 December 1900, their daughter was born. Theresa ordered them to call 'the brat' either Edith Florence or Theresa but Edith, backed by Charley, held out for Maureen Helen. Delighted as she was with her first baby, it was clearly her duty to become pregnant again soon in order to achieve the longed-for heir.

By the beginning of March she was enjoying Lady Warwick's hunting party where, while she was out in the field, a farmer told her that to see the Warwick party reminded him of the Empire. In April she joined her uncle Strath for a cruise to Spain in the ducal yacht, the *Catania*, writing to Charley happily and flirtatiously: 'Mind you don't ogle anyone with your darling goggle blue eyes. You are like a beautiful peacock. I would bite you if I could. I am sure I shall never last five whole weeks away from you.' Autumn meant Dunrobin again while Charley soldiered at

Windsor. And winter, Londonderry House ('I am miserable up here by myself').

During the first few months of 1902, in the routine they had now established for themselves, their base was Springfield. Edith would hunt all week while Charley was on duty at Windsor, and he would join her towards the end of the week for a day or two's hunting together. Occasionally, he was unable to come. 'It seems ages since I had a canoodle with you,' she wrote wistfully in April.

Two circumstances combined to raise her morale dramatically. At the end of April 1902, the Blues returned to the Regent's Park Barracks in Albany Street, and the young Castlereaghs acquired a London home of their own, 21 Cumberland Terrace, just round the corner. Now, surely, she would see more of Charley. Even more exhilarating, she was pregnant again. 'A little joke,' she writes chirpily in late April. 'Have you heard about the new peers, Sir Thomas Lipton and Dr Williamson the Queen's accoucheur? Lord preserve us and Lord deliver us.'

When, after the coronation of King Edward VII on 9 August, Charley went off as usual to shoot grouse – at Allendale, in Northumberland – Edith cheerfully accepted an invitation to Lowther Castle. Here she was clearly the belle of the party, with an old flame sighing over her and her host, Lord Lonsdale, confiding in her that the velvet for his coronation robes came out at five pounds a yard and asking her to call him by his Christian name, Hugh. 'Colonel Putty is here – a merry little man, and the little Wilson, who at one time used to love me dearly.' Colonel Pulteney, born in 1861, had joined the Scots Guards, and had served in Uganda, where he had become a keen big-game shot, and throughout the South African War which had ended only ten weeks earlier. In twelve years' time, Edith was to make full use of this new friendship. At the end of the visit, Lonsdale pressed on her four photographs of himself as a parting gift.

From Lowther she went on to Dunrobin, where the Sutherlands were entertaining the new King and Queen ('both very well and so pleased to see this place again') who were greeted by a pipe band which played outside the Castle. There were picnics, a deer drive and photography. 'The Queen would insist on Kodaking Millie and me the other day and I heard the King go up and say in an audible whisper "Take the heads, my dear."' Charley, at Windsor, received reports on the beauty and charm of his little daughter. 'Maureen is too angelic. Everyone is in love with her, and you have no idea how pretty and wicked she is. You have never seen such mischievous eyes. She won't look at a woman!' The little girl would not go near the Queen, said Edith, but liked the King. Charley responded, as always, lovingly if more briefly ('Bless you, my precious darling, Always your loving Charley'). All Edith hoped was that the coming child would be a boy or, in their private language, a 'buck'.

It was. Their son, Edward Charles Stewart Robert, was born at Cumberland Terrace on 18 November. It was a quick and easy birth; 'Edith has just had a boy in about two minutes', ran the pencilled note Charley sent round immediately to Londonderry House. Two days later, a letter came from Windsor Castle. 'My dear Charlie,' it read, 'I must write a few lines of congratulation to you and Edith on the birth of a "son and heir" as I know how pleased you must both be. It would give me great pleasure to stand as godfather to your little boy, and trusting that "mother and child" are doing well, Believe me, Yours very sincerely, Edward R.' The baby, always known as Robin, was baptised at the Chapel Royal in St James's Palace the following month, by the Reverend Angus Bethune, who had baptised three generations of the Londonderry family and had been chaplain to the famous Frances Anne; born in 1810, he claimed to remember hearing the first news of Waterloo. The King, who stood sponsor in person, gave his godchild an antique gilt porringer. It was a charming present and a handsome tribute to both families.

With a newborn son, in a London house of her own and her husband stationed only a few hundred yards away, 1903 opened happily for Edith. Her relationship with Charley had settled down into one of loving tenderness that coexisted with a powerful physicality – Edith was never shy about expressing desire. She was also on excellent terms with Charley's parents, often mediating when Charley was reluctant to comply with his father's wishes, and obediently appearing whenever Theresa wished her to be at Londonderry House. Theresa found her two grandchildren just as fascinating as did their mother. 'Your mother came to see me yesterday and suggested that I should have three daughters, one of whom was to be entirely adopted by her,' Edith told Charley. It was a more accurate prophecy than any of them realised: three more daughters were in fact to be born – though none of them was brought up by Theresa.

Very quickly, Edith was well enough to go down to Springfield again and hunt as usual. She continued feeding her baby boy, as she had done her daughter, until, when he was four and a half months old, she was advised to wean him. 'I am rather fussed about it all. It is rather anxious work for the first few days.' Two days later, on 4 April, she was able to report: 'Robin is doing well, and there is no more bother with him. He loves his bottle, and holds it to him with his little hands.'

Three months later, Edith developed double pneumonia, complicated by pleurisy. For eleven days her life was in danger and she was forced to miss the King and Queen's visit to Mount Stewart at the end of July. It was the first time the royal couple had stayed there and everything in the rooms set aside for them was new, with the linen and hangings specially woven by the girls and women on the estate. The Londonderrys gave the King their own rooms, which were on the ground floor (and incidentally possessed the only bath with running water in the house), while the Queen was given a bedroom and sitting room on the first floor. As Mount Stewart was not large enough to accommodate the King, the Queen, Princess Victoria, the ladies and gentlemen of the Household and all their servants – the Queen alone was always accompanied by her maid, dresser and a sergeant footman – some of this throng had to be put up in tents. But everything ran like clockwork, thanks chiefly to the Mount Stewart housekeeper, a majestic figure, swathed in grey alpaca in the mornings and black silk in the evenings. A widow with two children, so strict that the housemaids were never allowed out alone, she ran the place like a small kingdom with the aid of the house steward.

Mount Stewart, with its wide lawns and woods through which an occasional silvery glimpse of the Lough could be discerned, worked its usual spell. After Sunday morning service in the private chapel, the King and Queen called Theresa into their sitting room and gave her what she described as 'a most lovely bracelet, their two miniatures set in diamonds, with the Royal crown and cyphers, and green enamel shamrocks on the sides'. Even if Edith had been well enough to travel, Mount Stewart would probably have been the worst place for someone convalescing after pneumonia. 'Beautiful place, but very damp', wrote Queen Alexandra in the visitors' book.

It took Edith a long time to recover from her illness, and she was ordered by her doctor to winter abroad. The Castlereaghs decided to go out to India, travelling on the same ship as Lord Curzon. The Viceroy was returning to India after coming back to England to see his wife, who was seriously ill; she died three years later. Early in December they arrived in Bombay, where Edith and Charley stayed with Lord and Lady

Lamington at Government House on Malabar Point before making a round of visits to various princely states.

It was a period of intense pro-British feeling among the Indian princes, after the high point of the Durbar in January at which they had affirmed their loyalty to the new King Emperor. One with whom the Castlereaghs stayed wore Victoria's miniature set in diamonds instead of an aigrette on the front of his turban. Many of them had been educated in England, and some had sent their sons and daughters to school there or employed English governesses.

They entertained the Castlereaghs with all the magnificence of which they were capable. There was pigsticking in the marvellous Indian dawn – Edith rode a beautiful little Arab horse which ran away with her through a prickly-pear hedge – hunting blackbuck with a tame cheetah, a tiger shoot laid on by the Nizam of Hyderabad and crocodile shooting from the banks of the Jumna. Charley got a good one, which was brought home, stuffed and put in the nursery as a toy for Maureen and Robin. They spent Christmas with Lord Curzon, a friend both of Edith's father and her parents-in-law, at Barrackpur, the viceregal country lodge, returning from early service to find breakfast spread under a giant banyan tree on a terrace festooned with morning glory.

After India, the Castlereaghs travelled on to Japan, to be fascinated by the cleanliness, the beautiful teeth, the happy children ('you never saw or heard a child cry') and the sight of Japanese businessmen wearing bowler hats with kimonos.

They also had themselves tattooed. For a soldier, this was not particularly unusual, especially as Charley had chosen a conventional design for a conventional place – his regimental badge on his left forearm.

Edith's tattoo was another matter: a snake climbing up her left leg. Both, naturally, would have been ignorant of modern psychological views on the sexual symbolism of snakes; yet this twisting serpent perfectly expressed Edith's innate freedom of spirit and her powerful sexuality, both safely cloaked by her observance of the conventions. For Charley and Edith, though, these tattoos must have held a special significance – tattooing, especially for a large design such as Edith's, was a painful process – a mutual romantic decoration to serve as a permanent private reminder of this 'second honeymoon'. At the time, of course, neither Edith nor anyone else foresaw the shortening of skirts; when the snake eventually appeared in public, curling up from her ankle round her calf to disappear into the shortish hemlines of the twenties and thirties, it created a sensation.

They came back via Canada, crossing the Pacific to Vancouver in the *Empress of Ireland* (later sunk in the 1914–18 War). The voyage took fifteen days with a following sea that seemed to Edith as if 'great walls of water on all sides, hundreds of feet high, must break over the ship'. After briefly stopping in Toronto and New York, they sailed home on the *Kaiser Wilhelm*. The long, romantic months alone with Charley were over. Edith returned to the children and Charley to regimental duties.

VII

C HARLEY WAS an efficient adjutant, and enjoyed the work, especially in the chance it gave him to widen his experience. 'It is here I gained what little knowledge I possess of handling men,' he wrote later. His own natural elegance made him especially effective on the question of smartness of turnout, a particular concern of the King's, as this letter written by his Private Secretary Sir Frederick ('Fritz') Ponsonby, on 4 August 1903 shows. '. . . The King feels that the smart appearance of the Escort and the excellent manner in which they performed their duties during his visit to Northern Ireland is in no small degree due to your work as Adjutant of the Regiment. To mark his appreciation he therefore wishes to confer on you the Victorian Order . . .'

Charley answered by return, a punctiliousness which appealed greatly to the King. 'Your letter and the promptness with which you sent it received full marks. The King said only an adjutant could send an answer in so short a time,' wrote Fritz Ponsonby on 7 August.

Almost at once, there was another honour for the family. When the Prime Minister, Lord Salisbury, had resigned on 11 July 1902, he was succeeded by the Leader of the Conservative Party in the House of Commons, his nephew Arthur James Balfour, Chief Secretary for Ireland during Lord Londonderry's viceroyalty and the darling of the Souls – 'To each is dear Arthur the dearest,' said Curzon. The Duke of Devonshire was Lord President of the Council, a position which also carried the responsibility for Education. Balfour separated the two posts, creating the Board of Education and making Lord Londonderry its first President, with a seat in the Cabinet. In 1903, the Duke resigned the Lord Presidency, which was then offered to Londonderry, thus again linking the office with Education.

The King, who was going to stay with the Londonderrys at Wynyard in October to shoot, decided that the appointment of Londonderry as Lord President should be made at a Privy Council held there. The usual large house party of the King's intimates and those likely to amuse him had been invited. But not everyone was pleased. 'I shall have to travel 500 miles in 24 hours, at a moment when I am particularly busy, in order to assist at a ceremony that will occupy 10 seconds,' grumbled Sir Almeric Fitzroy, Clerk to the Privy Council.

Theresa, of course, was overjoyed. It was a signal honour: not since 1625, when Charles I held a Council at Wilton (the Lord Pembroke of the day was his Chamberlain) had one been held in a subject's house. Adding to the sweetness of this accolade was the fact that the Duchess of Devonshire was to be of the house party. Louisa Devonshire alone could claim with justice to excel Lady Londonderry as a social and political hostess. Only that June she had given a dinner at Devonshire House to celebrate the King's birthday at which thirty peers and Privy Councillors sat down. (On the King's left was his old friend Henry Chaplin, who said afterwards that he had never had a better dinner in his life except for one trifling point: the grapes with the ortolans were not stoned. Chaplin asked his host the Duke to convey a message to this effect to the Duchess. What the Duchess said is not recorded.)

The King travelled north on 18 October by special train, leaving London at 2.00 p.m. and arriving at Thorpe Thewles – the nearest station to Wynyard – at 6.55. Here he was met by Lord Londonderry and Charley. The only other passengers were the Duke and Duchess of Devonshire and Count Mensdorff, the Austrian Ambassador. The rest of the party, already at Wynyard and lingering over tea in the library while they awaited the King's arrival, were Lord and Lady Shaftesbury, Lord and Lady Crewe, the Earl of Kintore, Mr Walter and Lady Doreen Long, the Hon. Sir Seymour Fortescue, Fritz Ponsonby, Sir Edward Hamilton and the woman without whom no party for the King was complete, his mistress Mrs Keppel.

The next day the King held two Councils at Wynyard. The first was at 11.00 in the morning, the second at 10.30 in the evening, and the Orders in Council were headed in the time-honoured fashion 'At our Court at Wynyard', which further delighted Theresa. The second Council, at which Lord Londonderry was made Lord President, took place in the dining room as soon as the ladies had left; immediately afterwards, the King sat down to bridge with Mrs Keppel, the Duchess of Devonshire, and Sir Seymour Fortescue. Most of the others settled down to poker. After bridge, the King gave the ladies permission to retire for the night, and spent half an hour talking to the men of the party.

By now, Edith was an established beauty. '*The Lady Castlereagh held court nearby/A very Venus, goddess fair of love* . . .' is how she figures in one ode to famous beauties of the day. Men frequently pursued her; and looking at her face with its rounded chin, clear, faintly amused eyes and air of youth and gaiety as it appears in contemporary photographs, it is easy to see why. But, passionately in love with her own husband, she was emotionally insulated from the advances of her admirers, treating them with a genuine, relaxed friendliness. With no romantic interest to give her pause, she was able to cultivate such friendships, which often became lifelong. She was always at home in male company, openly avowing a preference for it, and, indeed, all her great friends were men ('she is not a great friend,' she once wrote of some female acquaintance, 'for that is not a thing a *woman* will ever be to me'). Charley, perhaps with his own behaviour in mind, sometimes cautioned her against this freedom but Edith was able to reply that his advice was unnecessary – and turn it quickly to her own advantage over her perennial complaint, his frequent absences.

'I am yours only and belong to no one else. All the same, I don't think you must go off and leave me alone any more as naturally a lone woman is always considered fair prey and it irritates me to feel someone else wants me too. I am so jealous of *you* as you are so beautiful and attractive. . . .'

It was in many ways a halcyon period. Their letters of this time are filled with private nicknames and expressions, little shorthand messages of passion and euphemisms for making love. His notes to her breathe adoration and devotion ('Can't you understand, my darling, that I worship you? and that I love you? I would give up anything just to make you happy. . . .'). Hers to him, though they express the longing of a woman deeply fulfilled in her love, still reiterate her underlying belief that she is somehow not good enough for him. One of the loving letters she always wrote him on their wedding anniversary, no matter whether they were apart or in the same house, declares: 'What a darling you are and how happy we have been – and I love you more than ever I did and never cease to be thankful to the Almighty for arranging our fates as he did. I know you are much the better horse of the two – you are really, and you have no idea how I admire and respect you.' Again and again, this theme is repeated. Expressions like 'I know you are too good for me. I do really know this' recur constantly, giving the impression of a lurking anxiety that was, in the event, to be harshly justified. For within the next few years, there were to be two major changes in her life. The first would change the channel in which their lives ran – 'the lovely life of soldiering and hunting' – the second would cause Edith an anguished reassessment of her marriage.

For the present, the closeness of their Indian idyll infused their relationship, though for Edith some of the old torments remained. 'You must always love me, otherwise you know you would break my heart. You are the only creature that I could love, and I feel this so strongly that it makes me quite angry sometimes with myself and you, because I feel so helpless and at your mercy.'

Nevertheless, she felt certain enough of Charley's constancy to take the children happily off to the seaside (Maureen had been ill), where the post brought notes almost every day saying how he loved and missed her.

Edith's sense of emotional security must have been further enhanced when, in October 1905, after an evening at the theatre with his father, Charley wrote dismissively of his former love and mother of his first child. '. . . Father and I sat next Fannie Ward at the Palace last night. I did not tell him because she looked so odd and was with a very seedy-looking man. I think she has come down in the world. I think she wanted to say something to me but I looked right through her.'

In fact, far from being down on her luck, Fannie's career was prospering. She was an established stage star and within ten years would make her first film. From 1902 onwards she appeared in a string of hits in London and New York, in the society parts she had made her own, including Nance in *In the Bishop's Carriage* in 1906, Fanny in *Fanny and The Servant Problem* in 1908 and Ethel Toscani in *The Price* in 1912. Playing Lady Gerrard in *Who's Who*, at the Savoy in 1904, she wore diamonds said to have been worth £200,000 given to her by her husband, Diamond Joe Lewis.

Lord Londonderry's evening out with his son may have been to discuss Charley's future in a more relaxed way than Theresa's presence would have allowed. Charley had been aware for some time that his parents wished him to enter Parliament. When, during the summer of 1905, it became evident that a General Election was imminent, Lord Londonderry told his son that he expected him to leave the Army and find a constituency. Both Edith and Charley had known that 'one day' Charley would be expected to enter the House of Commons, as his father had done before him, but they had not expected this to happen so soon.

When Lord Londonderry first made his wishes known, Edith, always good at grasping the nettle, had written to Charley: 'Just because I hate the idea so I feel there must be something in it, and I shall wait eagerly to hear what Colonel Fenwick [Charley's commanding officer] thinks. After all, I cannot see that there is really an urgent hurry to enter politics. It is only the question of it being a real chance, as it undoubtedly is but it is a cruel case to decide as I do so want to see you play polo in the [Inter] Regimental. All my sympathies are with this. And yet I feel it is I who ought to help you do the thing I loathe – I love your being in the Regiment. At the same time, nothing that is worth doing or having is ever attained without some sacrifice. I really cannot advise you in the matter, as I only feel I tempt you, like I do in other ways sometimes, of which I am very proud. I only know I love you harder every day, and you are the only man in the world and looked so beautiful today, with large googly eyes.'

Though today it might seem strange that a grown man in a profession that he loved and in which he was doing well should be arbitrarily ordered into a new career by his father, both saw it as part of an inevitable, ordered, pattern. At the beginning of the twentieth century a comparatively small group of people, of similar birth and background, related to each other by blood or connected by marriage, formed 'Society'. It was from this class that most of those who governed the country were drawn, their network of kinship and friendship cutting across party lines.

Even in Society there were several distinct circles: the old-fashioned aristocrats, territorial grandees who wielded enormous local and political power; the Souls, intellectual, sensitive, given to tender friendships between the sexes expressed in extravagantly romantic and affectionate language, equally aristocratic and also rich; the set that revolved around the King, pleasure-loving, fast, often regarded as vulgar by the first and second groups, smart and entertaining. The King's friends were in general the richest of all, including as they did men who knew how to make money rather than just spend it: the King was the first member of the royal family to befriend financiers like Lord Burnham, Sir Ernest Cassel, Arthur Sassoon and the Rothschilds. Indeed, entertaining him bankrupted some of the less wealthy of his friends.

All these circles overlapped, in a way that could be seen in Edith's own immediate family. Her uncle the Duke of Sutherland was a great landowner who, while primarily concerned with the running of his estates, offered Stafford House as a venue for meetings to further political objectives he favoured, such as Tariff Reform. Her Aunt Millicent, languid and exquisite, with her apricot pekineses settled on her lap or swirling round her feet, was a Soul, as well as being a blend of Victorian aristocratic hostess and social worker. Her father was a sporting countryman, a politician, a man who had remained faithful to the memory of his dead wife in the highest Victorian tradition, yet a close friend of the King's. Apart from wealth, pleasure and, with a few exceptions, birth, the common denominator among these people was involvement to a greater or lesser extent in the business of government: in those days if you were born into a certain social circle politics played a big part in your life.

This was as true for the women as for the men. Attending Parliament was a regular part of their social round. They sat behind the grille in the Speaker's Gallery in the Commons or in the Peeresses' Gallery in the Lords, listening to the great debates and the speeches of husbands, lovers, brothers or friends, which they talked about when they met the same men at dinner that evening. Edith herself had heard politics discussed all her life and, through her father, who sat in the Cabinet as the first President of the Board of Agriculture, had met all the prominent politicians of the day. She was familiar also with the mechanics of elections. She had seen her father galloping from meeting to meeting in his two-horse fly, its sides pasted over with sheets of pink paper as he exhorted the voters of Sleaford to support him once more, and she had played a part herself by driving constituents to the polling station in a small carriage drawn by a pair of Shetland ponies with long pink streamers flying from their tails and behind their ears.

Lord Londonderry wanted his son to represent County Down, a safe Unionist seat which he regarded almost as a pocket borough, but here Charley, backed up by Edith, jibbed. Both of them wanted a constituency nearer London and their friends, from which they could continue their social life and their foxhunting. Lord Londonderry next tried to interest his son in a constituency near Wynyard. 'Father is most anxious I should fight a forlorn hope at Hartlepool of all places. He wants to get me to stay the winter at Wynyard but I don't think I shall comply.'

Eventually, Charley was invited to contest the borough of Maidstone (once briefly Disraeli's seat), a small constituency of only 6,000 voters, and by the beginning of December had decided to accept. His election seemed unlikely as the sitting member, the Liberal Sir Francis Evans, was popular and all the signs were that the Liberal Party would be returned to power. The most important issues were Free Trade versus Protection, and the question of Home Rule for Ireland.

Charley had barely a month to prepare his campaign. 'Your vote and interest is respectfully solicited on behalf of Viscount Castlereagh', ran the message on his election literature, below an oval portrait of Charley in uniform with the Union Jack on one side and the harp of Ireland on the other. He was launched with the good wishes of the Prime Minister, Arthur Balfour, who sent him a telegram saying: 'Wish you every success. You have a name which should rally all Unionists to your standard now that the Union is again in peril.' What rallied them even more were the speeches by Sir Edward Carson – originally his parents' protégé during his father's viceroyalty and subsequently introduced by them into London politics and society. Charley worked out an effective speech which he delivered at meetings and – there were no women voters to bother about – at all-male gatherings such as 'smoking dinners', after which Sir Edward, formidable, eloquent and witty, drove home the Unionist message.

Edith, with two small children, took little part in the campaign. In any case, her efforts would have been overshadowed by the dramatic and imposing method of canvassing favoured by her mother-in-law. Theresa campaigned for her son in the grand manner, playing the marchioness for all she was worth and sweeping round the constituency in her barouche, with its four horses and postilions. Charley, staying at the Royal Star Hotel in Maidstone, was delighted, and convinced that no one could withstand such a glamorous canvasser. 'It is splendid your coming down here & I am sure your presence will do me no end of good; of course I will make out a programme for you but the fact of your being here and driving about, in fact giving the Maidstone people a show, will assist me a great deal,' he told her on 28 December.

Theresa's unorthodox tactics worked, though watching the grand equipage with Theresa inside, her proud Talbot nose raised in the air beneath one of her huge feathered hats, addressing the Maidstone voters with her customary blend of imperiousness and charm, the local chairman of the Conservative Association was moved to remark: 'I should think it was almost the last time when such an argument was brought to bear on an English electorate.'

The election of January 1906 was a Liberal landslide, bringing to an end over ten years of Conservative rule. Against the prevailing tide, Charley scored a spectacular triumph, defeating the popular sitting Member by just 132 votes to win back Maidstone for the Conservatives.

His defeated and furious opponent immediately filed an election petition, alleging ninety-seven separate charges of corrupt practices, but was unable to prove any of them.

By contrast, Edith's father, who had held his Lincolnshire seat for thirty-eight years without a break, now lost it. Sorrowfully, his Sleaford supporters gave him a portrait and a commemorative address. In 1907 he got back into Parliament as Member for Wimbledon with a majority of almost 7,000, defeating the Hon. Bertrand Russell, who fought under the unpopular banner of Women's Suffrage. Chaplin commented that he 'might be very old-fashioned', but he 'drew the line at that'.

Charley made his maiden speech on the third day of the new session, speaking on Home Rule. Edith sat with her mother-in-law in the gallery and Lord Londonderry was in the Peers' Gallery. The main thrust of Charley's speech was that, while no one was more in sympathy than himself with the view that Ireland ought to be governed in accordance with Irish ideas, he believed that those ideas must be consistent with the unity of the Empire. His speech was well received. 'While disagreeing with the views expressed by the Noble Lord,' said the new Chief Secretary for Ireland, 'we on this side recognise the talent and grace with which his speech was composed and delivered.' However graceful Charley's speech had been, though, it would have stood little chance against next day's maiden speaker, F. E. Smith, who burst upon the House in electrifying fashion. Carson introduced F. E. to Theresa, and from then on he was one of the Londonderry House circle.

Unfortunately, oratory was not the only thing on which Charley had been concentrating. His second cousin, the ninth Duke of Marlborough, had married a beautiful American heiress, Consuelo Vanderbilt. She was a captivating creature, with pale, almost translucent skin, long black hair, the swan neck then so much admired, oval face, languid dark eyes and graceful deportment. From the nursery she had been groomed to become the exquisite wife of a man who fulfilled her mother's ideal of social importance. She was never allowed out into even the mildest sunshine without a parasol or gloves, had a steel rod strapped to her spine during lessons to ensure an upright, elegant carriage, had at all times to converse in French with her mother, and had her dreams of going to Oxford to study literature – she was extremely clever – ruthlessly squashed.

Her marriage to the Duke of Marlborough in November 1895 was little more than a straightforward business deal: his title for her millions – the day after the wedding, the Duke received from his father-in-law 50,000 shares in the Beech Creek Railroad, conservatively valued at $2.5

million. The nineteen-year-old Consuelo, forced into the marriage by her mother, was deeply in love with another man at the time. Although she did her best to fulfil her side of the bargain, bearing her husband an heir and playing the role of chatelaine of Blenheim with grace and charm, this loveless union inevitably contained the seeds of its own destruction.

Edith and Charley, who was a second cousin of the Duke, were frequent visitors to Blenheim, though after their return from India Edith, busy with her small children and their house at Springfield, went there less frequently. The Marlborough marriage was disintegrating. Consuelo, adrift, beautiful and alluring, was too much for Charley. Caught in the throes of a sudden passion, they ran off to Paris.

A discreet affair would have been one thing; an elopement was quite another. Theresa, determined to save her son from a scandal that might ruin his life as well as destroy his marriage, realised that this was the moment to make use of her friendship with the King and Queen – the only people whose disapproval would be even more effective than her own. The culprits were summoned and castigated so effectively that the affair was quickly scotched. Charley's marriage was saved, but the Marlboroughs went their separate ways and separated in January 1907.

Edith's misery over the Consuelo affair can be imagined. This was quite different from the discovery of a previous love in her husband's life. If he could not resist someone already married to his own cousin, whom could he resist?

Charley himself was deeply penitent, terrified that he might lose his wife's love. 'My own darling Edie . . . I feel you are beginning to hate me. I don't think I have been nice to you. I have been cruel and unkind to you and now I believe you do not care about me at all. It is very sad and I feel it very much. Your face always used to light up when you saw me and you always used to look at me across the table and now you never want to see me and you never want to talk to me and you seem to want me to go away from you. . . . Forgive me, my darling, and do love me again. Always your loving and just as devoted husband.'

Edith could not stand it. 'Please don't be unhappy any more, I can't bear it,' she wrote in a letter that must have heaped coals of fire upon Charley's head. 'You are the best and most unselfish husband that exists, and I love you very much. But I don't think, darling Charker, that it is quite fair to say that other people have made the mischief. What has been done has been done by ourselves. I did experience a real deep shock in the early summer and it showed me with a clearness and abruptness how foundations which one imagines to be firmly built on rocks seem

73

as nothing when a great wave of – what shall I say? – feeling anything you like, comes along.

'After this happened, I set out to alter the old conditions of things to the new. It is not in my nature to do otherwise. God alone knows what I expected in the summer when I felt that everything was slipping and sliding away from me. Then I said to myself that I knew there was another side to you which was mine for always, no matter what you said or did, and that I would stick to that and keep it come what may. Insensibly and almost imperceptibly to me, in fact far less apparent to me, darling, than to you, my feelings had to undergo a change, unless I was going to make a public ass of myself. But ... I love you as I shall never love anybody else, because after what we have been it is impossible not to. Nothing will ever alter this. I admire you, I am proud of you, I would do anything for you and I shall be for ever grateful to you. If you think I am indifferent to you in other ways, you of course are the best judge. I only know, darling, that I had to choose one way or the other.'

Her long and analytical letter shows that she has fully realised one unpleasant truth that from now on would be integral to their marriage: her husband was an incurable philanderer.

'... for some time, darling husband, I have realised that yours is a nature to which in some ways a wife cannot be everything. I did realise this before [the summer] and even though I think I loved you in every other way more, I never liked you less for this because you are such a darling. Still it is bound in the long run to, not destroy, but lessen a little one's sentiments in this respect. I always felt you must have some girl to play about with, though I kept saying to myself, and I fear I often annoyed you openly about it, that it didn't matter. It didn't really, only eventually I suddenly found that I myself did not so much care even if I thought you fancied you liked someone else.' It was a bitter lesson for a girl of twenty-six to learn.

It took Edith some time to recover from Charley's betrayal. Her letters to him throughout the subsequent months continued to show undiminished affection, but affection as to a dearest friend rather than a lover: the earlier, unmistakable note of passion was missing. In early summer it appears again. The truth was that Edith simply could not keep her distance from Charley. She found him far too attractive; and to both the relief of forgiveness was immense.

Their reconciliation probably took place during a glamorous and dramatic visit to Madrid. King Alfonso XIII of Spain had proposed to Princess Victoria Eugenie ('Ena') of Battenberg during a ball at Londonderry

House, and Charley and Edith were invited to their wedding. Princess Ena was a granddaughter of Queen Victoria, and her uncle King Edward VII and Queen Alexandra were to be represented by the Prince and Princess of Wales – the Prince highly disapproving of his cousin's conversion to Catholicism in order to marry into the Spanish royal family.

After the nuptial mass, everyone except those in the royal procession went straight back to the Palace, where they awaited the arrival of the King and Queen. Edith, standing on the grand staircase facing the entrance, could see directly through the archway by which the royal coach would enter the Palace courtyard. Suddenly, a coach and horses dashed through the archway at full gallop, pulling up at the entrance in a cloud of dust. 'Oh, my God!' whispered Edith, clutching Charley's arm as Alfonso, deathly pale and in tears, got out and half-carried, half-supported his weeping, fainting Queen into the Palace. Her dress and the white lace mantilla covering her head and shoulders were full of holes from gunpowder burns and spattered with blood and grisly fragments of matter – two bombs had been thrown from an upstairs window and one had exploded under the horses. It was the anniversary of an attempt on the King's life the previous year in the Rue de Rohan, Paris.

The King and Queen showed great bravery when, immediately after the wedding breakfast, they made their planned tour of the city in an open carriage. Edith, who admired courage more than anything else, was overcome. Later, she and the King became close friends, a link that endured all their lives. Whenever he was in England he telephoned her, and she and Charley were often his guests in Spain where they would race one of his six-metre yachts from the Royal Palace at Santander. Edith's extraordinary strength and fitness made their mark here too: once, when a Basque deckhand fell overboard she grabbed him by the seat of his trousers before the swell could carry him away and pulled him back to safety. The sailor, astonished by such strength in a woman, later remarked disapprovingly to the King: 'It must be a desperate bad thing for any man to have so strong a wife.'

VIII

CHARLEY WAS a reluctant Member of Parliament. He was bored by the debates and took little interest in the business of the House ('I made a speech today, not a good one as I had not prepared it as carefully as I ought to have done'). Once he even attempted to offload his seat. 'I travelled with Sir Reginald Macleod to Inverness. I tried to find out if he would like to take Maidstone on but could not discuss much as I was unwilling to show my hand.'

His unwilling entry into politics was followed shortly afterwards by his father's equally unwilling departure. The rout of the Conservatives had given the new Prime Minister, Sir Henry Campbell-Bannerman, an overall majority of 114, and he could normally also rely on 136 Labour and Irish Nationalist votes (the Conservatives and the Liberal Unionists held on to only 157 seats). Lord Londonderry, affable, distinguished in manner and bearing, his vagueness about education often cloaked by volubility, ceased to be Lord President, surrendering the seals of office on 11 December 1906. Theresa did not disguise her regret at this change of fortune for both the Tories and her husband, though she carried it off in her usual grand manner.

The political scene was in any event changing rapidly. The Prime Minister was a sick man. He spent most of the autumn of 1907 resting quietly in Scotland. On 13 November, less than two weeks after his return, he had a massive heart attack. He weighed twenty stone and the prognosis was not good. His doctors ordered him to Biarritz to convalesce and he remained there until 20 January 1908, returning to preside over the Cabinets leading up to the King's speech at the opening of the 1908 session. He seemed fit and well – but on 12 February he made his last speech in the House of Commons. That night he had another heart attack.

For the next fortnight or so it was thought he might recover. The King, in Biarritz for six weeks with a party which included Mrs Keppel, did not want any changes while he was away. But Campbell-Bannerman's doctors told him that he could not go on, and on 1 April he wrote to the King resigning. The King, determined not to break his own holiday, acknowledged his Prime Minister's letter and then wrote on 4 April to Herbert Henry Asquith, asking him to form a government. The King would not return to London, and Asquith, to his annoyance, had to travel to Biarritz to kiss hands. The King was much criticised for this, and his suggestion that Asquith's new ministers should likewise come to Biarritz to receive their seals of office was successfully resisted. Campbell-Bannerman, too ill to be moved, remained at 10 Downing Street where he died on 22 April.

Asquith's premiership introduced an era when political differences would no longer be fought out only in the Palace of Westminster but would break up friendships, disrupt families – and, where female suffrage was concerned, divide husbands and wives.

At first Edith missed their previous army life as much as did Charley, despite diversions such as the Duchess of Westminister's polo week with its house party of forty. She soon found that her husband's new career sparked her own first glimmerings of political interest – or rather, the realisation that any effective political action was out of reach of her and of any other woman. Bold, dashing, self-reliant, as used to taking an independent line in conversation as across country, she did not hesitate to make it clear that her sympathies lay with those struggling to achieve female suffrage. Her father, parents-in-law and most of her circle took the opposite point of view and disapproved heartily. Charley wisely remained neutral; later he was more supportive.

The first demand that women should have a vote had been put forward by the Chartists at the time of Queen Victoria's accession – though the Queen herself was a bitter and lifelong opponent of 'this mad, wicked folly of "Women's Rights", with all its attendant horrors', once exclaiming furiously that a peeress who had attended one of the movement's conferences 'ought to get a GOOD WHIPPING!'

Despite royal disapproval, the feminist movement grew rapidly in the second half of the century. The Earl of Carlisle presented a petition to the House for female suffrage in 1851 and the first Women's Suffrage Committee was formed in London in 1861. But as John Stuart Mill, who had himself presented a petition for female suffrage to the House of Commons in 1866, pointed out in his essay *The Subjection of Women* (published in 1869), 'A woman who joins in any movement which her husband disapproves, makes herself a martyr, without even being able to be an apostle, for the husband can legally put a stop to her apostleship. Women cannot be expected to devote themselves to the emancipation of women until men in considerable numbers are prepared to join with them in the undertaking.' And to date, men were not only not so prepared, they were fighting the prospect tooth and nail – often aided by women themselves. For most men and many women firmly believed that the Almighty had ordained that woman was inferior to man in every respect – except, perhaps, in beauty and goodness – and from childhood women absorbed the doctrine of subordination and submissiveness. Many books laid down the canons of correct female behaviour and the need to 'render homage to her husband as a superior'. As late as 1895 a Royal Commission seriously doubted whether 'a girl's brains were able to grapple with the difficulties of vulgar fractions'.

Nevertheless, there were various advances, most notably the Married Woman's Property Act, 1882. Until then, despite piecemeal improvements (in 1877, a married woman's earnings were safeguarded in Scotland) all that a woman owned outright automatically became the property of her husband, and remained so even if he deserted her (the only way round this was for her property to be held in trust for her). The Bill putting forward the revolutionary idea that what a wife owned outright should not become her husband's property was widely opposed: honest men opposed it because they could see no reason why their wives should cease to trust them with their property, dishonest husbands because they could see every reason. The heart of the objection was most clearly expressed by Lord Fraser in 1881. 'The protection which has been thrown around a married woman already is sufficient,' he declared in Parliament, 'and why she should be allowed to have money in her pocket to deal with as she thinks fit I cannot understand.' When the 1882 Act became law the property of the married woman was protected but her vote was as far off as ever.

By the turn of the century the struggle was hotting up. The supporters of 'Woman Suffrage', as it was generally known, wrote letters, lectured, held meetings, lobbied Members of Parliament and sent deputations to Cabinet ministers. Again and again Bills were presented to Parliament, again and again they were outvoted, dismissed or talked out on any pretext however frivolous. The year Edith came out, for instance, one such Private Bill lost its chance when filibustered by a member speaking on a Bill relating to 'verminous persons'.

More subtly, the energy, conviction and determination that had brought women's cause to the centre of the stage had the effect of polarising opinion, thus rendering all opposition more determined and entrenched. Much of that opposition came from other women, hitherto more or less silent. Mrs Humphry Ward's Appeal Against Female Suffrage – also signed, to her later chagrin, by Beatrice Webb – was made to counter the work of the International Council of Women, formed in 1870.

By 1903, the campaigners had split into two camps, popularly known as suffragists and suffragettes. The goal of both was the same: votes for women on the same terms as votes for men. This was, in fact, a very limited claim as not all men had the vote. Only rate-paying householders, occupiers of shops, offices and farms, landowners or leaseholders of land with an annual value of £5 a year or more, and those who had an unfurnished tenancy (provided this cost a minimum of 3s 6d a week) were enfranchised. Graduates could also vote for their University Members. So few women compared with men fulfilled these qualifications that if the franchise had been extended to women on these terms only about 300,000–400,000 of them would have received the vote.

The methods employed by the two wings of the movement were quite different. The suffragists, under Mrs (later Dame) Millicent Fawcett, relied only on constitutional means; the suffragettes, led by the inspiring Mrs Pankhurst, believed that women had been patient too long and that the time for action rather than talk had arrived. The suffragettes were the first to use the slogan 'Votes for Women', and embarked on a campaign of action which gradually escalated up to the outbreak of war. They chained themselves to railings outside Parliament, Downing Street and elsewhere. They disguised themselves as charwomen to get into buildings where political meetings were to take place – women, not having the vote, did not normally attend such meetings – and hid there, emerging to interrupt and heckle the speakers before being bustled out. From boats on the river just above Westminster Bridge they harangued MPs on the Terrace. They shouted through megaphones from scaffolding. They broke windows and set fire to empty buildings. They were subjected to abuse, physical violence, and prison sentences. They went on hunger strike in prison and endured the horrors of forcible feeding or lying in irons for hours with a bravery admitted even by their detractors. In 1908, they organised a demonstration in Hyde Park which was attended by 250,000, the majority of them brought from all over England by thirty special trains. It was the largest public meeting ever held in England and immediately after it a resolution in favour of female suffrage was sent to the Prime Minister. He ignored both the demonstration and the resolution.

Edith, always strongly motivated towards the freeing and emancipating of women generally, was by now openly involved with the suffragist movement. It was a time when most women in her position sought to influence through men – if they sought to influence at all. Both her father and her mother-in-law strongly disagreed with the idea of female suffrage and disapproved of Edith's attitude. 'Like a young hound running riot,' remarked Theresa sniffily.

Edith was an excellent public speaker and made her reasons for supporting female suffrage clear again and again. In 1909, for instance, she said: 'It is all very well for those women who have comfortable homes to live in, and owing to their circumstances lead sheltered and protected lives, to pronounce in deprecatory tones that "women were not meant to compete with men". But women, in these days, are compelled to go out to work in their thousands. Many have to support the home. I believe I am not wrong when I say that the number of daily workers closely approaches five millions, and that a third of the children attending the London elementary schools are maintained by their mothers alone. It is asked how the vote is going to affect these women. It will affect them in the same way that it affects the men. It is well known, and surely it is only human nature, that a Parliamentary candidate attends to the wants and wishes of a voter in preference to a non-voter, and it is only through the possession of a vote that pressure can be brought to bear on the legislature. And this is only the material aspect of the question. How many laws are passed of vital importance to women, concerning their work, affecting their liberty, the education of their children, and in a hundred other ways relating to their moral and social welfare?'

She was equally adamant that peaceful means only should be used, differentiating herself sharply from the suffragettes. 'Our army has its own standards and must act accordingly. The ultimate goal of all may be the same but our tactics and methods are absolutely and entirely different to theirs and I wish to emphasise this fact in the strongest possible terms.'

Opponents of the women's movement used every argument they could think of to discredit it, from general shouting down to accusations of immorality, with words like 'disgusting, indecent, obscene' bandied about freely. Opposition to female suffrage had been a Liberal tenet since Gladstone declared himself against it, while Conservatives, from Disraeli on, were traditionally more sympathetic. But violent opinions, both for and against, cut right across party lines. In May 1909, for instance, Lord Curzon, the Conservative ex-Viceroy with whom the Castlereaghs had stayed in India, enunciated 'Fifteen sound, valid and incontrovertible arguments against the Grant of Female Suffrage'. These arguments were put forward in a speech at a meeting of the Men's League for Opposing Woman Suffrage, a body which fielded many of the eminent and influential among its members; its president was Lord Cromer (formerly Sir Evelyn Baring, the all-powerful High Commissioner in Egypt) and its vice-presidents included such respected public figures as the jurist Sir William Anson, Mr Austen Chamberlain and Mr Rudyard Kipling.

Lord Curzon's arguments against giving women the vote were as follows: political activity would tend to take away woman from her proper sphere and highest duty, which is maternity; it would tend to break up the harmony of the home; woman suffrage would pave the way to adult suffrage; women had not, as a sex or as a class, the calmness of temperament or the balance of mind or the training necessary to exercise a weighty judgement in political affairs; the vote was not desired by the large majority of women; the change was not approved by the large majority of men; women would probably not use the vote, but in emergencies, or on occasions of emotional excitement, their numerical superiority would mean that a preponderant force of women voters might be mobilised; woman suffrage would tend to weaken Great Britain in the estimation of foreign powers; it would be gravely misunderstood and would become a source of weakness in India; women would demand the right to become MPs, Cabinet ministers, judges, etc; woman would forfeit much of that respect which the chivalry of man had voluntarily conceded to her; the vote was not required for the removal of hardships and disabilities from which women are known to suffer; women ought not to make laws because they could not join in enforcing them – they could not become soldiers, sailors or policemen; there was no necessary connection between the vote and the intellectual emancipation of women which was proceeding; and, finally, no precedent existed for giving women as a class an active share in the government of a great country or empire. If the suffrage were once granted, he concluded, it could never be cancelled or withdrawn.

Edith, with considerable shrewdness, had realised that the real battle was not about exercising power but about the immediate and irreversible improvement to women's status. 'The talk about the vote raising or not raising wages is misleading,' she wrote in an article in the February 1910 issue of *The Conservative and Unionist Women's Franchise Review*. If, as men complained, women were ousting them from the labour market, she continued, it was nothing to do with their growing political consciousness but because, as they received only two-thirds of a man's wage, they were naturally preferred by employers. What the vote did do, she said, was to 'raise the status of that person ... It is the mark of complete citizenship, which alone is the real meaning of the word Liberty.'

But every attempt to achieve the franchise for women foundered on the rock of Asquith's opposition, often with success almost in sight. In 1910 an all-party group was formed, under the chairmanship of Lord Lytton, which drafted a bill (the Conciliation Bill, so called because both the women's organisations and parliamentarians approved of it) to enfranchise women householders, including married women. In May 1911 it passed its second reading in Parliament by a majority of 167 on a free vote; but then Asquith announced that he was about to introduce a new Male Franchise Bill and the Conciliation Bill was thrown out (after two General Elections in 1910 the Liberals were still securely in power though with a reduced majority). 'Of course you are supporting the universal suffrage, as I see Ramsay MacDonald is one of the patrons of it,' Charley wrote to Edith on 5 September 1912.* But in December the Prime Minister, while receiving a deputation led by Lord Curzon from the National League for Opposing Women's Suffrage, said that the grant of the franchise to women 'would be a political mistake of the most disastrous kind'.

The result of all this was a stepping-up of the suffragettes' campaign, which weakened their case in the eyes of moderates. 'They are doing no end of harm to their cause,' wrote Charley sadly. 'I can't see what good they do in attacking private property. It only means that the whole of the trading classes lose all sympathy for them, though I'm all for their rooting up park palings and devastating public buildings if they are so minded.'

The Conciliation Bill was introduced again in March 1913, this time to be defeated at the second reading – a rumour had swept the House that Asquith would resign if it were passed, so many Liberals sympathetic to the cause voted against it. The suffrage movement now pledged its support to the Labour Party, which had made giving the vote to women part of their official policy.

* Although Edith and Ramsay MacDonald did not meet until 1924, she plainly already admired him. I believe this letter, dated 5 September but without a year, to have been written in 1912. MacDonald, who entered Parliament in 1906 as MP for Leicester (for which he sat until 1919), was Leader of the Labour Party from 1911 to 1914.

On 28 March, a few days after the defeat of the Conciliation Bill, a long letter appeared in *The Times* from Sir Almroth Wright, a distinguished bacteriologist at St Mary's Hospital, London. It contained a swingeing attack on the whole idea of female suffrage and the sort of woman who wanted the vote, together with his ideas for a return to 'peace'; one was the suggestion that surplus spinsters should be shipped overseas.

This letter caused an immense stir. Sir Almroth was one of the great figures of his day. He was a Fellow of the Royal Society and a brilliant and revolutionary scientist, who had invented the anti-typhoid innoculation – in its effect upon the health of nations in war and peace a medical advance as epic and far-reaching in its day as was Sir Alexander Fleming's later discovery of penicillin. Strange reading as Sir Almroth's views on the physiology and psychology of women make today, in 1912 they commanded respect because of his pre-eminent position in the medical and scientific worlds. *The Times* considered them important enough to spread over two and a half of their correspondence columns. (The following year Sir Almroth expressed them even more fully in his book *The Unexpurgated Case Against Woman Suffrage*.)

'Sir, For man the physiology and psychology of woman is full of difficulties. He is not a little mystified when he encounters in her periodically recurring phases of hypersensitiveness, unreasonableness and loss of sense of proportion. He is frankly perplexed when confronted with a complete alteration of character in a woman who is child-bearing . . . the serious and long-continued mental disorders that develop in connection with the approaching extinction of a woman's reproductive function.

'As for woman herself she makes very light of any of these mental upsettings. She perhaps smiles a little at them. The woman of the world will even gaily assure you that "of course half the women in London have to be shut up when they come to the change of life". None the less, these upsettings of her mental equilibrium are the things that a woman has most cause to fear; and no doctor can ever lose sight of the fact that the mind of woman is always threatened with danger from the reverberations of her physiological emergencies. It is with such thoughts that the doctor lets his eyes rest upon the militant suffragist. He cannot shut them to the fact that there is mixed up with the woman's movement much mental disorder; and he cannot conceal from himself the physical emergencies which lie behind. The recruiting field for the militant suffragists is the half million of our excess female population – that half million

83

which had better long ago have gone out to mate with its complement of men beyond the sea.'*

Sir Almroth went on to describe the female types of whom the militant suffragists were composed. Briefly, they were 'the sexually embittered, in whom everything has turned into gall and bitterness of heart and hatred of men'; the incomplete ('one side of their nature has undergone atrophy'); the intellectually embittered; and young girls indoctrinated with 'the idea of being married upon their own terms'.

He went on to attack the 'fatuous doctrine' that women should receive equal pay for equal work, noting *en passant* that it was uncertain whether the institution of matrimony would survive without 'willing subordination' on the part of women.

'In addition to the element of mental disorder and the element of the fatuous,' he continued, 'there is also a very ugly element of dishonesty. But in reality the very kernel of the militant suffrage movement is the element of immorality.' This, he explained was because 'as woman stood in quite a different position from man in her relation to physical force, out of that different relation there must of necessity shape itself a special code of ethics for woman. And to violate that code must be, for woman, immorality.' Put simply, it was that woman was outside violence and that if she broke this taboo it might 'embroil men and women' in a never-ending battle.

Peace would come again, he concluded, only when woman 'ceases to resent the fact that man cannot and does not wish to work side by side with her. And peace will return when every woman for whom there is no room in England seeks "rest" beyond the sea, "each one in the house of her husband", and when the woman who remains in England comes to recognise that she can without sacrifice of dignity give a willing subordination to the husband or father who, when all is said and done, earns and lays up money for her.'

The reaction to Sir Almroth's effusion was as sharp as to one of his own vaccines. Letters poured in to *The Times*. Mrs Pankhurst's furious rebuttal appeared the next day (Friday 29 March). Another female correspondent drew the conclusion that women should be abolished, signing herself 'One of the doomed', and Mrs Humphry Ward predictably sprang to Sir Almroth's defence.

Edith must have spent much of that weekend drafting a letter which

* Sir Almroth's figures were as suspect as his logic. According to the 1911 census, out of a total population of 36,070,492 in England and Wales, there were 17,445,607 men and 18,624,884 women, a 'surplus' of 1,179,277 women.

appeared on 1 April. Coming from a young woman whose life was supposedly devoted to foxhunting and frivolity, and written in the teeth of family opposition, her letter was remarkable for its foresight and its comprehension of the needs and difficulties of her poorer sisters. Again she showed her awareness of the growing population of working women (the 1911 census gives the number of working women as 4,830,734 compared with 11,453,665 male workers). The letter, once composed, must have been dashed off in a mood of high emotion – for the first time, her English is faulty and occasional words are omitted – but the steel and the perception that underlay her public image as society beauty devoted to a life of pleasure were beginning to show.

Sir Almroth Wright's letter on Woman Suffrage may be almost regarded as a classic by some people, but on such a complex subject there are even more sides than the proverbial two. Without in the least wishing to be presumptuous in regard to such an able critic, I should like to put forward a few suggestions from another point of view.

Sir Almroth Wright deals with the subject as if the entire movement was based on militant hysteria, instead of its being but a small proportion of fanatical persons, which has by the way included several male supporters belonging to the militant branch. Much the same criticism, I venture to say, may be applied to the sweeping remarks of the physiology and psychology of woman.

When we take into consideration the great army of women workers, nurses, etc, and sturdy country women, surely it is of a minority that Sir Almroth is speaking when he refers to the grave disorders that are attendant on the sex, as if they were the rule and not the exception. Were this not the case, very few among the poorer women would be capable of being not only wives, but housekeepers, managers and holders of the purse, in addition to [attending to] the cares of the family. In actual fact, *they* are the householders, although not in name, for financial and political reasons, they bear all the household drudgery, and have scant time to consider their own health; and yet in how many homes do we find that these women are both capable and willing to bear their own share as well as those of all the family burdens on their shoulders faithfully and well.

I do not deny for a moment that both in the upper classes and middle classes may be found far more neurotic subjects, liable to all the ills Sir Almroth Wright mentions, owing to a great extent to heredity, their upbringing and mode of life, but I maintain that in relation to the entire sex these are the exceptions.

Sir Almroth Wright says he is appalled by the terrible physical havoc which the pangs of disappointed love may work. He is right, but his remarks apply also in regard to the mental state of the other sex. How else are we to account for the frequent mention in our daily papers of terrible crimes, under lurid headings, such as the following: 'Husband Murders Wife and Family', 'Father Runs Amok and Shoots His Children', and other similar horrors, not to mention the numerous other murders by persons calling themselves the lovers of their victims? Are not these persons suffering from some mental derangement, and without any of the 'physiological emergencies' which Sir Almroth thinks lie behind all similar actions relating to women? May not we leave this aspect out altogether? Man is the highly strung animal, capable of more sustained energy in any given direction. To him also belongs physical force, and, if you can get the perfect article, man as such is the finer all round animal. But woman has far greater powers of endurance and her energies are more diverse. Neither sex is complete without the other; they are complementary, not in the least identical. These are the lines on which this movement should develop, and not as an 'epicene' institution.

Sir Almroth Wright thinks the aims of suffragists immoral. Such is hardly fair to the great bulk of suffragists in this country, the large band of earnest thinkers and workers who have been striving steadily to achieve their cause by Constitutional means for 50 years. Because some women may have immoral aims (I don't say that they have) and wrong ideas of matrimony, this need not 'tar' all the members of the movement 'with the same brush'. After all, a great many men, especially amongst the very poor, have no idea of the sanctity of the marriage tie; the woman is regarded as often as not as the beast of burden, seldom as the companion that marriage intended her to be. The word 'obey' has been responsible for so much misunderstanding, quite as much with the men as with the wives. I certainly hold that wives should obey their husbands, but this is entirely different from women being subservient to men. Marriage is a bond of partnership, and man is the rightful head, but nowhere in Christian teachings is it laid down that husbands should treat their wives as household slaves. I often think in this senseless and foolish controversy over the marriage question that the husbands who omit 'to love and to cherish' are placed in exactly the same category as the wives who refuse to obey them.

I only digressed thus far as Sir Almroth Wright has made the usual incursions into the matrimonial side of the suffrage question and would further add that marriages would be far more successful than they are now if it were not for the very fact, to quote Sir Almroth Wright again, that 'marriage is the great instrument in the levelling up of the financial situation of women'. Further comment seems unnecessary; it explains itself why this necessarily unnatural mating so frequently is a dismal failure. In fact, economics are the basis of the whole of the woman's question.

With all Sir Almroth Wright's arguments against physical force I heartily concur, and all suffragists, except the few who are indicted by him, will feel grateful to him for putting the case so clearly against militant tactics. With regard to the vote, I have only this to say: We all agree what an astonishing disappointing instrument it is, but until there is a better one, the weaker sex will continue to strive to obtain the same protection that it affords to working men. It is not 'for the noblest women in England' as such that the vote is really desired, except for the recognition of the principle, but it is chiefly wanted for her poorer sister. When deputations at election time can bring pressure through the united votes of their trade unions, for or against a member or a candidate, it is obvious to all that the wants of such bodies are attended to before others, however large, if they cannot bring any such pressure to bear; and it is almost beside the mark to tell her that the vote is intended to hang a murderer or shut a public house, when she knows she could use it for all the factory laws and housing laws – in fact in a hundred ways in which legislation deals directly now with women. It is commonly supposed that only in the last 50 years have women taken part in industrial enterprise. True it is that only in the last 50 years have they been forced into the open labour market, as all the home industries, which she did at home, have gradually been absorbed by the factories, and for this very reason, she requires the extra protection of the vote.

The industrial woman and professional woman have come to stay. But I feel certain that the best suffragist is equally capable of being the best wife and can give a 'willing subordination' to her husband, as well as exercising her full rights as a citizen, and, let us hope, one of the mothers in our great Empire.

Yours faithfully, Edith Castlereagh.

Edith continued to reply to letters in *The Times* when she felt her views were pertinent. When, in January 1913, her mother-in-law's friend F. E. Smith repeated the familiar argument employed by opponents of female suffrage that as only Man could defend his country in War, so only Man should have the vote, she quickly countered by writing: 'Nothing to my mind has been more regrettable than the attitude of the House during the past week. There was a paragraph in Mr F. E. Smith's anti-suffrage letter in which he might have been describing the attitude both of the Ministers and the members themselves, although, in fact, he thought he was describing the women. It ran as follows: "Their judgements and opinions are coloured by emotional and personal considerations and might in moments of public excitement prove a source of instability and disaster for the State."' She also turned her sharp pen to more overt ridicule, with mocking verses, read, no doubt, by most of her friends.

In 1913, a further Bill with amendments on women's suffrage was debated. This too made no headway: it was withdrawn when the Speaker announced that if any of the amendments were adopted, they would so alter the Bill as to kill it. Outraged, The National Union of Women's Suffrage Societies issued a letter which said that 'Mr Asquith's proposed action with regard to Woman Suffrage in the Reform Bill had been before the House and the Country for five years, during part of three Parliaments and two General Elections. It has also been well known throughout this period that a majority of the House of Commons were pledged to support Woman Suffrage. Yet it is only 24 hours before the time comes for making good the Government's promise that the Speaker makes known his intention to render it abortive.'

Harassment and destruction now became the suffragettes' watchword. They attacked the Prime Minister with whips as he was playing golf, damaged golf courses, threw acid into pillar boxes and slashed a Velasquez painting in the National Gallery. One, Emily Davidson, was killed when she flung herself under King George V's horse in the Derby; the King himself had to abandon his daily ride in Rotten Row. Asquith retaliated by passing the infamous 'Cat and Mouse Act', whereby any woman whose health was seriously endangered by going on hunger strike in prison (some had already died) was to be released ... and re-arrested as soon as her health improved. It was a black and bitter period, only to be ended by the outbreak of war, when Edith, like other members of the movement, diverted her energies into the nation's struggle.

IX

EDITH'S WORK for women's suffrage may have been a welcome distraction from the difficulties in her private life. When she had become reconciled with Charley after the Consuelo affair, all had seemed set fair. From the summer of 1906 onwards, there was a constant interchange of loving messages, telegrams and letters between the Castlereaghs. 'Darling little Doody,' Charley would write, 'I am in the nest sitting on the eggs but no mate. Please come back soon.' He carried her letters about with him, he told her, and – possibly the highest compliment of all – reread them in his grouse butt. Only one hope was delayed in its fulfilment: it was not until 9 March 1910 that their third child and second daughter was born, at Londonderry House, and Edith could write jubilantly: 'I think I appreciate her more than I did the others, the seven years' waiting, I suppose!' Even so, no one could decide what the baby was to be called – Janet? Theresa? But both were disliked intensely by Charley. It was not until the christening party reached the church door that Theresa's compromise suggestion of Margaret was finally accepted, with Frances and Anne as second and third names.

Almost at once, Edith set off for Sutherland to work in the garden of their house in Scotland. She was already a keen gardener, an interest further stimulated later in the year by a visit to the Duchess of Leeds' villa at Bordighera; she thought this combined 'the beauty of an English garden with the rarer plants of the Riviera, without the curious but unsightly cactus'. Later, aided by the climate of the Ards peninsula, she was to put this combination into effect at Mount Stewart, with Italianate terraces and mimosa planted round the house as well as more conventional English features like borders and lawns.

She and her six-weeks-old daughter were still in Scotland when, on 6 May, Edward VII died. The night before, there had been a violent thunderstorm, and Edith was woken by the howling of her dogs. After one tremendous thunderclap and 'the most vivid flash of lightning I had ever seen' her dogs, a bloodhound, a small Scottish terrier and a dachshund, leaped through the window and bolted. They were traced by the baying of the bloodhound down by the river – but it was two more days before the news of the King's death reached that remote spot.

The following year, the Castlereaghs' fourth child and third daughter, Helen Maglona, was born on 8 July; and in September, Edith and Charley decided to revisit Canada, making the magnificent train journey through the Rockies and returning home on 3 November.

Edith was glad to be back, not only to see the children but because she was worried about her father's health. In 1907 he had taken a house called Pickwell in Northamptonshire. Two years later he moved to the Hall Farm, Brixworth, formerly a hunting box, in the Pytchley country. His daughter Florrie, as keen on hunting as Edith and her father, kept house for him until she began to train as a nurse in 1910. He was looked after by his devoted manservant William Northwood, who acted as valet, nurse, and secretary (Northwood taught himself to type) and whom Chaplin regarded almost as a son. Pictures of his children and grandchildren, his best hounds and favourite hunters, lined the walls; he knew everybody; old friends and awestruck young alike came to visit one of the most popular and famous foxhunting men of the day; and he had six splendid hunters, all well up to his weight. Of those Brixworth days, George Lambton wrote*:

To see him thundering down at a fence on one of his great horses was a fine sight. I remember on one occasion we were all held up in a field close to Melton, the only way out being where a young sapling had been planted in the fence surrounded by an iron cage, which stood about 4 ft 6 in, the thin tree growing up several feet above it. There were shouts for a chopper or a knife, when down came the Squire, forty miles an hour, with his eyeglass in his eye, seeing nothing but the opening in the fence. There was no stopping him; neither did the young tree do so, for his weight and that of his horse broke it off as clean as you would break a thin stick, and away he went with no idea that the tree had ever been there.

Chaplin's energy was phenomenal. When Parliament dissolved at the end of 1909 he had retained his Wimbledon seat, this time against a former Mayor of Wimbledon – a much more likely candidate than Ber-

* From *Men and Horses I Have Known*.

trand Russell – whom he defeated by about 5,000 votes; in the second 1910 election, he was returned unopposed. In 1911 he wrote to Edith: 'When the House was up yesterday, I went down to Leicester, slept at the Bell, got up at 6 to see two horses belonging to a 19-stone man I know well in the Quorn country, one out of a mare they swear is got by Hermit. . . . I bought the other – an Irish horse, up to 18 stone good, 6 years old and cheap too. Caught the 7.00 train to London and arrived in time for a meeting at A.J.B.'s house in Carlton Gardens which lasted nearly 3 hours. . . .' (Later the same year Balfour retired and Bonar Law became Leader of the Conservative Party.)

Chaplin was, however, riding too hard for a man of seventy with a weight problem. In addition, he had painful varicose veins, his knees were so riddled with arthritis and gout that most of his grip was gone and his hands too were clumsy with gout – he had always had perfect hands, hunting his horse in a double bridle rather than a snaffle without fear of jabbing the animal's mouth. It was inevitable that he would soon take a serious fall.

It came at the beginning of the hunting season of 1912. He was taken by surprise when his horse stood right back at a high boundary fence, before sailing high and wide into the ploughed field beyond. Chaplin came off and, although the landing was soft, he broke two ribs, one of which pierced a lung, and he developed pleurisy. This lasted a month, and he had to sit up the whole time in a huge armchair, issuing commands to the nurses who tried to keep him in order and insisting on eating what – and as much as – he wanted. His appetite was huge and he was a great meat-eater; he always had a cold chicken or, in season, a cold partridge by his bed. The story goes that when an old friend, the noted surgeon Sir Alfred Fripp, came to see him, he looked despairingly at the luncheon Chaplin had ordered for himself – a goose, a hare and a snipe – and, having whispered to Edith that it was 'kill or cure', said sternly that Chaplin should not eat so much. Chaplin replied amiably that he would give up the snipe.

His extraordinary constitution pulled him through. By Christmas he was recovering, though still weak, and writing as copiously and affectionately as ever to his children. 'Bless you, my darling – and every happiness be yours, with Charley and your sweet children for this and many years to come is the daily prayer and loving wish of your devoted Father,' he wrote to Edith on Boxing Day 1912, to follow this note with another five days later. 'One line, my darling, to wish you all love and a really happy new year. That is one thing, and another is to tell you again how sensible I am of all the love and thoughtful care you have given me through my illness and the thousand and one things great and small you have done and so effectually to help me through it, and without which I really think it would have gone very much harder with me than it did.'

By now Edith had troubles of her own again. Charley's affair with Consuelo had not been a single, isolated, infatuation; his philandering had become a constant in their married life. Margot Asquith, whose husband the Prime Minister was also very susceptible, held the view that 'no woman should expect to be the only woman in her husband's life. The idea of such a thing appears to me ridiculous . . . I not only encouraged his female friends, but posted his letters to them if I found them in my front hall.' Although such an expectation did not seem ridiculous to Edith and she did not encourage Charley's forays, ultimately she too accepted him on his own terms. 'I want you so much', she told him, 'that I do not mind what you do.'

This seemingly complaisant attitude may seem puzzling today, when divorce or at the least disenchantment would be the inevitable consequence. But the parameters of marriage almost a century ago were very different – especially for women. For a start, even if Edith had wished to divorce Charley, this would have been impossible: a husband's adultery was not then sufficient grounds for the dissolution of a marriage. Although a man could divorce his wife for adultery alone, she could only divorce him if his unfaithfulness was accompanied by another cause such as desertion or cruelty.

The dictates of faith backed up the diktat of the law. Edith was a Victorian, born, brought up and married in an era when religion held a central place in national life to an extent almost impossible to imagine now. In the days when family prayers were not simply an obligation performed out of a sense of duty but a deeply felt part of family life, a Christian marriage meant exactly what its vows said: 'To have and to hold, from this day forward, till death us do part'. Edith herself, whose faith had been profound since childhood, viewed the marriage bond as sacred, mystical – and indissoluble.

Marriage was virtually the only career open to women, with motherhood held up not only as the highest goal but also as a preordained duty. A few exceptional and brilliant women became doctors, teachers, nurses or writers but, as a general rule, women of all classes, economically dependent and psychologically subservient, passed straight from the care of a father to that of a husband. This was as true for a duke's niece like Edith as for a dustman's: although the upper-class girl would, of course, never suffer real privation if she remained single, without marriage she would never achieve everything that made her life worth living – children, status, a full social life. She would, in other words, be a failure; and a married woman who divorced would be *déclassée* into the bargain.

Edith was well aware of the advantages of wealth and position. In the world in which she had been brought up, success, for a woman, meant making a good match; and her whole upbringing had been geared to preparing her to become the bride of such a man, the richer and more aristocratic the better. In Charley she had found him.

As the daughter of a man who was an intimate of Edward VII, she must also have been aware that the partners in these dynastic alliances often looked elsewhere for love. Among the rich and pleasure-loving Edwardians who surrounded the throne such affairs, though discreet, were commonplace. The women married young and had little experience before marriage; instead, everything from amorous flirtations to deeply passionate liaisons came afterwards. To Charley, whose parents were in the Court circle and whose own mother exemplified such behaviour, unfaithfulness must have seemed, even if reprehensible, something that a marriage could be expected to digest.

But Edith had grown up in an atmosphere in which romantic love was an essential part of marriage. Her parents, she knew, had been blissfully happy during their brief years together, her father had felt so deeply about her mother that he had never remarried, her Uncle Strath had fallen head over heels in love with her Aunt Millie when Millicent was still in the schoolroom. She too wanted love: love that was close, deep, warm, binding, generous, enduring, articulate, lavishly affectionate – and monogamous.

What she had not anticipated was feeling quite such a depth of passion for her handsome husband. Twenty-five years or so after their wedding she was to write: 'You have no idea really how silly I feel about you. I might have been married yesterday to you. That is how I feel – I just worship you.' The physical attraction that held and bewitched her all their life together not only made her jealous but also made it impossible for her to indulge in affairs herself.

In addition, there was the psychological handicap that from the beginning she had felt the luck was all on her side, often secretly wondering – despite the attentions of the many other men who fell in love with her – how Charley, this godlike creature, could have chosen her. When his infidelities began it was the start of a period of intense and anguished inner struggle, while his need for other women imbued her with a sense of failure. All in all, she was in no position to issue an ultimatum to Charley – indeed, what would the answer have been? – though all her instincts and beliefs rebelled against his behaviour. Yet she was determined to keep their marriage alive in the truest sense, as well as maintaining it as the most important relationship in both their lives.

It was an emotional dilemma that could have torn a weaker character apart. Edith resolved it with characteristic pragmatism: if Charley's womanising was an unalterable part of his character – very well then, she would simply rise above it. She would treat his 'girls' as passing peccadilloes, to be discussed with her husband, to be laughed over, sympathised with, even asked to stay, but above all, never to be considered as on the same plane.

Gratefully, Charley fell in with this concept, frequently expressing his genuine devotion. 'Doodie darling,' he wrote on 27 November 1911, 'when this reaches you it will be our wedding day. I hope we will have many more together, as I couldn't do without you.' She even managed to rationalise sharing him physically with other women. As she pointed out to Charley himself years later, if *she* found him irresistible, how could other women not? 'I don't blame you because the women hunt you to death. You are so beautiful and so attractive. . . .'

It was, perhaps, inevitable that one of the 'girls' would become more serious than any of the others. This was Eloise Ancaster, the alluring and predatory American wife of the Earl of Ancaster. The elder daughter of a rich New Yorker called Breese, she had vigorously embraced at least one of the customs of her husband's milieu, producing four children in the five years after her marriage in December 1905. Now, with her duty done, she was free for a more amusing life. The Ancasters lived at Grimsthorpe Castle, only two miles from the Castlereaghs' house at Springfield, and hunted with the same packs; sometimes, too, Charley would stay at Grimsthorpe to shoot. Eloise was lively, sporting – she was a good shot – with an excellent figure, the transatlantic vivacity and freshness that had so appealed to Charley in Consuelo, and few scruples about pursuing any man she set her sights on. It was a lethal combination.

At first Edith treated the affair with her usual tolerance, not even protesting when Charley went on his own to stay in the same house party as the Ancasters in Scotland in the autumn of 1912. This altruism was repaid by a letter (dated 15 September) saying: 'It was very good of me coming here but I was rewarded by a warm greeting and the Countess seems in an excellent temper. But she is not nearly as nice as my Doody, in fact I would not confuse the two, only you foolishly do.'

But Eloise was possessive, and anxious to flaunt a conquest as glamorous as Charley. Gossip began. This, with its sting of public humiliation, did distress Edith, though even then she was careful not to blame Charley. 'Really, you and I are very unlucky. If we are left alone we can manage very well indeed. I can't see why our kind friends must always be repeating things. . . .' For the moment, though, it was still possible to regard the Eloise affair as just another of Charley's repeated but fleeting amours. There were, too, other preoccupations.

The question of Home Rule for Ireland, which had split the Liberal Party when Gladstone brought in his Home Rule Bill, and divided the country since, was approaching crisis point; and the Londonderry family, as leading Unionists, were deeply involved. Asquith had been determined from the beginning to introduce Home Rule. The Protestant majority in Ulster, violently opposed to the idea of Catholic-dominated rule by a parliament sitting in Dublin, were equally determined to resist at all costs. They were backed by the Conservative Party, and the Liberal Unionists, many of whom believed that the grant of Home Rule to Ireland would be the first step towards the breaking up of the Empire. Most of the peers were Unionists but, with the passing of the Parliament Act in August 1911, which broke the power of the Lords, Home Rule could no longer be prevented by constitutional means.

Resistance strengthened rapidly, led nationally by Sir Edward Carson, chairman since 1910 of the Irish Unionist Parliamentary Party and holder of one of the two Dublin University seats. In Ulster he was supported by politicians, led by James Craig (later Lord Craigavon), and landowners, led by Charley's father and the Duke of Abercorn. Lord Londonderry became chairman of the standing committee of the Ulster Unionist Council, the body responsible for the movement's policy. The new King and Queen had paid a state visit to Dublin in 1911, but unrest quickly became so widespread and so deep-rooted that they were unable to visit Ireland again until the King opened the Ulster Parliament in 1921.

The decisive step towards rejection of Home Rule for Ulster took place on 28 September 1912, when nearly half a million men and women signed the Solemn League and Covenant (more generally known as the Ulster Covenant) pledging themselves to stand firm against what they saw as the handing over of their country. The feelings roused were so deep that many signed in their own blood, cutting fingers or wrists for the purpose. Mass meetings, at which the chief speakers were Carson, Craig, Bonar Law, F. E. Smith and Lord Londonderry, were held throughout Ulster. The Belfast magistrates now openly allowed Orange lodges and Unionist clubs to 'practise military exercises, movements and evolutions', and the Ulster Volunteer Force was born.

The week before the Ulster Covenant was signed Charley came over to join his father at Craigavon. He entirely missed the significance of the occasion, merely feeling bored and supernumerary trailing along in the entourage of his seniors. 'It is damnable here and I am bored to tears, nothing in the world to do; I am simply loafing about. As yet I have done nothing, tomorrow evening a meeting and the same on Thursday and then I sign on Saturday. I wish I had just come over for the signing; for all the good I have done or will do I might have been at Timbuckto [*sic*]. I hate swelling the train after Carson and F. E. There are so many anxious to do it.'

He was equally unenthusiastic at his dispatch back to England to welcome the Leader of the Opposition at Wynyard. 'Disaster, Bonar Law goes to Wynyard and the parents are most anxious I shall be there. It is a great nuisance and I wish there was no need for it but under the circumstances I don't really see what else I can do,' he wrote on 25 September. 'If I can't go it is a grievance at once. . . . I really am in a huff. The last week here has put me all wrong, never again do I undertake a week like this unless I am the central figure and I fear that Ulster interests me less and less.' It was an opportunity missed: years later, Stanley Baldwin told Charley's son Robin that politically his father had failed to make the impression he should have, 'especially on Home Rule when it became a vital issue'.

By contrast, Theresa Londonderry felt herself deeply involved, and sought to proselytise for Ulster whenever possible. She had long talks on the Province's problems with the new Editor of *The Times*, Geoffrey Dawson,* in October; and kept in constant touch with its Defence correspondent, Colonel Repington, frequently asking him to lunch or dinner at Londonderry House.

The Home Rule Bill had its first reading in the House of Commons in January 1913. Asquith told the King that when the Bill became law (in June 1914) there would be 'the certainty of tumult and riot, and more than the possibility of bloodshed', a euphemistic way of describing what would undoubtedly have been a bloody civil war. Ulster reacted immediately, declaring that the moment the Bill became law a provisional

---

* Then Geoffrey Robinson; he changed his name to Dawson in 1917. His first day in the Editor's chair was 23 September 1912, 'beginning at about 11.00 a.m. and getting to bed about 2.00 a.m.'

government would be set up in Belfast, and stepping up her military organisation.

Not only Parliament but Society were now split into two bitterly opposed factions. Friends cut each other, families were riven. Lord Londonderry as an Ulsterman was one of the most fiercely partisan. He asked his sister Lady Allendale, married to one of the Liberal whips and a near neighbour in London, not to call at Londonderry House any more; refused an invitation to stay at Windsor for Ascot Races as it might have meant driving down the course in the same carriage as Liberal fellow-guests like the Chesterfields or the Granards; and, at one of Millicent Sutherland's evening receptions, went red in the face and turned angrily on his heel just as his hostess was about to receive him – he had spotted the Liberal Lord and Lady Lincolnshire in the press of people ahead. Similarly, the Duchess of Abercorn, staying in a house party which included the King, refused to sit next to Lord Crewe – a member of the Government and previously a great friend – at dinner and the seating had to be quickly rearranged. The King was so annoyed at the insult to one of his ministers that when the house party was over he invited the Crewes, but not the Abercorns, to travel back to London with him in the royal train.

In Ulster, there was now a disciplined, highly trained citizen army under the command of Lieutenant General Sir George Richardson, a retired Indian Army officer selected for this post by Field Marshal Lord Roberts. Short of arms and ammunition these volunteers might be but nobody doubted their fighting spirit, professional ability or a morale stiffened by the knowledge that half England was on their side. So, too, they believed, was the Almighty. 'A great churchgoing has been arranged for today, the Primate and the Bible to sanctify our cause,' wrote Charley from Mount Stewart on 14 January 1914 ('Of course, I haven't brought a tall hat, so I shall try and cry off').

The King, deeply unhappy at the increasing likelihood of civil war in Ireland, kept up a steady pressure on his Prime Minister to compromise. Throughout the winter of 1913/14 Asquith held talks with Bonar Law and Carson and the leader of the Irish Nationalists, John Redmond. At first neither side would give an inch but finally, with Carson and Bonar Law still holding out for the total exclusion of Ulster, Redmond reluctantly agreed to the introduction of Home Rule by stages.

This was enough for Asquith. Early in 1914, the Government introduced an Amended Bill designed to give immediate Home Rule to the South but allowing the Six Counties of Ulster to vote, county by county, every year for six years, on whether to accept Home Rule or reject it; at the end of the allotted six years they would automatically come under the Dublin Parliament. Not surprisingly, the anti-Home Rulers fiercely opposed this Bill too. 'We do not want sentence of death with a stay of execution for six years!' thundered Carson when the Bill received its second reading on 9 March 1914. He was, of course, supported by all the Conservatives – Henry Chaplin, a dedicated imperialist, made impassioned speeches against Home Rule.

On Saturday 14 March Winston Churchill, then First Lord of the Admiralty, made a speech at Bradford describing the Ulster Provisional Government now installed in Belfast as 'a self-elected body, composed of persons which, to put it plainly, are engaged in a treasonable conspiracy', hinted at a 'revolutionary purpose' and concluded by saying: 'Let us go forward together and put these grave matters to the proof.' To many, these provocative words sounded like a deliberate threat to use the armed forces of the Crown to coerce Ulster. This led to the so-called 'Curragh mutiny'.

In 1914, there was a considerable garrison in Ireland. The Commander-in-Chief was General Sir Arthur Paget. Edith's friend Major General William Pulteney commanded the 6th Division in Cork. The 5th Division, under Major General Sir Charles Fergusson, covering the centre and north of Ireland, had its headquarters at the Curragh in County Kildare, thirty miles southwest of Dublin, where the cavalry brigade, commanded by Brigadier General Hubert Gough, was stationed.

The Ulster Volunteer Force was now a formidable body some 100,000-strong but despite constant gun-running was still short of weapons. Although there had been no 'incidents' of any description the Government feared that the Ulstermen would seize the arms and ammunition stored in various British Army depots in the north, especially now that the Bill was nearer law than ever. Churchill prepared to send eight warships to anchorages within reach of Belfast. One of Lord Londonderry's Liberal relatives made a speech in which he declared that 'the guns of the Fleet should be trained on Belfast and the brains of Lord Londonderry and others like him should spatter the streets'.

Sir Arthur Paget, a brave but excitable man with a tendency to view things in black and white, was summoned to London to confer with Colonel Seely, the Secretary for State of War, and Sir John French, the Chief of the Imperial General Staff. He was ordered to move troops to protect the vulnerable arms depots. Paget was worried about the position of officers who lived in Ulster: if the worst came to the worst, would they be expected to fight their own brothers and relations? He put this question to Seely and French, who told him that in the event of hostilities such officers could 'disappear' and return later without it affecting their careers; but that all other officers must obey lawful orders. This assurance was given by word of mouth only.

On his return to the Curragh, Paget immediately summoned his senior commanders and told them to pass this ruling on to their officers in the form of an ultimatum requiring a decision by the evening of Friday 20 March. The damage was done.

Paget's words appeared to offer harsh alternatives to all but those officers who lived in Ulster: instant dismissal or, as they believed, full-scale hostilities against the Ulster Volunteer Force. They were given no chance to consult their families, most of them were in any case sympathetic to Ulster and, above all, no one had even hinted that the whole question was at that time hypothetical. 'Can you imagine a subaltern of 22–26 making up his mind in an hour as to whether he should shoot down Loyalists in Ulster or try to start a civil career without a bob?' wrote one to his father.* It was even worse for those older officers who were married, had children, and, without private means, were living on their pay: were they to give up their careers and their eventual pensions rather than serve against Ulster?

The officers of the Cavalry Brigade, including Gough, resigned more or less *en masse*, and their example was infectious. The story broke when a Curragh correspondent wired Fleet Street that the War Office had said that any officers not prepared to serve against Ulster must immediately resign or be dismissed the service, and that about 100 had sent in their papers. The War Office, horrified, wired to Paget that 'Resignations of all officers should be refused', but only minutes later, at midnight on Friday 20 March, it received a telegram from him saying, 'Regret to report Brigadier and 57 officers, 3rd Cavalry Brigade, prefer to accept dismissal if ordered north.' In all, resignations were received from 58 cavalry and 280 other officers.

The situation was largely retrieved by General Fergusson, who pointed out that the primary duty of every soldier was loyalty to the King. But the Cavalry remained obdurate and Gough, who had come to London, refused to return to Ireland without a written promise that the Army would never be used to crush opposition to Home Rule. Seely gave this promise, which the Cabinet later repudiated. Seely was forced

---

* Quoted from *The Curragh Incident*, by Sir James Ferguson of Kilkerran.

to resign and the Prime Minister took over the responsibilities of Secretary of State for War.

In County Down, Charley went with Carson to call at the Barracks 'where the Norfolks and Dorsets are posted in case of disturbance. There is no doubt that a great coup was intended by the Government and that it was intended to arrest 120 people and make the revolution a failure. Gough frustrated all this. The next move will be an interesting one.'

The next move was to end inconclusively. As the time for the Bill's third reading approached, the Government was coming to realise that Ulster would have to be excluded from Home Rule. 'I had a long buck with HM yesterday about the political situation', wrote Charley to Edith in May. 'He is jubilant at the prospect of a settlement as he feels he will not be called in. He detests Winston. He favours exclusion and thinks the rest of Ireland must have Home Rule. So pleased was he with me that he asked me to lunch and the lunch lasted so long I missed the 1,000 [Guineas] fillies in the paddock and had a plunge on the wrong one.'

By June it was clear that exclusion was the only alternative to civil war. After yet more talks had failed, a conference was called to settle the boundary between the Province and the rest of Ireland. The King, delighted that a compromise seemed in sight, offered the hospitality of Buckingham Palace. Negotiations began between Asquith and Lloyd George for the Government, Bonar Law and Lansdowne for the Opposition, Redmond and Dillon for the Irish Nationalists and Carson and Craig for Ulster; the Speaker of the House of Commons took the Chair. The conference started on 21 July, and broke down three days later when Carson and Redmond, both of whom had demanded Tyrone, refused to give way. Waiting to say goodbye to the King, the Speaker picked up the evening paper. It contained the fatal ultimatum from Austria to Serbia.

Eleven days later, on 4 August, Great Britain was at war. The Irish question was shelved, the suffragettes in prison released, the women's organisations agreed to halt political activity, and Redmond pledged the support of the Irish Nationalists. The nation was once more united.

X

WAR WITH Germany had been feared and anticipated since the beginning of the century. Germany, jealous of Britain's Empire and already the greatest military power in Europe, had embarked on a naval building programme which could have only one object: to challenge the Royal Navy's command of the seas, uncontested since the Battle of Trafalgar. But the imminence of the outbreak of war took even the Cabinet by surprise, so much had the mounting crisis in Irish affairs obscured all other issues.

Britain and Germany were ostensibly on good terms, and their royal families closely linked. The Kaiser was King George V's first cousin and had supported Queen Victoria on her deathbed; there were many Anglo-German marriages and friendships; it was quite unremarkable that the German Prince Louis of Battenberg (the grandfather of Prince Philip, Duke of Edinburgh) was First Sea Lord. In June, British naval visits to the High Seas Fleet's home ports of Kronstadt and Kiel had taken place in an atmosphere of fraternal *bonhomie*. Britons and Germans competed against each other in a regatta, dined in each others' ships and walked arm in arm in the sunshine.

Seen through German eyes, though, the picture was very different. As Winston Churchill wrote: 'Britain was rent by faction and seemed almost negligible, America was three thousand miles away, Germany, her fifty million capital tax expended on munitions, her army increases completed, the Kiel Canal opened for Dreadnought battleships that very month, looked fixedly upon the scene and her gaze became suddenly a glare.'*
Der Tag was near.

On 28 June, the Archduke Franz Ferdinand of Austria and his morgan-

---

* *The World Crisis, 1911–14.*

atic wife were assassinated at Sarajevo, but the significance of this was not immediately appreciated. It was only on Friday 24 July, after the conference to decide the Ulster boundaries had broken down, that as (again in Churchill's words*) the Cabinet, 'turning this way and that in search of an exit, toiled around the muddy byways of Fermanagh and Tyrone . . . the quiet grave tones of Sir Edward Grey's voice were heard reading a document which had just been brought to him from the Foreign Office. It was the Austrian note to Serbia. This note was clearly an ultimatum but . . . as the reading proceeded, it seemed absolutely impossible that any state in the world could accept it, or that any acceptance, however abject, would satisfy the aggressor. The parishes of Fermanagh and Tyrone faded back into the mists and squalls of Ireland and a strange light began immediately, but by perceptible gradations, to fall and grow upon the map of Europe.'

The mud and blood of the trenches, the wholesale slaughter of a generation, were not then foreseen. The greatest naval power in the world was going into battle, with her Empire beside her. The general consensus was that the war would be over in a matter of months if not weeks, but certainly by Christmas – one of the few dissenting voices was Kitchener, who said that it would last at least three years – and many of the young and patriotic were terrified that they would miss the fighting.

Charley, who had sent in his papers when he stood for Parliament, was on the Reserve of Officers. Conscious that he had not been on active service in the South African war, he immediately volunteered to rejoin his regiment, hoping to get across to France with them. There was no chance of this, however: only one regiment, made up from the First and Second Life Guards and the Royal Horse Guards, was sent out, and no extra officers were needed. When, three weeks after the war had begun, Edith's friend Lieutenant General Sir William Pulteney was sent out to France to command the Third Army Corps and offered to take Charley with him as his ADC, it seemed an ideal solution to everyone. Edith – who had used her charm and friendship with Putty to arrange it – felt that her beloved Charley would be safe, while Charley saw it as one step nearer the Regiment in France. As for the General, it must have been agreeable to have two scions of the nobility (his other ADC was the Earl of Pembroke) acting as personal assistants and companions, while simultaneously doing a favour to a beautiful woman he admired.

Separation, paradoxically, drew the Castlereaghs closer together. Their

* *The World Crisis, 1911–14.*

letters are those of lovers rather than a couple married for fifteen years. 'My darlingest little angel,' writes Charley, 'I have no news except to say what a sweet little pet you are and how I should love to hug you,' or 'I am missing you dreadfully. I am starving for a look.' Edith, determined that her husband should lack for no creature comforts that she could provide, sent him cigarettes, jams, biscuits – and letter after letter. 'I gloat over everything,' he wrote (on 24 August). 'I turn them over and think that you have touched every one of them. I hate the separation from you but it was bound to come in some form or other, and this for me is very pleasant to be going with Putty. All my love my sweetest pet. You are the very best and truest and I know it. . . .'

He frequently put this to the proof by asking her to forward letters to other women. 'You might send the enclosed on to Eloise. I haven't written to her at all. Put a stamp on and just send it off. That would be very sweet and dear of you.' For 'the girls', in particular Eloise, were still in Charley's life, though he constantly sought to reassure Edith by swearing his overwhelming love for her, beside which his feelings for them were of the most trivial. 'You, and you alone, count in my life . . . I have never realised so much how nothing whatsoever matters to me except your sweet self . . . It is a relief to me that Mollie does not write. Eloise continues to do so but I could quite well dispense with her letters.' For these, though affectionate, contained what Charley described as 'a sort of undercurrent of venom which rather bores me'. Expecting his mistresses to regard these liaisons in the same light-heartedly amorous light as he did, he shied away from any form of possessiveness – especially when expressed in the form of an angry reproach. 'Why can they never make the best of things?' he asked Edith plaintively (in January 1915), quickly adding: 'I have never mentioned anything you have told me to her.'

He had also begun a correspondence that was entirely unexceptionable, with one of the most fascinating and best-known women in English society, who was to become his lifelong friend and confidante.

Lady Desborough, tall, slim, graceful, elegant, was a remarkable woman. She was a person for whom the word 'charm' might have been coined. Born Ettie Fane, she was co-heiress to the barony of Butler, a granddaughter on her father's side of the eleventh Earl of Westmorland and on her mother's of the sixth Earl Cooper. She grew up in an ambiance that combined wealth and politics – while still in the schoolroom she met and became friends with Arthur Balfour and Alfred Lyttelton – but her personal life was scarred by tragedy from the start. She was orphaned at the age of two, her only brother died when she was eight and the grandmother who was bringing her up when she was thirteen. More cruel still, she was to lose two of her three sons in the war, in agonisingly protracted circumstances, and the third in a motor accident eleven years later, in 1926.

In 1887, at the age of twenty, she married Willie Grenfell, Lord Desborough's heir, a notable sportsman and athlete. It was the start of her life as a great hostess. Everyone of note came to stay at Taplow Court, a large red-brick Tudor manor house set in a 200-acre park, with a celebrated avenue of cedars. It was here that the Souls as a recognised entity first came into being; and it remained their chief and favourite meeting place. Here Arthur Balfour, George Curzon, George Wyndham, the Duke and Duchess of Rutland, Harry Cust, the Duke and Duchess of Sutherland, Lord and Lady Elcho, Lord and Lady Ribblesdale and Margot Tennant (later Asquith) read – and wrote – poetry, and discussed metaphysics, emotion, destiny, politics and above all the power, demands, obligations and pleasures of friendship, in an atmosphere quite different from the lavish, unthinking hedonism that characterised most grand Edwardian houses.

It was, perhaps, the awareness that she would have to depend on others for her emotional needs that helped Ettie Desborough develop the formidable powers of attraction which fascinated and allured men and women alike. Curzon described her thus: 'Ettie riding on top of her wave of spirituelle and graceful pre-eminence, always gentle, always thoughtful of others, always well equipped for any call either of brain or heart; always incomparably dressed and an epicure's feast for the eye.' She was at the heart of that network of romantic friendships characterised by a chivalric devotion expressed in extravagant language that linked the men and women of the Souls. Her friends were legion, and worshipping, like Balfour, who adored her – indeed, many of the men were abjectly devoted. Here is Curzon again, six years after his marriage, writing to her in 1901 from Viceregal Lodge, Simla, in a perfect example both of Ettie-worship and Soul-language. 'For a whole night I have dreamed of you – no hope of reciprocity – they were wonderful dreams, lover's dreams, in which things never contemplated in life were realised in that glowing fancy haze. Now that I am awake again and am respectable it is a heavy shock to find that there is no love, no triumph, no embrace; not even the fugitive consolation of a kiss. Ah me!' Both, it is hardly necessary to add, were happily married.

Ettie was intelligent as well as being beautiful. 'Lady Desborough is the cleverest woman in London,' declared Mrs Keppel. She was also brave: even Cynthia Asquith, usually a hard critic of her own sex, admitted: 'I give Ettie very good marks in wartime.' Above all, though, she had a genius for friendship. She was a marvellous listener and none of her friends was ever in doubt as to her devotion to them and her understanding. Her correspondence took her one and a half hours a day; her letters, expressing exactly what she felt, are full of warmth, emotion and the belief – usually stated but always implicit – that her correspondent was brilliant, charming, compassionate, kind, and in all ways worthy to be beloved. It was an irresistible approach.

Ettie's correspondence with Charley began against a background of family intimacy. She was eleven years older than he and already a great friend of his father and Edith's. Their first 'real' talk was in the gardens of Stafford House one summer's day. They poured their hearts out to each other; so enwrapped in conversation did they become that no interruption could disturb them ('Constance came up in the middle to show us a horrible snake wrapped round her neck'). Both had romantically complicated lives. Charley must have just begun his affair with Eloise – from the start, his wartime letters to Ettie contain many references to this – while Ettie herself had recently lost the lover of several years' standing. This was Archie Gordon, youngest son of the seventh Earl of Aberdeen, eighteen years younger than she was and a mere three years older than her son Julian. He was driving home from a day's shooting in Hampshire one late November day in 1909 when his car collided with another, overturned, and pinned him beneath it. He survived for nearly three weeks, before dying with his family and Ettie beside him.

Such was the formality of the age that Charley never wrote to the woman who rapidly became his dearest friend as anything except 'Dear Lady Desborough' or, as their friendship deepened, 'Dear Lady S' (Maurice Baring had nicknamed her 'Lady Sottise' after she had misread the name Madame Sottine). Ettie's greetings, from the vantage point of one who had known him as a child, quickly graduate from 'Dear Charley' to 'Dearest Charley'.

Their correspondence began almost immediately after the outbreak of war when Ettie sent him a parcel. It was, said Charley truthfully, very nice to be thought of. 'You divine my wants, too, because I could only bring a few things and mine [socks] were all thick ones. The boracic ointment is invaluable and I hadn't got any. We have had a strenuous time, especially when we began. The retreat [from Mons] was very disheartening but we are facing in the right direction now and I hope we shall continue to do so ... Yours always sincerely, Castlereagh. PS I saw Maurice Baring yesterday for a moment, looking very well.'

He told her about his general: 'Putty has been more than charming and makes everything very easy'; he sympathised with her own worries: 'I feel so much for you in your anxiety and pray heaven a merciful Providence will watch over your Julian. I expect I shall soon see the Royals and will send you a line at once to say how he is looking.' He confided in her about Eloise: 'I have had some very nice letters from her.' When he came home on a few days' leave he told her penitently of a spat with Edith: 'I suppose you will say it was my fault that I was aggressive.' And at Christmas he sent her his best love, 'and you know what is in my heart'.

Pulteney's corps missed the battle of Mons but was involved in the retreat southwards. 'This retiring is dreadfully disheartening,' wrote Charley to Edith on 2 September. The French, he thought, were useless ('I do not believe they ever put up a fight') and he feared the morale of the men would be severely damaged by 'the continual bolting'. However on 9 September came the battle of the Marne, when the Allies counter-attacked, capturing 160 guns and 38,000 prisoners. The Third Corps took part in the fighting on the Aisne and the advance north to secure the Channel ports. By 14 October, the line had stabilised and Pulteney established his Corps Headquarters at Bailleul. One incidental benefit was the planting of the Wynyard vinery: the vines at Bailleul were famous and one of Charley's brother officers, James de Rothschild, brought Edith cuttings when he came home on leave. (When the Germans recaptured Bailleul in 1918, they destroyed every vine.)

Charley quickly became disenchanted with life as an ADC and loyalty to Putty warred with the urge to be taking an active part in the fighting. Even Edith, desperate that Charley should be safe, had to admit that his duties were not very onerous; and one can imagine how regimental officers serving in the line were contemptuous of these two well-connected young men dancing attendance on their general in the safety of Corps Headquarters. Charley felt this keenly. 'How much better I should have done if I had remained in the Army and done the Staff College instead of stagnating for eight years in the House of Commons,' he wrote to Edith on 26 September. 'It is very irritating to see people in important positions, no better than me, and to feel that I am a sort of mixture of a footman and a clerk.' All his life Charley, born in the days when aristocrats believed their natural place was at the head of things, intensely disliked the idea of playing second fiddle.

When, in their plentiful spare time, the two ADCs visited the trenches, Charley noted on 9 January 1915: 'The rain is still going on and the trenches are flooded. I believe there was some fraternising yesterday and the day before between the two sides but the authorities are very down on that sort of thing.'

Those first few months of war also saw the first hint of what was to become one of Charley's chief interests and keenest joys, flying. For the rest of his life, he was fascinated by everything to do with aviation. 'The thing that has most impressed me here has been the aeroplane service,' he had written to Edith on 24 September when Third Corps were fighting on the Aisne. 'A splendid lot of boys who really don't know what fear is.' Three days before Christmas he had his first flight, lasting ten minutes. 'A delightful sensation. I seldom enjoyed anything more.'

But by the beginning of 1915 his initial good spirits had given way to depression. He wanted to rejoin his regiment, and felt useless and frustrated in his comfortable ADC's job. His letters to Ettie breathe the boredom of his circumscribed life – one highlight was a visit by the Earl of Lonsdale, in a 'superb khaki outfit different from everyone else's', come to check on the welfare of the horses for the Blue Cross – and to Edith he reiterates his longing to rejoin the Blues. Though still fond of Putty, he is rapidly becoming intensely bored by him. '. . . and what is so tiresome, no conversation. It is all "Oh, yes, top-hole, what!" and filth. Not that I blame him for a dirty mind, but there is nothing else, and the ADC's job is to laugh and endeavour to cap his stories. He has a good heart . . . but I don't think he can understand our feelings about the ridiculous position he keeps us in.' Charley would even, he told Edith, be prepared to take a job at home, so hopeless did he think the duties of an ADC. 'It is rather sad and I have been in the downs lately.'

For Edith the opposite was true. She had perceived instantly that war would revolutionise the status of women and, with it, everything from their general attitude to their dress. The clamour of the suffragettes gave way to a different voice: that of women seeking to play their part in the war effort. Edith realised that there was room for some kind of organisation of women on a grand scale. Almost at once, the vehicle for it appeared. When the Women's Emergency Corps came into being and, affiliated to it, the Women's Volunteer Reserve, she was asked to become Colonel-in-Chief of the Reserve. She hated the military-sounding title ('I think it a mistake, and misleading') but she recognised the opportunity and seized it.

The Reserve grew rapidly. Edith, believing that if it were to increase to the size essential to replace large numbers of men it would have to be run on less military lines ('I was confirmed in this opinion by a fresh batch of abusive letters early in 1915'), now forced the issue by resigning as its Colonel-in-Chief. Once she had broken her direct connection with the Reserve, she was free to found a breakaway organisation. All the members she had personally recruited followed her, and thousands more quickly joined. The Women's Legion was born. They wore a khaki uniform, with a badge depicting the bronze figure of Victory holding a laurel wreath (known by many of them as 'the lady with the frying pan') and the motto *Ora et Labora*.

Forming a pool of women prepared to undertake work previously done by men might seem a praiseworthy contribution to the war effort deserving of nothing but assistance and good wishes. Yet in the context of the times and in the wake of suffragette violence it was seen by many in quite a different light – as an attempt by women to break the boundaries of feminine behaviour, and thus an offence against God and (probably more important still) Man. When Edith wrote to *The Times* in February 1915 on the subject of employing women in agriculture she received a shoal of anonymous abusive letters; and the idea that women should wear breeches instead of skirts for farm work was considered perverted, immoral and obscene. Until then, domestic service, working in shops, some factory work, nursing, cooking and sewing were the main occupations open to women – apart, of course, from marriage and the supreme goal of all right-thinking females, motherhood. Even in August 1915, Horatio Bottomley's scurrilous magazine *John Bull*, as it hailed the prospect of a land fit for heroes to live in once the war had ended, was saying: 'In all this, Woman will take her true place. No more hysterical shriekings after power; no more stifling of maternal instincts. She shall learn to glory in the role of Mother and House Ruler ... and to make herself efficient in her proper sphere – the greatest mission of all.'

The question of the public attitude to women doing what was perceived as men's work was a delicate one. In December 1914 a large meeting, attended by hundreds of women, was held at the Mansion House at which Edith (still Colonel-in-Chief of the Reserve) and her father, as a former Minister of Agriculture, spoke. Both knew it was as important to reassure the audience and the sceptics outside as to promote the idea of women in agriculture. Their message was that they were not seeking to bring into being some kind of quasi-military body, simply one that would do work formerly done by men so that the latter could be released for active service. Even this objective drew denunciations ('women masquerading as men') and abuse, but it was agreed that such a body should be formed. Most of the audience wanted it called the Women's Corps, until Edith asked them if they wanted to wear shoulder straps decorated with the initials WC. In April 1915 Chaplin and Walter Long, likewise a countryman, Master of Foxhounds and former Minister of Agriculture, formed a committee to forward the employment of women; it succeeded in placing many women on farms before it was taken over by the Agriculture section of the Women's Legion. By 1916 women did harrowing, potato picking, haymaking and even heavy work like ploughing.

From the start, the Legion had clearly defined sections, gradually increasing in both number and scope until by the end of the war women were doing something like eighty per cent of the work previously done by men. Edith rapidly found she had a full-time job organising recruitment, talking to the women, soothing the fears of the men they had to work with, finding new ways in which women could replace male workers and overcoming the numerous moral objections raised, as well as persuading, cajoling and, if necessary, out-arguing those in authority.

She did not hesitate to use every scrap of influence and charm she possessed, writing to those she had met at dinner or house parties or, in default of any personal contact, simply heading directly for the top. Generals, officials and politicians, faced with a beautiful young peeress pleading for their help, found it difficult to resist; friendships were sealed by invitations to luncheon or dinner at Londonderry House. Soon there was a network of influential men on whom the fascinating Lady Castlereagh could call for assistance. Many of them fell romantically if one-sidedly in love with her, a state of affairs summed up by one rueful admirer in five stanzas that began: 'There are Percy and Maxie and a great many more/Who for love of the charmer are all very sore/But she cares not one jot for them or the others/She treats them all as if they were brothers.'

One of them was General Sir John Cowans, Quartermaster General from 1912 until 1919. Cowans, formerly of the Rifle Brigade, was a consummate ladies' man. 'He possessed two dominant qualities that endeared him to many women: he wasted no time and he was never ambiguous,' wrote Princess Daisy of Pless, one of his greatest friends, '. . . but if he became a woman's friend, he remained her friend.' To Edith, his assistance proved invaluable, since he not only held the key to extensive use of the Legion by the Army, but was prepared to advise her on its organisation and help her with travel arrangements when she wanted to go to France (she took hospital supplies to Boulogne in November 1914).

He also gave her a beautiful little Colt revolver in case she should ever need to defend herself – a highly acceptable present to Edith, used to handling rifle and shotgun.

The first of the Legion's sections was devoted to military cooking. This was launched in February 1915, shortly after the Mansion House meeting, through the simple expedient of a visit by Edith to Sir John. 'I approached him on the matter,' she wrote demurely of this first meeting, 'and asked him whether he would not consider having women cooks under their own women officers at camps, etc. He agreed to the idea.'

At first women cooks were tried at a few convalescent camps, where their work was so appreciated that by July 1915 Sir John had agreed to allow the Legion to provide cooks for the convalescent hospitals at Eastbourne, Epsom and Dartford – at £26 a year, with free rations and accommodation. The scheme proved such a success that after a few months' trial this section of the Women's Legion was taken over by the War Office and put under the control of the Inspector of Army Catering. After the cooks, the next section to be formed (in 1916) was the Army Service Corps drivers, who drove anything from generals' cars to heavy lorries. They wore General Service buttons and the ASC badge in addition to their Women's Legion badges, had the same hours and did the same work as men but, of course, were paid less. They were quickly followed by women dispatch riders and mechanics.

By now most of Edith's friends were in uniform. One particular admirer was Lord Hugh Cecil, nicknamed Linky, the youngest son of the former Prime Minister Lord Salisbury, Member of Parliament (at the beginning of the century he had been one of a small ginger group of Tory MPs, of whom Winston Churchill was one, known as the Hughligans), High Churchman and theologian; when in doubt on a point of doctrine or conscience, Edith would seek his opinion, as he sought hers on secular matters such as hunting clothes ('a dark-coloured coat – what colour? Black? and what shape? Cutaway? Then, what waistcoat? And as to collar and tie, must I wear those strange swathing bands called stocks?'). He had joined the Royal Flying Corps and was attempting – disastrously – to learn to fly. 'Flying sometimes reminds me of bicycling and sometimes of boating on the sea,' he confided, knowing Edith's fondness for both.

Lord Hugh was a safe friend but other men had to be kept at arm's length. Sir John Cowans (often known as Merry John) was clearly very smitten with her, writing her affectionate letters ('You would despise me if I didn't say "Duty First" even before an angel!') and inviting her to luncheon at the Ritz or Berkeley, bringing anyone she liked. But Edith was well aware of the need for a young married woman on her own to observe the proprieties. 'John, Birdie, Hankey and I dined at the Carlton. Merry John is going to take us over to Calais and for a trip,' she wrote to Charley on 27 January 1915. 'Do you mind? It will be quite private and it will be such fun. I meant to ask you if you think it matters my seeing so much of Hankey and M John and taking the former out hunting.' Lieutenant Colonel Cyril Hankey was a King's Messenger and brother of Maurice Hankey, who became Secretary to the Cabinet in 1916.

Charley did not mind; in any case, there was a much more serious worry. His father had been ill and miserable for several months. Lord Londonderry was convinced that Charley, his only son, would be killed in the war, and was also worried by the wild and bloodthirsty threats against himself because of his active opposition to Home Rule. Anxious, wretched and despairing, he began to drink. In October 1914, Edith had written to Charley to suggest leaving the children at Wynyard, when she had to return to London. 'Your father seems so miserable about their leaving tonight, and I somehow feel we ought to let them stay, because he does love them and we should be so sorry later on to think we had perhaps not let them be with him as often as they might.'

At the end of January Lord Londonderry caught flu, which quickly turned to pneumonia. It was a comparatively mild bout, so that Edith wrote to Charley: 'I am not anxious about him yet and when he has seen the doctor I will tell you faithfully what he says. But this drink business must be stopped. If they think you could do any good by coming over and appealing to him for yourself and for your sake not to do it, I will tell you ... He is such an angel but he takes no further interest in anything except you, I think, and has no desire or wish to do anything at all.'

It was perfectly true. Figuratively speaking, he had turned his face to the wall. Normally so quick to answer any letter from the son he was so proud of, he had let two go past without a response. Anxiously Charley wrote to Edith on 2 February (1915): 'I hope you will be able to give me better news of my father.' The full account that Edith promptly dispatched did nothing to reassure him. 'It is very sad indeed and paralysis is really too awful to contemplate. Old Blandford seems to have done well but I don't know how he can be kept away from the drink.' The seriousness of Lord Londonderry's condition only dawned on those close to him at the last minute – he was only sixty-two and had always been a fit man – but by now Charley had begun to think of trying to get leave to see his father. 'I know Pa hates to be seen when he is ill and I don't think he wants us really but I feel I might be able to cheer him up a bit.'

It was too late. Lord Londonderry died on 8 February 1915. He was buried in the family vault at Long Newton in County Durham. Charley's letter to Ettie not only summed up his feelings for the father he had so suddenly and unexpectedly lost, but showed Charley at his best, full of sweetness, self-knowledge, humility and disinterested love. 'I can't bear to think of the world without him, without his loving help in everything I tried to do. I knew whatever happened I always had a friend, ready always to believe me in the right and fight all my battles to the end. I have been carried all my life by him and I know it. The Home Rule Bill broke his heart. He has never looked up since and his only interest now as it was my and Birdie's success and happiness. Oh, it is foolish to write like this but you are so understanding and sympathetic, at least I always feel you are, that I feel I can just tell you what I am going through now. I know I am not the only person in trouble, there are scores and scores with far greater trouble, but no one has ever lost a truer friend and affection of that quality is so rare in the world that we none of us can afford to lose it. He was the dearest and most loving father any son has ever had.' Carson described him as 'a great leader, a great and devoted public servant, a great patriot, a great gentleman, and above all the greatest of friends'. Theresa, as she had done when she lost her son Reggie, spent much of her time out of doors in an attempt to exorcise her grief. 'Walking is the only thing you can do when you are unhappy,' she told her little grandson Robin.

Almost at once there were financial differences. Only a month after his father's death Charley, who had never really trusted Theresa over money, was telling Edith that his mother's grabbing attitude made him sick. In particular, he was anxious that the marvellous family jewels be passed intact to his wife. 'You must be firm about the jewels,' he wrote from France. 'She has bagged anything she could and she will take advantage of your good nature. Please have a list made out of what she has got and have the remainder very carefully gone into as I have no faith in her at all.'

Lord Londonderry had in fact provided generously for all his family, as they quickly learned – probate of his will was granted within three weeks of his death. Both Birdie (now Lady Ilchester) and Theresa got legacies of £100,000 as well as annuities; Theresa was also left any one of his carriages, pair of carriage horses and set of harness that she wanted, any one of his cars, and any two of his brood mares with foals or yearlings at foot. Everything else, apart from bequests and legacies to servants, went outright to Charley. As well as the houses, with their furniture and pictures, the jewels and the stud, there was, of course, the income from the coal mines: even though when war broke out a great number of the miners enlisted, mostly in the Durham Light Infantry, profits from Seaham averaged £22,792, from Silksworth £10,118 and from Dawdon £73,988 during the years 1912–17.

The role of deposed queen was not one to which Theresa took kindly but Edith was exquisitely tactful in dealing with her formidable mother-in-law. 'My darling Mother,' she wrote a few days after Londonderry's death, 'I do hope you are going on all right and not feeling too utterly lonely and desolate. I know well what splendid courage you possess & that you will pull through, but I also know what it will cost you. I feel it myself all the more, as not only have you & beloved Pa always treated me as if I was your own daughter, but I had come to regard all the houses, all the homes, in the light of a daughter too, & the shock is all the greater, when thro circumstances over which one has no control one is forced to step into other people's shoes. I feel exactly as Birdie wd do on the position of taking your place but you know how I adore your Charley (and mine) and wd do anything to help him, & also I will always try & do what I know Pa liked, & he was so devoted to Wynyard.'

Nonetheless, with Charley in France and Edith busy with the Women's Legion, Londonderry House was turned almost at once into an officer's hospital. It was subsidised by the Government but still cost Charley about £1,200 a year. Edith supervised it, dealing with any misbehaviour; some of the officers were suffering from shell shock – one used to hurl his tray of food on to the floor at every opportunity, others would decorate the statues of Venus and Apollo in the hall with lipstick or articles of clothing when they came back in cheerful mood from an outing. The day-to-day running was left to Mrs Harris, Theresa's superb cook, who was used to large-scale catering.

Theresa did not like these changes. 'You never told me my rooms would be used or that anybody would go into them,' she wrote indignantly on 29 April 1915. 'It is so nice of you offering me the gold brackets in the sitting room but I do not think Charley would like them removed, and I would leave them as they were put there in Frances Anne's time, seventy years ago or more, with the blue velvet.... I own it gives me a great pang to feel my friends are able to run in and out of Londonderry

House before three months are over without one thought for me or one who has gone.'

Charley had also put Seaham Hall, in Durham, at the disposal of the authorities, who used it as a convalescent home. It was supervised by Theresa, at the suggestion of Edith, who realised that here her mother-in-law's powerful personality could be put to good use ('The men have been giving a lot of trouble everywhere as they are just too well to be in hospital and not sufficiently ill to wish to obey orders'). The grant for Seaham was more generous and cost Charley nothing except free coal from his mines nearby.

Despite his huge new wealth, Charley was still worried about money. Not that this was anything new, his reproaches on the score of Edith's extravagance had several times reduced her to tears of misery – once, she wrote wretchedly offering to give up her chief joy, hunting, if this would help – but now, he told her apologetically, he was the one who was giving her trouble as he really did not know where the money would come from to pay the previous year's supertax, a sum of about £14,000. 'And on 1st April begin Mother's and Birdie's and Olive's legacies, nearly £16,000 a year. But it's no good complaining and I would not like them to think I minded.' He hoped, he said, that Edith would be able to manage on £1,000 a month. 'Out of this should come food, servants' wages at Londonderry House and Springfield. All Springfield and Wynyard horses would be out of this, children's accounts, hospitals, convalescent homes, racing stud, all new bills. Rates and taxes at Londonderry House and Springfield would be paid by you.' It must have been a relief for Edith to read on and find that the upkeep of Wynyard and Mount Stewart was to be met from a different account.

XI

ALMOST AT once, the new Marchioness put her own original stamp
on Londonderry House entertaining. Every Wednesday, from
early 1915, the group of friends known as the Ark met for a late
dinner on its top floor, the rest of the house, apart from two rooms on
the ground floor, having been turned over to the hospital.

The Ark was originally formed to give Edith's friends a chance to relax
away from their wartime work. It quickly became the nearest thing to a
salon in wartime London. Not everyone approved: it was stigmatised by
Lady Cynthia Asquith, perhaps a trifle jealously, as 'ridiculous'. And
certainly there was something of the school secret society about it: you
had to be invited to join; every member, however august in private life,
had to take the name of a real or mythological beast and was given a
matching 'address'; silly games were played; jokes were told, gossip
exchanged, verses written, skits acted. It was a long way below the lofty
intellectual and spiritual plateau on which the Souls resided; but then, as
Edith had rightly judged, for a Cabinet minister or a general who had
spent all day grappling with the arduous and depressing realities of the
war the chance to drink the excellent Londonderry House champagne –
laid down by Theresa in the days of lavish pre-war parties – to be
frivolous, playful, even absurd, in the company of beautiful women,
painters, writers, politicians and soldiers on leave or convalescing, was
irresistible. What the Ark offered, above all, was *fun*. (By contrast, the
King, gloomily, had just given up drink at the behest of Lloyd George
– who had not – to set an example to the shipbuilding and munitions
workers. Windsor Castle on the wagon was a sad affair, reported Ettie,
one of the Queen's ladies-in-waiting. 'Tempers but little improved by
temperance and a crepe wreath fastened to the cellar door. . . .')

Ark appellations had to begin with the first letter of Christian name or surname, or they had to rhyme, or be amusingly apropos. The Quartermaster General, Sir John Cowans, was Merry John the Mandrill (he lived, naturally, at the Monkey House), Princess Helena Victoria* was Victoria the Vivandiere, Hankey was Cyril the Squirrel (telegraphic address, Knuts), Charley was Charley the Cheetah – serving in France, his telegraphic address was *Sans Purr*.

Edith found herself christened Circe the Sorceress, no doubt because she fascinated so many of the men. Here are some of the verses one wrote in her commonplace book.

> Oh, would I were Ulysses
> Embraced by Circe's arms!
> I'd seek no other blisses
> However sweet their charms
>
> No more should ventures lure me
> Upon the kindly seas
> If Circe would immure me
> With her in Cyclades
>
> In Lotos Isle the diet
> Brings sleep and peaceful rest
> I'd much prefer to riot
> In Circe's downy nest
>
> With Circe for a pillow
> I'd need no other kind
> Nor would I rest until, oh! –
> The maid rolled up the blind
>
> Let others strive for honour
> Let fools fight for a name
> My heart is quite a goner
> Would Circe's were the same!

Through the years, the Ark had a diversity of members. Sir James Barrie (Barrie the Bard) was an occasional visitor; so too was Edith's elderly

* Princess Helena Victoria, usually known in the family as Thora, was the daughter of Queen Victoria's fifth child, Princess Helena, and her husband Prince Christian of Schleswig-Holstein.

and faithful admirer Sir Edmund Gosse, who had encouraged her in the women's suffrage campaign – in 1927, his New Year present to her of his book *Father and Son* was inscribed 'To the divine Circe, from her infatuated Gos-hawk'. Winston Churchill was Winston the Warlock, Edward Wood was Edward the Woodpecker, Sir Samuel Hoare, a keen skater, was Sam the Skate, Lady Astor was Nancy the Gnat, and the painter Sir William Orpen was Orpen the Ortolan. Carson and Balfour (Edward the Eagle and Arthur the Albatross) battled with each other in a childish card game called Chase The Ace for the prize of a box of Bryant and May matches. It was on one such Ark Wednesday – 31 May 1916 – that Balfour, then First Lord and fresh from the Admiralty, which was in wireless contact with Jellicoe, gave the rest of the Ark guests the first news of the Battle of Jutland. It had begun a few hours earlier but as this was ten years before the age of broadcasting the public knew nothing about it until the first reports appeared in the newspapers two days later. As Edith already knew the Secretary of State for War, Lord Kitchener, well enough to choose furniture for his seventeenth-century house while he was in Egypt, she must have been one of the best-informed women in Britain on the progress of the war.

After the war, the Ark Wednesdays became more formal. At 9.30 p.m. members would meet in the great ballroom. Liveried footmen with powdered wigs kept the champagne flowing; Ark members like Harold Macmillan (Harold the Hummingbird) and John Buchan (the Buck) chatted over delicious food. As the Ark grew more famous still, and its members more numerous, the dinners were replaced by suppers, at which habitués could drop in after a dinner party, a late vote in the House or simply for half an hour's gaiety before bedtime. By now, three more Prime Ministers past and present belonged: Ramsay MacDonald, Stanley Baldwin and Neville Chamberlain (the last two with their respective wives). Invitations always said 'Dress optional' in order not to discourage the more Bohemian guests – Sean O'Casey, for instance, always insisted on wearing a black polo-necked sweater and plum-coloured trousers and asking for a pot of tea at midnight. Later, when the Castlereagh daughters Helen and Margaret were growing up, these suppers were transferred to the gallery, with dancing for the young.

More conventional hostesses were still confining their invitations to those people who constituted 'Society', but Edith was fascinated by artists and writers no less than by politicians long before it became the fashion to lion-hunt. What gave the Ark its peculiar flavour right from the start was the eclectic mixture of guests. As usual, an Ark member put this into verse:

> You will find there a Queen,
> A jockey, a Dean,
> With perfect affinities sorted;
> A sculptor, an actress,
> A world's benefactress
> By crowned heads and clergymen courted.
>
> The Bench and the Bar
> The latest film star
> Hob-nob with young bloods diplomatic;
> While foreign artistes
> Play tunes to the 'beasts'
> In time with their movements erratic.

And so on for another eight verses.

After his father's funeral, Charley, by now promoted to Major and with a mention in dispatches, had returned to France, where he found himself touched by Putty's obvious efforts to cheer him and the general atmosphere of chaff and friendliness.

In April, Curzon came out to France. 'He has just been taken to within 170 yards of the Germans and has looked at them I expect through a periscope,' wrote Charley to Ettie. 'I should like to have gone with him as I am sure his sonorous sentences would reverberate through the trenches.' A week later, though, he got the chance to accompany Balfour. 'AJB . . . looked tired, I thought, but it was very nice seeing him; I have been brought up in an atmosphere of adoration of AJB as my poor father worshipped the ground he walked on and, though an obstinate man, he had not a will of his own in Mr Balfour's presence.' He felt, he said, quite cheerful, though, unlike many of his friends who were still talking in terms of victory within the next few months, he himself did not see an early end to the war.

Three days after Balfour's visit, the Germans made their first attack with poison gas. There was fierce fighting, and a British withdrawal to southwest of Hooge, with casualties of 58,000 other ranks and over 2,000 officers. One of these was Julian Grenfell, who had earlier won the DSO in the first battle of Ypres. He was wounded in the head on 13 May and taken to a British military hospital. Ettie travelled to France immediately and sat by his bedside until he died on 26 May. 'I am haunted by the thought of Ettie seeing her glorious son die by inches,' wrote Lady Cynthia Asquith.

Although they had barely met each other, Julian's death may have brought Charley's suppressed frustration and wretchedness to a head, for all his discontent with his job as ADC now flooded back. 'I cannot persuade myself, try though I will, and I have tried very hard, that I am doing anything but evading those duties . . . that are incumbent on everyone certainly under 40. I see all my contemporaries and friends running risks and taking their part and I cannot see where I am different.' Charley was a brave man, hunting, playing polo and point-to-pointing with immense dash, and he had all the brave man's dislike of seeming to appear a coward. Additionally, as a man conscious of his own good looks and elegance, he had the touch of vanity that meant he was always conscious of the figure he cut in the eyes of others. Underscoring his intense dislike of appearing to shelter behind his general was his accurate suspicion that Putty was determined to keep him not because of any affection ('he has no personal feeling for me') but out of a desire to please Edith. For, like so many, the good Sir William appears to have been a little in love with her. 'I feel years younger for having seen you,' he told her after one of their meetings. 'The devil there is in you, the risks you will take; if only I had a dozen brigadiers like you we should be in Berlin by Christmas.'

Charley, stuck in Corps Headquarters, wrote letter after despairing letter to Edith. 'Putty I feel is quite hopeless, and cannot understand how I can object to continuing for another year in this ridiculous post, and I cannot see how I am going to withdraw without a certain amount of unpleasantness. He will not discuss it, in fact he is quite impossible. Now you must not write to him about me. I don't trust you very much about this.' He was right not to: Edith, desperately worried at the thought of her Charley in the trenches, confided these anxieties to her friend Sir John Cowans. He reassured her that Charley would have to stay with Putty as, if he went back to the Regiment, he would have to go as Second in Command, and he had not sufficient recent experience in soldiering to do this job. 'So you will have to tell him it is his duty to stay with Putty,' concluded Merry John.

Edith passed on this advice as tactfully as she could, leavening it with praise and loving support. 'It may be galling for you as you are worth so much more but I think honestly it is your duty to remain [with Putty]. . . . You have struggled to do your best to return to your Regiment and failed and I think you really should do your best where you are – not that you don't always but you should accept the position. I don't know what I would give to be in your arms now, but as I can't, I must just tell you once more that I love you more than anything in the world and shall count the hours till I hear from you again. I kiss your letters all over.'

But Charley's thoughts had crystallised. 'I want to fight and if I can't fight I want to go home,' he wrote to Edith in June 1915. 'I realise that except for the role of being at the front there is no object in my being here when I can be usefully employed at home. Billy [Lambton] thought I was under no obligation to Putty and advised me not to hesitate about as he put it "carting" him. And there I think he is quite right. I feel I have just wasted a year, with everybody thinking how ridiculous I have been the whole time.'

He applied to go home as Second in Command of the Reserve Regiment of the Blues. 'As second in command in a reserve regiment I become of military value. At the present moment and as long as I continue with Putty I am of no military value whatsoever. The moment I become of military value I shall seize the opportunity and I might get anywhere if this cursed war is going to continue. From here I can get nowhere and I am running a serious risk of being stamped as a loafer for the rest of my life.'

Eventually, Putty had to concede defeat and let his unwilling ADC go, writing dolefully to Edith: 'It will mean a very different menage; because I can't have pals again as ADCs but just "beck and callers".' Charley, delighted, returned to the Reserve unit of the Regiment, which was stationed at the Regent's Park Barracks and due to go out to France the following spring. Finally Edith, too, accepted his decision. 'If I clutch at straws and appear weak it is because I am your wife, and I love you so much I cannot contemplate existence without you. But I shall equally rejoice with you whatever you do, now or in the future, if I know it is what you want and think right to do.'

Charley's decision, and Edith's fears, can only have been strengthened when, on 4 August, Julian Grenfell's brother Billy was killed. Ettie's bravery was almost superhuman; true to her philosophy that everything was always for the best, she refused to wear black, and continued with her normal life, talking and writing to friends in the style so many mistook for frivolous. There are harrowing descriptions of her chatting on some topic of the day while tears streamed down her cheeks. It was not that she was attempting a grisly façade of normality: she truly believed that her sons were still close to her; yet these cuts to the heart were too much. 'I feel often like a dead woman, still able to move and speak and eat and laugh, but the real person has gone far away. It is *all wrong*. I am always fighting and shall prevail at last.' Charley, who wrote to his 'Dearest Friend' straightaway, could find no words of comfort, and even to him she was only able to speak of those devastating losses after two years had passed, in one brief and tragic sentence. 'It is ... like being bled to death inwardly.'

Asquith's agreement, under duress, to include a Conservative and Labour element in the Government did nothing to alter the feelings of the hard-line Unionists. Shortly after this first coalition was formed, the Prime Minister had been to France. Charley wrote sheepishly to Edmund Gosse that when Asquith had visited Third Corps, he (Charley), consulted by the brigadier as to whether three cheers was not a fitting end to the proceedings, had, 'would you believe it', 'feebly said Yes. For heaven's sake don't tell my dear Mother or that the cheers compared very favourably with those accorded to Carson to the accompaniment of the Orange drum.'

What did delight Theresa was that shortly after Charley's return from France the King offered him the position of Lord Lieutenant of Down. 'I cannot describe the joy it gave me. It would have pleased his Father beyond everything,' she wrote in a diary entry which described her grandchild Maureen's beauty ('like her Mother with her Father's eyes') and Robin's prowess, 'top of his class, a clever and most interesting child, full of sport and games'.

In September, Zeppelin raids began. Edith saw one of the Zeppelins clearly; it was, she thought, about two miles up. Everyone at Londonderry House, where the patients ran out on to the balcony in their pyjamas, heard the anti-aircraft guns in St James's Park, Hyde Park and Green Park blaze away but their shells burst far beneath it. Later Edith drove down to the City, where incendiary bombs had started fires. She saw Bartholomew Close, where there had been many casualties, the smashed windows of the nurses' quarters in St Bartholomew's Hospital, the crater outside Great Ormond Street Hospital and the hole in Liverpool Street Station where a bomb had gone straight through it into the Underground below, smashing water pipes and flooding the tunnel. 'The results of these huge bombs are not at all reassuring. From what I saw myself, I am convinced that if one struck this house it would go through it as if it were paper.'

Fortunately the Londonderry convalescent hospital at Seaham was well away from danger. Here Theresa, who had remained at Wynyard since her husband's death, was now taking an active part, playing hymns for the Sunday evening service, visiting the wives of Durham soldiers and sailors, giving talks to the eighty-three patients ('they seem to enjoy being talked to very much'). She must have described her visit to Beatty's flagship, the *Lion*, lying off Rosyth dockyard, on 3 September 1916. She was taken on board by Lady Beatty, in the Admiral's barge.

'It was a most glorious day with half a gale of wind blowing, which made the Forth look beautiful. To me, who love the sea and have not been on it for two years, it was a real joy to feel myself dashing through the water. I can hardly describe the thrill it gave one, on going on board the Lion, to be on a battle cruiser which had so lately been in action [the Battle of Jutland had taken place on the night of 31 May 1916]. She was minus a turret – the turret in which Molyneux and 59 men were killed. We were shown a screen through which a shell passed, and a broken piece of shell. We were also told that some hazelwood fenders caught fire in the action, also that there was a fire blazing on board while it was going on. Also a shell was fired into the middle of the fire by the Germans, but for some reason it did not explode. The Admiral told me that he saw this from the bridge but knew that nothing could be done till the fire slackened. Mercifully the shell did not go off and when the fire ceased it was rolled overboard. I believe that the Lion would have experienced the fate of the Queen Mary, namely going down because a shell had fallen into the ammunition hold owing to the flap being open but a seaman jumped on the flap and shut it down and I hear that his legs were blown off. We were shown some photographs of the Jutland Battle. There was one of the Invincible three minutes before she was sunk, and one as she sank, with her three funnels close together and her back broken. We also saw one of the Lion, with all the shells falling the other side of her.'

Earlier, she had organised a New Year theatrical entertainment in the drawing room of the Hall. It proved to be one of Charley's last engagements before he left for the front. It was a real family affair, with Edith, her young cousin Lady Rosemary Leveson Gower (Millicent's daughter), Robin, Maureen and a neighbour, Sir Hedworth Williamson, all taking leading parts. The hit of the evening was Sir Hedworth's rendering of 'Keep The Home Fires Burning'. Patients and their friends occupied the front rows, and the rest of the seats were sold for half a crown each for the benefit of the Soldiers' Comforts Fund.

This time, Theresa was determined not to put her oar in to prevent Charley going out to the front. 'As I promised him I would not interfere with his plans, after the South African affair, I cannot do anything. He must please himself and there is nothing to be said, but I hope against hope.' She realised it was only a question of time before Charley got what he wanted, noting proudly in her diary that while she wished he would be content to stay in the Reserve unit 'it is impossible that any child of mine could be content with doing nothing'.

On 9 January 1916 came the longed-for telephone message: Charley was to join the Expeditionary Force 'as soon as possible'. He was to be Second in Command of the Reserve Regiment (in London, he had commanded them for the last few months). He left on 13 January, suffering a horribly rough Channel crossing – the ship had to make three attempts to get into Boulogne harbour, eventually entering stern first. After a slow, day-long train journey Charley joined the Regiment in billets, writing to Edith the same night to tell her that 'I miss you dreadfully and my righteous feelings that I am doing my duty does not nearly make up for it. I think you now know how I feel.' For the five months Edith and Charley spent together had cleared up much that had sometimes made their wartime meetings miserable.

'You have been a sweet and darling angel about my tiresomeness,' he now told Edith, '. . . but I think you attach too much importance to it, I do really.' Even in this wartime context, it must have been difficult for Edith to think of Charley's philandering merely as 'tiresomeness', but she was as determined as ever to treat the Eloise relationship, though long-standing, as trivial – in their letters, she and Charley often referred to Eloise as his 'wife'.

For all his seeming wish to escape Eloise ('Relations are very strained with "my wife" so I shall not tell her anything at all. I think I must be in disgrace.' 'Don't ask Eloise to meet me. I shall not tell her I am back but I expect she'll find out') his feelings were clearly ambivalent. He protested that he did not want to 'pay homage' to her; he declared somewhat disingenuously that their correspondence was one-sided: 'My "wife" has been writing to me, and I am sure she is very angry now that she has had no reply!!' Yet she was still in his life and he still saw her when he came home on leave.

But when, after that leave, he went back to the front, all the Londonderrys could think of was their feelings for each other. He wired to Edith when he landed and wrote to her the following day. 'Never have I had such a lump in my throat as I had yesterday when you walked away down the platform, and I know you had too. God Bless You, my best and sweetest, remember I love every little bit of you, soul and body, and your lovely unselfish nature. Your very loving Charley Husband.'

His letter crossed with one from her, written the day he left. 'I hope you are warm and comfy and asleep. I shall just think of how nice you look and our last night together here. We have had a delicious time anyhow, haven't we? and I am so proud of you going out and I am really very pleased and never think I am frightened about you, beloved thing. You know it is not in my nature to worry. I only feel I cannot bear to think you are in the cold and I am all warm . . . but it was hard, darling, parting from you and I fear I did not make it easy for you. I dared not look round when I left.'

He wrote to Edith almost every day. The Blues were in the 8th Cavalry Brigade with the 10th Hussars and the Essex Yeomanry. Half the Regiment were with their horses at Aix-en-Issart (a few miles from Montreuil), and the other half were in the trenches, alternating places every fortnight. He described the endless rain, the mud, the intense cold down at the bottom of the trenches, the constant sound of gunfire, the dirt, the monotony, and his own good spirits. Shells were landing round his dugout and the British lack of ammunition disquieted him ('we did not have a bad time in the trenches but the Boches were rather active and as we lack rifles, grenades and trench mortars it was difficult to keep upsides of them. It is rather tiresome after 18 months of war to be short of these essential methods of defence'). He remarked on how well the French did themselves ('I have just been out to lunch with the officer of the French troops quartered here for training. I never saw such a lunch'); he asked for cigarettes and a box of gingerbreads – 'I eat them at all times, and they are very good. Last night I ate one in the middle of the night.' And when he learned that Robin had taken Remove at Eton, it filled him with pride and pleasure. 'I have wearied everyone here with the ecstasy of a foolish parent,' he wrote to Ettie, 'though I will not dilate on it to you. But he is a good lad.'

He also dispatched a letter to the *Sportsman* on hearing that the War Cabinet was thinking of stopping racing for the duration. After pointing out that the sport still continued in Germany and Austria, he wrote that 'The stoppage of racing carries with it the immediate depreciation of bloodstock, the ruin of the small breeder and the destruction of a number of thoroughbred horses . . . this check to the horsebreeding industry will operate in the direction of transferring the centre of this valuable market to some other country whose foresight will have prevented them from adopting the destructive measures contemplated by our Administration'.

Eventually, a compromise was reached: racing could carry on, but only at Newmarket. Here, one of Charley's horses, Coup-de-Main, was killed by a bomb during a raid by German planes minutes before the running of the Newmarket Cup, for which it was the hot favourite. So censored were the newspapers that Charley did not learn of this for some time; the papers only reported that 'owing to an accident Coup-de-Main was unable to run'.

Edith kept her husband's letters under her pillow, told him repeatedly how proud she was of him but, despite her presentation of herself as a good and obedient wife, refused his suggestion that she should go to some safe spot well away from the possibility of bombs. 'It never does to run away from danger, and you would not like to make me a coward, would you? If I was that sort of woman, how should I live with you away all these months?'

A year or so after the war had begun, Chaplin's health had seriously deteriorated. He had sat continuously in the House from 1868 onwards, except for a break of a few weeks in 1906 – a break which had cost him the Fathership of the House. In 1915, when he was seventy-five and extremely overweight, getting to Westminster from his flat in Charles Street – and, worse still, back – in wartime conditions was very difficult. Cabs had become few and far between and, though kind friends would sometimes lend him their motors, his manservant William often had to come and fetch him and walk him slowly home. In the winter of 1915/16 he had a slight stroke, but still refused to give up going to the House every day – in many ways it was his life.

Edith realised that something had to be done. She wrote as tactfully and charmingly as she could to George V telling him of the situation and her fears, and soon afterwards, when Chaplin was staying with his daughter at Springfield in the hope of getting some hunting, a special messenger arrived from Buckingham Palace. He carried a handwritten letter from the King, offering Chaplin a peerage, 'to relieve him of the strain of further work in the House of Commons and in the hope that he would be able to continue in the less arduous Lords for many years to come'. After initially demurring – he would no longer be 'the Squire', the name by which he was known and loved by so much of England – Chaplin accepted gratefully. On 10 April 1916, he became Viscount Chaplin of St Oswald's, Blankney.

On 24 June, the Blues left Aix-en-Issart to move into the Somme valley, and on 1 July the Battle of the Somme began. It lasted four and a half months in all and resulted in huge casualties – over three-quarters of a million men on the British side and more than half a million on the German. Charley lost his two best friends, Harold Brassey, best man at his wedding, and his cousin Charlie Helmsley. 'Charlie was my cousin and my life's friend.'

Charley himself, who had hoped for command of a battalion, was not considered senior enough. Instead, he was made second in command of one drawn from the 8th Cavalry Brigade. Its main duties were digging the reserve trenches and the dispiriting task of burying the dead of the Somme battlefields. The sight of this vast number of dead young men, overrun by rats intent on a meal, affected Charley profoundly. 'Personally, I should end the war now,' he wrote to his confidante Ettie on 22 July, 'as there is nothing to be gained by either side, and I should think the Germans would accept terms which, shorn of Asquith's rhetoric, are the status quo ante. Why not send it [out] on the wireless every day? It is a question of "saving faces" and while the rulers are deciding how best they can do it, I suppose some two million on all sides will be killed or maimed for life.'

In November Edith managed to get a *laissez-passer* to Paris, where Charley met her for a week's leave. It was the third time she had crossed the Channel in wartime; she had no trouble in obtaining vouchers exempting her from the usual search at Victoria Station from Sir John Cowans, only too pleased to render this favour to his 'Beloved Circe'. In December Charley was given a further fortnight's leave; during this, Asquith resigned and the King sent for Lloyd George, who became Prime Minister of the second wartime Coalition Government. Theresa, thrilled that the political *bête noire* of the Londonderry family had stepped down, instantly had dreams of a Government post for her son. But, as Charley pointed out, there were 'certain difficulties' in the way.

One, of course, was that he was a serving soldier, now back with his regiment. As Second in Command of the Blues, he took part (on 10 April 1917) in the attack on Monchy, a village between Cambrai and Arras. From the cavalry point of view it was a disaster: the going was very heavy over snow-covered ground and they galloped into such a barrage that they lost about 500 horses. The commanding officer of the Blues was killed by a machine-gun bullet as he stood in a nearby trench; and Charley took over command until the new commanding officer arrived.

Edith, despite her promises, had been intriguing ceaselessly to have Charley sent home. By now she knew just about everyone who mattered, and it was not long before her efforts were crowned with success. On 8 May 1917, she received a letter from the Londonderry family's adored AJB, saying that he had written to the Cavalry Brigade Commander, Brigadier General Kavanagh, suggesting that he should send Charley home as 'he does not realise how very necessary it is that he should come back and look after his own affairs'. It was a very strong letter, and Balfour was Foreign Secretary. Kavanagh acted on the suggestion.

As for Charley, he was by now thoroughly disenchanted with the part he was playing and with his military prospects. The conditions of warfare prevailing in France were such that the cavalry were regarded as cumbersome and outdated; their role was no longer one of dash and glory but, in general, of performing comparatively menial tasks for which others could not be spared. Charley much preferred the idea of throwing himself into Irish politics to fight for a satisfactory settlement of the Home Rule question.

Since the Easter Rising in 1916, the spectre of civil war had arisen once more. Lloyd George now proposed two possible solutions. The first gave immediate Home Rule to Ireland with the exclusion of the Six Counties, such exclusion to be reviewed after five years; the second (characterised by Lloyd George as 'the last resort') was 'a convention of Irishmen of all parties for the purpose of producing a scheme of Irish self-government'. The first plan was turned down immediately by both Nationalists and Unionists; the former because it involved partition, and the latter because exclusion was only temporary. Both sides, however, agreed to a Convention.

The opening meeting of the 100-odd delegates, mainly leading business and professional men and the representatives of public bodies, county councils and the Roman Catholic hierarchy, was at Trinity College, Dublin, on 25 July 1917, under the chairmanship of Sir Horace Plunkett. Charley, there both as Lord Lieutenant of Down and secretary of the Ulster Unionist delegation, was one of only two or three delegates under forty, but he made an excellent impression on Sir Horace when he first spoke. ('He had all the charm of his father and a good share of his mother's brains.') The delegates argued, negotiated and wrangled for eighteen months, with Sinn Fein – which had boycotted all the meetings – an invisible but powerful presence. One November night, Charley ran into Lord and Lady Fingall at the Theatre Royal; immediately, Daisy Fingall, an Irish Catholic and a Nationalist, attacked him with all the vigour at her command, accusing him of a closed mind and a stubborn refusal to compromise. When he got home that night he wrote her a long letter that was an exemplary mixture of affection, chivalry, explanation and firmness, concluding with a paragraph that summed up his own beliefs:

'My views are contained in a few sentences. I am absolutely convinced of one thing, and that is that, so long as the British Empire exists, Ireland must remain politically within the circle of the United Kingdom; and whatever path is chosen, long or short, or through whatever intermediary stages, man in his wisdom or his folly may ordain she shall pass, that Ireland will be politically governed in exactly the same manner as England or Scotland or Wales. My plan is a Federal one with which I need not weary you now....'

Thinking it over, Daisy Fingall found that she agreed with Charley that complete separation between England and Ireland would be fatal to both countries. Both must have thought, too, of the many Irishmen fighting for Britain in this third year of a bitter war.

Unofficial exchanges of views were possible thanks to a fellow Ark member. Hazel Lavery (known in the Ark as Hazel Hen), the beautiful Irish-American wife of the painter Sir John Lavery, was an ardent Home Ruler who was also a society hostess. In her South Kensington house Charley and his cousin Winston Churchill encountered many of the Irish politicians informally.

Even before it was presented, Charley's Federal plan was rejected by his fellow Ulstermen. Meanwhile Lord Midleton, leader of the Southern Unionists, had said that he would be agreeable to an Irish Parliament that had the equivalent of dominion status. More important still, the Nationalist leader John Redmond was prepared to accept such a settlement. But each was disowned by his own party. Because he could carry neither the Nationalists nor the Catholic hierarchy with him, Redmond withdrew altogether, saying, 'I feel I can be of no further use to the Convention.' Less than two months later he was dead.

'The Irish Convention is doomed and the sooner it is wound up the better,' Charley wrote to Ettie on 16 March 1918. He was lame, from water on the knee, he told her, the result of a kick on the knee while out hunting. 'I then processed behind Redmond's remains for two and a half hours and this did the mischief. The stout Protestants of the North with whom I am associated look on this as a direct visitation for associating myself with Papistry.'

Following the breakdown of the Convention and Midleton's refusal of the Irish viceroyalty – he would have had to enforce conscription, which he profoundly disliked – Sir John (by now Lord) French became Lord

Lieutenant. After the Armistice, Lord French carried on in effect as military governor of Ireland, appointing seven political advisers, one of whom was Charley. With Irish politics once more brewing up a storm, Charley may have recalled his private words of six months earlier. 'Ireland has always been a tragedy. . . . It is a pity that [it] cannot be pushed a little further out into the Atlantic.'

XII

A S CHARLEY and the other delegates to the Ulster Convention
travelled from meetings in Dublin to meetings in Belfast, from
meetings in Belfast to meetings in Cork, and back to Dublin
again in pursuit of the will-o'-the-wisp of Irish unity, Edith's work with
the Women's Legion had increased in scope. The Legion, under her
leadership, had come to do virtually all the everyday jobs that men had
done. Its 30,000-strong military cooking section became the nucleus of
the Women's Auxiliary Corps* when this was formed in February 1917;
it provided drivers for the Army Service Corps and later for the Royal
Flying Corps, with its own driving training school for 200 at Teddington;
it supplied mechanics, draughtswomen, clerks and instrument-makers to
replace men in factories. Its members drove ambulances at night through
the air raids, provided canteens for munition and transport workers; and
worked on the land. Women drove horses and tractors (the Women's
Legion bought and owned some of the first farm tractors in England),
lifted stones, harrowed, spread manure, picked fruit, cabbages, potatoes,
milked cows, made hay, and thatched cottages and barns.

On 16 March 1918, the Legion was inspected by the Queen in the
gardens of Buckingham Palace. Edith led the march past of 160 drivers
on foot followed by sixty-five in their vehicles. Sir John Cowans, writing
formally to congratulate her on the parade, continued his letter with an
appreciation of the Legion's contribution to the war effort. 'I say without
possible contradiction that your Women's Legion has been of the greatest
possible assistance to the Army generally since the beginning of the War
... I remember so well at the beginning of the war how you insisted
upon the introduction of women to military duties. We ought all of us

---

* Renamed the Queen Mary's Auxiliary Army Corps in 1918 just before it disbanded.

to be most thankful to you personally. The Army owes to you and your organisation a deep debt of gratitude.'

It was a most desperate point in the war. Germany had subdued Russia during the previous year and transferred an enormous army from the Eastern to the Western Front. On 21 March 1918, the Germans launched a tremendous attack and Sir Hubert Gough's Fifth Army, heavily out-numbered, was almost overrun.

By now women were working on buses, railways and tramways, delivering the post, and bottling fruit and vegetables for Service canteens. There were also remount girls. These girls, young, fit, efficient and often very pretty, were responsible for changing Henry Chaplin's hitherto set prejudice against the vote for women. All his life unable to resist either a beautiful woman or a good-looking horse, when he saw the remount girls' combination of looks, bravery and horsemanship he was bowled over. 'Bless their little hearts!' he exclaimed. 'They deserve everything!'

Edith herself had worked tirelessly at expanding the Legion's role, visiting depots, writing articles, speaking, interviewing, encouraging and seizing every opportunity to show that, when given the chance, women could do almost any job as well as a man. She herself wore uniform constantly, although it was still the cause of much prejudice – she was often shouldered out of the way and once told to wait in a friend's basement as the maid who opened the door refused to recognise such a person as a 'lady'. She tackled controversial subjects such as self-defence for women, despite the reaction these roused among the rigidly conven-tional even in a war that by now did not spare civilians. 'If we sit down and seriously think what war means to women, when by "war" we mean "invasion", when the state of Belgium is contemplated and the fate of the civilian population recalled, is it not time to look the facts in the face and ask ourselves exactly what would be the fate of women in these islands if an invasion on a large scale ever took place?'

Her work was briefly interrupted by a narrow escape from death that last summer of the war. At the beginning of July she and Charley had gone down to Combe to stay with friends for a golfing weekend and she, Charley and a friend had jumped out of the train at Malden station while it was still moving. Edith, who had jumped last, slipped, and fell under the train's footboard between the nearside rail and the platform. Two carriages had passed her safely when a projection from the third struck her on the back of the head as the train came to a halt. She bled so much that a doctor had to be called to stitch up her head in the Ladies' waiting room. Then, bruised, limping, the back of her dress in tatters but still calm and cheerful, she was driven back to London by a distraught Charley, who wrote to her later: 'The whole thing is a nightmare and I find myself continually putting my hands to my face to shut out the awful scene. I shall never forget it.'

The war ended on 11 November 1918, but the Legion's work continued. Edith's own contribution had been recognised when, on 25 August 1917, she was made a Dame Commander of the Order of the British Empire, one of ten women so honoured in this new Order of Knighthood. The following January, greatly to her delight, her DBE was transferred to the military side to recognise the fact that not only was the Legion's primary object to free men to fight but that much of its work was directly military.

Shortly after the war ended Edith set up a branch (under the Ministry of Pensions) to train disabled ex-servicemen in the art of gold and silver embroidery for naval and military uniforms. Several hundred Legion drivers went out to France to replace men drivers, in order to speed up demobilisation. These women lived in tough conditions, three or four to a hut in isolated spots during the icy winter months. 'Really, they are splendid,' reported Edith who, naturally, went out to see and to share. 'I haven't had a bath for three days, as we arrived so late each night that I did not fancy going to cold outhouses in the camps. I am housed in a delightful Nissen hut. Tomorrow we go to Poperinghe. We have been to Peronne, Saint Paul, Meault, Cambrai, Douai. . . .'

In the Victory Parade of July 1919, the Legion was represented by a detachment of 120 of these drivers, led by Edith. They must have been picked for size as their average height was 5 ft 8 in, Edith's own. It was a seven-mile march, on military lines, and, as no woman had ever taken part in such an event before, Edith had to learn the necessary drill and words of command. Her instructor was the Regimental Corporal-Major of the Blues. This distinguished and senior warrant officer, a terrifying figure to the men, drilled her on the barrack square of the Albany Street Barracks. 'Imagine my feelings, knowing as I did only too well, that all my husband's brother officers were looking on laughing from the windows of the Messroom,' she wrote later in her memoir *Retrospect*.

The march, which began near the Albert Memorial, made a circuit south of the river – where local people offered them oranges and bananas on their halts for rest – then returned through Admiralty Arch and up the Mall to the front of Buckingham Palace. 'This was almost worse than the barrack square! for at the end sat their Majesties the King and Queen, the Court, and the Cabinet, and I had to give the salute and eyes-left.

To add to my terror we were between two bands, playing different tunes.'
However, it was all a great success.

As the King had said:* 'When the history of our country's share in
the war is written, no chapter will be more remarkable than that relating
to the range and extent of women's participation.'

What women had done, of course, was to produce the most cogent
argument possible for the franchise. Even before the war had ended, their
heroic efforts, their efficiency, stamina and intelligence, proved across
the whole spectrum of jobs hitherto done only by men, their independence and sense of responsibility, made it impossible for anyone to use
the old arguments that they were unfit for the vote because of inferior
performance, lack of intelligence or emotional instability.

In January 1917 a Speaker's conference had recommended that the
franchise be given to women householders and wives of householders
provided they were thirty-five or over – an age barrier quickly dropped
to thirty. The Prime Minister allowed a free vote on a Bill granting this
limited female suffrage, which on its second reading was passed with a
majority of 350. The grille in the Ladies' Gallery in the House of Commons, behind which women visitors always had to sit as if in the purdah
of harem quarters, was taken down. The one obstacle remaining was
the House of Lords, which had always been strongly against women's
suffrage. But even Lord Curzon crumbled in the face of expediency.
'Although I thought the House of Commons was mistaken, although I
think the majority of my Party in that House is mistaken, although I
think both will rue the day when they acted in the manner they have
done', he could not, he said, advise the noble Lords to vote against the
Bill unless they were prepared to come into conflict with the Commons.

On 6 February 1918, the Bill became law and, in the first post-War
election, on 14 December 1918, six million women were on the electoral
register for the first time. Waiting in the mud and rain outside polling
booths for voting to begin, they easily outnumbered male voters, but the
fears of those who had opposed the measure proved unfounded. The
female vote did not lead to a change of government and Lloyd George
won the Election. In the new House of Commons his supporters numbered 526, there were 63 Labour members, and Mr Asquith's Independent
Liberals won only 33 seats. Asquith himself lost the seat he had held for
thirty-two years. The dramatic change was the drop in the Irish National-

* In July 1918, in his response to a Procession of Homage and Address on the occasion
of the King and Queen's Silver Wedding.

ist vote, down from 71 and 76 in 1910 to only 10 in 1918, and the emergence of Sinn Fein. The new party won 73 of the 105 Irish seats.

The new Lord Chancellor (F. E. Smith, Carson's right-hand man, and now Lord Birkenhead) decided to appoint women magistrates. Edith, along with Mrs Humphry Ward, arch-opponent of the suffrage campaign, and Beatrice Webb – who still, despite her egalitarian stance, called herself Mrs Sidney Webb – was on the Chancellor's advisory committee formed to choose suitable candidates. Edith herself was quickly sworn in as the first woman Justice of the Peace for County Durham, an appointment celebrated by one of her men friends in the doggerel verse so fashionable.

> When sitting on the Woolsack
> After dining far too well
> F. E. began a'dreaming
> Of Law in a Fairy Dell.
>
> He woke with a start and muttered
> 'We must not the women flout
> They can sit in the House and make laws –
> They shall help us carry them out.'
>
> So he looked around the country
> In search of women fair
> Who could help the hand of justice
> The drunkards to repair.
>
> In Durham he found a lady
> With a stubborn methodical push
> To sit by that cunning old hero
> Who goes by the name of 'the Bush' . . .
>
> The lady's name is Circe
> Her effect on the Bench will be????
> We do not like to prophesy
> So we'll sit down and wait and see.

She was still working to extend both the franchise and the place of women in public life. In 1919 she published a pamphlet, *Woman's Indirect Influence and its Effect On Character: Her Position Improved by the Franchise*

Morally and Materially. 'What we are struggling for', she summed up, 'is to remove the sex disability and to extend the franchise to all duly qualified women on the same basis as that possessed by men at the present day.' When Nancy Astor contested and won her husband's Plymouth seat in 1919 on his elevation to the House of Lords, to become the first woman MP to take her seat in the House of Commons, Edith was delighted. 'I feel you realise what a great responsibility it is,' wrote Lady Astor in reply to Edith's letter of congratulation. 'I shall hope never to let you down. We may not always agree about politics but we will each know that the other is trying to be honest ... I cannot express myself in "Parliamentary language", only I do deeply appreciate your letter.'

Popular mythology held that women could not work together smoothly but always caused trouble – especially if a man was involved, when they would almost inevitably quarrel. Edith's own experience with the Women's Legion had shown her the opposite: that women could, and did, cooperate successfully with each other. It was a message she reiterated at every opportunity, as in this plea for a fairer post-war world for women.

'In our struggle to be allowed to act openly and independently we must show that given the opportunity women can and will act loyally and honourably towards each other. We must remember that a house divided against itself cannot stand and that combination means strength ... Woman, in demanding to be released from the indirect bondage of her position, should always endeavour to raise the tone of her life and surroundings higher and as her responsibilities increase, so will her loyalty and sense of honour respond.'

She herself had found that when women were given an outlet for their energies and intelligence they were just as capable and level-headed as men – and often more so. 'Women have an uncommon share of common sense. In a crisis they can make up their minds quickly and stick to a decision.' Nor was she bound by conventional ideas of what was, and what was not, a suitable profession for women. She believed, for instance, that they would make excellent diplomats because of their skills in both negotiating and in getting on with other people – a revolutionary thought in those days when all affairs of state were considered a purely masculine preserve.

Similarly, although flying was in its infancy, and there were no women pilots, she did not see why this should remain so. 'Women have light hands, a great asset in horsemanship and nearly as essential in the air.'

She knew also, from her observation of the agricultural side of the Women's Legion, that 'the power of endurance with which woman has been endowed is outstanding'. For all these reasons, she declared, she disliked the idea of drawing a hard and fast line between 'men's' and 'women's' jobs, though she cautioned that 'in her eagerness to have her just political rights accorded her, [woman] must never, never surrender the position she already occupies, and with it the best, the highest, and most sacred duties, which woman and woman alone can fulfil, in her home, her children and her surroundings'.

But the public did not see it this way. The Government, returning servicemen, employers – all were determined that women should go back to 'women's work'. What this meant, of course, was either domestic service or poorly-paid labour. With the male half of the country determined on this, and with many women glad to welcome their men home and return to their own former domestic role, there was little option for the rest. Edith's efforts to secure immigration into Australia and New Zealand to work on the land for the women who had achieved such miracles in the agricultural branch of the Legion came to nothing: employers there, too, would only accept them as domestic servants. Instead, she was forced to do what she could through the Household Section of the Women's Legion, trying to negotiate better conditions and offering help and advice to ex-servicewomen.

Meanwhile, there had been an unexpected increase in her family circle. During the last months of the war and the winter of 1918/19 an epidemic of Spanish flu ravaged Europe. One of its victims was a pilot called Jack Barnato, who left a beautiful eighteen-year-old widow. This was Dorothé, Charley's natural daughter by the actress Fannie Ward, born less than three months after his marriage to Edith. Edith herself, who had once wanted to adopt the baby Dorothé, had kept in touch with her over the years. Now she took her into the family circle.

Little is known about Dorothé's early childhood, when Fannie Ward was crossing and recrossing the Atlantic to star alternately on the London stage and on Broadway. Dorothé's ostensible father, 'Diamond Joe' Lewis, lived at 3 Berkeley Square from 1904 to 1910, and presumably Dorothé was brought up there. But by 1912 Fannie's marriage to Joe had collapsed: she had fallen in love with John Dean, her leading man in the company of players she had now gathered round her, and in 1913 she divorced Joe. Dean was tall, handsome, eight years younger than the age Fannie gave as her own, and talented – he wrote many of her songs in the musical comedies in which she acted. After surviving a lawsuit by his wife for $100,000 for 'alienation of affections', Fannie married John Dean in 1915 and the same year gave up the stage for the cinema.

It was a tribute not only to her beauty but to how staggeringly young she looked that in her early forties she was able to compete with screen beauties like the 22-year-old Mary Pickford and the nineteen-year-old Lilian Gish. Sam Goldwyn is said to have met her in the elevator of the Hotel Claridge in New York and offered her a contract on the spot. He remarked later: 'She was not in her first youth, but if Ponce de Leon had seen her that day he would surely have cried "Ho, man, we're getting warm!"' Her first film, *The Marriage of Kitty*, was a dreadful flop but Goldwyn gave her another chance and, in *The Cheat*, she was a huge success – especially when she dramatically ripped her dress off her shoulder to show the brand printed on her arm. She never looked back.

Dorothé, now without a parental home, had been placed by her mother in a good school. Here she met the girl who was to be one of her closest friends, Margery Madge, whose doctor father ran a fashionable practice from his flat in 11 Mount Street – Queen Marie of Rumania was Margery's godmother. Dorothé stayed with them constantly, and often joined them on family holidays. Other holidays were spent with the former governess of the Barnato family.

The Barnatos had been friends of Joe Lewis since their South African days – Lewis had been an associate of Barney Barnato, king of the Rand diamond mines. Barnato, whose surname was originally Isaacs, had started his career on the East End stage as assistant to his older brother. (Barney Isaacs became Barney Barnato, so the story goes, when the stage manager called him out to join his brother for a curtain call with the words 'Barney too! Barney too!'). The newly discovered South African diamond fields beckoned; by 1876 Barney had made £3,000 and bought a block of four claims in the Kimberley diamond field; by 1880 he was a millionaire. In June 1897, sailing back from Capetown to London for the housewarming party at his new house in Park Lane, planned for 22 June (Diamond Jubilee Day), he fell overboard in mysterious circumstances and drowned. He left a window, Fanny, who settled in Brighton, where she brought up the three Barnato children, a daughter, Leah, and two sons Isaac and Wolf (later known as Babe). Isaac, always called Jack, was born on 7 June 1894.

Jack Barnato was a tallish, slight young man with a fair skin. He had been educated at Charterhouse and Cambridge, had joined up as a private soldier when the war began and had then transferred to the Royal Naval Air Service, finally becoming a flight commander in the Royal Flying

Corps. He had been mentioned frequently in dispatches and was one of the four naval airmen who bombed Constantinople in the early part of the war.

One day when he went to visit his old governess, Dorothé was staying there. She was fifteen or sixteen, and he fell in love with her instantly.

It was not surprising. She was an exquisite, fragile-looking little creature, with a slender, supple, dancer's figure – she later became famous for her dancing – a heart-shaped face, large violet-blue eyes and a sweet expression. Her long, thick, ash-blonde hair was tied back in a big bow, as was then customary for girls still too young to have 'come out', and put their hair up. It was a fashion that gave rise to the name 'flappers' for girls of sixteen or seventeen, from the way these bows flapped on the neck. To Jack, throughout their brief marriage, she was always known as 'the Flapper'.

Once he had met Dorothé, he spent as much time with her as he could, both in Brighton and during her prolonged visits to the Madges, who treated her like a daughter of the house. He married her at the first possible moment, on 13 October 1917, when Dorothé, 'only child of Mr and Mrs Joe Lewis, of London and South Africa', was just seventeen and a half.

Jack adored his young bride, treating her as a mixture of beautiful woman to be worshipped and child to be teased. His happiness breathes from this letter, written on 19 June 1918, to his sister Leah, married and living in New York. 'This is the second time this year I have written, still the first wasn't a proper letter really, was it; all my writing time in France was taken up writing to the Flapper, the great one and only, and reading hers ... my old woman is fine, you really ought to see it. It's awfully bucked at the moment because its Pa's coming home soon. It really is too wonderful for words. You simply must see it before it is grown up. We make it take its hair down sometimes but it is getting more dignified every day.'

Jack now had a staff job in London. He and Dorothé took a house near Richmond, with two cows, rabbits and a large garden, near enough to the Underground for Jack to travel in easily. 'Isn't it wonderful Jack's being home again?' wrote Dorothé to Leah. 'If only this job will last. I do wish we could see you again, darling, it would be so ripping. Why can't this filthy war end? We went to see Mother on the pictures yesterday. She really is *too sweet*, and makes me cry so much every time I see her that I always swear I'll go alone next time. I'd give anything to see her again. Does she ever come to New York? Fondest love to you both, Your loving sister.'

Four months later Jack caught Spanish flu. He died on 16 October 1918, after only a few days' illness, and was buried in the Jewish cemetery at Willesden. The million pounds his father had left him was almost intact. Apart from annuities of £2,000 a year each to his mother and to Joseph Lewis, 'the father of my said wife', who had gone back to South Africa, and a freehold flat in Hove to his brother Babe, he left everything to Dorothé. She was now that most desirable of persons, a rich and beautiful young widow.

It was, perhaps, not only a distraction but a real comfort for Edith to have this sweet and affectionate young girl to console. Her own private life was becoming steadily unhappier as the quality of her relationship with Charley was again deteriorating. He was as usual pursuing every pretty woman who crossed his line of vision. One to whom he was laying siege was Lady Diana Manners. 'Lord Londonderry continues his attack,' she wrote to Duff Cooper in the autumn of 1918, 'and has now reached the gambit of open discussion as to whether he could make me happy.' (Sure of Lady Diana's love, Duff Cooper could afford to reply: 'There are few whom I could better pardon you for casting eyes on. There is no one whom I would sooner look like.')

But the real cause, once again, was Charley's long-standing mistress, Eloise. She had tried for some time to lure Charley away from Edith but without success; now, she attempted to drive a wedge between them by busily spreading the story that Charley had foisted his daughter by a 'common tart' on Edith. 'It is boldly done, to annoy me,' wrote Edith to Charley on 7 July 1919, 'but by belittling you she annoys me far more, because she has been blackguarding you to everyone, all the Season. But it is useless to tell you these things. Myself, I should refuse to discuss anything with your woman.'

For once, though, Eloise succeeded in getting under Edith's skin to the point where the Olympian detachment she practised over Charley's women cracked. 'You know I am devoted to Dorothé and sooner than Eloise making trouble I would have a real row with her. I don't often get roused but if she drives me too far she had better look out. I'll have her up for libel. Just tell her to mind her own business and that Dorothé is a personal friend of mine. Of course Dorothé's story is just what your female wants, damn her. But no one believes a word she says, so it does not matter. If Dorothé is *my* friend that is quite sufficient. It is all done to annoy me and make you appear disreputable, which I know for a fact is her amiable habit. Bless you, darling, don't worry, nothing can upset us or Dorothé now.'

Anyway, she concluded, she would much prefer any son of hers to marry a 'common tart's' daughter rather than a society strumpet's, 'and you can tell her so from me direct if she gives any further trouble. One is a necessity, the other a nuisance.'

The following day, however, she had reverted to her more usual stance of adoring wife, ready to forgive her beloved Charley anything. 'I was very worried after I sent you my letter yesterday but I lost my temper,' she wrote apologetically. 'It really was a case of protecting my young. You know I adore you so much that anything that belongs to you I cherish, and for poor dear little Dorothé to be attacked like that, who has more breeding and ladylike intentions in her little finger than Eloise has in the whole of her body, drove me crazy. Please forgive me, Doody, for adding to your worries. What a beast I feel that I have attacked you also as well as your "wife". But I don't mean it and I will do anything I can to help in any way.'

It was a wretched, miserable situation. The strenuous and fulfilling life of the wartime years was over and the links that had bound her and Charley so closely during those anxious days when neither knew if they would see the other again had loosened. Charley had reverted briskly to his pre-War attitudes and, with the gradual disbanding of the Women's Legion, a certain aimlessness appeared to stretch ahead in her own life. But all was soon to change.

At the end of the war, Theresa had seemed as robust and vigorous as ever. In January 1919, visiting Mount Stewart, she had danced a Highland schottische at the servants' ball – partnered by the butler – and gone out sailing most days on Strangford Lough ('The Widgeon, to my mind, is a little small for squalls and rough weather').

She caught flu, could not throw it off, and at the end of February went out to a dinner party with a temperature of 101. The infection got worse but it was useless for her friends to try and persuade her to lie up. All of them knew it was the last thing she would ever do. She remained indomitable to the end. Colonel Repington, now a great friend, took her out to lunch at Claridges and remarked afterwards: 'She is still the best company of any woman in London.' She died a week later, on 15 March, and his were the words that best summed up her impact on the age: 'A great figure gone and a real true friend. A grande dame of a period which is passing: one of the most striking and dominating feminine personalities of our time, terrifying to some, but endeared to her many friends by her notable and excellent qualities.' She was sixty-two, the age at which her husband had died. She was buried in the Londonderry family vault, beside the man she had loved, betrayed, and finally mourned deeply.

Edith was now, without question, *the* Lady Londonderry. The shadow of her powerful mother-in-law had finally passed, and with it the fear of disapproval of any alterations or changes she might wish to make. She was now at the centre of the stage; soon, the stage itself would be in her hands. By the end of 1919 Londonderry House was no longer required as a hospital. It was a house, as Theresa had amply shown, made for entertaining.

The Ulster Convention had been adjourned 'indefinitely' in February 1918. After the General Election of December 1918 Winston Churchill became Secretary of State for War and Air in Lloyd George's new Coalition Government, with Colonel Seely as Under-Secretary for Air and Vice-President of the Air Council. Charley, at his cousin Winston's instigation, was appointed unpaid Finance Minister of the Air Council in January 1919 (becoming Under-Secretary in Seely's place in April 1920) and in November 1919, now an *ex officio* member of the Government, he was approached to find out if the Londonderrys would give a political reception for the Coalition Government. He agreed.

It was the start of a new career for Edith: that of the foremost social and political hostess of her day – a dazzling symbol of wealth, power, glamour and influence to all those who walked up the great staircase of Londonderry House, and to the many more who aspired to.

XIII

THE CIRCUMSTANCES of the rich had been little changed by the war. Before it, most of the wealth in the country had been owned by a tiny fraction of the population and this was still so. Class barriers had remained reassuringly firm; accents, dress, behaviour, attitudes and above all expectations were virtually unchanged. Although the number of domestic servants had dropped, there were still well over a million of them to maintain pre-war standards. In 1919 there was no hint of the slump to come two years later; businesses prospered, fortunes had been made, and the very rich grew steadily richer. Relief that the slaughter was finally over enhanced the delight felt at being spared to savour remembered pleasures, among them entertaining, which, though less ostentatiously extravagant, reverted to its pre-war pattern. The first post-war Londonderry House reception was eagerly awaited.

For Edith, 18 November 1919 was an auspicious moment for her debut as a hostess on the grand scale. Two weeks short of her fortieth birthday, she was a glamorous and impressive figure. Her splendid bosom ('*beaucoup du monde au balcon*' as one admirer put it), seen to advantage in the *décolletée* dresses she favoured, could have been made for the Londonderry family jewels; her height and upright carriage gave her an imposing, almost regal quality. The wartime years running the Women's Legion had edged her powerful personality with authority, strengthened her natural decisiveness and removed the last traces of hesitancy and shyness. The hecklers she had had to deal with when she spoke in public had given her a quick-witted poise and the ability to project both personality and a voice which, though not loud, was distinct enough to be heard at the other end of her long dining table if she wished. Already a charismatic personality known to a wide circle of the influential and the interesting, she was also, thanks to the regular Ark dinners she had given since 1915, an experienced and perceptive hostess.

Above all, she possessed an almost mesmeric charm. It was felt as keenly by the debutantes, to whom – remembering her own terrifying debutante days – she was far kinder than most hostesses, as by her huge circle of friends and the men she continued to enthral. Her physical vitality expressed itself in a spontaneous flirtatiousness that many found irresistible: she exuded an aura of warmth, welcome, generosity, and the promise of enjoyment, fun and excitement. Her sparkling eyes expressed a gaiety and love of life that drew like a fire. Her manner was bright, frank and natural, dissipating shyness in others, her gift of response made them, in turn, feel cleverer, wittier, more attractive. She laughed often, and there seemed always to be an undertone of amusement in her voice. Those who drew near her found themselves unconsciously beginning to smile. Though she could terrify, neither then nor later were crossness or moodiness any part of her character.

As well as her unassailable position at the top of the social hierarchy, she possessed two incomparable assets for any hostess entertaining on the grand scale: Londonderry House and the Londonderry jewels. Both added immeasurably to the aura of wealth, power, glamour, position and prestige that now surrounded her.

The history of the Londonderry jewels is romantic. The most significant part of the collection, the Down diamonds, brilliant stones almost barbaric in their size and splendour, had been in the family since the Stewarts were simple country squires.

These diamonds first appear in the possession of the heiress Mary Cowan, mother of the first Marquess of Londonderry. Mary and her brother William were the children of Anne Stewart, the second daughter of William Stewart, who had married a widower, an alderman of the City of Derry called John Cowan, in 1700. Alderman Cowan also had a son, Robert Cowan, by his first wife. Robert Cowan went out to India and was eventually appointed Governor of Bombay by the directors of the East India Company. When he finally returned to England in 1736 it was to a knighthood and a seat in Parliament. More substantially, he brought with him an immense fortune including the Down diamonds.

A few months after his return, Sir Robert Cowan died, leaving his fortune to his half-brother William. William Cowan in his turn died suddenly, unmarried and intestate. His sister Mary inherited everything. She was quickly snapped up by her first cousin Alexander Stewart, who married her in 1737. The diamonds now belonged to the Stewarts, and when Alexander and Mary's son Robert became the first Marquess of Londonderry, they became Londonderry family heirlooms.

The collection was increased by other diamonds, mostly Brazilian in origin, presented to Lord Castlereagh by grateful foreign monarchs and ambassadors. Contemporary records describe a star and badge of the Order of the Garter, the jewelled hilt of a Sword of State, a clasp, various ornaments, a scroll necklace, collet (recessed-gemstone) bracelet, waist clasp and waistband, containing in all 3,349 large diamonds. In 1854 the crown jewellers Garrards reset many of them into more manageable pieces. The waistband alone (which can be seen in a portrait of the Foreign Secretary Castlereagh's wife Emily) was at least three inches wide and yielded 1,225 brilliants. Almost all of these stones were used to make what Theresa called 'the family fender' – the dramatic, dazzling Londonderry tiara.

Other important pieces made from the original hoard were the stomacher, a large square-link bracelet, a pearl and diamond bracelet and a corsage. One of Theresa's favourites – later worn often by Edith – was a necklace of enormous stones from which depended a huge Latin cross. This cross was made from some of the diamonds that at one time surrounded a miniature of Castlereagh worn by his wife Emily after his death.

There were also the Antrim jewels, inherited by Frances Anne: a huge and beautiful emerald and diamond *parure* (a suite of matching necklace, earrings, brooches, hair ornaments), a diamond *parure* (this was given to Edith's sister-in-law Birdie and passed out of the family) and a ruby necklace that could be worn as a tiara.

Her inheritance was not enough for Frances Anne. Few people were more passionate about jewellery and, since she was sufficiently a child of her time to believe that grand jewellery should only be worn with grand clothes, she did not hesitate to don full evening dress in mid-afternoon. When her son was born in Vienna in 1821 during her husband's ambassadorship, she celebrated his birth by buying a famous suite of teardrop pearls set in diamonds called the *Gouttes de Perles*. It cost her £10,000 and she had it reset into necklace, diadem, comb and earrings, which she first wore at her son's christening. Mrs Bradford, the wife of the Embassy chaplain, described her as receiving the guests in 'Brussels lace over white satin, a profusion of diamonds on her head, ten thousand pounds worth of pearls on her broad expanse of neck and shoulders and a bouquet of flowers in precious stones, without exception the most beautiful thing I ever beheld'.* Her most spectacular purchase was made the following year: a marvellous suite of turquoises (her birthstone) also set, almost needless to say, in diamonds.

But this was not the last of her acquisitions. While in Vienna, she met the Russian Emperor, Alexander, who fell in love with her. 'I can only rejoice and wonder that we came out of the ordeal free of guilt,' she said afterwards. He gave her jewels to remember him by, enormous purple Siberian amethysts to wear Russian-fashion as a chain across her dress, a deep pink topaz set in gold and diamonds, a yellow diamond and a delicate and exquisite Russian cross.

She wore many of these jewels indiscriminately together, in rainbow-like profusion. As she became very fat the display was awe-inspiring. Disraeli – who later became a great friend – remarked of his first meeting with her at the fancy-dress ball she gave in 1838 to mark Queen Victoria's coronation: 'Lady Londonderry as Cleopatra was in a dress literally embroidered with emeralds and diamonds from top to toe. It looked like armour and she like a rhinoceros.'

Londonderry House had been designed for entertaining on a palatial scale. The main rooms had been decorated at a time when aristocratic life was at its most lavish and ostentatious, to the order of Frances Anne, who was considered flamboyant even by the standards of the 1820s. These rooms were huge, high-ceilinged and magnificent, with pillars, gilding, rich plasterwork on cornices and ceilings, crystal chandeliers, white marble classical statues on plinths in arched niches, damask on the walls and deep windows framed with roped, tasselled and braided Geno-ese velvet curtains. The walls of the state drawing room (originally three rooms) were hung with green damask, its doors were gilded, nine Lawrence portraits of members of the Londonderry family gazed over the gilded French chairs, the palms, the screens and the collection of Sèvres porcelain. Edith had stripped this room of the clutter fashionable in Theresa's day, removing the screens so beloved of Victorians and Edwardians and getting rid of excess furniture, so that its beautiful pro-portions, pillars and superb pictures could be seen. (Theresa, arriving unexpectedly one day soon after the change, looked round the now barer room and remarked disapprovingly: 'Some people like to live in a barrack! *I* don't!')

In the great square hall stood busts by Nollekens of the younger Pitt and the great Castlereagh. Two sculptures of reclining nymphs flanked

* The flower brooch subsequently disappeared.

Wyatt's staircase, with its mahogany rail and gilded balustrading, up which four could walk abreast ('like a musical comedy staircase', remarked Lady Cynthia Asquith with characteristic acidity). At the top of this staircase, which divided halfway up, was a wide gallery running round all four sides of the house at first-floor level. This was a place designed for spectacle: to parade upon and to be seen doing so. Here those who had arrived earlier or made the circuit of the great rooms could watch Lady Londonderry receiving those still arriving. Off this gallery led the immense, interconnecting rooms which allowed the guests to move freely.

Through a pair of glass doors on one side of the entrance hall was the banqueting hall, with its magnificent mahogany table that seated sixty. At an important dinner, its polished surface reflected the gleam of gold and silver. Silver epergnes full of flowers – pink and white rhododendrons, freesias or roses – stood between the high Paul Storr candelabra. Guests ate off gold plates, with gold knives and forks (which made a nerve-jarring rasp if scraped sideways over one of the gold plates by the unpractised). Geoffrey Dawson, Editor of *The Times*, had described one of Theresa's pre-war dinner parties as: '. . . a very rich and sumptuous affair – glorious plate and glass and flowers and "soft music without", though of the food, alas, I can remember little except that it included salmon caught by our hostess, who only arrived from Ireland this morning. After dinner we all went up to the picture gallery at once and stood about and talked and smoked. The King, to my great trepidation, sent for me at once and you may picture me carrying on a very conspicuous conversation with His Majesty in the middle of this throng – he mercifully doing most of the talking – about the Times and the changes in the Navy and the Midland Railway trouble and the feeling on the Continent. Then the Queen came up and I had a much more difficult 10 minutes with her; and then the King went off to play bridge and then the Queen sat down and we all thankfully did the same. He had said (very kindly) that he hoped I would go when I liked, as he knew I had to work, but it was rather a difficult thing to do – as a matter of fact I stayed to the end and had a very interesting hour or so talking books with Lord Rosebery. I had practically done with my leading articles in the afternoon and got to the office by midnight just in time to finish them off.'

When Edith, with the Prime Minister, Mr Lloyd George, and the Leader of the Conservative Party, Mr Bonar Law, stood at the top of the famous staircase of Londonderry House to receive her guests on the evening of 18 November 1919, she was determined to continue the tradition of magnificence laid down by previous marchionesses. Her clinging black satin dress was festooned with diamonds and pearls. On one side of the deep vee of her *décolletage* was the Down diamond corsage, down the other a double row of large diamonds. Theresa's favourite Latin cross hung from a rope of heavy pearls which fell below her waist, with a diamond 'crown' worn low across her forehead. The becoming black dress – she was still in mourning for Theresa – came from Paris. 'I have bought a rather naughty black frock here, it is not expensive, 850 francs* which is much less than London prices. It is a very pretty one with lots of jet about it, and they are altering another black one of mine and making it quite evil-looking too.' She looked, said one report, 'absurdly young' to be the mother of Maureen, who was flitting about in a white dress fringed with ostrich feathers.

It proved a spectacular return to pre-war tradition. There were 2,500 guests and all the jewellery of London was out in force. The Spanish Ambassador was so fascinated by the finery of the English grandees that instead of circulating through the drawing rooms he stayed in the gallery to stare down at the procession steadily mounting the stairs. 'Just like old times, only three times as many people,' said Lord Curzon, also gazing down from the gallery as he stood near his hostess. He was glad, he added, that he had escaped being 'classed with the climbers' by coming up in the lift.

But the party was different in several respects. Some were comparatively minor: for the first time there was music – Casano's band was playing at the far end of the ballroom – and an entertainment by Mr George Robey, who had performed in front of King George and Queen Mary at one of Lady Curzon's parties. For the first and only time, this was a Londonderry House party without flowers (save for a few bowls of yellow chrysanthemums) as greenhouses had not yet recovered from the lack of both heating and gardeners during the war. The guest list was more catholic: among the ministers, ambassadors, peers and parliamentarians who wandered through the great rooms admiring the blue Sèvres vases, the gold plate and the tall pier glasses were the doctors and nurses who had staffed the Londonderry House hospital and the officers who had been their patients.

The contrast with Theresa's magisterial grandeur was quickly noticed. 'Happy unselfconsciousness' was how *The World* described Edith's manner. 'She most certainly stands for modernity in general. Does not

* Then just over £23.

her record in the war, not less than as the young Lady Castlereagh, prove this up to the hilt? "Oh father!", she cried, running down a few steps when she saw, slowly mounting the stairs towards her, that portly institution Lord Chaplin.'

Most significantly, though, this first post-war Londonderry House reception demonstrated Edith's flexibility – and her pragmatic approach to politics. At the last great reception, in 1914, her father-in-law was in active opposition to the Government, and Londonderry House was a meeting place for the opponents of Home Rule. Now, as Edith reflected ironically, here was the Liberal Prime Minister of a coalition government standing beside her – and, even more to the point, beside Charley – at the top of the staircase. True, Lloyd George had arrived late and most of the time the politically unexceptionable Mr Bonar Law had been at her side, but it was Lloyd George she took down to supper; on the way they ran into George Robey, who promptly turned round and came down with them.

Successful though their party was, it also represented one of the increasingly rare occasions on which Edith and Charley were together. To Edith's misery, they were still drifting apart. Charley had gone back to leading his life as it suited him best, sometimes travelling north for two months in Scotland with a baggage train of guns, rifles, fishing rods and golf clubs, sometimes accepting last-minute invitations for a luncheon party, dinner or a sporting weekend exactly as if he were a bachelor, and expecting Edith to accede to or fit in with his plans. She was no longer the eager, inexperienced, still uncertain girl he had married, but a woman who had founded and run a great movement, a woman accustomed to independence with a busy life of her own, a woman now used to admiration and friendship. But she was as vulnerable as ever where Charley was concerned.

The past ten years had, however, shown her one important truth: much of her emotional sustenance had perforce to come from friendships – friendships which she was careful to keep only as friendships. When Charley, who, despite his own philandering, believed in total discretion in his wife, taxed her with one of them, she stood up for herself vigorously.

'You talk of "my" friend. Well, I cannot have a friend who is not one of yours. My friends mean a lot to me and they would do anything in the world I asked them, either for you or me, so I do not want to give them up for nothing. I think it is difficult for you to realise, darling, because I don't tell you, how often when you have arranged to do something and your plans change, I throw mine away or vice versa.

148

Often and often I make no plans at all because I do not want to miss you and at the last moment you say you are dining or lunching somewhere. It is too late then for me to ask anyone. I can only get hold of a tame cat like Cyril [Hankey] who is seldom doing anything. The other reason when I seem to have a long-standing engagement is that now I am busy I have to make plans ahead – and yours do change more often than mine. If I make a plan I usually stick to it. I really thought you were a certainty this time.'

Characteristically, she immediately excuses him. 'It is no fault of yours, I know. Your women never leave you alone, and if I had no friends I could rely on I should so often be left.'

She tried to encourage him politically, she sought to draw him to her with news about the children. 'Everyone vies with each other in praising Maureen for her brains and beauty. Everyone likes Robin wherever he goes. I know he is clever. I have made great headway with him recently. Margaret really is clever. The Churchill governess told Clemmie that she had a most remarkable brain, and is an unusual child and far ahead of the Churchill children, one of whom is 10. Helen is a real beauty.'

She still took the responsibility for any failure in their relationship while reiterating her love for him. She blamed herself for coldness: 'Darling, don't say you do not "please" me because everything you do and say always does. The fault lies with me, constitutionally – and I feel always that I make "married" life very difficult for you. You told me so years ago and I have never forgotten it. But it is not because you don't attract me. I have always told you that you are the most attractive and best-looking man I have ever met and I shall always think so.' Only a month before the Coalition reception, she was apologising for irritating him. 'I think I have become very selfish, living so much on my own and I know, beloved one, that I get on your nerves sometime. You have sometimes said and done things very like your father used to be towards your mother, but quite unconsciously, I am sure. I could laugh at it if I did not mind so much just because it is you.'

More than anything else, and in the face of their increasing separateness, she reiterated her love for him, though for the first time there is a note of bitterness in the loving message she sent, as always, to reach him on the anniversary of their wedding, just ten days after they had stood together welcoming their guests. 'Twenty years ago tomorrow I was a virgin, and I still am, I think. But you are not.'

XIV

EDITH'S FIRST political reception in Londonderry House marked the beginning of two years when much changed in her life. She and Charley drew close again and he broke off his affair with Eloise; the first of their children, their eldest daughter Maureen, married; their youngest child, Mairi, was born; Mount Stewart, the Londonderry property in County Down, now became their main home, and Edith started her creation of the marvellous gardens there.

The Ulster Convention adjourned 'indefinitely' in April 1918; it had been, as Charley commented wearily, 'a complete frost'. When, in 1918, Winston Churchill became Secretary of State for War and Air, Charley was made the Finance Member of the Air Council and acted as Government spokesman on Air matters in the House of Lords. Though an office of honour, the job, unpaid, was no sinecure – he worked five days a week from 10.00 a.m. to 5.00 p.m., with a half-day on Sundays – and it further fuelled his growing enthusiasm for the Air. He found everything to do with flying exhilarating, describing a trip to Lille 'in literally one hour 40 minutes!', and was always both stimulated and soothed by it. 'A flight . . . smothers or partially smothers things I won't let myself worry about. Literally and metaphorically, it is very beneficial.'

It was an anxious time. Apart from his governmental duties and the continuing question of Eloise – who was now being more troublesome than ever – there was a threat to the basis of the entire Londonderry fortune.

For years there had been unrest in the coal mines. Mining was not only the dirtiest but the most dangerous job in Britain: the previous year 1,300 miners had been killed and another 160,000 injured, and miners' children suffered the highest infant mortality in the country. The hundreds of individually owned or run mines meant widespread differences in pay and conditions, unnecessary duplication of distribution and machinery costs, and numerous boundary disputes. Immediately after the war prices began to rise sharply, and the miners put forward a claim for higher wages and shorter hours. The Lloyd George government, which had controlled the coalfields during the war, bought off a threatened strike by agreeing to set up a Royal Commission to look into all aspects of the industry – including the possibility of nationalisation, for which the miners' leaders had been pressing.

The coal-owners, however, had no intention of seeing the fortunes that lay beneath the land they owned wrested away from them. Most of them were Conservatives (seventy per cent of the House of Lords voted Conservative) and their generalised distrust of the Prime Minister now boiled up into a campaign waged against the prospect of nationalisation. Accusations of 'Bolshevism' were flung about; with the murder of the Russian royal family fresh in everyone's minds, Bolshevism was to remain an ogre throughout the next decade. 'Unless the people come to their senses it is my belief that we are in for a disaster similar to that which befell the Roman Empire in its last days,' thundered Lord Brassey, initiating the debate on the Commission's report in the House of Lords on 16 July 1919. Charley's attitude, as he told the Commission, was altogether simpler. 'I believe in the private ownership of property . . . in holding my own, like the coat on my back or the coat on yours.' His suggestion for improved efficiency was the amalgamation of the industry district by district, to reduce overheads and distribution costs.

In the face of such pressure Lloyd George, who depended on Conservative support for his survival, backed down, and the Government announced that it could not accept nationalisation of the mines.

In April 1920 Charley was promoted to Under-Secretary for Air. The same year, following on the failure of the Ulster Convention, a new Parliament of Northern Ireland was created by the Government of Ireland Act. This Parliament, which had limited powers of self-government, had an elected House of Commons of 52 members and a Senate of 34 chosen in proportion to party representation in the Lower House. The Unionists won 40 out of the 52 Commons seats but their leader, Carson, refused the premiership on grounds of age and the office went to his lieutenant, James Craig. Craig invited Charley to become Leader of the Senate and Minister of Education in the new Ulster Government. The Ulster Parliament then adjourned, to reassemble on 7 June 1921, when its first session was opened by the King.

At the same time, Charley became aware of a third possibility – a distant, alluring, awe-inspiring mountain peak of a position, to achieve which would truly be the summit of ambition. The question of a new Viceroy of India was in the air: Lord Chelmsford, the incumbent, was about to retire.

To become Viceroy of India, to occupy that position so glamorous and magnificent, so redolent of imperial power, had been a half-acknowledged longing at the back of Charley's mind for some time, perhaps ever since the days when he and Edith had stayed with the Viceroy, Lord Curzon, in 1903. In 1916 he had written to Lady Desborough: 'I agree it is very good of Victor* going to Canada, a very unattractive post and a foul life, as you rightly say. India is quite different, and I aspire to that with the arrogance natural to me.'

In many ways, he was a suitable candidate. He was a grand seigneur to his fingertips; he possessed distinction, elegance, charm; he was rich; he had a wife who would have filled the position of vicereine superbly; he was a soldier, an all-round sportsman noted for his horsemanship – all attributes that would undoubtedly have appealed to the Indian love of magnificence and spectacle as well as to the rulers of the princely states. But it was not to be: Rufus Isaacs, Lord Reading, the Lord Chief Justice who had been the wartime British Ambassador in Washington, was appointed.

The viceroyalty had never been more than a distant golden dream. Now another, more likely, prospect of advancement appeared, only to vanish equally quickly. In the immediate post-war years the Air Ministry was also in charge of civil aviation, by now beginning to expand. But the emerging airline companies found the services they had inaugurated to the Continent were so uneconomic they were threatened with insolvency. The thought that the new cross-Channel flights might cease caused an outcry, and the Government was forced to make a grant of £600,000, distributed by a committee under Charley's chairmanship, towards restoring them. When this had been done, the London to Paris fares by air were the same as those by rail: six guineas single and twelve pounds return. The Prime Minister, realising the growing importance of the air, decided to take the responsibility for military and civil aviation away from the War Office and created the post of Air Minister. Churchill, who thought highly of the work his cousin had done, pressed for Charley to be made Air Minister, but Lloyd George wanted a Liberal. Charley

* The ninth Duke of Devonshire was appointed Governor-General of Canada on 9 August 1916.

Top left Theresa, wife of the sixth Marquess of Londonderry, photographed in 1903 when she was 47. She wears one of her favourite jewels, a diamond necklace made from some of the largest of the Down diamonds from which hangs a diamond cross made from brilliants that surrounded the miniature of the Foreign Secretary Castlereagh worn by his widow after his death.

Top right Henry Chaplin, the father of Edith Helen Chaplin, later Marchioness of Londonderry, as a young man of 24.

Dunrobin, seat of the Dukes of Sutherland, where Edith Chaplin was largely brought up.

Top left Charles, Viscount Castlereagh, at the beginning of the 1914–18 war.

Top right General Sir William Pulteney ("Putty"), to whom Charley Castlereagh was ADC during 1914 and 1915.

Edith Londonderry in her uniform of President of the Women's Legion in 1915.

Top left Lord and Lady Londonderry leaving the House of Lords after the State Opening of Parliament, 1926.

Top right Edith in 1926, aged 47.

(l. to r.) Lord Londonderry, Sir Bruce Porter and Lady Londonderry at the wedding of the Hon. R. E. B. Beaumont and Miss H. M. C. Wray at St George's, Hanover Square in 1926.

Top (l. to r.) Lady Londonderry, the Prime Minister Stanley Baldwin, Mrs Philip Snowden, and Lady Bigge at a meeting of the Y.W.C.A. at Carlton House Terrace in 1926.

Above left Edith Londonderry at the Chelsea Flower Show in 1927.

Above right (l. to r.) Lady Londonderry with her daughter, Lady Maureen Stanley, and son-in-law the Hon. Oliver Stanley M.P. at Epsom on Derby Day, 1927.

Top left   Lady Cunard (left) and Lady Londonderry at the exhibition and sale of work by the War Legion Guild of Sailor and Soldier Broderers held by Edith Londonderry at Londonderry House in 1929.

Top right   The Londonderrys and their youngest daughter Lady Mairi Stewart (later Lady Mairi Bury) who took the part of the 3rd Marquis of Londonderry at a Victorian Court Matinee at the Cambridge Theatre in 1931.

Above left   Edith Londonderry in period dress for a ball at the Austrian Embassy in 1931. She was accompanied by the Marquis Alphonse ("Fono") Pallavicini, First Secretary at the Hungarian Legation and a regular escort.

Above right   Lord and Lady Londonderry talking in the library at Londonderry House. In the shelves behind are the volumes containing the Castlereagh papers.

Top left   Lord and Lady Londonderry leaving the House of Lords after the Opening of Parliament in November 1932, a fortnight before Edith Londonderry's 54th birthday.

Top right   A portrait of the 7th Marquess of Londonderry, wearing the Garter Star that belonged to Castlereagh, by Sir John Lavery. It was painted in 193?

Mount Stewart, from the Strangford Lough side.

Top   (l. to r.) Lady Mairi Stewart, Lady Londonderry, Ramsay MacDonald and the Londonderrys' son Robin, Lord Castlereagh, in the garden of Mount Stewart during the Prime Minister's visit in 1932.

Above left   (l. to r.) Lord Hailsham, Ramsay MacDonald, Prime Minister of the National Government, and Lord Londonderry on the steps leading to the Dodo Terrace at Mount Stewart in 1932.

Above right   Edith Londonderry in 1934.

Top Lord Londonderry, Lady Mairi Stewart and Lady Londonderry leaving by air for Aintree in 1935.

Above left Lord Londonderry as Air Minister about to fly himself to Paris in 1933.

Above right Edith Londonderry campaigning in May 1934.

Top left Lady Mairi Stewart (l.) and Lady Londonderry at the Saturday Meet of the Cottesmore at Whissendine, Rutland in 1933.

Top right Lord and Lady Londonderry in Court Dress, May 1935.

Above left Lady Londonderry in 1933, the first time her snake tattoo was publicly noticed. At first it was mistaken for patterned stockings.

Above right Lady Mairi Stewart and Lady Londonderry at the opening of the Dresden State Opera Company's season with *Rosenkavalier* at Covent Garden in November 1936. Mairi was then 15.

Top left Edith Londonderry talking to
Hermann Goering, Commander in Chief of
the Luftwaffe and President of the Reichstag,
at the International Congress of Air Travel
in Berlin, in June 1938.

Above Lord Londonderry with Hitler and
Ribbentrop during the Londonderry's visit
to Germany in 1936.

Above left (l. to r.) Joachim Ribbentrop,
Lady Londonderry, Frau Ribbentrop and
Lord Londonderry during the Ribbentrops'
visit to Mount Stewart at Whitsun, 1936.

Left Edith Londonderry sitting next to John
Buchan during a banquet (probably 1934).

Top left Dorothé Lewis, daughter of Lord Londonderry and Fannie Ward, aged 12, and her friend Margery Madge, 13, in 1912.

Above Dorothé, after her marriage to Jack Barnato and recent widowhood, in 1919.

Left Dorothé and her second husband Terence (Teddy), Lord Plunket, in the mid-Thirties.

Below Lady Helen (left) and Lady Margaret Stewart in the dining room in Londonderry House at a party for the Personal Service League in 1933.

Top left Edith Londonderry with Princess Helena Victoria (Thora) at a sale of work for the Personal Service League at Londonderry House in 1932.

Top right Lady Londonderry with Prince Rainier of Monaco, aged 12, in 1935. He frequently spent holidays at Mount Stewart.

Above left Edith Londonderry receiving at the top of the Londonderry House staircase during an Eve of Parliament reception. She wears the purple Siberian amethysts given to Frances Anne, wife of the third Marquess, by Czar Alexander. Beside her is the Prime Minister, Ramsay MacDonald.

Above right Lady Londonderry receiving at her Eve of Parliament reception in 1937 with the Prime Minister, Neville Chamberlain, beside her.

Top Lady Londonderry enrolling women recruits as motor transport drivers in the drawing room of Londonderry House towards the end of 1935 (the Women's Legion had been maintained on a reserve basis since the end of the 1914–18 war).

Above left The famous staircase at Londonderry House, with the Gallery in the foreground.

Above right The octagonal hall at Mount Stewart, on which the hall at Wynyard is modelled.

Top Edith Londonderry with her pony Rogart (named after a place in Sutherland) in 1930.

Above left (l. to r.) The Hon. Alexander McDonnell, Lady Londonderry and her son Lord Castlereagh at the opening of Newtownards Airport in 1934.

Above right Lady Londonderry pointing out features of one of the aeroplanes at the flying display at Redhill airfield, Surrey, in July 1939.

Lord Londonderry on his sixtieth birthday in May, 1938.

Edith, Lady Londonderry in 1957, aged 68.

Edith, Marchioness of Londonderry, on her
eightieth birthday.

Edith Castlereagh, aged 22, from a painting by
Ellis Roberts published in The Book of
Beauty, 1902.

meanwhile had made up his mind to accept Craig's offer. 'There was a real call of the blood,' he wrote to Lady Desborough. 'If I had turned my back on the offer which James Craig had made to me, I should never have forgiven myself.'

Gradually, the focus of the Londonderrys' lives shifted to Mount Stewart, hitherto opened up only for visits at Easter, Whitsun or in the summer, or for grand house parties, usually when members of the royal family were visiting Ireland.

Of all the Londonderry houses, Mount Stewart was the one to which Edith gave her heart. It was *her* house in a way that none of the others was: she had brought it to life, she loved it passionately. It was special, a place of magic, enchanting and enchanted, the spot where her love for Charley and his for her flowered again; in his will, it was left to the child who sealed their *rapprochement*, their youngest daughter Mairi. Edith felt physically well there – whenever she was ill, she was sure a visit to Mount Stewart would cure her – and almost always happy. She filled its beautiful rooms with air, scent, light; she created the marvellous garden in which trees, flowers and plants seemed to grow larger and more luxuriantly than anywhere else. As she grew older, she spent more and more time there, sitting in the window sorting out plants, seeds or bulbs, writing her never-ending stream of letters, mixing handfuls of the fragrant pot-pourri she made in a large drying-room off the hall. Indeed, one of the chief characteristics of Mount Stewart was its smell; gusts of rose or carnation fragrance that drifted out when the door of the pot-pourri room was opened, the heavy, intoxicating scent of lilies, the perfume of roses or polar-bear rhododendrons in pots or in containers specially made to fit the angles of the stairs and, everywhere, the scent of sweet briar from the bunches that stood in every room and passage. Even her beloved Highlands now took second place: Mount Stewart was equally imbued with the Celtic aura of legend and myth that appealed to Edith at some deep level of her being; it had, as well, a lush Italianate charm unexpected in a northern island encircled by a rough and dangerous sea.

The house itself is large, built of the local dark grey stone, on the site of an earlier timber house called Mount Pleasant, erected by Alexander Stewart, husband of the heiress Mary Cowan, soon after he acquired the estate in 1744. The earliest part of the present building, the west front, overlooking the sunken garden, was built for Alexander's eldest son, the first Marquess, in 1804–5; most of the rest, including the giant Ionic portico, was built in 1825 by the third Marquess, the great Castlereagh's half-brother. Pillared and porticoed on its south side, it is approached by the road that runs south from Newtownards along the edge of Strangford Lough, past small fields brilliant with clumps of yellow gorse. Across the seventeen-mile stretch of the Lough, its silvery-grey surface ruffled by the prevailing southwesterly breeze, seabirds flying and calling, between the Ards peninsula to the east and the mainland to the west, the Mountains of Mourne can be seen blue in the distance on a clear day.

From the road, the house might not be there: behind the mile-long grey stone demesne wall lies an impenetrable planting of tall trees and rhododendrons. When Edith first stayed there she thought it dark, gloomy and sad. Even to set foot on the winding drive, the dark leaves of its rhododendrons lugubrious when the flowering season was past, was to enter a melancholy, *belle-au-bois-dormant* kingdom. Dark ilexes, huge and flourishing like everything else that grew there, almost touched the house in many places, other enormous trees blocked out almost all the light and air. The garden, as with most large Irish houses at that time, was well away from the house. It was reached by a path through the pleasure grounds called The Ladies' Walk.

Theresa had found it a place of peace and solace. 'The eucalyptus trees tall and silver and the firs – a walk up through ilexes and the red and yellow sallies – up to the lake covered with duck and other waterfowl, the foreground all yellow and white with narcissus, tulips and daffodils and a wealth of rhododendrons, pale pink and crimson,' she had written of her arrival one April day. 'Two hours saw me on board the Red Rose, running along with all sails set before a light south easterly breeze. Evening came, a glorious sunset and the moon shining as it does shine in Italy and Mount Stewart, Sirius flashing in the south, the curlews and brown gulls calling, a weird sound as if they were wishing and longing for an answer. The ilexes with the moon through their leaves turning them silver reminded me of olive trees.' But for most there was little hint of the warm south; rather, the sea mists, the frequent rain and the absence of the owners for much of the year combined to make the house damp, chill and often unwelcoming. Charley and his father preferred Wynyard.

When Charley succeeded, Edith looked at Mount Stewart with a fresh eye. 'This is the most divine house. Why do we ever live anywhere else?' she wrote in May 1915, in a letter that foreshadowed the lifelong passion that was now to take hold. 'I will be very good and stay with you at Wynyard whenever you like in case you refuse to let me come here.' During the war, Mount Stewart had been a convalescent hospital. As soon as she could, Edith set about the work of transformation.

She began with the drawing room. As she had done at Londonderry House, she allowed its beautiful lines and splendid pictures to emerge by removing much of the general clutter that reflected the era when Theresa had begun her reign – the room had been full of chairs or small sofas in conversational groups, their backs protected by antimacassars, tall screens and bamboos and palms in pots. She did the same thing outside, letting in light and air by cutting down the ilex trees which grew in front of the house.

It was some time during the winter and spring of 1919/20 that Edith and Charley drew together again. The probability is that their reconciliation took place during those first spring months together at Mount Stewart, aided by Edith's loving, almost sublime, gift of forgiveness. This time, she was able to exercise the magnanimity of the victor: Charley – no doubt with the pretext of now living in Ireland – had finally broken off his long affair with Eloise. She sent back all his presents in a great sack, and it soon became apparent that she had not taken kindly to being dropped.

There were, however, other emotional preoccupations closer to home for both Edith and Charley. The first was the seemingly wilful refusal of their eldest daughter Maureen to think of Prince Albert, then at her feet, as a serious suitor. Both Edith and Charley felt that their dazzling daughter would be a fit bride for royalty – and there were at that point four unmarried princes. What they did not know was that Maureen was already engaged to Oliver Stanley. Well aware that in her parents' eyes a second son, even of so great a potentate as Lord Derby, was no match for a royal prince, she kept her engagement secret.

Though only nineteen, Maureen had no trouble in withstanding parental pressures. As well as the good looks inherited from her parents, with the true Londonderry colouring of fair hair and blue eyes, she had her mother's forceful personality coupled with a self-confidence that had been lacking in the nineteen-year-old Edith. Nothing and no one frightened Maureen: she had her parents' physical courage and dash spiced with a recklessness and flamboyance all her own. She had Edith's gaiety and high spirits, she was witty, intelligent and uninhibited – later she became an excellent public speaker, able to turn the laugh against any heckler who dared tackle her, later still she ran a 'salon' similar to her mother's. Extrovert and sure of herself, she fascinated those who were quieter, shyer and more timid. One of these was the King and Queen's second son, the future King George VI. He frequently came to the Wednesday Ark evenings, which now included dancing for the benefit of Maureen, Robin and the younger guests. Charley and Edith did what they could to further Prince Albert's suit by asking him to shoot at Wynyard and hunt from Springfield. But Prince Albert – or the Unicorn, as he was known in the Ark – sighed in vain.

Oliver Stanley, tall, quiet, dignified, scholarly and shy, was a stock-broker and a rising MP. But he was a younger son and from Edith and Charley's viewpoint, if their beautiful daughter would not marry a prince, an eldest son was the least they could expect in his place.

Maureen was unabashed. Basically serious-minded, from a family that, like her future husband's, had always been deeply engaged in the political life of the country, she shared her fiancé's interests and admired his approach to life. She bent her powerful will to persuading her parents that her destiny and happiness lay with Oliver Stanley. Soon both Londonderrys were looking forward to the wedding, planned for November 1920.

Maureen was not the only Londonderry daughter falling in love. Two months before Maureen's wedding, Dorothé had bought a house in Cleveland Square – No. 15, the biggest house in the square – but spent most of her time at Mount Stewart. Young, lovely and rich, she was not surprisingly a target for several fortune-hunters. One, Bobbie Cunningham-Reid, a good-looking former pilot who had shot down ten German planes in the 1914 war and was a friend of Jack Barnato's, came fairly close to success until 'seen off' by Edith, who by now regarded Charley's daughter as her own. Within two years Cunningham-Reid had married Mary Ashley, the younger sister of Lady Louis Mountbatten, in spite of her family's opposition.

A more suitable admirer now appeared. Terence Conyngham Plunket, always known as Teddy, who in 1920 became the sixth Baron Plunket, was one of the six children of a neighbouring landowning family. He was quiet, serious and shy. He was a serving soldier, having joined the Rifle Brigade in 1918, and an excellent painter. He was all that Edith could have wished for Dorothé. 'She and Lord Plunket have become friends,' Edith wrote to Charley, 'and I have great hopes.'

By the early autumn of 1920 Edith was distracted by finding herself, in her own words, 'unaccountably seedy'. With all the organisation and arrangements for Maureen's wedding ahead of her, she found this sudden malaise annoying and depressing. But the mystery was soon resolved: her reconciliation with Charley had been so wholehearted that another baby was on the way. 'I don't think I mind about the infant,' she wrote a trifle dubiously to Charley. 'As long as I feel you want another "buck"

156

I shall be only too pleased. It is only such a surprise and awkward just now, and having been so seedy made me feel rather appalled at the prospect. But now I am in rude health it amuses me.' When Maureen married Oliver Stanley in Durham Cathedral on 4 November 1920, the bride's 41-year-old mother was four and a half months pregnant.

After Edith had got over the shock, she was delighted. 'We shall both dote on it, like two old sillies. Besides, it will be the best Easter Egg that Margaret and Helen have ever had.' With three daughters already, she hoped for another son. 'I should be far more pleased at being able to produce a buck for you than any of the other things I have done, because this really will be for you, and only I can do it.' She added triumphantly, 'You can't make use of all your others, can you?'

The wedding over, she returned to Mount Stewart as soon as she could. 'Do let us come together and see if we can get away before the others next month, quite alone, and have a honeymoon,' she wrote to Charley on 2 January 1921. 'Wouldn't it be fun? all the way in the train last night I kept going back over the old days ... I fell in love with you first just because you looked such a gentleman, and like your ancestor, and because, of course, as all your family say, you are the most attractive man that ever lived. Oh, my thoughts at going to bed the night before I married and wondering what the next would be like. What a pair of babies we were really!'

Her own baby, born on 25 March 1921, was a girl. She was christened Mairi Elizabeth. Despite Charley's reassurances, Edith castigated herself for her failure to produce the longed-for 'buck'. 'I promise not to worry any more about the baby,' she wrote a fortnight after the birth. 'But I could not help trying to put myself in your place and realise how very annoying and disappointing another girl must be for you, and the morti-fying feeling that only I could produce you a son – just the one thing, my Doody, that you can't do better without me – and I couldn't even do that.' It was the last time she would mention such a thing: within a week or two both Londonderrys were equally besotted with their new daughter. 'She is going to be a real beauty with the most lovely eyes, great big bulgy deep blue ones, and so like you,' wrote Edith.

For Eloise, hurt, furious and humiliated by her lover's defection, this public proof that he had abandoned her for his own wife was more than she could bear in silence. Though Charley's behaviour had been sufficiently discreet for no word of their liaison to emerge beyond their own circle, and though no obvious conventions had been broken, all their friends knew of it – just as all their friends now believed it was over. She would prove them wrong.

She embarked on a campaign to get Charley back while simultaneously concealing from the world that their affair had broken up. The simplest way of maintaining the fiction that she, Eloise, was the love of his life was to cast doubts on his relationship with Edith. Accordingly, her loyal sister Alice put it about that Edith's new baby must be an illegitimate child by a lover since, 'as everyone knew', Charley was in love with her sister Eloise and entirely faithful to her. These rumours were spread so briskly that for once the rule of *pas devant les domestiques* fractured: Mairi's nanny, a Scotswoman devoted to Edith who had looked after the baby's older brother and sisters, would say to anyone peering in at the pram she was wheeling: '*Isn't* she like her father?' At the same time, Eloise did her best to lure Charley back – little knowing that the object of her affections faithfully reported her every move back to his wife. 'Your talk about the Countess is amazing,' Edith commented to him that June, while she was still at Mount Stewart with her two-month-old baby. 'She thinks if I am safely away she might still get you whilst Billy is hors de combat.'

Eloise's machinations were of little avail, though her constant, carefully publicised efforts to reassert her hold over Charley sometimes got through Edith's guard ('Was I nasty to you? Please forgive me, as you are so beloved always. I expect I was annoyed at hearing gossip. It always bores me so'). But from now on, although Charley would continue to have a succession of 'girls', no other woman would have the hold of Eloise – and none would ever again seriously challenge his feelings for Edith. Henceforward, they were sure of each other in a way that neither had really experienced before. A month after Maureen's marriage, Edith poured out her feelings to her husband of twenty years in a letter that could have been written by a bride. 'You know I love every little bit of you, inside and out. I love you so much, as everything – as a lover, a wife and a mother. I love you in a thousand different ways. I admire you, I respect you, I almost worship you. I have never found anyone like you and I just adore you, so that's that. And as for friendship, you are my best friend, and don't we love it when we get away together here. I do, anyhow. Bless you, I wish I could hug you.'

There was only one flaw in the idyll. Quite apart from the necessary refurbishing of Mount Stewart – it had needed rewiring, decoration and the central heating which both Londonderrys felt essential to counteract the chill dampness of the Irish air – the garden had begun to eat money. Edith was also extremely generous, giving frequent presents to everyone she loved. Throughout their marriage, her extravagance was a constant refrain of Charley's, though there never seems to have been a need to curtail his own expenditure on shooting, polo and racing. Early in 1921 he wrote chidingly: 'Your overdraft is more than at the end of the last quarter so I fear you are overspending. I am authorising Dillon to pay off this and to deduct £100 a quarter from you for a short time.' Edith, desperate to avoid anything that could damage their new closeness, as usual apologised. 'I do want to tell you, darling, how deeply distressed I am at my extravagance. It is always the same old story and I feel so ashamed of myself. It is not as if I was entirely an idiot and irresponsible, so it becomes a worse fault. I was under the impression I had done quite well this year, and have told you so repeatedly, and it was a great shock this morning.'

But Charley was not really perturbed – nor had he need to be. He had an enormous income from the family coalfields and the capital value of the various Londonderry properties and possessions was immense; and (by January 1922) his holding of Victory Bonds alone was worth £439,000 and he was buying more.

The summer of 1921 was productive in every way. Maureen too was now expecting a child and arrived at Mount Stewart to be with her mother while awaiting its birth (her son Michael was born in August). While Mairi slept or gurgled in her pram, Edith was busy with another creation: the gardens of Mount Stewart.

The previous year, almost as soon as she arrived, she had sent for catalogues of plants and roughed out designs. The mammoth task ahead required an equally massive input of labour; here, she was helped by the economic situation of the country. During the difficult period immediately after demobilisation, when returning servicemen flooded the labour market, Ulster landlords were asked to employ as many as possible; in the months ahead, as Britain drifted towards the slump of 1921/22, unemployment rose to its highest for 100 years – between the wars, it was never to sink below one million.

Twenty ex-servicemen were assigned to Mount Stewart. Their first task was to level and clear the site of what is now the Italian garden that stretches along the south front of the house. With these men, working beside them whenever possible ('I have just transplanted a huge rhododendron from outside to near the house. It looks magnificent and with plenty of water it is sure to live'), Edith set about what was nothing less than a full-scale re-landscaping, followed by complete replanting.

She made a wild garden, a paved garden, a lily wood, a rock and shrub garden, the Italian garden with its flagged terrace and beds edged with heather similar to the formal garden of her childhood home, Dunrobin. She planted camellias, rhododendrons, azaleas, magnolias, bulbs from South Africa and, against the wall of the house, mimosa. In a sunny alfresco 'room' of tall yew hedges she made a Shamrock garden, at its centre the Bloody Hand of Ulster, the crest of the MacDonnells of Antrim (if Frances Anne had been a boy she would have been the Earl of Antrim). All the stonework was done by local craftsmen, some of it adapted from the Villa Gambaraia near Florence and the Villa Farnese at Caprarola, some – like the balustrades, parapets, monkey pillars and large pots – to Edith's own design. Within a few years she had also built a loggia, a salt-water swimming pool set in an exquisite, secluded garden on the lough side of the Newtownards road, and the Dodo Terrace which, with its stone animals, commemorated the Ark. She had also begun the planting of the hill leading to Tir N'an Og (Gaelic for 'The Land of the Ever Young'); this, with its pavilions, walls, cypresses and roses, was conceived as a private burial ground for Edith, Charley and their family.

She was, of course, helped enormously by two factors: her invariable practice of going straight to those who were the most expert or powerful in their fields; and the remarkable climate of the Ards peninsula. Twenty-one miles long but never more than four miles wide, bounded by the Irish Sea to the east, Strangford Lough to the west and with Belfast Lough sweeping right round its north coast far inland, it is virtually an island, with the Gulf Stream, running up the Irish Sea, washing all its shores. Its climate is sub-tropical, its atmosphere humid – in hot weather, the dews are extraordinarily heavy – and all vegetation flourishes luxuriantly. Eucalyptus, bamboo, tree heaths, rare Chinese plants grew with a speed and extravagance that Edith, who until then had only had experience of gardens in the coldest part of England and the northeast of Scotland, found amazing.

One of her mentors was Sir John Ross of Bladenburg, owner of the famous gardens of Rostrevor House, at the southern end of County Down among the Mourne mountains country where many of the inhabitants supported Sinn Fein. As the Troubles were raging, visits were dangerous; when Edith took a house party there they were preceded by an armoured car. Once arrived at the Rostrevor garden, known to its owner as 'Fairyland', there was much for the keen gardener to see. Edith's first visit began with a gaffe: overcome by admiration at the variety and exuberance of its planting she exclaimed, 'I have never seen such shrubs before! It might be the gardens at Kew.' The elderly Sir John stopped dead and said in pained tones: 'Dear Lady Londonderry, never mention Kew to me again. I can grow things here Kew has never heard of.' But they became fast friends and he gave her countless seeds and cuttings as well as encouragement.

Her other adviser was Sir Hubert Maxwell of Monreith, in Wigtownshire, whose wonderful garden was also full of rare and delicate species. Like Sir John, Hubert Maxwell urged her to take full advantage of the Ards climate, and plant much that was normally only seen in greenhouses. In went acacias, lapagerias, a huge tree called *Drinys winteri* covered with large, fragrant ivory umbels, Himalayan blue poppies, a camphor tree, a pomegranate, trees from Australia, California and China, and a massive replanting of different varieties of rhododendron.

The Mount Stewart gardens were a success from the start, ceasing – thanks to the speed at which everything grew there – to look 'new' in an extraordinarily short time. Jealous neighbours, regarding the number of gardeners and the lavish planting, might claim that the Mount Stewart gardens were 'manured with money' but this is not to take into account Edith's own hard work and expertise. Her approach was that of a professional. She became immensely knowledgeable about plants, and supported plant-hunting expeditions such as those by Kingdon Ward to China; in return she was given many of the plants he brought back. She kept copious notes, recording every detail about a new arrival: where it was put, what the weather was like that day, which way it faced – she believed it was essential that when a tree or shrub was transplanted, the part that originally faced north should do so again in its new home.

She was busy, happy and fulfilled, absorbed in her Mount Stewart life and conscious always of the happiness of having won Charley back again. Every glance at Mairi was a reminder of this joy. 'She is a gift of God to us, surely, yours and mine. It is such joy we both have in her, now don't we. The truth is, we should not be separated.'

XV

MOUNT STEWART was an island of joy and tranquillity in an increasingly wretched and strife-torn Ireland. The Troubles were at their height. A month after the election of December 1918, the seventy-three Sinn Fein members had met in Dublin, adopted a declaration of independence and a provisional constitution, and formed a parliament, the Dail Eireann. Michael Collins, the 28-year-old Minister for Home Affairs in the provisional Government set up by the Dail, organised the escape of De Valera from Lincoln gaol. De Valera then became the Dail's President, or *Taoiseach*. In September 1919 the Dail had been declared illegal by the British Parliament and thenceforth its meetings were held in secret. In 1920, the Irish Volunteer Organisation had proclaimed its allegiance to the ideal of a Free State. The violence against the visible signs of the 'occupying power' rose to a crescendo. By the autumn of 1921, the IRA – the active wing of Sinn Fein – had shot more than 500 British officers, soldiers and police.

To maintain law and order, the British Government recruited unemployed ex-servicemen as auxiliary policemen. These quickly became known as the Black and Tans – from their khaki uniforms and black berets – and their reprisals were as brutal as the outrages they were trying to prevent. Feelings grew increasingly embittered, more houses owned by the Protestant Anglo-Irish ascendancy were burned down, the ambushes continued and a network of gun-runners smuggled in still more arms.

Even in the 'black Protestant' county of Down, one of the few where not a single Sinn Fein member had been returned, Sinn Fein was active. Already Edith's friend and Ark member the portrait painter Sir John Lavery, commissioned to paint the Protestant Archbishop of Armagh and staying at Mount Stewart to do so, had received an anonymous letter.

Beneath the heading 'The Londonderry Air' Shelley's verse below was written in block capitals:

> I met murder by the way
> He had a mask like Castlereagh
> Very smooth he was yet grim
> Seven bloodhounds followed him.

'Do you have no sense of shame?' the letter continued. 'Parasites like you should be exterminated.' Nor had the Irish love of sport prevented 200 farmers, who sympathised with or were threatened by Sinn Fein, telling the Master of the County Down Harriers and Staghounds that they would not allow hounds on their land if anyone who had been a soldier came out with them.

As 1921 drew to its close the campaign was stepped up. Masked men marched on the undefended house of Lady Una Ross at Strangford (on the mouth of the Lough), forced Lady Una and her maids into the garden, and made them watch the burning of the house and all its contents. Nearby Castle Ward, the home of Lord Bangor and his family, was defended by the B Specials (volunteers enlisted for this purpose); and any visiting member of the Government was guarded constantly.

Edith and Charley refused to behave as if under siege. Friends and politicians still came to stay, although there were certain concessions to the situation. B Specials guarded the house, and Edith always slept with a set of day clothes by her bed and the revolver Sir John Cowans had given her in a bedside drawer. One night, with a full moon blazing into her room (she always slept with the blinds up), she was woken by a fusillade of shots. She rushed to the night nursery, where she found all three of her younger children in their nanny's bed, then tore down to the servants' quarters, where one of the maids was having hysterics. Emerging into the hall, she met two of her male guests in their Jaeger dressing gowns, each holding a candle. Noticing that one guest did not have his false teeth in, she coolly sent him back to his bedroom to fetch them, saying that otherwise, should they all be captured, he might never see them again. Finally, as the raid appeared to have fizzled out, everyone retired to bed again – but when Edith got to her room, put out the light, and looked out of her window, a bullet whined past her ear and the branch of a rose beside her fell to the terrace below. She drew back quickly, to hear more firing . . . followed, mercifully, by the noise of men running away. It was useless to follow them: she knew that, even if terrorists were caught red-handed, it was extremely difficult to convict them, as witnesses were too frightened to give evidence.

It was not a situation that could be allowed to continue. In any case, Lloyd George had been consistently in favour of Home Rule, though even he did not envisage an Ireland completely divorced from Britain: on the eve of the 1918 General Election he had issued a joint letter with the Conservative Leader Bonar Law stating that: 'two paths are closed: the one leading to a complete severance of Ireland from the British Empire, and the other to a forcible submission of the six counties of Ulster to a Home Rule Parliament against their will'. Tentative steps towards a negotiated settlement had been taken at the end of 1920 and fresh impetus was given when the King, in his speech formally opening the new Ulster Parliament in June 1921, appealed for the strife to end, for forbearance, conciliation and forgiveness. 'May this historic gathering be the prelude', he said, 'to a day in which the Irish people, North and South, under one Parliament or two, as those Parliaments may decide, shall work in common love for Ireland upon the sure foundation of mutual justice and respect.' A truce (to be frequently violated in the coming months) was declared in July, and De Valera and Sir James Craig were invited to London to discuss a settlement.

Negotiations began in Downing Street on 10 October. De Valera remained in Dublin, but five Irish delegates, with plenipotentiary powers, met the representatives of the British Government – three Liberals and three Conservatives – to hammer out what they hoped would be a satisfactory solution. The Irish delegates included Michael Collins, by now Minister for Finance in the Dail and a legendary figure on account of his skill, daring and brilliance in the organisation of guerrilla warfare against the British. He was extremely good-looking: tall, fit and energetic, with dark brown hair, square jaw, and a brooding, almost truculent expression that frequently gave way to an engaging grin. Women loved him.

During the months of negotiation, prolonged because so much had to be referred back to De Valera in Dublin, Collins came backwards and forwards to England, usually staying with Sir John and Lady Lavery at 5 Cromwell Place. Both the Laverys were Catholics, and Hazel Lavery was an outspoken supporter of Sinn Fein. As a glamorous figure in London society and a member of the Ark, she was on close terms with many leading or influential politicians, including Winston Churchill. In 'Hazel Hen's' white-marble dining room with its black and gold furniture, Collins met politicians of all parties on an unofficial basis, while his aura of romantic, courageous patriotism made him an attractive figure even to his political opponents.

Finally, on 6 December 1921, articles of agreement for a treaty between Great Britain and Ireland were signed. Almost at once, it became apparent that the months of hard work, bargaining and compromise had failed to bring peace to Ireland. When the negotiators returned to Dublin, De Valera repudiated the Treaty.

Once again, the sticking point was the British concept of Empire. The Treaty provided that Ireland was recognised as having 'the same constitutional status in the community of nations known as the British Empire as the Dominion of Canada, the Commonwealth of Australia, the Dominion of New Zealand and the Union of South Africa, with a Parliament having powers to make laws for the peace, order and good government of Ireland and an executive responsible to that Parliament'.

The Dail split, with a narrow majority (64 to 57) in favour of the Treaty. This more or less even balance was reflected in the country, also split between Free Staters (those in favour of the Treaty) and Republicans (those against it). De Valera resigned, and a provisional government was formed on 14 January 1922, of which Collins became chairman. But opposition to the Treaty hardened and those against it began to organise their forces.

One of those who had met Collins at the Laverys' house was Edith. Charley had not wished to. 'I refused deliberately to meet Michael Collins in a social atmosphere and I gave as my reason that, whereas I would certainly meet him in the conference chamber, I was not willing to meet anyone who, whatever his motives and reasons may have been, had been a party to the murder, sometimes in cold blood, of brother officers of my own and many friends who lived in Ireland.'

As Collins began the task of taking over the functions of government from Westminster, he continued to visit London. At the same time, the unrest in Ireland was escalating, with deepening divisions in the South itself as well as sectarian violence. It was clearly imperative that peaceful conditions be restored, and the conference Charley had spoken of was now arranged. The leaders of the North and the South and representatives of the British Government met on 30 March 1922 in Churchill's room at the Colonial Office, with Charley as one of the two representatives of Ulster. Agreement that violence must cease and on how this was to be achieved was reached remarkably quickly – by 8.00 p.m. the same evening – but, as Churchill pointed out to the House of Commons next day, there would be those 'anxious to wreck these arrangements . . . we must be prepared for attempts to mar all this fair prospect'.

Edith believed that if Michael Collins and Charley could meet privately it would help each to understand the other's point of view, and she persuaded Churchill to suggest this to them both. Charley was captivated by Collins's fervour, directness and patriotism. 'I can say at once that I spent three of the most delightful hours that I ever spent in my life,' he wrote afterwards. '. . . his enthusiasm was delightful as he unfolded his plans for the future in stirring phraseology. Perhaps I knew history a little better than he did and perhaps also I knew the power which he had over his followers and also the power which I had over mine when he entreated me to join with him in a really big conception.'

Collins's relationship with Edith must have been more complicated, to judge by the following letter – the only one written to her by him to survive. From its deeply personal tone, its misery and its realisation of the gulf between their worlds, it reads as though Collins had against his will fallen in love with her. There are, of course, other interpretations but that it stemmed from any feeling of social inferiority is unlikely – Collins's background had never troubled him during the Treaty negotiations, however well bred the members of the other side. His note, written obviously under the stress of emotion, is in pencil on a piece of battered blue writing paper savagely torn across the second page – almost as if Edith had started to tear it up and then thought better of it. It runs:

'Forgive me. I bitterly regret my outburst about L. You were very kind to try to arrange the meeting and I am well aware that I was very miserably minded to listen to W [Winston Churchill].

'It is all very well to tell me as you do that he has no "interest" in you. But how can you expect me to believe that, feeling as you know well I feel? So you must forgive my bitterness, and try to imagine what it means to be a man like myself, entirely self-made, self-educated, without background and trying to cope with a man like Lord L., a man who has every advantage that I lack. This is not self-disparagement, a mean quality that I think I do not possess, but I cannot help recognising the fact that you and he speak the same language, an alien one to me, and he understands to perfection all the little superficial things that matter in your particular world. Unimportant things maybe – but oh! my God, not to be underestimated with a woman like you. I know that instinctively.

'I feel savage and unhappy and so I blame you for a situation for which I alone am to blame. But I contrast myself with him, my uncouthness with his distinction, my rough speech with his unconscious breeding, and the worst of it is I like and admire him and feel that he is brave and honest. On one point alone I believe myself his superior.'

What this was we will never know.

Collins strove hard to pacify Ireland and to heal the breach between Free Staters and Republicans. He called an election for 22 June. But, even though 94 of the 128 newly elected deputies supported the Treaty, the Republicans refused to accept the verdict of the electorate and the civil war in the Free State continued. The Republicans seized key buildings and Collins issued an ultimatum: all buildings illegally occupied should be evacuated. When this ultimatum expired on 28 June 1922, the Free State lapsed into civil war. Collins took command of the Army and, after a battle in Dublin, broke the revolt there. 'I see that in the Dublin battle 700 or 800 were taken prisoners,' Charley wrote to Edith on 8 July. 'No doubt a few patriots will be sacrificed but after all if as I believe Michael is an IRB [a member of the Irish Republican Brotherhood], this is all in the day's work. Meanwhile my firm conviction is that supported by Winston with substantial help, aeroplanes, etc, Michael will be able to raise and equip an army for use in the next two or three months.'

Michael Collins paid for the signature of the Treaty with his life. On 22 August 1922, as he was returning to Cork with some of his staff, they were ambushed in wild country near Macroom and Collins was shot dead.

In Britain, too, the political scene was changing. Disenchantment with the Lloyd George Coalition had been growing in Conservative circles. Without the cohesion forced by the wartime years, the growing scandal of the traffic in honours, the Prime Minister's personal control of what was supposed to be the Coalition's fighting fund, the irregularities of his private life and divergences in policy all combined to produce Conservative unrest. In peacetime, too, the essentially different qualities of the Conservative Leader Bonar Law and the Prime Minister had begun to work against rather than complement each other as they had previously done. Bonar Law, who both as Chancellor of the Exchequer (1916–18) and then as Lord Privy Seal and Leader of the House of Commons, had supported the Prime Minister unstintingly, was a moderate, kindly, balanced man, impassioned only on the subject of Ulster he was the son of an Ulster Presbyterian minister who had emigrated to Canada – whose formidable grasp of detail and excellent memory had fitted him admirably for the chancellorship. Above all, he was a man of the utmost probity. Lloyd George was visionary, flamboyant, a brilliant orator, devious and unscrupulous. Nonetheless, when Bonar Law, exhausted after years of overwork and a heavy smoker, resigned because of ill health on 17 March 1921, the Prime Minister lost his strongest support.

Many Conservatives had begun to believe that the Party was losing its way and should return to the original concept of Conservatism – impossible if Lloyd George continued to dominate the political scene. The first to state this publicly was the influential elder statesman Lord Salisbury, who declared in a letter to the *Morning Post*, on 20 June 1921, that 'the Coalition Government no longer possesses the full confidence of the Unionist Party'. Carson expressed similar fears more strongly still to Edith in December: 'I feel so certain that the permanence of the Coalition under any name will be a disaster and indeed prohibitive of free action and criticism.' The Unionist leader was one of a small group of politicians already plotting action: their goal was the formation of a group of 'true' Conservatives within the main body of the Party. Charley, as a staunch Unionist, was one of them; and it is a mark of how deeply involved Edith had now become in the world of politics – and how respected was her judgement – that most of the men concerned confided in her, like the Duke of Northumberland, writing on 23 December:

'. . . I quite agree about Salisbury. He has far more experience than anyone else in the Lords and would carry more weight. Also, it is a great thing to have a man one can really trust and who is not thinking of himself. That is in my view his greatest asset. As to Horne [see below], I like him and I think his instincts are Tory but I am afraid he has gone too far to turn back.

'But don't you think that what we ought to do is just to keep our small "die-hard" party together for the next few months in view of the probability (and I should regard it almost as a certainty) that the whole Conservative Party will eventually come round to us? . . . in the meanwhile, there must be some rallying point for Conservatives that we must provide.'

He concluded with a postscript which showed quite clearly the part Edith was playing. 'I am so glad you are taking the lead in getting all those who think like us to meet. It is not at all pushing and there is nobody else who could do it so well as you.'

Lord Salisbury produced a list of six peers ('Buccleuch lives a long way off but is staunch and very useful in Scotland; Erskine would, I am sure, help in any whipping work'), Lord Wolmer suggested meeting her at the Duke of Northumberland's seat, Alnwick, for further discussions and Robert Horne, a member of the Ark, wrote to her on Christmas Day with a story that vividly illustrates the atmosphere of plotting and intrigue that surrounded the last months of the Coalition. Horne, formerly President of the Board of Trade, had been made Chancellor of the Exchequer by Lloyd George on 17 March 1921 in place of Austen Chamberlain, who had become Leader of the Conservative Party on Bonar Law's resignation.

'My dear Circe . . . On Wednesday morning I start for Cannes to join the Prime Minister at Grasse where a villa has been lent to him. Winston turned up at No. 10 on Friday and, on hearing that the PM was starting on Monday, insisted on joining the party. F. E. is to debouch on Grasse from St Moritz next week so we shall be swelling with eminence and distinction. I'm rather looking forward to this meeting for a reason which I had not meant and ought not to tell you but I know I can trust you *never to give it away*.

'The story is this. Austen Chamberlain came to me one day last week to tell me that he had been present at a dinner with the PM, F.E. and Winston when Winston demanded that he be made Chancellor of the Exchequer in the near future. He said he was not going any longer to serve in a subordinate office and, if he didn't get the Exchequer – well, he was a "soldier of fortune" and he was going "to keep his sword free". In this demand he was supported by F.E. (evidently these two people feel that their positions have been greatly strengthened by the Irish negotiations). Austen broke in to say that "It would be monstrous to put such a proposition to Horne. He, poor devil, had been forced to leave an office which he didn't want to leave and put to the Exchequer to which he didn't want to go and it would be unconscionable for the PM to ask Horne to step down and look as if he had been a failure when in fact he had done well at a very difficult time." It was then further discussed and the proposition is to be made to me at Cannes that Winston goes to the Exchequer and I to the Colonial Office; *with a peerage*(!).* Austen says that if I refuse, as he thinks I should be entirely justified in doing, he will support me with all the weight of the Unionists who follow him.

'I told Austen that if the proposition is made to me by the PM I should at once put the Exchequer at his disposal. I have twice intervened to prevent a rupture between the PM and Winston because I have been so keen to prevent the Coalition breaking up and I am not going to let my

---

* He was elevated to the House of Lords although not until 1937, when he became the first Viscount Horne of Slamannan.

personal position affect the situation now. But I am not going to take either the Colonial Office or a peerage. The real question is whether I shall stay in the Government. I don't want to do anything that looks like sulking or being peevish because I don't feel that way. But twice since I have been in the Government I have made great personal sacrifices out of a feeling of loyalty from which I am now clearly absolved; and I may take this opportunity to go out and look after my own interests.

'This is a tiresome tale to tell you and you must forgive me pouring it out to you. I wish I could have talked to you ... unfortunately the truth of the business can never be disclosed and whatever course I take the public opinion will be that I must have proved unfit for my job. Quite frankly, my vanity rather revolts at that; but it can't be helped.' In the event, Horne's fears were unfounded and he remained Chancellor until Lloyd George was toppled. His loyalty to Lloyd George prevented him from taking office in the new Government.

Conservative unease grew steadily, centred mainly round the right-wing, die-hard Unionist core though a more generalised dissatisfaction was now spreading. When Stanley Baldwin, who had a deep, almost mystical belief in and love of his country and the English character, was appointed to the Lloyd George Cabinet in his own first Cabinet post – in April 1921, as President of the Board of Trade – he was shocked by what he saw as the cynicism and levity of his colleagues.

After the political excitements of the winter, Edith had spent the spring of 1922 at Mount Stewart. She was, as usual, blissful there. Maureen and her baby son Michael were staying with her, there was the garden, and there was Mairi. 'I feel so happy having got a small thing to play with, and now I can see she is really going to be very like you it is an additional pleasure.' She was, though, exhausted and physically depressed. She suffered sporadically from sinus and antrum trouble and was now laid low by a particularly bad attack; in addition she was still feeding her youngest child ('I howled buckets at intervals all day long. The doctor says it is a perfectly natural and to be expected reaction and all that sort of thing'). By May, she had recovered, and visitors were arriving at Mount Stewart. One was her father, another was Dorothé, who spent much of her time sailing with her half-sisters and seeing her suitor, Teddy Plunket ('Things are working with Dorothé and P,' wrote Edith happily), and another was Field Marshal Sir Henry Wilson.

Wilson was a great favourite of Lloyd George, who had made him Chief of the Imperial General Staff in February 1918, a Field Marshal in

July 1919 and a baronet a month later. He was an Ulsterman and a fanatical Unionist, and throughout the Home Rule crisis of 1914, when he was Director of Military Operations at the War Office, had leaked much secret information to the Conservative Opposition. In February 1922 he had been elected Conservative Member for North Down. In May, he came to visit his constituency, and to make a series of speeches there. Before the first one, in Newtownards, he dined with the London-derrys and their house party; as they sat down, Edith realised that they were thirteen at table. As her father, who was staying with them, was over eighty years old, she reflected that if he were to die within the year this could hardly be laid at the door of superstition – in which, in any case, she told herself, she did not believe.

The party set off for Newtownards, where Henry Chaplin, Charley and Robin all spoke, to introduce the new Member. Then Sir Henry rose to his feet. He and Lloyd George had worked together for many years, he told his audience, but recently Lloyd George had tended more and more to make terms with 'murderers' – as he described the Republicans. He made similar inflammatory speeches at other meetings.

Shortly after he left, Edith dreamed that he was murdered. She woke up at 4.00 a.m., to find herself sitting up in bed and shouting out: 'Good God, someone must go and tell Lady Wilson!' She felt, she told Charley and Lord Dufferin, one of the house party, the next morning, as if she had received a violent blow. Both told her not to be such an 'old croaker'. Four weeks later, on 22 June 1922, Wilson was gunned down by two Sinn Feiners on the doorstep of 86 Eaton Place, his London home.

For the Unionists, this was just further proof of Lloyd George's mistaken policies *vis-à-vis* the south of Ireland. For the rest of the Conservative Party, what brought matters to a head was the 'Chanak crisis'. Mustapha Kemal, now seizing power in Turkey – Britain's former enemy during the war – was threatening to invade the neutral zones which had been created around Constantinople, the Bosphorus and the Dardanelles. Lloyd George's confrontational reaction to this convinced most of the Conservative majority in the House of Commons that he was determined to take the country to war again, or at least dangerously near it. The crisis was eventually resolved by the courage and tact of Sir Charles Harington, a brilliant and distinguished soldier who was then the Military Commander of the Allied Forces of Occupation in Turkey. For Lloyd George, it was too late.

On 19 October 1922, a meeting of Conservative Members of Parlia-ment was convened at the Carlton Club. The Leader of the Party, Austen

Chamberlain, recommended that the Coalition Government should go to the country and it would be time enough to talk of changes then. But when it was realised that the senior members of the Party – Austen Chamberlain, Balfour, Horne, Birkenhead and Curzon – were pledged to the support of Lloyd George and would go into the election under his banner, the rank and file rebelled; and a motion was proposed that the Conservative Party should be 'an independent Party with its own leader and its own programme'. Baldwin's speech, which said of Lloyd George that 'a dynamic force is a terrible thing; it may crush you but it is not necessarily right', carried the meeting, and the presence of Bonar Law, who had risen from his sick-bed to support the motion, clinched the victory of the rebels.

With his Conservative support gone, Lloyd George had no option but to resign. Austen Chamberlain, who as Leader of the Conservative Party had refused to carry the message of dismissal to him, also resigned; and on 23 October Bonar Law became Prime Minister. Curzon, going back on his word, agreed to serve in Bonar Law's administration, retaining the Foreign Office and causing Lloyd George to comment: 'The Proconsul has ratted.' The following month there was a general election and the Conservatives secured an overall majority of seventy-five, resulting in the formation of the first purely Conservative Cabinet for seventeen years.

The fall of Lloyd George faced Charley with an agonising dilemma. Bonar Law invited him to join the new Government as Air Minister. It was, of course, unutterably tempting on every count: a seat in the Cabinet, and the portfolio of the Air, his real love. He asked for forty-eight hours in which to think it over, writing immediately to tell Lady Desborough of the offer. She replied by return, ecstatically. 'Our friendship has become such an integral part of my life it's all I can do not to say to the strangers in this train "He's got Cabinet!"' But her rejoicing was premature. Charley refused Bonar Law's offer: he felt duty-bound to continue as Minister of Education in James Craig's administration in Ulster.

Just how much this meant to him can be seen in his response to Ettie Desborough, who clearly believed that Craig had used moral blackmail to persuade Charley to stay in Ulster. 'I am in complete despair,' she wired. 'It seems to me the saddest lost opportunity there has ever been. No one now will be in the Government who either knows or cares about Ireland. Think what you could have done, and what help you would have been to poor Jim.* No, it may be bigoted but I cannot see any other point of view. I feel cold with anger against Craig.'

The following day (25 October) Charley replied: 'I fully appreciate your wire and all it meant, and I feel deeply grateful and appreciative of having such a real friend. But I *have* made a sacrifice this time. I have never made one before that was purely disinterested. This may destroy my prospects altho' if I am really good enough it cannot do that, and if I am not good enough it doesn't matter. But judging dispassionately at this moment, as I have done, I have followed the right course. I came here to help deal with a crisis; that crisis is not over, and it amounts to running away if I follow the path of my personal ambition. I can always let myself go in conversation with you, and I need not adopt the garb of false modesty, so I will say this. I knew I was of a certain value here, that I filled a place which no one at the moment could fill, but I did not realise that my suggested departure would really create consternation. Craig had a reception at Stormont last night and I have expressions from colleagues, friends, officials which I never anticipated; it was a revelation to me; and James Craig himself too. It really felt like leaving the front line for a soft billet at GHQ.

'You must judge me as your knowledge and wisdom dictates but I want you to realise what I have given up; the summit of many ambitions, a post in the Cabinet, a partnership with a real true friend like Jim, and a renewed association with Trenchard. Nothing but conviction could have compelled me to make the sacrifice.'

This conviction was that peace between Catholics and Protestants in the Province had to start in childhood, and through education. There was no use expecting help from parents, already set in a tradition of implacable hostility; any change in attitude must therefore start in the schools. These were sectarian, forcing-grounds for later bigotry and prejudice. Here the root of the trouble, Charley believed, was the difference in the way the Bible was taught to Protestants and Catholics. His view was that not only should Protestant and Catholic children attend the same schools but that, in order to avoid any early confrontation, no religious instruction should be given.

On 14 March 1923, he put the fruit of these ideas into practice in a new education bill, called the Londonderry Act, which established a non-sectarian basis for schools and teacher-training colleges. '. . . I look with confidence to the future believing that in the new spirit of the new

---

* Bonar Law, whose Christian names were Andrew James.

era dawning before our eyes, tolerance and a mutual respect will replace prejudice and jealous mistrust,' he said.

Unsurprisingly, both Catholic and Protestant churches joined in opposing the Londonderry Act. Stormont finally bowed to Orange pressure and allowed the education authorities to adopt a simple programme of Bible instruction – taught, naturally, the Protestant way. Naturally, too, the Catholics refused to allow their children to attend such schools. Charley's unselfish loyalty to Ulster had cost him dear. Sectarian education persists in Northern Ireland to this day.

XVI

EDITH WAS now staying at Mount Stewart as much as possible. She loved it, she was busy there and she had her three youngest daughters with her. Her new baby was a constant delight: fourteen months after Mairi's birth she was writing to Charley to ask if he would feel neglected if she stayed with the baby while he was in England. 'I would give up nursing her tomorrow if you really wanted and fly to you, although I do love nursing her. It is such a very real joy, especially when you are away. I can't explain it, as I have never felt like this before. But it is like having a little piece of you to cuddle and feed.'

Another happiness was Dorothé and Teddy Plunket's engagement. They were married in the Church of St Mary's, Denham, on 2 December 1922. Discreetly, neither Charley nor Edith went to the wedding. Dorothé, as a widow, did not wear white; instead, powder-blue chiffon velvet and a silvery veil set off her ash-blonde hair and huge blue eyes. The bridesmaids were the nieces of her first husband, Jack – Diana and Virginia Barnato and Patricia Lyon – and Teddy's first cousin Lady Veronica Blackwood. A month later, Maureen's former admirer Prince Albert became engaged to Lady Elizabeth Bowes-Lyon, soon to become one of Dorothé's closest friends.

The Plunkets started their married life in Dorothé's large house in Cleveland Square. Here they stayed for a year or so until they bought their first home together, 38 Upper Brook Street; Fannie Ward, by now a successful film actress, took over the Cleveland Square house. Dorothé's talent as a dancer soon became known, and she was much in demand. 'Cabaret by Lady Plunket' was a great attraction at charity balls. Her first appearance was at a party given by Bucks Club, whose founder, Captain Buckmaster, was collecting funds to give East End boys the chance to learn dancing. She danced a Strauss waltz with 'Frankie' Leverson, who often partnered her.

Soon after Dorothé's marriage, there was another change in Edith's family circle. Henry Chaplin was now eighty-three and had been getting weaker for some time. Too much weight and too little money had made him give up stalking some years earlier but he had returned to Sutherland in 1921, thinking that the Highland air would help him in his battle with insomnia – he had been lying in bed for a month, with a clot of blood in his left leg, awaiting a pair of elastic stockings, and the pain and lack of activity made sleep elusive. When the stockings finally arrived he set off for Dunrobin with the faithful William, making a detour on the way to stay with the Duke of Westminster at Loch More. Here he fell ill again, but finally arrived at Dunrobin, where the Prince of Wales was staying. By now Chaplin's memory was beginning to play tricks, though his charm and engaging courtliness never left him. One day, as a shooting party assembled in the hall, the Prince saw Chaplin waiting there and asked, 'Aren't you coming with us, Harry?' 'Sorry sir,' replied the old man, 'but I am waiting for Florence Paget.' His memory had gone back not to his courtship of the daughter of the house who had become his wife, but to that earlier Florence, whom he had introduced to an earlier Prince of Wales, and who had later jilted him so cruelly.

His last visit to Newmarket had been on 13 October 1922. 'Your father was in great form yesterday,' Charley had reported to Edith. 'I found him in the Jockey Club stand, without a single button done up and a piece of shirt sticking out. I told him of this and he said "Yes. The thing is, what with salts and physics I am always undoing my trousers and I somehow omit to button them up."' Charley, who was deeply fond of the old man, was not above teasing him. 'I said I thought the reason he gave would not be appreciated and that his intentions might be misunderstood.' Everyone tried to smooth Chaplin's path, from the King downward. 'The King is always so good and thoughtful to me that when I arrived for the Derby dinner the first thing he said was, "Now mind you are to sit after dinner," and the last time I was at Windsor for Ascot he had a chair for me to go round the State Rooms in.'

Five days after that Newmarket expedition, it was announced that Viscount Chaplin had given up his house at 6 Charles Street, Mayfair, to live with the Londonderrys. Edith, who adored her father, now had to watch him growing weaker by the hour. 'He reminds me painfully of the picture at Wynyard, the Dying Lion, but he still tries to keep his old head up, and raises it quite up to look at anyone. He is talking a great deal to himself and chuckling to himself. This morning he was making a speech but this afternoon he can't pronounce his words. I don't really think he can last very long. Darling, you have been angelic in having Father here but it does make everything so much nicer. I can never thank you enough for all you have done. It has made the whole difference to the end of his life.'

Her gratitude to Charley was emphasised by her belief that she had inherited her father's extravagance ('Look what you are doing about Father and how tiresome he is to you . . . at times I feel terribly ashamed of him and then myself, always getting into debt . . . and yet you are always the same and so sweet to me').

By the beginning of May 1923 Chaplin had become so much weaker that Edith thought he would soon be completely bedridden. 'All one can hope for and yet what I don't expect, nor does the doctor, is a speedy end, although the old thing is quite peaceful in every way, muddled, but in no pain.' She was able to make a quick visit to Charley in Mount Stewart, then returned to Londonderry House to report that the doctor felt it could not be much longer. She missed Charley's steadying presence. Her brother Eric, who unlike Edith had not watched their father's daily decline, was extremely distressed at the pathetic sight he now presented, and unable to concentrate on the inevitable arrangements. Edith's own sadness was tempered by relief that he no longer seemed to be suffering. 'Father is very peaceful and does not look ill or sad or drawn and his own wonderful complexion and hair just the same. I somehow feel all is well with him,' she wrote on the morning of 23 May 1923. He died that evening.

Chaplin left £4,800, all that remained of the vast estates he had inherited. He was not only Edith's last link with her childhood but a national figure: the epitome of an earlier, more spacious age and one of the last of that intimate circle who dined, raced, gambled with and entertained Edward VII.

Racing had been one of the bonds between Charley and his father-in-law. He had been elected a member of the Jockey Club after his father's death and had kept the Wynyard stud going as best he could during the war. In the post-war years, he had had a series of successes, in particular with his colt Polemarch, a son of The Tetrarch. As a two-year-old Polemarch won the Gimcrack Stakes in 1920. In the customary speech made by the owner of the winner at the Gimcrack dinner in York, Charley said: 'We are passing through an era of unrest and discontent, the necessary aftermath of the greatest upheaval the world has ever seen. . . . I feel that racing, which engenders sportsmanship and which unites all classes, is one of the factors which it is folly to underrate.' Polemarch went on to win the Rous Plate in Doncaster and, the following year, the St Leger, and made the Londonderry colours of lilac and yellow with black cap once more familiar to racegoers.

Unfortunately, racing provided an opportunity for Eloise to continue her pursuit of Charley. Although Edith was now fundamentally sure of Charley, she hated his absences as much as ever and, when she felt tired or ill, 'I get depressed and imagine all sorts of silly things, that you don't like me any more and get used to being without me and get to prefer "your wife", etc.'

In general, she showed an almost superhuman tolerance of Charley's philandering. Immediately after her father's funeral she had returned to Mount Stewart and, just before Ascot Week that year, she wrote to Charley to commiserate with him over the difficulties he was having with Eloise. 'I am sorry your "wife" is not being pleasant, because you know I want you always to be happy. Nothing worries me except when she worries you and I think you have been made to look foolish.' For Edith was still extremely sensitive to any hint that there was a continuing rift in her marriage. When a gossip columnist mentioned that Charley and Eloise had been seen together at Ascot that year, it upset her badly. 'What I minded, and still do rather, was about you and your "wife" walking in the paddock. I expect it is small-minded of me but I hated it, as it is such public property now. Still, I quite realise that you can't help that paragraph any more than I can.'

Part of the trouble was that Eloise, still furious and jealous, refused to allow her past relationship with Charley to mellow into the uncomplicated, undemanding friendship for which he now hoped. Their social circles overlapped to such an extent that any kind of complete break was impossible; far better to be able to meet easily, without embarrassment, quarrels or emotional scenes. As early as the previous October, Ettie, a past mistress at the art of turning admirers into friends, had written to Charley: 'It is so sad not to be able to share freely as you would like this triumph with the Countess. Could you not write a friendly letter and tell her – say you wanted to tell her yourself, and why should not friendly feelings continue all round, even if circumstances are altered? (Or would she be quite deaf and non-understanding?) It seems to me that you should remain friendly and should absolutely refuse to quarrel whatever she may do. It is so far the strongest and most unassailable attitude.'

The 'triumph' to which Ettie referred was Bonar Law's October 1922 offer to Charley of a Cabinet post. Now, several months later, all was in the melting pot again. Bonar Law, who admitted that he had 'hesitated up to the last moment' before accepting the premiership, was a very sick man. In April 1923 Stanley Baldwin took over the leadership of the House of Commons; on 20 May, Bonar Law, wretchedly ill with the cancer of the throat that was to kill him, resigned. He had been Prime Minister for exactly 200 days.

'Poor Bonar is said to be as bad as possible, and Eddie Derby, with whom I lunched on the way through London, says it is a question of *days*,'* wrote Ettie to Charley a week later. 'The situation was still quite undecided last night about Horne and Austen. Willie [her husband] had a long talk to Horne late yesterday afternoon, and did all he could to persuade him in. They are all very annoyed with Austen for "sulking and skulking" in Paris, but I really don't quite see what else the poor chap could do, do you. If he had come over they would have abused him equally. They are still angling *unsuccessfully* for AJB – Cabinet without Portfolio. I do not know what to wish about it – one's whole heart and brain are on the side of his being there, but I really do not think he is well enough. . . . Oh how I wish you hadn't self-sacrificed yourself out of all this, Charley, but it's only for the moment.'

On 22 May, to the acute disappointment of Lord Curzon, who had felt the position was his right, Stanley Baldwin became Prime Minister. Baldwin's remark of a week earlier, that he wanted to return to Worcestershire 'to read the books I want to read, to lead a decent life, and to keep pigs', can have done nothing to soften Curzon's disappointment.

Baldwin, destined to become Prime Minister three times, could not have provided a greater contrast to Lloyd George – indeed, according to a colleague his idea of what a prime minister ought to be was 'to begin with, to be as unlike Lloyd George as possible – plain instead of brilliant; steady instead of restless; soberly truthful instead of romantic and imaginative; English not Welsh. . . . Above all, he must be patriotic, a lover of his fellow-countrymen, of his country's history, of its institutions, its ancient monarchy, its great Parliamentary tradition, its fairness, its tolerance.'

His whole persona bore this out. Baldwin looked like a sturdy countryman, broad-shouldered, open-faced, sandy-haired, standing foursquare with his ash stick on his return from one of the long country walks he loved, pipe clenched firmly between his teeth. Under his shaggy brows

* He died five months later, on 30 October.

his eyes were blue; his hands were broad, his expression shrewd and faintly quizzical. He went in for being what he called 'a plain man', and he spoke simply and plainly, often using rural similes or metaphors. He played the sturdy-countryman card for all it was worth, and as the population grew increasingly urban with the new industries springing up after the war, this twanged a nostalgic chord on the national heartstrings – and recalled, to those who had fought and suffered, the green and beautiful land they had been fighting for.

One secret of his popularity was that, in an era dominated by the public-school ethos of reticence on emotional matters, he was not afraid of expressing his feelings. Through his commonsensical approach there ran a vein of bluff emotionalism which he tapped to great effect. He was warm, intuitive and sympathetic, but the guile of which he was often later accused was all in the service of his vision of his beloved country. There was nothing false about either Baldwin's patriotism or his idealism. In 1919 a letter appeared in *The Times* signed only FST, urging the rich to tax themselves voluntarily for the benefit of the country and revealing that the writer, estimating his own fortune at £580,000,* had decided to realise one-fifth of it and give it to the Exchequer by buying War Loan for cancellation. Only later was it discovered that 'FST' shrouded the identity of Baldwin, at the time Financial Secretary to the Treasury. His attitude was probably best expressed when he said (in a speech in January 1925) during his second premiership: 'There is only one thing which I feel is worth giving one's whole strength to, and that is the binding together of all classes of our people in an effort to make life in this country better in every sense of the word. That is the main end and object of my life in politics.'

Baldwin called a general election within months – a move inexplicable to many Conservatives, who could not understand this chancing of a safe position. 'I think Baldwin has gone mad,' wrote Birkenhead to Austen Chamberlain in 1923 (both, supporters of Lloyd George at the time of the 1922 rebellion, were out of office). 'He simply takes one jump in the dark; looks round; and then takes another.'

Baldwin's reasoning was both high-minded and pragmatic. The vast debt to America incurred during the war and the post-war slump had left the country poor; though there had been a partial recovery thanks to new industries and technological advances – there was a building boom and the beginning of the mass manufacture of cars and electric equipment

* In 1919 £580,000 had a purchasing power equivalent to over £10 million, in 1992.

– the major industries, coal, cotton manufacture, shipbuilding, iron and steel, were still depressed and their difficulties were accentuated by the Government's deflationary policy. To counter the prospect of continuing high unemployment Baldwin wanted to introduce protection, but he felt it dishonourable and risky to do so without a mandate from the electorate. Accordingly, he asked for a dissolution of Parliament and, on 6 December 1923, went to the country.

He had miscalculated. Massive gains by the Labour Party brought them 191 seats; the Liberals won 158; and the country's view of the lack of unity in the Conservative Party was reflected in their total of 258 seats – gone was the overall Conservative majority. On 17 January 1924, a vote of No Confidence was carried in the House, and the Government fell.

Whichever of the two major parties was to form a government would have to have the support of the Liberals. Asquith, the Liberal leader, gave his support to Labour. He thought that, as the Conservatives had failed to get a mandate for the introduction of tariffs, they could not simply carry on as if nothing had happened; and he believed that, if the two 'middle-class' parties combined to refuse the Labour Party office, this would encourage class antagonism and so exacerbate the difficulties between employers and a disenchanted workforce. The King sent for the Labour leader, James Ramsay MacDonald, and the first Labour Government of Great Britain was formed.

Nobody thought it would last very long. As Asquith commented, if a Labour government ever were to be tried 'it could hardly be tried under safer conditions'. Edith gave a reception for the defeated Conservative administration on 12 February 1923, wearing amethyst-coloured velvet edged with skunk fur, a girdle of diamonds and pearls round her slender waist, and Czar Alexander's huge amethysts like an insignia on one shoulder. Up the stairs came the Curzons, the Astors, the Austen and Neville Chamberlains, the Buchans, the Beaverbrooks and most of the *corps diplomatique*. It seemed as though nothing had changed. 'You made many people very happy,' wrote Baldwin in his letter of thanks, 'and I thought you played your part marvellously.'

What no one could have foreseen, least of all Edith herself, was that the country's new leader would become her closest friend and that, within a few years, she would be accused of luring him away from his own Party.

XVII

RAMSAY MACDONALD, Leader of the Labour Party and Britain's first Labour Prime Minister, was in many ways a man of contradictions. He was warm-hearted, deeply affectionate, cordial, even playful, yet his outward persona was aloof and unapproachable. Throughout the war he was reviled by the British public and ostracised by many, yet four years later he was a revered figure in his own party and the leader of the nation. He was an idealist who was deeply committed to the purity of early Socialism with its concepts of freedom, justice and equal opportunity for all, yet he was happier all his life with the friendship and in the homes of those who were his political enemies. He was a cultivated man who loved books, pictures, antique furniture, fine china, exquisite jewellery, rich colours, beautiful surroundings and elegant society. 'An intellectual aristocrat, he was driven by the accident of class and fortune to herd with the common people,' said Harold Laski. Or, as Bernard Shaw put it: 'He was not really a Socialist in the academic sense; he was a seventeenth-century Highlander who was quite at home in feudal society and quite out of it among English trade unionists.' He was sensitive, reserved, autocratic, shy, self-conscious, generous, kindly, honourable and romantic. He possessed at one and the same time severe intellectual honesty and a misty romanticism based on the myths and legends, the heroic figures and superhuman deeds of Scottish history, all diffused through the melancholy haze of a Celtic twilight.

There was the same dark, romantic glow about his appearance. He looked like a leader and he had the presence of one. He had a natural distinction and elegance; when he left Buckingham Palace as Prime Minister after his first audience with the King, he looked immensely distinguished in glossy top hat and wing collar. He was very handsome (and a cartoonist's dream), with his faintly brigand-like looks – wavy, tumbling hair, black moustache and flashing dark eyes. The musical tone of his baritone Scottish voice, with its dramatic risings and fallings, its emotional richness, its expressive cadences, could hold a crowd spellbound. His flow of oratory, by turns imaginative, scornful, romantic or cynical, and almost always lengthy, inspired many though it bored others. 'I looked upon his speeches in the House as tea intervals,' said Margot Asquith; Harold Laski called him a great platform orator whose speeches 'state great platitudes with an almost theological enthusiasm. Indeed, it might well be argued that Mr MacDonald's hold over the populace is essentially that of a lay preacher, with an immense power of moral fervour.' Anthony Eden thought he 'reeked too much of the soapbox, emphasising the last words of every sentence as though for rounds of applause'. As he grew older, he became more prolix, more inclined to diverge in whimsical fashion from the main path.

The strains of earning a living from freelance journalism sufficient to support a large family while working full-time as Party Leader meant that he suffered chronically from fatigue and overwork. This was compounded by an inability to delegate: essentially, MacDonald was a loner. Though he was on friendly terms with all his colleagues, few were intimates. 'MacDonald remains the "mystery man" to all his colleagues – who know little of his thinkings and doings,' wrote Beatrice Webb in her diary. Much of his thinking, if not of his doing, was informed by a passionate Celtic mysticism that sprang from his deep love of the Highlands and the songs and stories of Gaelic mythology. It also meant that he almost always made up his mind without consultation and often intuitively rather than by logic. 'Mr MacDonald and logic have never been on friendly terms,' said Harold Laski. 'By treating it with hauteur he hopes to reduce it to a proper sense of its subordination.'

He was born on 12 October 1866, in a tiny cottage – a two-room 'but and ben' – in Lossiemouth, Morayshire, a grey Lowland village of fishermen and farmworkers at the mouth of the Lossie, five miles from Elgin. His grandmother, Isabella Ramsay, a woman of enormous character, had brought up four daughters by herself after her husband had left her. The youngest, Anne, when working at a nearby farm, became pregnant by the head ploughman, a Highlander called John MacDonald. They did not marry, and Anne's son, James, was born at her mother's cottage. To be fatherless and brought up in a household of women was difficult.

Ramsay MacDonald was educated at a board school, in the sound Scottish tradition of respect for learning: although the fees were only eightpence a month he learned Euclid and Latin. As was customary for many brilliant but penniless students, he became a pupil–teacher at his old school, with the run of his scholarly headmaster's library, where he fell upon Shakespeare, Carlyle and Ruskin. At eighteen he left for London, where eventually, after much difficulty, he found work as an invoice clerk at fifteen shillings a week. As he was to do all his life, he read voraciously and incessantly, spending much of his money on books, sending some shillings home, and still managing to pay his fees to Birkbeck College. But the relentless regime of underfeeding and over-work – he was spending every spare moment studying science – broke him down and he had to return to Lossiemouth. Two years later he was back in London again, where he was taken on as private secretary by Mr Thomas Lough, the Liberal parliamentary candidate for West Islington, at the princely sum of seventy-five pounds a year.

This apprenticeship taught him much about the practical side of poli-tics. He was already well versed in theory. Soon after arriving in London he had joined the Fabian Society and many of the other small Socialist groups that then flourished, where his gift for public speaking was quickly discovered. From the start he was at home on a platform. He was also asked to write for Socialist newsletters and papers, and when, after four years, he left Mr Lough's employment, he earned his living as a journalist. He was a prolific writer, always in demand, but he consistently undersold himself. By the time he became Prime Minister the highest fees he had received for an article were £50 from *Answers* and £60 from *John Bull*, though later he was to turn down an offer of £50,000 to write his memoirs ('there is nothing I shrink from more than making public personal impressions of people').

In 1893 he played a leading role in forming the Independent Labour Party, and from 1900 to 1911 he was secretary to the Scottish Labour Party. As a popular speaker and a Socialist deeply involved with the foundation of the Party, he had often travelled abroad to represent Britain at international Socialist gatherings. This varied and well-rounded experi-ence put the final polish on his gifts, and in 1906 he entered Parliament as Member for Leicester. From 1906 to 1909 he was also chairman of the Independent Labour Party.

In 1895, he married Margaret Gladstone, the daughter of John Hall Gladstone, a girl who came from a milieu far removed from the two-room Lossiemouth cottages of MacDonald's boyhood – his father-in-law was a Fellow of the Royal Society, a distinguished scientist and a social worker. It was an extraordinarily happy marriage. Margaret's warmth and gift for friendship perfectly complemented her husband's more inward-looking nature, and her secure social and financial background introduced him to the objects and tastes that fulfilled the love of beauty that had hitherto seldom been indulged in his life of overwork. Her money gave him, for the first time in his life, a certain financial security. The MacDonalds were able to entertain their growing circle of friends at their house in Lincoln's Inn Fields, where their six children were born, and to travel. In 1906 he and Margaret went on a world tour and in 1909 they visited India; each summer from 1907 to 1916 MacDonald visited the Continent for Socialist gatherings.

This happy life ceased abruptly. In 1910 their youngest child, a boy, died. Then, eighteen months later, on 11 September 1911, Margaret MacDonald died of blood poisoning. MacDonald was devastated. Always a solitary, confiding in at most one or two people, he now withdrew even further into himself. He recognised this – 'I am one of those unfortunate people who sorrow alone' – but it did not help him. He could not armour himself in indifference, and he now had no one to talk to when grappling with emotional problems that his beloved Margaret would have solved with understanding, warmth and love. There would be no one to replace her; although a man who loved deeply, he did not love easily. When an attractive dinner partner said to him years later: 'Oh, Mr MacDonald, you are so handsome, so clever, so able, so attractive – why have you never married again?' he replied simply: 'I buried my heart in 1911.' But he loved the sympathy and understanding of female company and was immensely susceptible to beautiful and charming women – especially aristocratic ones – enjoying their friendship, basking in their smiles, flattered by their interest, soothed and amused by their frivolous, light-hearted gossip.

He had been a supporter of the women's movement since the 1890s, believing that the state 'must be created from the same experiences, motives and sentiments from which the family itself has been built up'; therefore women deserved the vote just *because* they were women, with a different family experience from men.

During the war he was a pacifist, which in those frenzied days when even dachshunds were chased in the streets required enormous courage. Stones were thrown at his meetings, the House of Commons heard him in icy silence, he was expelled from the Moray Golf Club – he never played on the Lossiemouth links again – and there was a relentless press campaign against him. The *Spectator* asked, in sober and reasonable tones: 'Is it a right thing that Mr Ramsay MacDonald should be drawing £400 a year from the British taxpayer when so far as we can judge by his correspondence in the Press, the chief work he is doing for the country at the moment is heartening the enemy?' Horatio Bottomley's *John Bull* said the same thing but with no pretence at moderation when it quoted 'an officer', supposedly writing from the front, as saying: 'For Heaven's sake, lock up Ramsay MacDonald. It is irritating to read his sentiments when on all sides there are graves of those who have *done* – not talked – for their country.' Under the letter was the editorial comment: 'If we had our way, there would be one more grave over here.'

John Bull (masthead motto: 'Politics Without Party – Criticism Without Cant – Without Fear Or Favour, Rancour Or Rant') went further still. In August 1915 it printed a replica of MacDonald's birth certificate showing his illegitimacy. This vicious public disclosure of what was then a matter for shame and humiliation caused MacDonald acute misery – especially as his first sight of it was in the company of the woman who was at the time the object of his romantic affection, Lady Margaret Sackville. 'On the day when the paper with the attack was published, I was travelling from Lossiemouth to London in the company as far as Edinburgh of the Dowager Countess De La Warr, Lady Margaret Sackville and their maid. Breaking the journey at Aberdeen I saw the Contents Bill of the paper announcing some amazing revelations about myself and when I rejoined the ladies at the station, I saw the maid had John Bull in her hand. Sitting in the train, I took it from her hand and read the disgusting article. From Aberdeen to Edinburgh, I spent hours of the most terrible mental pain . . . the first time I had ever seen my registration certificate was when I opened the paper at Aberdeen. Never before did I know that I had been registered under the name of Ramsay, and cannot understand it now.'

For a sensitive man, the enmity roused by his pacifism in those days of war fever and white feathers must have been difficult to bear, especially as he was naturally courageous. He joined Lady Dorothy Fielding's First Aid Yeomanry Corps, and served in France and Flanders, but none of this negated in any way the suspicion caused by his opposition to the war. He found some comfort in the society of others of like mind, staying frequently with Lady Ottoline Morrell at Garsington, then a refuge for pacifists, and often suggesting that Lady Margaret Sackville be asked at the same time. His host, the MP Philip Morrell, was not as taken with him as was Lady Ottoline. 'RM told long, long stories very slowly about his walking tours and his journeys. They were quite trivial and of small interest. His mind seemed so blurred and vague and he was so vain that he didn't see clearly about anything. I became so irritated I could hardly bear it.' But he read poems by Walt Whitman beautifully, and the rest of the house party enjoyed his company.

As one of the most unpopular men in Britain, MacDonald lost Leicester in the 'Coupon' Election of December 1918, and was out of Parliament for four years. He had always been a moderate, and in 1920 he used all his considerable influence to persuade both the Labour Party and the Independent Labour Party (at their annual conferences) to reject Communism. He was instantly savaged by the Far Left, which had the effect of improving his position with the general public, and when he stood for East Woolwich in a by-election in 1921, he was only narrowly defeated. But in the General Election of 1922, he became the Member for Aberavon, Glamorgan, with a comfortable majority, upon which he was at once elected Leader of the Labour Party. Since the Labour members outnumbered the Liberals, he also became Leader of the Opposition. 'The work is prodigiously heavy but I flourish under it. I am lonely though,' he confided in his diary.

Upon Baldwin's defeat in the House of Commons on 17 January 1924, the King sent for MacDonald. When MacDonald arrived in Downing Street he had one problem to face unknown to any previous prime minister: how to manage financially. His salary was £5,000 a year* but this was reduced to just over £3,600 by income tax and supertax, he had spent £350 out of his own pocket on his election expenses and even Beatrice Webb was moved to remark that he would not make ends meet on this. His children had to walk to school – though their pocket money was raised from three pence to six pence a week – and he himself frequently travelled on the underground. His eldest daughter, the twenty-year-old Ishbel, dark, pretty and resolute, kept house for him and acted as his hostess. Fortunately, her 'Daddie's' term of office began in January, when the sales were on, so she was able to buy the necessary everyday china, linen and household items to equip the private part of the forty-room house at bargain prices. Government Hospitality provided what was needed for official entertaining. Combining economy with good Socialist principles, groceries were bought from the Co-op – it was the first time a Co-op van had drawn up at the august door of No. 10 – and the delivery boys were from the Army and Navy Stores rather than fashionable establishments. Coal was strictly rationed out, and to save

---

* From 1831 to 1937 the Prime Minister's salary remained at £5,000. On Ramsay MacDonald's, after personal and children's allowances, income tax worked out at £1,025 13s. In 1923/4 supertax (assessed separately) began at £2,000; calculated on a sliding scale it amounted to a further £362 10s.

fuel, the family ate in those rooms which were heated at Government expense. Servants were a problem: the MacDonalds had never had any before and, as good Socialists, did not approve of them. His youngest daughter, Sheila Lochhead, remembers that 'we did not have a butler as we felt we couldn't cope with one. The head parlourmaid was a girl from Lossie, and we had a very experienced cook and two other maids, also very good – we were determined to justify the expense by not making a mess of it.'

Almost at once, MacDonald had his first experience of a difficulty that attends the new Prime Minister: dealing with the clamour for office. 'All but two or three were disappointed,' he wrote in his diary on 19 January 1924, in an entry that shows his mixture of the sensitivity that appealed so powerfully to women and the slightly martyred attitude that would always characterise his approach to the trials of office. 'One after another behaves as if I had insulted him by offering anything but a Cabinet place. Today a wild letter has come from the wife of one who has refused subordinate office which will give me a sleepless night. I feel like an executioner. I knock so many ambitious heads into my basket. After this every man will be my enemy. Somebody has to do it but probably no one but myself would be disturbed so much by the pain I am causing.'

One difficulty that many expected – how would a Labour leader, from a background so far removed from the circles familiar to the Sovereign, get on with the King? – was notably absent. From the start, they got on marvellously together, MacDonald responding to the King's kindliness with the respect and affection of a Highlander for his chieftain, the King enjoying his Prime Minister's instinctive grace of manner and vein of poetic imagination. In April MacDonald stayed at Windsor ('the kindly homeliness was that of a cottage and sat well in gilt halls') when Monarch and Prime Minister talked of Scottish history, of Ireland, the Marseillaise and other 'revolutionary matters'; in May he was recording in his diary: 'The King has never seen me as a Minister without making me feel he was also seeing me as a friend.' And when his children taxed him with working too hard he would reply: 'It is very encouraging to think your Monarch thinks you are doing the right thing.'

Almost immediately, the King had made a gesture that was designed not only to inspire confidence in the new, minority, Labour Government but to show that, even if most of London society disapproved of them, he certainly did not. Unprecedentedly, he invited the entire Cabinet to dinner at Buckingham Palace. It was at this dinner that Edith first met

MacDonald, and the foundations of the intimacy that was to puzzle some, scandalise others and intrigue many more were laid.

The omens for such a friendship were not auspicious. Not only did Edith come from the heartland of Unionism, she was in the opposite camp on virtually every issue. She detested MacDonald's dealings with Russia, her husband and most of her friends had fought in the war while the Prime Minister was notorious for his pacifist views, her husband owned coal mines and collieries while MacDonald and his fellow Socialists believed they should be nationalised, she was a rich capitalist while he was a poor Socialist.

Thus when she arrived at Buckingham Palace on the night of the dinner to be told by a somewhat flustered Master of the Household that she was to be taken in to dinner by the Prime Minister, so well known were her political affiliations that she was asked if she had any objections. 'Certainly not,' she assured the embarrassed official. 'Mr MacDonald is Prime Minister and as such he holds a position which in itself is sufficient to command respect.' On the Prime Minister's right was Queen Mary, also known to be very anti-Socialist. It is impossible not to feel a moment's sympathy for MacDonald as he seated himself at that dinner, hemmed in on either side by two powerful and strong-minded women who disagreed with him on virtually every count. But he charmed them both; politics were never mentioned; and an instant rapport sprang up between himself and Edith. They talked of her Mackenzie ancestors on her mother's side, out in the '45, they talked of their common love of the folklore, songs and scenery of the Highlands. Another link may have been MacDonald's great fondness for her father, who had shown marked kindness to him as a new MP.

It quickly became apparent that the new Prime Minister did not feel that fraternising with the Conservatives infringed his Socialist principles in any way. Many of his Party felt otherwise. One who disapproved from the start was Beatrice Webb, whose husband Sidney, having been the member for Seaham since the 1922 Election, was well aware of the Londonderry influence. The very day after the dinner at Buckingham Palace Mrs Webb was warning MacDonald against Edith. 'Lady Londonderry of all people! Why, she's a most dangerous woman.' Three weeks later she was writing in her diary. 'What MacDonald can be thinking about in taking his daughter into this vortex of luxurious living and silly chatter I cannot understand: it will make it impossible for Ishbel to do her duty to the party and it will undermine his influence with the left, and undermine it in the ugliest way.'

What Beatrice Webb would have said if she had known that Mac-Donald had not only already invited the Londonderrys to Chequers – their names are the first in the visitors' book after he became Prime Minister – but that he had embarked on a lively correspondence with the dreaded Lady Londonderry hardly bears thinking about. In April he was suggesting Edith invited herself again to Chequers, in June he was telling her ruefully that he was being criticised for being seduced away from House of Commons business ('You may have noticed that the papers have been attacking my "social engagements" and accusing me of neglecting my Parliamentary duties'), in August he was engaged in a serious discussion with her on the perennial Irish question and urging her to use her influence for the cause of peace, in a letter that is at once appealing and confiding, gentle and humorous.

'. . . The burden of Atlas was nothing to mine. His was the world; mine is the follies of the world. Between the weights of the two there is no comparison. This new Irish trouble is most worrying. I am rigidly opposed to hasty legislation, but I must make it clear that the Government intends to keep faith. I know you will do your best to get your friends to meet us reasonably within the period between now and the end of September. Do not let us revive these evil passions of hate, strife. We were not meant to be torn by such things, and I shall not countenance in any way the too evident intention of Mr Lloyd George and his miserable-minded following to make party capital out of a grave tragedy. . . . You are all on the other side of the world of people and ideas from me and when I go from this I hope never to emerge again from my own fireside; but whilst the sun is up and I am doomed to bear these burdens, and because I really *did* enjoy our talks, I beg you to help like a dear good woman, to give us peace. I slave here for the time being to make France reasonable' – the Prime Minister was also Foreign Secretary, and there were difficulties over German reparations – 'but in the words so often groaned out by its poor nerveless Prime Minister "C'est terrible". . . .'

Edith's response was immediate, a long letter written from Mount Stewart. 'The Southern Irish can be very charming but they certainly are an inconsequent race – in fact very like children – and when given too much latitude they get out of hand. It does not really signify what government they have, they must always be "agin" it. . . . You ask me to do my poor best to help towards peace; and get my friends to meet you reasonably. But to do this you must be reasonable too, and keep the faith with Ulster. So far Sir James Craig has always had his people under control (the South never) but there is a point beyond which men of Scottish blood will not be led and that point will be reached when they think that the British Government has not kept its word to them, pledged in the 1920 Act. If those who signed the Treaty regard it as a debt of honour which Great Britain owes to the South, she owes an equal debt of honour by the 1920 Act to the North.'

She concluded with an appeal involving one of the Gaelic tales they both loved.

'The original North East Ulster (Uladh) was won by a MacDonald who was the first to touch these shores by cutting off his left hand and throwing it from the boat on to the land which he claimed. Hence the bloody hand of Ulster. Won't you, another MacDonald, extend to us the other hand, the right hand of fellowship and maintenance, and throw us the olive Branch? I am on the other side of the water, but not of the world, as you suggest, nor do I think that, though we certainly are in opposite camps, that our ideas are necessarily so wide apart or that we may not have the same goal in view. I certainly did not receive this impression at Chequers, and I shall be surprised if the future makes me think otherwise.' It did not.

MacDonald's life was simple and, as far as he could make it, devoted to his children. The family breakfasted together every morning and went to Chequers every weekend. The children spent their holidays at Lossie-mouth, joined as often as possible by their father; and when in Downing Street the Prime Minister lived quietly, entertaining scarcely at all. His lack of means increased the strain of his life: when, for example, he was returning to Chequers after making a speech at the Pilgrims' Dinner in London on a Saturday, he had to go, late at night and presumably very tired, first by underground to Baker Street, then by Metropolitan Line, finally from the station to Chequers by a small Ford car. This so worried an old friend and admirer, Alexander Grant, the chairman of McVitie and Price, that in March he gave MacDonald the use of a Daimler and a life interest in £30,000 worth of shares in the company to provide the income necessary to run the car and pay a chauffeur. Two months later, Grant was given a baronetcy.

In September several newspapers carried this story, and the Prime Minister was forced to defend himself, pointing out that Grant was one of his boyhood friends – his uncle and Grant's father had been fellow guards on the Highland Railways – and that both the Daimler and the shares were to revert to Grant's family when the Prime Minister died. It was soon clear that there was no hint of corruption here; rather an attempt to alleviate a situation which should never have occurred. And in any case, Sir Alexander's name had been put forward for his baronetcy long before: he had been a notable public benefactor for many years – he had given £100,000 to the Edinburgh public library alone. But the whole affair rubbed the bloom off MacDonald's reputation, recalling as it did Lloyd George's unsavoury practice of selling honours, and the Prime Minister himself was deeply hurt.

MacDonald's attempts to seek a *rapprochement* with Russia, by recognising the Soviet Government and recommending the guarantee of a loan, had already caused unease. Then came the Campbell case. On 25 July the Communist news-sheet *Workers' Weekly* published an article urging soldiers not to shoot their fellow workers in a class or international war. Campbell, the acting editor, was charged with sedition but the Attorney General, Sir Patrick Hastings, withdrew the prosecution. It was suspected that this was as a result of ministerial pressure, and fears of extremism and Bolshevik influence intensified. When Parliament reassembled on 30 September, the Conservatives tabled a motion of censure. MacDonald decided to treat this as a vote of confidence and, on 8 October, the Government fell and Parliament was dissolved.

Just before polling day, at the most crucial point of the Election campaign, the 'Zinoviev letter' was published. This letter, urging increased Bolshevik pressure on the MacDonald Government by means of infiltration of the trade unions and insurrection in the armed services, purported to be signed by Zinoviev, president of the Third Communist International. It was later proved to be a forgery – probably the work of White Russian *émigrés* – but it did for the Government. Fear of the Red menace wiped out all disunity in the Conservative Party, who won 413 seats to Labour's 151, and on 4 November 1924 Stanley Baldwin became Prime Minister for the second time. 'This election would have rejoiced your father's heart,' the new Prime Minister wrote to Edith a fortnight later. 'To have ridden from Lincolnshire to Land's End on Tory territory! What a dream! Now to work, and I will try to keep both eyes open.'

Not everyone was glad to see Labour defeated. 'I am sure the King is sorry to part with MacDonald,' remarked Lord Esher shrewdly. 'Radicals and Socialists are much nicer to Sovereigns than Tories.'

XVIII

S O PERSISTENT were Eloise's attempts to inveigle Charley back
into her arms that eventually the Londonderrys realised the only
solution was to put more distance between them physically. They
must give up Springfield. Both Eloise and Charley hunted several days
a week with the same packs for up to five months a year, and while in
London encounters could be kept to a minimum, with the occasional
formal meeting at dinner parties stage-managed with decorum, and invitations to the same house parties refused, the hunting field was different.
Any manoeuvring there took place under the interested gaze of a hundred
pairs of speculative eyes. In 1924 Springfield was sold. For Edith it was
a miserable wrench; it had been her first real home with Charley, it was
where she learned to love gardening, and the children had done much of
their growing up there. It was to be a year or two before they found
another hunting box, Ranksborough.

Much the most expensive of their five houses was Wynyard. Once
again they wondered, though not seriously, whether to sell it. Edith,
writing to tell Charley that she had been asked to head the column of
women's services at the Cenotaph on Armistice Day, added: 'I don't see
Robin in the future wanting to farm at Wynyard, do you?' She was not
to know how Robin would come to love Wynyard and develop a real
sympathy with the mining community at Seaham.

As well as giving up Springfield Charley resigned his office as Minister
of Education in the Northern Irish Government. At the end of 1925 talks
were held by the Boundary Commission on the border between Ulster
and the Free State, notably on the 'difficult' counties of Tyrone and
Fermanagh with their high proportion of Nationalists. Charley was
deeply offended at not being asked to take part in these talks – he would,
indeed, have been an obvious choice, with his experience both in the

Ulster Convention and in the Northern Irish Parliament – and early in 1926 he resigned, giving as his reason for doing so the need to look after his coal-mining interests.

It was not entirely a pretext: the mines – or, rather, the men who worked in them – were now in ferment. Mining had always been a dangerous, unhealthy and dirty industry and grime and poverty were the chief characteristics of mining towns and villages. In 1924, one of Beatrice Webb's friends described Seaham, the heartland of the Londonderry coal fortune, as 'a town on a beautiful coast and all defiled with soot in the air, old boots, dirty paper and broken things on the ground; romantic ravines looking like newly made railway cuttings, no music, no public library, no hospital' [and this in an industry with the highest injury statistics of any], 'the large unkempt picture palace in a back street, and a suspicious smell pervading back courts and closed-up corners – railway lines and coal trucks everywhere. . . .'

Britain's million-odd miners had been saved from the worst effects of the 1921–23 slump by a coal strike in America in 1922 and by the French occupation of the Ruhr in 1923, both of which reduced imports of cheap coal. When there was once again competition from the Continent, intensified by improved efficiency in France and Germany, the livelihood of British miners was threatened once more by a surplus of coal. In 1925 the Government gave the mining industry a temporary subsidy and, on 31 July 1925, set up the Samuel Commission. This was ordered to report on 11 March 1926, with more specific, long-term answers to the problem.

Everyone recognised that the mines were badly run and inefficient. Quite apart from the inadequate and dangerous conditions under which the miners laboured, much production was lost because, where there were several small adjoining mines under different ownership or management, the boundaries underground were so imprecise, and the difficulties of co-ordinating tunnels so impossible, that for safety's sake wide areas between the mines were left untouched. The Commission recommended drastic reorganisation and streamlining of the entire industry in the long term and, in the short term, wage cuts – leaving the individual employers and miners to work out the details of these for themselves. It was a recipe for disaster: the festering bitterness left over from the abortive Commission of 1919 erupted once more. Both sides, which had been up against each other for years, stuck rigidly to their respective points of view.

On 13 April, Charley wrote to the Prime Minister to ask for guidance on an important point not mentioned by the Commission: if there was already a surplus of coal, was increased output really necessary? 'If it is true that only a limited production is required, then all theories of increased output fall to the ground. I put this to you with all respect and humility because we collectively, owners and men, have failed to do what I earnestly hoped and prayed we could do, which was to join together and work out a solution of the problem.'

His reference to failure was all too true. Immediately on publication of the Commission's report advocating a temporary reduction in wages, the coal-owners had demanded wage cuts, combined with longer working hours, to take effect from 1 May (the date when the Government's subsidy was to cease). With no guarantee that these would be only a temporary measure and, more importantly, no guarantee that the Government intended to carry out the main recommendation of the report – complete reorganisation of the industry – the miners refused to accept any drop in wages. 'Not a penny off the pay, not a second on the day,' they chanted, confident in the knowledge that they had most of the Trades Union Congress leaders behind them.

Neither side would budge an inch. On 1 May the owners locked the miners out. On 3 May the TUC, knowing that the Government had proclaimed a state of emergency and that if they did not support the miners now they would never be forgiven, called a general strike. Though most of their leaders sympathised with the objectives of the strike, they were also heavy-hearted and somewhat apprehensive. 'I picture it as a whirlpool,' said one of them, J. H. Thomas, 'knowing I cannot help being dragged in, knowing that the State must win on an issue like this.'

The General Strike was perhaps the most serious industrial confrontation seen until then. Three million workers came out, though essential services were kept going by volunteers who drove trains and buses and kept the mails moving. It lasted until 12 May, when the TUC, aware that its funds were melting away and that the Government would not give in, accepted an unofficial settlement proposed by Herbert Samuel.

But the miners stayed out. They were determined not to accept a reduction in wages, even if this meant closing mines and further unemployment. Baldwin and Churchill, the Chancellor of the Exchequer, tried all autumn to bring the two sides together and on 21 September it looked for a moment as though agreement was near. If wages were held above the 1921 minimum, said the miners' leaders at a meeting in Downing Street, and all local agreements were subject to arbitration by a national tribunal, they would order an immediate return to work. But

Baldwin did not want to commit the Government to arbitration – or to upset the owners – and again it was left for owners and miners to sort out between themselves. Once more there was deadlock – F. E. Smith (now Lord Birkenhead), after meeting the miners' representatives, said: 'I should call them the stupidest men in England if I had not previously had to deal with the owners.' The strike dragged on until finally, in December 1926, cold, starving, impotent and angry, the miners were forced back on the worst of terms – the lower wages and longer hours against which they had fought so hard.

Industrial relations in the coalfields had always been bad; now they were worse. Instead of the gradually improving conditions the miners had wanted, a benevolent paternalism was the best that most could hope for. As Sean O'Casey was later to write to Edith: 'I read that Lord Londonderry has kept an unprofitable mine open to save the miners from hardship of unemployment, & this, even to my fierce, jagged Communistic outlook, was a very good deed indeed.'

That June, Robin had been involved in a car accident. He and a friend, a member of the Danish Legation called Torbin de Bille, were driving along the Great West Road in Hounslow when their car ran into the back of a market-garden wagon. M. de Bille's skull was fractured and he died two days later. Robin was deeply cut about the neck. It was the Wednesday of Ascot Week, and Ettie, racing there, wrote to Charley that night. 'I don't think I ever knew quite *how* much your happiness mattered to me. You do not know how sorry people were – some quite indifferent people – nothing else was spoken of. But oh, what the thankfulness is, for after talking to you this evening I really do feel quite comforted and hopeful. . . . But I thought of nothing but you every hour and every moment, and what that waiting must have been, and the drive to London, those awful moments, every one an eternity. I am so thankful. One simply cannot envisage what might have been. Bless you.' Four months later, Ettie's third and last surviving son, Ivo, died after a similar motor accident. He was driving home late one night when the steering went and his head struck a wall. In an agonising echo of his brother Julian's death in 1915, he lingered for thirteen days with his mother at his bedside.

With Robin recovering, Edith was now entering a period of happiness, consolidation and growth. Her already large circle of friends grew wider and more varied. King Alfonso regularly visited Wynyard; once, anxious to see a coal mine, he was taken by the Londonderrys to Seaham Harbour, where they donned overalls and leather caps, and went down the 1,800-

foot shaft of the Dawdon mine that ran out under the sea. Harold Macmillan, usually shy with women, was devoted to her and all their lives they lunched together regularly. Politicians like Balfour, Carson and Churchill, painters like Sir John Lavery and Sir William Orpen, writers like Shaw, O'Casey, Gosse, St John Gogarty, musicians like Rutland Boughton, came to the Ark dinners, usually thirty or forty strong, that still took place every Wednesday. Lord Hugh Cecil wrote often, sometimes on theological subjects ('the Church of England will once more be exhibited to public contempt as having nothing to say which is any use on a great moral issue'), sometimes frivolously. 'My dear Edie: Rouse yourself from your degraded sloth. Cast aside the dilatory self-indulgence that besets you. Realise that on June 29 the sun will be eclipsed totally and that the central line of the eclipse passes over Wynyard and that such a phenomenon happens in Great Britain only once in 200 years!!! Resolve at once that you will be at Wynyard on June 29 and that you will have a party there; that you will ask me to be one and that, hand in hand, each with our smoked glasses, we shall gaze at this rare sight. It happens, such is the tactless selfishness of these luminaries, at 5.30 a.m. or thereabouts. Hateful thought! but once in 200 years. . . . No bath, no shaving, perhaps even pyjamas and a dressing gown. It must be faced. England expects it.'

One of the friends who now drew closer was John Buchan, then at the height of his fame as a historian and best-selling novelist. He came of a Liberal family and most of his friends were Liberals though he eventually entered Parliament (in May 1927) as a Conservative, representing one of the Scottish University seats. He was also a great friend of Ramsay MacDonald. Though he had an idealistic, Puritan streak, Buchan's books were frequently set in the grand houses where so much of the business of the country was discreetly conducted. Half-amused by, half-disapproving of Edith's flamboyance, grandeur and insouciance, he was romantically drawn to the aura of history and tradition emanating from Londonderry House, and fascinated by the glamour of the whole glittering scene. Although he talked of 'Circe's antics', he quickly fell under her spell, coming to stay at Mount Stewart for weeks to help her write the memoir of her father which was published in October 1926. It was Edith's first book, and received generally good reviews although, as she wrote to Charley, 'Harold Macmillan, and I confess myself too, are chuckling over the remarks on Buchan's part "having no literary merit". I know it would have been different had they known it was him and not me.'

She was also responsible for launching into London society a woman who quickly became known for her parties and her eccentricities. This was Laura Corrigan, immensely rich, immensely snobbish, given to malapropisms, kind, generous, well-meaning and unstoppable in her pursuit of social success. Stories about her were legion: she called her house in Grosvenor Square 'my little *ventre-à-terre*', she had a wardrobe of wigs, from a dishevelled one for wearing first thing in the morning through different styles for day and evening to a 'must-go-to-the-hairdresser' one. In the war, when she had generously financed a hospital in France, to which she went for the official opening, she greeted all the wounded soldiers in her abysmal French with '*Dieu te blesse, Dieu te blesse*'; when a man she had placed on her right at dinner, in the belief that he was the Duke of Lancaster, told her he was plain Mr Lancaster, she replied: 'Oh my dear, what a terrible mistake!', shouted down the table 'Who's the next-ranking dook?', and changed their seats accordingly.

Mrs Corrigan had met the Londonderrys through their son Robin. When he visited America, Laura Corrigan's husband James, a steel millionaire, had been kind to him; when, after James Corrigan's death, his widow sold the steel mills, invested the proceeds and came to England, Edith repaid this debt of friendship by introducing her to London society. Such was Edith's prestige and influence by this time that any friend of hers was automatically acceptable.

Laura Corrigan, presented at Court by the wife of the American Ambassador, was now ready to embark on the way of life to which she had chosen to devote her widowhood: the scaling of the highest peaks of London society. Her parties were lavish, famous and original, with cabarets and marvellous presents – it was not uncommon for guests to find a gold Cartier lighter or compact by their plates. Her rule of thumb for this generosity was simple: the grander and more aristocratic the recipient, the more lavish and expensive the present. 'One must always be kind to the poor,' said her rival hostess Lady Cunard. 'It's only Mrs Corrigan who's kind to the rich.' Edith, who did not give a fig for other women's opinions, genuinely liked Laura Corrigan and often had her to stay at Mount Stewart. Mrs Corrigan, who knew what was expected of her, gave freely to Edith's favourite charities.

Edith's friendship with Ramsay MacDonald was now firm-rooted and thriving, and for MacDonald an alleviation of the straitened and depressing circumstances in which he found himself. The loss of his prime-ministerial salary had meant that he reverted to the £400 annual salary of an MP; and the Labour Party could only allow him £800 a year to cover his expenses as Leader. He had had one piece of good fortune: early in 1925 he had received a legacy from a friend which had enabled him to buy for £6,000 Upper Frognal Lodge in Hampstead (now 103–105 Frognal). This impressive twenty-room Georgian house had a large and lovely garden and a panoramic view of London. 'Books everywhere, the home of a scholar and a gentleman,' said Beatrice Webb (for once approvingly). Faced with earning a sufficient income to maintain his house and provide for his family, while simultaneously carrying out the duties of a Member of Parliament and Party Leader, he had to go back to freelance journalism. 'Weekend interruptions devastating to my income. Last week not a penny made. This week will be different – writing an article on Gladstone.'

The strain was appalling and worst of all was the effect on his health, already damaged by the overwork of his premiership when he had held the additional office of Foreign Secretary. At his house-warming party in September 1925 he looked ill and depressed; his diaries are full of references to his chronic exhaustion and lowered vitality. 'To keep up with the business of the House of Commons and *think about it* and work at it, to speak in the country, and even faintly satisfy the demands of the Party, to write every week and enough to keep the house going, it is impossible almost, and means an incessant drudgery with no rest, no gaiety, no lilt in life,' he wrote in April 1927. He summed up his position with a simile that accurately describes the anxieties of the freelance. 'It cannot go on and yet what can I do? I am like a man wading a river, with the water up to his neck and not knowing but that the next step will take him out of his depth.'

His health, his fears that his physical and mental powers were declining and the difficulties of earning a living became a constant preoccupation. 'How tired I am!' he wrote in January 1928. 'My brain is fagged, work is difficult and there is a darkness on the face of the land. I am ashamed of some speeches I have made but what can I do? I have no time to prepare anything. It looks as though it will be harder to make my necessary income this year. I wonder how this problem of an income for political Labour leaders with no or small independent incomes is to be solved. No one seems to understand it. To be the paid servant of the State is objectionable, to begin making an income on Friday afternoon and going hard at it till Sunday night, taking meetings in the interval, is too wearing for human flesh and blood. On the other hand, to live on £400 a year is impossible.' One result was that insomnia, soon to become chronic, was plaguing him. 'Last night surpassed itself for sleepless gloom. Every evil that could happen, happened; and I felt the horrors of it. The machine is not only rattling but rattling ominously.' He was sixty-one.

None of these black thoughts showed themselves in his correspondence with Edith, with its careful gradations of intimacy, from 'Dear Lady Londonderry' to (in 1926) 'My dear Lady Londonderry', from 'Yours sincerely' to 'Yours very sincerely'. They exchanged books ('I am sending to Mount Stewart the "Domestica"') and good wishes, she invited him to dinner to meet the King – but cancelled it when the King had influenza and suggested to MacDonald that he seize the chance of an early night instead – they talked of their Scottish heritage which was so much part of them. 'Sometimes I feel that love of the Highlands which is bred in the bone is almost a disease. Wherever one is there is the almost unreasonable wish to get back there. I find it a perfect nuisance!' wrote Edith, to receive the response: 'We have glorious weather and the land is arrayed in white and glistens like a bride. I have been a long walk by the shore and your native hills on the other side slacken my steps, they were so beautiful in the afternoon light. Why does one go back to London and politics and other dreary pursuits?'

By 1927 the former Labour Prime Minister had clearly overcome any scruples he might have had as to the propriety of a friendship with the leading hostess of the Tory party. 'His thoughts and his emotions are concentrated on his agreeable relations with the men and women, especially the women, of the enemy's camp,' grumbled Beatrice Webb. 'Nor did he want to talk to us about politics – he wanted to talk about old furniture and "Society" personalities.'

The truth was that while his Socialist beliefs were as strong as ever, an evening in Londonderry House was infinitely more agreeable than earnest, austere hours spent discussing the principles of Socialism with trade union leaders. The informality in the midst of grandeur, the ease, charm and gaiety that was Edith's special gift as a hostess, appealed to him powerfully. He was, in addition, fascinated by the literary and artistic scene – he much enjoyed having people like Max Beerbohm to tea at Frognal Lodge – and many of the leading artists and writers of the day frequented Londonderry House. The trifling matter of political differences was quickly disposed of: Edith affected to believe that he was 'a Tory at heart' or, if not, the best and purest kind of Socialist, with whose aim of improving the lot of the poor rather than destroying that of the rich she could readily sympathise; while he resorted to a note of teasing intimacy. 'I am writing this just to tell you that I am so glad that your son and mine [Malcolm] are to be thrown together on a Honolulu trip [a parliamentary deputation]. . . . If your son makes mine a Tory I shall never look with any favour on the name of Londonderry and when I come in I shall forfeit all your heirlooms without a halfpenny of compensation. And if my Left is too strong I shall allow you to be guillotined, though – as I could not bear to see it – I shall turn my back upon the scene. On the other hand, if yours becomes a decent Labour man, I expect to receive from you and your husband your warmest congratulations.'

By 1928 they had drawn closer still, and MacDonald's penchant for high society was causing further rumblings in his Party. In February Edith gave her usual reception for the State Opening of Parliament, with Stanley Baldwin standing foursquare beside her at the top of the stairs. Fragile clouds of yellow mimosa filled all the fireplaces and trailed along mantel shelves, its faint scent rising from huge containers in the hall; Edith wore a black, tight-bodiced velvet dress, and, as usual, glittered with diamonds – the long drop earrings Charley had given her, the family diamond rivière, necklace and tiara. The guest list took up a whole page of *The Times*. She had asked Ramsay MacDonald to bring any colleagues he cared to but the Labour Party, conscious of where the Londonderry fortune came from, took a more astringent view of this splendour than did their Leader. When MacDonald enquired if any of his colleagues would like to come, Arthur Henderson turned to Willy Adamson and asked: 'Well, Willy, would you like to go and see the inside of a coal-owner's hovel?'

Soon there would be another link between MacDonald and Edith. The National Executive of the Labour Party decided that MacDonald's Aberavon constituency was too demanding for the Leader of the Party and Sidney Webb agreed to hand over the safe Labour seat of Seaham to his Leader and went to the Lords as Lord Passfield (Beatrice Webb insisted on still being known as Mrs Sidney Webb rather than Lady Passfield). By now, as MacDonald confided to Sidney Webb in December, he and Edith were on Christian-name terms.

Although Edith continued to fascinate men, there was still no one but Charley for her. 'I had a saucy time in London. My "links" are all too amorous – and I have no love for anyone but you,' she wrote to him in October 1927 and when, in the spring of 1928, he left her halfway through a yacht trip to go back to London her letter from the SS *Ranchi*, off Finisterre, expressed the same adoration: 'I can't begin to describe the pain of parting from you. It eclipsed all else, real physical agony. I hope I shall never have to leave you like this again. It is at such moments as this that the real values assert themselves and my beloved little Mairi almost vanished from my sense. Darling beloved, I do feel so part of you it is cruel to be parted like this. I absolutely and utterly broke down and had to go to bed and even woke up sobbing in the night.' That May he was fifty; in the birthday letter she always wrote she told him: 'I shall never cease to love you more than anyone else in the whole world and I am convinced we shall be together some day, somewhere, always.'

XIX

I N THE General Election of May 1929 Labour emerged for the first
time as the strongest party, winning 287 seats to the Conservatives'
261, while the Liberals achieved a mere 59. The General Strike, the
miseries of the miners and the Trades Disputes Act of 1927 (which
made any repetition of a general strike illegal) had all polarised and
strengthened Labour support. As Robin Castlereagh, contesting Darling-
ton – where he lost by just over 1,000 votes – had prophesied: '. . . the
Conservatives will get it in the neck at the Election. The average voter
in the North has a simple mind. He sees that unemployment and distress
are as bad as ever and that dear old Baldwin with his record majority
has not cleared things up.'

Ramsay MacDonald's handsome looks, bearing and charismatic platform persona may also have helped by appealing to the important new
female vote. The Equal Franchise Act, 1928, had lowered the voting age
for women from thirty to twenty-one. About five million women benefited. In 1929 there were 14.5 million women voters, easily out-
numbering the 12.25 million men voters. Though the Bill's passage was
a foregone conclusion, a strong rearguard action was fought by its opponents, who included men as distinguished as the historian Sir Charles
Oman, Professor of Modern History and MP for Oxford University.
Fourteen years on from Lord Curzon's doom-laden prognostication
about the effect on India of enfranchising women, this argument was
once more brought into play, with a last-ditch plea by the diehard Tory
MP for Enfield, Colonel Applin. 'Among the Mohammedans, women not
only have no voice but are not seen. What will be the effect on the
greatest Mohammedan population of the world of granting the franchise
in this country – the governing country – to a majority of 2.2 million
women over men?' But this time, the response of the House was laughter.

As Labour did not have an overall majority, the Conservatives and Liberals could have combined to form a government. But from the Conservative point of view this would have meant giving the Liberals a disproportionate hand in government, with Lloyd George playing a pivotal role – and Baldwin detested Lloyd George. (MacDonald's opinion of him was little better. '... I have to deal with a man who never, eating your bread or sitting at your table, felt what devotion to loyalty was or who in trouble drew his sword and put his back to a friend's. You must know I refer to Lloyd George. He was born defective,' he later wrote to Edith.)

On 4 June, Lord Stamfordham telephoned Ramsay MacDonald, inviting him to Windsor the following day. Here he was received by the King, who had been ill and was wearing, recorded MacDonald, a 'Chinese dressing gown with pink edges and ground of yellow with patterns in blue and green'. He forgot to ask the Labour Leader to form a government 'but I had kissed hands'. The Baldwins moved to 10 Upper Brook Street, where Mrs Baldwin put yellow net curtains in all the windows to give an air of permanent sunshine.

The King was delighted to see MacDonald back, and their relationship quickly became more cordial than ever. The King's initial fear that on the minor but important matter of protocol and dress a Labour prime minister would refuse to conform had already been laid to rest: MacDonald loved dressing up, given a suitable pretext – or as he put it: 'A pageant is only justified when it expresses the soul and life, the sense of colour and beauty and romance, of the nation.' The King, a stickler for correctness in every aspect of ceremonial and uniform, found that his Prime Minister admired knee breeches, silk stockings, glittering orders and the dazzling jewellery exhibited almost as badges of rank at a state ball. Even the King's reluctance to meet representatives of the Government that had murdered his cousin the Czar (but with which his Socialist Prime Minister sympathised) was successfully accommodated. 'Went down to Sandringham yesterday, and Ishbel and I got genial welcome from King and Queen. Surroundings royal but house totally Victorian in its bourgeois round of unconscious dignity. King talked about our troubles and his. Begged not to be asked to shake the hand of a Russian and in consequence only a chargé d'affaires should be appointed,' MacDonald wrote in his diary.

The new Prime Minister soon received an accolade of a different kind. 'An invitation to enter your ark delights me,' he wrote to Edith on 8 July 1929. 'What ponderings it awakens! Am I to escape the Flood which is sure to come upon this ungodly nation? What am I to be? A bear? A serpent? A wolf (in sheep's clothing or not)? A lamb? What? . . . I am in the midst of a dispatch to a friendly power so I cannot pursue this speculation. . . .' MacDonald became known in the Ark as either Hamish the Hart or Ramsay the Ram, but it was another year before Edith and he were intimate enough to sign themselves as 'Hamish' (Gaelic for James) and 'C', for Circe. For Edith took no notice of MacDonald's playful protests that Circe was a '*wicked* witch. Witches I love. But they should be good and romantic . . . Circe is on the films, in the nightclubs, she is a vulgar jade, a bad egg, a snare *and* a delusion . . . she is in short a hussy. I love snares but not hussies.' Such letters, fanciful, joking, expressive of a growing intimacy and devotion, were the release of a mind that during every other hour of the day had to face doleful news and exhausting decisions.

For the new Labour Government could hardly have got off to a worse start. Prices were rising and so was the unemployment that Labour was pledged to reduce. Just ahead lay the biggest economic catastrophe of the century, beyond anyone's control to avert. On 28 September 1929, MacDonald left on the first visit ever made to America by a British prime minister; it was to discuss naval disarmament and was followed by a two-week visit to Canada. On 23 October, just as he was about to embark for home, the Wall Street crash began. It was the start of months of worry and strain as the country drifted helplessly in a downward spiral of recession.

Edith realised the strain on the Prime Minister and – as this typical note of 20 May 1930 makes clear – she also realised her own role in his life.

'Dearest, I have yours. I hope you won't go into a wilderness "to gnaw my own unhappy and unsettled mind". That is where I come in, although I say it that shouldn't. Time and time again, when you have come here very reluctantly – not that you did not want to come, but felt too disgruntled and tired – it has done you good. I have so much vitality now. I am well aware I do you good!! Now don't laugh – you have often told me you felt better after you have been here. Shall I burst in on you early on Sunday . . . ?'

Soon, he would be the one to comfort her. At the end of July, Millicent's daughter Rosemary, the young cousin whom Edith had always regarded as a cherished little sister, was killed in a plane crash. Rosemary and her husband Eric Ednam (later Lord Dudley) had been entertaining a house party in their villa at Le Touquet; earlier, their seven-year-old son had been killed by a lorry when riding his Fairy cycle and Rosemary was anxious to return home to see how the garden she had designed in her son's memory was shaping. In those days of scanty passenger air services and long, slow journeys in motors that often broke down, private aeroplanes were frequently chartered and Rosemary, with several of her guests, decided to return to England this way. The plane was a German single-engined Junkers owned by an air taxi service and piloted by Colonel G. L. P. Henderson, a well-known and experienced pilot. The plane, flying low in drizzle from thick clouds, exploded in mid-air above Meopham, showering the houses below with golf clubs, handbags, coats and suitcases. Rosemary's brother the Duke of Sutherland and Charley had the melancholy task of identifying her body.

'I thought of you when I read of that terrible accident and saw who was in it,' wrote MacDonald from Munich, where he was on holiday. 'These things seem so cruelly useless, apart from one's personal grief, that one revolts and at the same time feels so impotent. When one thinks of that crushing "no more" the whole world seems to come tumbling down under an earthquake of despair. We must just go on, with the curiosity in our hearts, which beats with a little catch in its breath, when the old Scottish pagan paraphrase of Ecclesiastes hums through our minds "The living know that they must die"'. From now on, like a thread through a tapestry, the air would be a constant theme running through Edith's life; and within three months, MacDonald himself would lose one of his greatest friends in an air disaster.

But this was still to come. Meanwhile, whenever he could, MacDonald chose the air rather than the railways for the 600-mile journey to Scotland or back, much to the perturbation of his Cabinet. His plane would take off and land from a clover field near the old village school of Drainie, where he had once been a pupil and then a teacher. This account of his return from Lossiemouth in August 1930 gives the primitive, risky, casual flavour of early flying. 'His plane was due to land on the usual field near the old Drainie school at 9.30 but was delayed for more than half an hour by mist over the Cairngorms. When it arrived, the Premier put on a warm leather coat, and helmet, strapped on his parachute, and set off.'

A fortnight later the uncertainties of air travel made themselves felt during his return to Lossiemouth prior to spending the weekend at Balmoral. Over Yorkshire the flight had to be abandoned because of a tremendous thunderstorm and they landed at the airfield near Catterick. The next train to Scotland did not run until the following morning, so MacDonald had to stay the night in Catterick. The storm still raged and lightning struck not only the house in which he was staying but his room. Next morning he caught the early train, only to have the engine break down at Newcastle, so that by the time they reached Aberdeen he had missed his connection to Elgin. He finally got to Elgin at 11.30, arriving at Lossiemouth at midday, too late to achieve his promise of opening the flower show (Ishbel deputised). Not surprisingly, he was reported as looking tired and travel-stained. But for him, Lossiemouth was worth the most appalling of journeys, with its quiet evening walks, the faces he had known from childhood, the games of golf played amid beautiful scenery, its very distance from Downing Street.

By now he and Edith were writing to each other regularly. They arranged meetings – 'My dear Ladye,' (his favourite salutation) 'I *have* had a good time with you and you must take this large sheet to symbolise the spaciousness of the thanks I should like to send to both of you for letting me come and have a rare day of peace and happiness. The folks and the place were delightful and I left you as Dugald in the story left the card table to go through the bothersome process of being hung' – she sent him a book of Latin lyrics, a box of the pot-pourri she made at Mount Stewart, and a bolt of cloth, for which he wrote ecstatically from Downing Street.

'I shall strut like a peacock with these feathers on my back. This morning my dressmaker comes to measure me for a new frock. I am now entitled to go to Buck Pal and wherever gay creatures foregather with eppie lets [*sic*] hanging fondly on my shoulders and I am having the appropriate dress made. Wait for the next Londonderry House rite when barn-door fowls are asked to come in cockatoo's feathers. I shall put this lovely and heart-moving cloth under his nose. I shall smell it, stroke it, pat it, hold it out at arm's length, put it against my leg, say "Did you ever before . . . ?" watch him expand, head up, glow with admiration, envy, professional appetite and finally suggest that he should make it up for me. I shall give him infinite trouble about the hang of this coat, the girth of the waistcoat, the droop and fullness of the other garment. He *shall* turn it out to be worthy of its giver and its maker. . . . When next I appear, they will from sheer necessity of appearance address me as "My Lord". . . . The shadow of that gloomy owd John Buchan and his kind lies over this sheet and in awesome (or is it awsome? no it is not) whisper reminds "Timeo Daneos [*sic*] et dona ferentes". I don't Timeo a bit. I just thank you with all my heart.'

Only three weeks later he was writing to her miserably. As a widower, he depended on his friends more than most people but as a natural solitary, the ones he loved were few, and those mostly women. He now lost the man who was possibly his closest male friend, the Secretary of State for Air, Lord Thomson of Cardington.

Christopher Birdwood Thomson had started life as a soldier. His war-time service had included serving for two years as Military Attaché in Bucharest, where he had fallen in love with Princess Marthe Bibesco – later one of MacDonald's greatest women friends. After twice standing unsuccessfully as a Socialist candidate, he was raised to the peerage in 1924 and made Air Minister in the first Labour Government. He was a great believer in lighter-than-air flying machines, using heavy oil as a fuel, and was largely responsible for a three-year scheme to design and build two airships. One, the R100, was designed and built by a Vickers team that included the novelist Nevil Shute and was headed by Barnes Wallis (later to design the Wellington bomber, and the 'bouncing bomb' that destroyed the Ruhr dams). The second was the R101, designed by Air Ministry experts.

By the time Labour returned to power the airships were completed. The Vickers R100 was fuelled by petrol, the R101 by Thomson's choice, heavy oil. On 28 July 1930, the R100 flew successfully from Cardington to Montreal in seventy-nine hours, returning on 16 August after a flight of fifty-seven hours. A flight to India was planned next and, because of the danger of fire, it was decided to use the R101 – heavy oil was safe to use and carry in the tropics. Thomson, whose interest in and involvement with the air had steadily grown in opposition, was determined to make this proving trip on the airship that was the vindication of his beliefs and theories.

The R101 left Cardington at 6.36 p.m. on 4 October. On board her were Thomson, eleven other passengers including the Director of Civil Aviation, and a crew of forty-two. By 2.00 a.m. they were over Beauvais, flying at 1,000 feet in bad weather with a fierce gusting wind that caused the airship to roll badly. Without warning, moments after the watch changed, she went into a dive, losing several hundred feet, and though the crew managed to level her off, she went almost immediately into another dive. This time she buried her nose in the ground and her hydrogen-filled envelope burst into flames. Thomson was not one of the eight survivors (two of whom died shortly after).

MacDonald was shattered. Thomson, who had never married, was a confidant, a supporter, a companion always at his disposal, a true friend allowed behind the wall of reserve the Prime Minister presented to his other colleagues. 'I am lonely and broken and just want to go away and be alone and try to forget what has happened,' he wrote to Edith. 'My devoted friend and companion has gone and I fear suffered. I do not know if you knew that Thomson and I were Jonathan and David. He was so gay when he bade me farewell on Friday. "I shall never let you down" were almost his last words, and they hum in my ears night and day.' The loss of this 'goodly companion who had the magic that resolved the world into an insubstantial thing and enabled us both to rule time and eternity with a cigar and a glass of Waterloo sherry in an easy chair in front of a fire' may have been one reason why he saw even more of Edith when she returned to London that autumn.

She was now an integral part of MacDonald's life. He loved her intelligence, sensitivity and warmth, while her light-heartedness and enterprise appealed to him irresistibly – though he had drawn the line when she had suggested swimming the Serpentine together on Midsummer's Day, dashing off his refusal in the doggerel then so popular. 'I am shocked and I must tune the harp – not of David, God forbid! but of Anna Maria Smith, the patron saint of the upright.'

> Ya! I took you for a lady
> With whom to lunch or dine
> H'instead of which you say ter me
> 'Let's swim the Serpentine'.
>
> I thought ye'd walk out with me
> In silks and nodding plume
> And here ye sez: 'Let's go out
> In a bathing scant costume.'
>
> I ain't a blinking Lansb'ry
> Whose moral sense is crackit
> I'm never seen in public
> 'Cept in trousers and a jacket.
>
> Stern rectitude is in me
> And in this I'm firmly fixed
> And the devil is the father
> Of all bathing that is mixed.
>
> I'll join ye in a charabang
> I'll walk ye in the Park

(Provided ye will meet me
Before it is pitch dark).

A night club that is upright
May be squeezed into my creed
But a MIXED BATH IN THE SERPENTINE!!!
St Columba! I'm d....d.

'I shall blush if the crowned heads let me see you tonight. I shall stammer my embarrassments. I shall be dumb and awkward like a yokel. . . . I am so confused that I do not know if I am Yours Ever, Hamish.'

They saw each other frequently, although the Imperial Conference held that autumn – for which Edith gave a reception – meant additional work for the Prime Minister. He would slip away to Londonderry House for lunch, returning to Downing Street by 2.30, or arrive at short notice for tea and when he could do neither he would write ('Now people come to lunch and I can say no more. I hear the laugh of the Chancellor [Philip Snowden] through the door and the gentle bleat of Mrs S through the keyhole'). Part of her charm for him was that with her he could allow the lighter side of his nature play, without fear of being condemned for frivolity. 'The week has been one party after another and long long days trying to reconcile the irreconcilable and incidentally I win fame as a chairman. Heavens! fame as a lover, as a thief, as a scallywag, that would be precious. A chairman! Like Wolfe, I would have rather written Gray's Elegy than sit in a chair and look the part. . . . How restful is rubbish.'

One reason the Prime Minister wrote rather than, as Edith often did, telephoned was the greater privacy a letter afforded ('This evening there were three journalists in my room when I was speaking to you. Didn't I manage it well?'), especially in the days of the manually operated telephone exchange. Another was that pouring out his thoughts and fantasies upon the page as he sat by the fire at Chequers or Lossiemouth served as the emotional release he often needed so badly. Sometimes his letters, with their occasional uncertain spellings, ran over page after page, sometimes they were mere isolated thoughts, occasionally they were in verse. Here is one forecasting the fall of his Government.

Alas, alas, 'tis only a vain dream
Born of the beauties of a Lossie day
The magic of the whin and broom in gleam
And like a dream 'tis doomed to fade away.

The sunlit earth will shiver into grey
The moment's peace die into lasting care.
Soon will the Tory archers bend their bows,
The Tory hordes wind up a Park Lane stair
And smirk at Circe (how she does 't, God knows).
The world will bow to Mrs Baldwin's plume,
A lonely outcast, I shall dream of broom.

His troubles were increasing. Unemployment had risen from 1.5 to 2.75 million (in America, it had reached seven million). In Germany, where the French refusal to cancel war debts had resulted in sky-high inflation, it reached five million, producing a climate of disintegration where the rise of Hitler would seem almost inevitable. The Depression was now in full swing, and the City was calling for economies, notably a cut in the wages of those paid by the State, and in the dole – both steps anathema to the Party of the People. In March 1931 the Government appointed the May Committee to look into methods of making up the budget deficit for 1932, expected to be £20 million. In the meantime, trade continued to fall and gold to leave the country, while the Party pledged to the betterment of the working man watched helplessly as the tide of unemployment rose and the working man's sufferings increased daily.

For MacDonald it was a miserable time. 'I feel as though I should throw in my hand, so heavy are work and responsibility, so difficult are the conditions, and so worn out is my poor head,' he wrote to Edith in February 1931. 'But a Highlander does not do that. And yet, and yet – it's hard making bricks without straw. You don't know how helpful you are. . . .'

By this time, MacDonald was exhausted. When the Government was attacked in the House of Commons he replied with a speech which, said the *Spectator*, had to be heard to be believed. Unfortunately, began the Prime Minister, 'the ship had only just been launched. The pace was not yet satisfactory but it was increasing. They had to put in petrol, heat up the engine, take off the brakes and take out part of the machinery [it must have been a very odd ship, commented the *Spectator*].' As for the land, said MacDonald, the intention was nothing short of 'recreating a peasant population. The problem was being worked on sympathetically by means of a scientific facing of the problem of production and the handling of such things as go to make a minor breakfast-table – eggs, vegetables, flowers and so on.'

There could have been a cause other than the fatigue which now seemed chronic. Four months earlier, when MacDonald, Edith, Mairi and the artist Brock were driving in the Cairngorms, there had been a curious incident. As Edith described it to Charley: 'We picked up Ramsay at Bullach. He showed Mairi the Trossachs and Rob Roy's grave. We went two and two, I in his, Brock and Mairi behind. Now comes the bad part. About four o'clock, he was telling me all about Samuel when suddenly he spoke exactly as if he were drunk. He could not pronounce his words or move his hand. I thought he was going to have a stroke. Luckily I had my little flask of brandy and poured it down his throat and he got all right as it sent the blood back to the brain. Will you tell this to Tommy [Lord Horder, MacDonald's doctor] and say I think he should always carry a flask. Otherwise when he has these attacks, unkind people would immediately say he was drunk. R. said Tommy told him it was brain anaemia, and he was very exhausted. . . .'

As the economic situation worsened Edith became even more acutely aware of the Prime Minister's suffering. On 2 May 1931, she wrote:

'My dearest H, I feel so worried about you. Shall I come and see you tomorrow morning, or what would you like me to do? You wrote me such a vy charming and dear letter – I cannot bear to think of you worried and wretched. This letter carries all my love to you, and the flowers. Ring me up some time this evening, about 9. o.c. Bless you, and more love from C.'

By now, MacDonald's devotion to Edith was becoming a subject of gossip. When Virginia Woolf met the Prime Minister at a dinner party for six that June, she noticed that he seemed to be completely absorbed by Edith. Beatrice Webb's diary contained a constant undertone of disapproval, emerging in complaints such as: 'Considering that he represents Seaham his friendship with the Londonderrys almost amounts to a public scandal.' Edith, worldlier and more sophisticated than the innocently besotted MacDonald, was well aware that their friendship was giving rise to talk, but the caution she enjoined was brushed aside and turned neatly on its head. 'Promise to let me judge whether accepting invitations from you damages me or not. My fear is that you may be injured among your folks by asking me to sit at your table,' was his response. 'And for harbouring these hesitations as to what people will say are we not fools?' Nevertheless, MacDonald's enjoyment of 'the aristocratic embrace' – as Beatrice Webb's husband, Lord Passfield, put it – was already harming him in the eyes of his own followers.

When Austria's biggest bank, Kredit Anstalt, shut its doors on 18 June

1931 – the French had refused to cancel German war reparations – there was a domino effect all over Europe. By the time the May Committee reported on 31 July it was found that the country's financial state was far worse than had been thought and that the Budget deficit it faced was in fact £170 million. The May Committee suggested raising taxes, reducing the pay of all employees of the State – the armed services, government ministers, judges, the Civil Service and all other public servants – and, crucially, cutting the dole (unemployment benefit), then thirty shillings a week, by 20 per cent. This gloomy report further weakened foreign confidence in Britain, provoking a run on the pound, and unemployment rose to three million. The only solution was to borrow, and the only way to persuade foreign bankers to lend was for Britain to show that she herself was prepared to make stringent economies in order to balance her budget.

On 19 August, with great difficulty and much argument, the Cabinet finally agreed the ratio of new taxation to cuts in social services in a compromise economy package. According to MacDonald's diary, the eleven-hour meeting resulted in grudging majority agreement that the dole be cut by a maximum of 10 per cent. Then, on 20 August, the Conservative and Liberal leaders told MacDonald that they would not stand for more than 25 per cent of these measures in the form of new taxation (the previous year, income tax had been raised from 4s to 4s 6d and supertax increased also). This threw three-quarters of the burden of necessary economies on to cuts in public services and wages – and the dole. The TUC, led by Walter Citrine and Ernest Bevin, was adamant that neither the dole nor the pay of lower-salaried public workers must be touched. It was deadlock.

MacDonald now faced two alternatives, each equally unpleasant. He could either accept the ratio suggested by the Conservatives and Liberals and force these cuts through with their support, thus irrevocably splitting his own party. Or he could resign, in which case not only would Labour lose power but – to MacDonald much more serious – confidence in Britain would be further weakened. Knowing that the crisis point was at hand, he advised the King, who had only just set off for Balmoral, to return to London. On 22 August, the Cabinet were informed that America would not help with a loan unless the dole was severely cut. The Cabinet revolted: if such draconian measures were necessary, let them be enacted by a Conservative Government.

MacDonald now realised that a Labour government could no longer remain in office. On the morning of Sunday 23 August he went to see the King – who had arrived back from Balmoral only two hours earlier – reported the position and said that he feared he would have to resign. The King tried to persuade him to stay. 'He was most friendly and expressed thanks and confidence,' recorded MacDonald in his diary. 'He said he believed I was the only person who could carry the country through.' MacDonald advised the King to send for the leaders of the other two parties to hear their views on who should form a new government.

As leader of the largest Opposition party, Baldwin should have been the first to see the King, but no one knew where he was – he had, in fact, gone to lunch at his club, the Travellers. Thus the first to be received was Sir Herbert Samuel (Lloyd George had had a prostate operation, much more severe and dangerous then than now, less than a month earlier). The King, anxious for continuity and personally fond of MacDonald, wanted him to remain in office; Samuel did not want to see a Conservative administration, and preferred the idea of a coalition, so when the King asked Samuel if he would serve in such a government under MacDonald, Samuel said that he would. Baldwin, eventually located, arrived at 3.00 p.m. at the Palace, where, presented with such a *fait accompli*, he had little option but to say that he, too, would serve under MacDonald.

That night the Labour Cabinet met again. MacDonald, distressed and unhappy, told them of the advice he had tendered to the King: that the Labour Government could no longer carry on and that the King should send for the other two Party leaders and ask their advice on who should form a government. The entire Cabinet placed their resignations in his hands and, at 10.10 p.m., with the words 'I'm off to the Palace to throw in my hand', MacDonald once more left Downing Street for the familiar drive up the Mall. Not surprisingly, the Cabinet were convinced he had gone to resign and, indeed, such was undoubtedly his intention at the time.

But the King was not going to lose his valued Prime Minister so easily. Again he pressed MacDonald to reconsider, telling him that he was the only man to lead the country through this crisis, and assuring him that as Coalition leader he would have the support of both Conservatives and Liberals. MacDonald asked if the King would receive himself, Baldwin and Samuel together the following day so that they could all confer. The King gladly agreed.

At 10.00 on that cold and cloudy Monday morning, the King received MacDonald, Baldwin and Samuel together. The King said that he hoped the Prime Minister would remain, with those colleagues who stayed faithful to him and with the support of the Conservatives and Liberals. Just before noon final agreement was reached, and at midday MacDonald told his astonished colleagues, waiting in the Cabinet Room in Downing Street, that he would be leading a national government, with a 'Cabinet of individuals'. One after another the Cabinet declined to serve in a government propped up by the enemy until by 12.25 the Prime Minister found himself deserted by everyone except an unhappy Snowden, J. H. Thomas and Lord Sankey. At 4.00 he drove yet again to the Palace, tendered his resignation as Prime Minister of the Labour Government, and was immediately invited to form a national government.

MacDonald accepted the King's commission, believing that he was genuinely doing his best for his country and that the National Government had been formed to do a specific job. 'Once that work is finished,' he said in a broadcast the next day, 'the House of Commons and the general political situation will return to where they were last week.'

But the Labour Party did not see his decision this way. To them, it was a treacherous volte-face. They had seen their Leader go to the Palace as they thought to resign rather than compromise the principles in which they all believed. Now here he was, top hat in place, emerging as Prime Minister of what was, in effect, a Conservative government. All their suspicions of his liking for the way of life found among the enemy, for smart clothes, grand houses, aristocratic company, epitomised in his friendship with Edith, now bubbled to the surface. They saw what he had done as a betrayal and as a betrayal they treated it. His colleagues never forgave him and nor did the rank and file: in his own village of Lossiemouth, 'Traitor' was painted on the door of his house, Hillocks. To a man bitterly hurt, feeling himself lonely and isolated, miserable at what he saw as the desertion of his colleagues, Edith's sympathy, support and loving affection were more necessary than ever. Subtly the balance of the friendship had shifted; the Prime Minister, Hamish the Hart, was not only in thrall to Circe, but dependent on her.

XX

A FEW days after accepting the King's commission to form a
national government, MacDonald wrote to Edith: 'I was glad to
have your good wishes and your encouragement in doing what
you can easily understand may have been the right thing but was assur-
edly an unpleasant one. It's done and that's that. And the choirs of the
earth praise me. I am a little weary but not a little buoyant. . . . I shall
take the liberty of kissing your hand when I see you, for have I not
defied all your pet horrors from the TUC downwards? But they have
hoisted the Jolly Roger and shots will soon be whizzing about our ears.
With you in the boat, I shall keep away from port as long as I can, and
what would you say if I ran you in the end ashore on a desert island?'

As the realisation that their leader had seemingly abandoned his Socialist principles overnight sank in, the hostility of the Labour Party crystallised. He had been formally expelled from the Party almost at once and
within a fortnight it was borne in on him that to them he was a dead
man. In a letter starting simply 'My best Friend,' he told Edith: 'The
general opinion among my friends here is that I have committed suicide.
. . . I shall welcome a sight of you again and put on a collar and shirt,
which will hide the hangman's rope now round my neck.' The difficulties
and depression in his private life were matched by the national gloom.
The economic crisis was gathering momentum. At the back of everyone's
mind was the recent collapse of the German mark.

On 10 September, Charley wrote to Edith with justified pessimism. 'I
am afraid the country is not really aware of the crisis. If the pound slips
anything might happen . . . if [it] loses its value we should find the cost
of food something enormous.' He continued with an example which
would not have impressed the Durham miners. 'You will remember the
amount we had to pay in March for our dinner at the Opera in Cologne

and the same thing might easily happen here unless confidence is restored.'

On 21 September Britain went off the gold standard. Three days later, Charley wrote: 'I am very worried about money at this moment. The French exchange has gone badly against us so I expect you will not stay in Paris [Edith was staying with Mrs Corrigan in the latter's palazzo in Venice]. I hope you have got your tickets to bring you here, otherwise they will cost you more. The situation is depressing. The pound's value is getting less and I expect it will go down before it improves. I never thought we should ever really see the pound go.' The King, to share his subjects' troubles, ordered that £50,000 be cut from the Civil List and the Duke of York, whose £25,000 a year was reduced, had to sell his string of hunters. 'The parting with them will be terrible,' he wrote glumly to the Master of the Pytchley.

Charley also was selling horses, though his plan that 'the stud must be scrapped altogether' was not fulfilled. Most of the horses in training, brood mares, foals and yearlings went but a nucleus remained. He was also, he told Edith, going to Ranksborough to 'comb out' the hunters. He concluded: 'I miss you so much but I am glad you are having a good holiday right away from all your bothers and worries, myself being one of them.'

The new National Government needed a clear mandate for pushing through the legislation necessary to overcome the crisis. Although Mac-Donald had agreed on the need for an early election, he was now dubious. 'The political situation is full of currents and counter-currents, reasonable and unreasonable, so how long we shall last I know not,' he wrote to Edith on 8 September, explaining why he could not accept an invitation to come and stay in Venice at the Corrigan palazzo. He was still undecided even by 23 September, mistrusting the Conservatives. 'I am in some doubt as to whether an election is inevitable. Your folks are not behaving too well. The chances they now have as a party are too tempting for them.'

Nevertheless, he asked for a dissolution and the General Election took place on 27 October. His own majority at Seaham (28,000 in 1929) was cut to 5,900 – a figure achieved with Conservative support, thus further identifying him, in the eyes of Labour supporters, with the Londonderrys. Much of this dramatic reduction was due to the efforts of the Webbs, well known in Seaham thanks to Sidney Webb's spell as its Member. As soon as she heard of the Election, Beatrice Webb had written a long letter to the Friends of Seaham, appealing for support for the official

Labour candidate – the Prime Minister was standing as the 'National Labour' candidate – and setting out Labour's view of his behaviour. The crisis was a very simple matter, she said, going on to pour scorn on the American bankers, and concluding with a withering resumé of what was now viewed as MacDonald's betrayal in becoming Prime Minister of a coalition government.

'At noon on Monday, 24 August, the Prime Minister informed his astonished colleagues that he had been asked by the King, and had agreed, to remain Prime Minister, with a new set of Ministers drawn mainly from the Conservative and Liberal Parties. He had taken this step without any consultation with the Labour Cabinet, still less with the Parliamentary Labour Party. Unlike Mr Baldwin and Sir Herbert Samuel, who immediately consulted the Conservative and Liberal Parties, Mr MacDonald never came near the Parliamentary Labour Party, which passed a resolution repudiating any connection with the so-called "National Government" and its policy. . . .

'At this point I wish to make clear that I have no desire to denounce Mr MacDonald. He is a man of charming personality: good to look at and delightful to listen to, with a rare gift of emotional oratory. For all these reasons his joining the enemy is a calamity for the Labour Movement. But as to the result of his actions there can be no dispute. The so-called "National Government" which he has created is acclaimed by the whole of the Conservative Party and newspapers as the one and only bulwark against the spread of Socialism, and against the coming into power of the Trade Union and Co-operative Movements. . . . Within the new Ministry are the most prominent enemies of the Labour Movement, such as Mr Baldwin and Mr Neville Chamberlain. Why should the late Labour Member for Seaham have superseded George Lansbury, as First Commissioner of Works, by the Marquis of Londonderry? I can only observe that, as the Bible says, "Evil communications corrupt good manners".' MacDonald had at first included Charley in the National Government as First Commissioner of Works (Charley had previously held this office in Baldwin's administration between October 1928 and the General Election of June 1929, when it had carried a seat in the Cabinet). In MacDonald's National Government, it was not a Cabinet post.

MacDonald's former opponents, for long his preferred social milieu, closed ranks around him. 'How much happier he was after 1931, when he carted all his old followers and began to breathe freely in the more capacious Conservative air. . . . I saw him sometimes in those early months of the first Labour Government, when London society very wisely decided to take him up rather than ignore him. Defiant at first, he soon took to grandeur and high life and wallowed in it like a man who has been starving all his life,' commented Chips Channon. MacDonald himself held the comfortable belief that, *au fond*, his views and those of his beloved Edith and her coterie were not so very different. 'We are queer folks who agree on practically everything which is fundamental and disagree on so much which is superficial,' he told her that summer. Even the upright and uncompromising Ishbel, thanking Edith for some of her delicious pot-pourri, agreed that 'I too believe we can be friends without besmudging our principles'.

The Election had produced a government that was Conservative in everything but name. The Conservatives won 473 seats – among the Conservative members was Robin Castlereagh, returned unopposed for Down – and other National candidates brought the Government's total strength up to 521 in the new Parliament. The Labour Party mustered only 52 seats.

Four days after polling day, Robin, now twenty-eight, married Romaine Combe, a small, dark, very pretty girl who was a niece of the Duchess of Sutherland and a great friend of his sisters Helen and Margaret. Their wedding had been postponed for a fortnight from its original date of 14 October because of the Election, and they also had to cancel their proposed honeymoon on the Riviera because the new Parliament was convened almost immediately. They were married at St Martin-in-the-Fields, Romaine in ivory velvet, with Margaret, Helen and Mairi among the ten bridesmaids. Dorothé's small son, Robin Plunket, carried the bride's train. Edith gave them, as part of her present, exquisite fine linen sheets in every colour, made near Mount Stewart. The linen industry in Northern Ireland was, like industry all over Britain, suffering from the scourge of unemployment and Edith was doing her best to encourage demand for the fine linens and embroidery made in County Down. From now on, she gave linen as presents wherever possible, often to those whose patronage might advertise its virtues. One was Queen Mary, who accepted 'with heartfelt gratitude' a large collection of fine blue and pink tea cloths and napkins, and suggested, so beautiful were they, that she might order more. Edith, of course, at once offered what she wanted as a present – which may have been in the Queen's mind all along.

Immediately after the Election, MacDonald went down to Chequers. He longed to see his 'dearest Friend' and asked her if she could drive down for a meal and a walk. Saturday was, of course, the day of Robin's wedding but she went down on Sunday. After luncheon they walked in what MacDonald, whose style frequently tipped over into a somewhat effusive sentimentality, later described as 'woods of gorgeous raiment and in a land of serene dignity and graciousness, and you made me forget everything which did not belong to that order of things. I was your attendant g[h]illie.' Edith also enjoyed the walk but for a different reason: five days later it was announced that Charley had been appointed Secretary of State for Air, with a seat in the Cabinet.

Baldwin may have wondered whether the Prime Minister would have the nerve to give Charley a seat in the Cabinet and face the inevitable gossip. It must have been galling for him, with 473 supporters in the House, to see the patronage being exercised by MacDonald, with 12 National Labour supporters. A week earlier Mrs Baldwin had written to Edith: 'It is a bad time for Stanley, who loves his friends, not to be able to give office to those who not only have earned it but ought to have it!' The King, however, fully approved of Charley's appointment. Anxious that all should go well for MacDonald in his invidious position, he felt it would be easier for his Prime Minister if 'the old Gang' [of Ministers] was cleared out. Among those who went were Sir Austen Chamberlain, Lords Crewe, Reading and Peel, and Lord Amulree, the elderly Air Minister, whose speciality was industrial arbitration. The King particularly wanted him replaced by someone younger, more active and who, like Charley, was himself a pilot.

At last Charley had the job he wanted. Earlier that year he had turned down the Governor-Generalship of Canada. In January 1931 Lord Willingdon, the then Governor-General, was made Viceroy of India. The Prime Minister of Canada, Richard Bennett, had met the Londonderrys at the reception Edith had given for the Imperial Conference in the autumn of 1930 and liked them, and the post was offered to Charley. But his opinion of it had not changed since he first disparaged it to Ettie in 1916. Now he wrote to her:

'As you know, I have always been consistent about Canada and Australia and I see no reason for changing my mind. . . . I wrote to the King in a long letter that I could not become a figurehead representative of the sovereign and could only contemplate India in that connection. Edie was even more emphatic about it than I was and was almost indignant at my being asked to succeed the Willingdons. Whether I have acted rightly or wrongly is not for me to say. Acceptance meant being completely extinguished and, by making what would be a real sacrifice, I could not see that I could do very much good or any more than many aspirants for the post could do.... So I have definitely chosen the arduous path of politics here and I believe you will say that if I am not right I am not altogether wrong.' As the new Air Minister, he felt this decision had been well justified.

Edith was now right at the heart of the political world, and Londonderry House a social centre for the new National Government. She gave her now-famous reception for the Opening of Parliament with Ramsay MacDonald in the place of honour at her side and Charley a few paces behind. Receptions during the National Government were held in the afternoon, when men wore morning dress (either a morning coat or, for the old-fashioned, a frock coat). It was thought that evening receptions, with their full-scale magnificence – white ties, tails, orders, decorations and tiaras – were too ostentatiously opulent when so many in the country were suffering real deprivation.

Edith was careful to keep her links with the Baldwin family, at the apex of the Conservative Party with its enormous Commons majority; as well as being Party Leader, Baldwin was Lord President, and lived at No. 11 Downing Street (with the agreement of the Chancellor, Neville Chamberlain). Unlike the Prime Minister, he wrote to her confidently rather than complainingly. 'I'm undoubtedly up against the job of my life to keep the majority happy and to make Ramsay's curiously composite government function. However, I shall do my best and honestly if I can't do it I don't know who can.'

As for the Prime Minister, his relationship with the Londonderrys, and in particular with Edith, was now more notorious than ever, with much speculation as to whether or not they were lovers. He himself told her of a remark he had overheard a Labour MP make about himself in the lobby of the House of Commons only a fortnight after Charley's appointment. 'Yes, a few months ago he sang The Red Flag, but now he whistles The Londonderry Air.'

XXI

RAMSAY MACDONALD'S attachment to Edith reached its height in 1932. A sight of his letters ('I just blush to tell you that I love you more and more and long and long to talk with you') would have convinced the most doubting that he had passed from romantic devotion to full-scale infatuation. He saw or wrote to her almost every day and on most Sunday evenings managed to call in for supper at Londonderry House on his way back from Chequers. His fascination with her looks, intelligence and sparkle, his reliance on her sympathy and moral support, were subtly transmuted from the affection of pure friendship to the more ardent feelings of romantic love. To use Stendhal's evocative metaphor, 'crystallisation' took place. An inner momentum had built up; now circumstances forced the pace.

The year had begun unpromisingly, amid intense diplomatic activity. In January the Japanese had bombed Shanghai, where Britain had enormous interests; and in February the International Disarmament Conference opened in Geneva. In a world which longed for peace, when neither America nor Britain was prepared to consider military action, diplomacy offered the only hope of preventing further such acts of aggression. In the run-up to the Conference, Britain, although militarily weak, could not afford to rearm. American goodwill was essential during the economic crisis, and the Americans were opposed to rearmament.

Charley, as Air Minister, naturally attended the Disarmament Conference. Baldwin led the British delegation as the Prime Minister was ill. Just before the start of the Conference it was discovered that he had a serious eye problem. Throughout the previous November and December the sleeplessness and exhaustion from which he now habitually suffered had been aggravated by appalling headaches. Glaucoma in his left eye was diagnosed and on 27 January he went into 17 Park Lane, a well-

222

known private hospital and nursing home. It had the added advantage of being next door to Londonderry House, whence Edith could visit him frequently.

Her presence enlivened and cheered him; when he was away from her he found he missed her dreadfully. Ordered by Horder to recuperate in the sea air of Newquay, he wrote to her from this quiet Cornish resort every other day, long whimsical screeds that poured out thoughts, feelings, jokes and, sometimes, his fears for her safety. 'I do not want to counsel you to be a coward but do not take up flying as your own pilot. Let others do that. Fly with someone else at the joystick.'

Although he was ill, MacDonald's views on the line Britain should take at the Conference over the Japanese outrage were decided. 'I have in my mind a perfectly clear policy with two guiding points,' he wrote to Charley in Geneva. '(1) the Japanese themselves should know privately exactly what we think about affairs; (2) the affair must be straightened out without bringing us into the conflict; and I might add a third point – we must keep our eye upon our prestige in the Far East and not allow Geneva diplomacy to lower our authority either in China or Japan.'

Charley soon realised that the Disarmament Conference would last for some time – at least until the autumn, he thought; in the event, it dragged on into 1934. He debated taking a house in Geneva so that Edith could come out to him, but then decided that it would be better all round if she stayed at home to run family affairs and be with the girls while he came home as frequently as possible ('a month here and ten days at home'). He was not enjoying himself much: he wrote of the grinding boredom of Geneva and of the rain pouring down so that golf was impossible. 'I long to be at home, hunting with you.' His letters to her usually travelled in the Foreign Office bag, and Edith would then collect them. Frequently they were scribbled in pencil between meetings or before setting off for dinner somewhere. Sometimes he would telephone her but the lines were not very good, and he had to remember that there was an hour's difference in the time.

As the days wore on his old dislike of the subordinate role emerged again. 'I am not liking the second-in-command business, especially as JS [Sir John Simon, the Foreign Secretary] is not altogether easy. However don't express a word of criticism to anyone as I don't want this to get about.' In any event, Edith had to be very discreet: her closeness to the Prime Minister meant that any opinion she expressed might be thought to be his. On 6 March Charley, well aware that Edith was now the Prime Minister's confidante in virtually everything, wrote:

'The Japanese are doing everything they can to upset the applecart. They have not a leg to stand on and the time will come when we have to say so. However, the Cabinet are very coy about consenting to this. I wrote the PM a note about it but only a short and vague one as I had to send it through the post. He is one of the few who understands foreign politics. I should like to take a stronger line than we are taking now but I doubt if we can move the Cabinet in that direction. However, there is time yet. If you see the PM, you can mention this to him, but . . . make him realise . . . we are just maintaining a conciliatory and non-committal attitude. The highhandedness of the Japs must have a bad effect so far as we are concerned on the East as a whole. Peace is all very well but it is not the role of Great Britain to be able to do nothing but plead. You had best say nothing about what I have written to anyone except the PM.'

MacDonald was now sixty-seven and, though both Edith and Charley were worried about his health, they hoped that a long rest would restore him. Charley in particular was anxious for his presence. 'I presume the PM will be escaping from his prison soon and then there will be no holding him. I am quite sure he will have to play a very big part in this conference, and you must impress upon him the necessity of getting really well for it because he is the only person I believe who really understands foreign politics.'

But the recuperation was to take longer than anticipated, and the weeks of enforced solitude and idleness, with little other purpose or distraction, had made him more than ever dependent on Edith. Weakened by illness, heading a government whose very elements promised strife, the Prime Minister was emotionally in a vulnerable condition. He was lonelier than ever: the knowledge that his former colleagues despised and disliked him had cut this sensitive, honourable man to the quick; his children, with whom his relationship was excellent, were grown up, pursuing their own careers or marrying. In any case, his intensely romantic nature demanded objects of worship, be these in human form, ideals to aspire to or, like his view of a distant, mythic Highland past, cherished visions locked away in some secret mental shrine.

As the months passed, the subtle shift from *amitié amoureuse* to romantic adoration continued. Back in 17 Park Lane for a further operation on his eye in May, MacDonald wrote Edith a much-quoted letter after she dropped in to see him on her way to a Court that evening. 'You were very beautiful and I loved you. The dress, dazzling in brilliance and glorious in colour and line, was you and, my dear, you were the dress.

I just touch its hem and pray for your eternal happiness, wondering at the same time what generous-hearted archangel ever patted me on the back and arranged that amongst the many great rewards that this poor unwelcome stranger to this world was to receive was that he would be permitted before he returned to his dust to feel devotion to *you*.' Underneath he wrote: 'This you will burn.'

It is easy to understand the ageing Prime Minister's infatuation. Edith in her early fifties had the naturalness of complete assurance, she was funny, vital, gay. Her physical allure was considerable: her skin was still fresh, her energy immense and she was extraordinarily youthful-looking. 'You *did* look young yesterday, and so well,' the devoted MacDonald told her at the beginning of that year. He was not the only one who thought so. 'My Lady, you are a freak!' remarked the Londonderrys' head groom, staring at her one hunting morning. She looked magnificent on a horse, riding side-saddle in a superbly cut habit that made the most of her excellent figure and erect carriage. Edith, true to form, merely laughed. Nor did a more formal setting extinguish this vivid quality. That summer, staying with the King and Queen at Windsor, her youthful appearance was so remarked on that fellow guests and the Household teased her with the running joke that she was 'coming out' the following year, a compliment she dismissed in private ('It is not difficult to look and feel young in this crowd of aged hags').

There was also the fact of her position in the highest circles of Court and aristocracy, the pageantry of which struck such a responsive chord in MacDonald's romantic heart. As Marchioness of Londonderry she was cloaked in an aura of prestige, history and aristocratic achievement; around her was the rarified atmosphere of great wealth. She knew everyone who was worth knowing, and everyone who was or aspired to be anyone passed through the doors of Londonderry House. When she stood at the top of its famous staircase, hung about with ropes of pearls and glittering with diamonds, she was a dazzling figure. All in all, if she set her mind on something, or someone, few could resist – certainly not MacDonald.

What Edith wanted was the Prime Minister as an intimate friend. Friendships are seldom completely straightforward and hers with the Prime Minister undoubtedly involved several strands. For years all her closest friends had been men and the whole concept of deep friendship between a man and a woman was to her entirely normal. Her letters to him are warm, devotedly affectionate, supportive, often loving – but never for one moment do they transgress the invisible bounds of decorum. 'If there is any chance of seeing you on Sunday next, after 5 p.m., I would come up, with Charley.'

She had liked MacDonald from the moment she met him – after the Labour Government had lost power in 1924 she was the one who took the lead in establishing a more lasting link – and she was deeply and sincerely fond of him. He was, after all, a man very appealing to women and he was one of the very few with whom she could share the passion for the Highlands, the longing to return there, that was so much part of her; as she wrote to him, 'this . . . you and I know and understand and share together'. Sometimes she fell into exaggerations of friendship that must have gratified the streak of vanity that lay beneath MacDonald's surface puritanism. 'However eminent you may be – and you are – yet you are the most human, lovable human being I have chanced to meet on this glorious earth.'

For a woman like Edith, situated at the pinnacle of Society, personally magnetic, already a social legend and able to command the presence and the allegiance of almost anyone she wanted, there were few challenges left. To have the Prime Minister at her feet must have been profoundly satisfying. Edith loved power, both because it was central to her concept of her own life and for Charley's sake. From the moment when she had used her charm and influence to try to keep Charley safe in the war, she had endeavoured to help him in every way she could. She had furthered his cause by making Londonderry House an unofficial centre for Conservatives, and by entertaining senior politicians with established reputations and rising young ones. With MacDonald under her spell, she could be more effective than ever.

She also loved power for its own sake. She was used to that most insidious of drugs: a position near the heart of things. She was the daughter of a politician who was a close friend of the Royal Family: knowing what was going on, being privy to the thoughts of government ministers as well as to the gossip of political circles, Court and Society, had been part of her life since her childhood. MacDonald's confidences on the day-to-day events of Government fascinated her, and by now they were coming thick and fast. He wrote to her constantly, from No. 10, from his study in Lossiemouth after dinner, or scribbled notes in pencil as he waited to play golf for the first time ('I could not go a whole round. . . . These operations weaken one more than one knows and I could not see the ball very well through darkened spectacles').

When, at last fit enough to travel, he left for the opening of the Lausanne conference (on German reparations) in June, the flood of letters continued. Even before he arrived there – with the Foreign Secretary, he had broken his journey in Paris for talks with their French opposite numbers – he was telling her of a change of heart by the Foreign Secretary ('Charley had better say nothing about this to our colleagues until we report ourselves'). But chiefly notable were the love and longing such letters expressed. 'I shall never see these places [Versailles, the Petit Trianon] unless I am alone or with one other person who is not likely to come. . . . I am well, naughty, and so terribly fond of you that I ought not to tell you how much. I only wish that there were lady Cabinet Ministers and that they (e.g. she) were on the Lausanne delegation. . . .'

While the Prime Minister was away Edith was involved in a serious car crash. On 19 June she had been dining with her cousin Geordie, the Duke of Sutherland, now living at Sutton Place. She had been driven there by another of her admirers, the Marquis Alphonse ('Fono') Pallavicini, First Secretary at the Hungarian Legation, who often escorted her when Charley was away. Coming back, just after they had turned into the Kingston bypass, they saw a Green Line coach coming towards them on the wrong side of the road. Fono twisted the wheel to the left and jammed on the brakes, but the coach smashed the right-hand lamp and mudguard and broke the right axle. Edith's head hit the windscreen and her left thumb was broken. She reassured an anxious MacDonald with a cheerful description of her injuries. 'I have three stitches in my scalp and they have shaved a bit off like a monk. It looks rather like the remains of an old rook's nest. Altogether what with bloody eyes and bruises I look most interesting.'

This unappetising description did nothing to dampen MacDonald's ardour. The letters continued, many – with an echo of Asquith scribbling away to Venetia Stanley during Cabinet – written during the tedium of endless speeches in foreign languages he did not understand. By the end of the summer of 1932, the Prime Minister was showing all the symptoms of an infatuation that bordered on obsession. He dreamt of Edith at night and he thought of her during the day. He daydreamed that she was talking to him or listening to him, that she was sitting beside him when he was alone at supper; when he was out walking in the hills he imagined her appearing over the horizon on a horse and galloping up to him.

He confided to her his worries, his increasing adoration of her, his longing for Lossiemouth and the simple life. He told her she was beautiful – always there is some flattering adjective attached to any mention of her person: 'your graceful fingers', 'I am pulling your comely leg'. He expressed worship ('I am the inferior one and shall remain so because I love you'). He asked for her photograph so that he would at least have that in Lossiemouth, and its arrival is the occasion for a positive spate of whimsical conceits ('I left someone in Lossiemouth asleep in lavender and musk and roses who I must just visit and kiss that a blush may warm her cheeks and her heart may stir in her slumber'). He reminisced about the first meeting with the beloved. 'I wonder what prompted the monarch to send us a command to put everything aside and go that evening to the Palace, sit by each other, rise with a sigh and depart, hoping that we might meet again. I laughed right to the centre of my heart when you told me once that I rose from the table having seen no vision!'

The faithful John Buchan attempted to prevent MacDonald becoming too involved, reminding the Premier where his duties lay and staying physically as close as he could to his friend. Often he would accompany MacDonald and his small black Highland terrier on their regular pre-breakfast walk in St James's Park, remaining vigilant in Downing Street afterwards. But Buchan's puritan conscience, and the strictures of Beatrice Webb, stood little chance against the flattery implicit in Edith's sentiment that: 'I tremble when I consider how many precious half hours of yours I have wasted – yet not wasted, because I have derived untold good from them.'

In August, back in Lossiemouth after staying at Mount Stewart during the first week in August, he sent her a love poem.

> Last night I went to see the moon
> Her golden path of glamour trace
> Across the lough – I saw no moon
> But just my lady's face.
>
> Last night I went to see the stars
> Bejewel night and flame the skies.
> But ah! I never saw the skies
> But just my lady's eyes.
>
> Last night I went to see the land
> Mysterious lights and shades of elf.
> In darkened sleep I saw no land
> But just my lady's self.

In September, he wrote quite simply '. . . the silly fact is that I love you. Isn't it a nuisance?'

The 'nuisance' of loving Edith was a motif that returned often. Her image came between him and sleep or distracted him from work, he could not see her as often as he wanted – and he knew perfectly well that this was a situation impossible of resolution. Yet for a man accustomed to lead, to occupy a solitary height, to present an immaculate public front, there was an immense relief in dropping his guard and appearing what he so often felt himself to be: a weak and fallible creature. Coupled with his natural tendency to place on pedestals the women about whom he felt romantically, this resulted in more than a touch of self-abasement. 'You say, "Tiresome creature, why this inferiority complex?" Why? Because I am a devotee. Do you think I can go up to you with a brazen face and treat you as an equal? Can a nice, properly-feeling blade of grass kiss the spring of refreshing water – the water that makes it happy and see visions – as an equal? No, its heart makes it tender; it approaches slowly and with glowing reverence; its kiss is worship ... I am the inferior one and shall remain so because I love you. ...'

Were they lovers? London gossip often made them so but this is almost certainly not the case. Though one of Edith's letters, filled with political chitchat, concludes 'Do, dearest, let us try and meet soon. I do want to see your dear self, and to hold your hand', that is probably all they did. Everything known about either of them points to the conclusion that physical love was not part of the bond that linked them. The Prime Minister was nearly seventy, in failing health, a sufferer from chronic fatigue and insomnia, recently recovered from two eye operations and a man who had already had what appeared to be one small stroke in Edith's presence, and it is unlikely that this was an isolated occurrence. His upbringing had been strict and moral, his keen sense of honour would not have allowed him to seduce anyone's wife, let alone the wife of a Cabinet colleague – especially as at the same time he was frequently writing in friendly fashion to Charley. He was in any case well aware of the complications that could follow upon such involvements. 'Every day in my life I have to remember that all Party leaders have had difficult colleagues and that they have had to keep a close eye upon les femmes,' he had written in his diary only a few years earlier. More telling still was the knowledge that he could express his feelings in perfect safety, knowing that they would not be misinterpreted and that there was no chance that Edith would either misconstrue his declarations as an avowal of passion or respond to them as such.

For Edith, as MacDonald was perfectly well aware, principle and inclination followed the same course. Her strong religious sense and unswerving passion for her Charley had meant a steadfast faithfulness even during the difficult earlier years when to seek consolation elsewhere would have been understandable; now, her marriage was once more a true partnership, her own devotion undimmed and her faith no less strong.

It was the very freedom from the guilt both would have felt over an illicit affair that allowed them to express their feelings so freely. Yet when Edith concluded one of her letters: 'My very fond love to you, you dear and great soul. I love you very much and admire you more', it was merely the spontaneous, if highly coloured, expression of a devoted friend. But when MacDonald told her: 'I live by hope and love', it was nothing less than the exact truth.

XXII

T HE YEARS 1931–5 were a plateau of fulfilment and content for both Londonderrys. They were busy and involved; they had the friendship of the Prime Minister; their place was at the hub of the wheel – Lord Hailsham flatteringly told Edith she had become the *via media* of the Cabinet. Their life together was established, their partnership secure and unshakeable, built on deep, unbreakable friendship, continuing attraction and the shared memory of great passion. As Edith told Charley, 'No one can rob us of what we have once had. We have it for ever and will always.' Even Eloise, once so potent a threat, had finally been reduced to a peripheral figure.

Staying with Laura Corrigan in her Venetian palazzo in the autumn of 1931, Edith had unexpectedly encountered the woman who had once so nearly wrecked her marriage. 'Last night Laura had an immense party, 65 to dinner. Alice Wimborne was here, Norah Lindsay, Hugh Sefton, Helen Fitzgerald and last but not least, Eloise. I heard she was longing to make it up and I went straight to her and said: "Do let us say How do you do, as I know Laura is just going to introduce us." She was delighted, and we met as if nothing had ever happened. I thought this would amuse you.' Charley, for whom any amusement must have been tempered with relief at not being there, was next regaled by the news that his former mistress was giving a party for his wife: Eloise, thrilled at Edith's public gesture of forgiveness, was now metaphorically gambolling round her like a puppy. 'All day yesterday she was quoting me to other friends and saying "Edie L told me this and said that".' Edith concluded the episode by explaining Eloise's new meek behaviour in hormonal terms. 'I think she has had the change of life. They [Americans] age earlier than we do.'

The family's usual routine had been to spend the summer at Mount

Stewart, leaving for Scotland and stalking at the end of August until the middle or end of October, when they returned to London for the Opening of Parliament. From November to March, they hunted from Ranksborough, where Mairi and her governess lived. Edith and Charley and their older daughters came down to hunt at weekends and whenever else they could manage. Christmas was spent at Wynyard, where the family also went in May, for Stockton races.

Now, even for Edith and Charley, money was getting shorter. In 1925 Charley's total assets were valued at £2,625,842 18s 6d;* by the end of 1931, when the Depression had bitten, they had dropped to £1,855,180 6s 4d. Londonderry House, with its grand parties, swallowed up £12,469 13s 3d that year. Outgoings on the Welsh property Machynlleth were £4,599 in 1931 and on the lodge at Loch Choire only £47 15s. Wynyard, the main Londonderry place, huge, immensely grand and cold – tons of coal were burned every week, with relays of footmen carrying coal scuttles to all the rooms – was disproportionately expensive at £7,649 for the few weeks it was opened up each year.

Ranksborough, used during the whole of the hunting season, was only a few hundred pounds more expensive at £7,982 – which included the keep of the string of hunters and the wages of the grooms. Both Edith and Charley had hunted all their lives and giving up their favourite sport was unthinkable. Edith did suggest shutting Ranksborough, lending some of their horses to friends until times improved, and staying with friends to hunt. Her idea of defraying expenses with paying guests was dismissed as too complicated ('they will need managing') as was Charley's of letting Ranksborough, since £500 was all they could expect for the season. Finally, it was agreed that keeping it empty with only a few horses fit would be the most satisfactory solution.

Mount Stewart cost most to run – £14,879 in 1931– because the family was now spending most of its time there. As Charley said, in these hard times the best way to economise was to have one establishment instead of keeping up several. Edith asked nothing better. 'I do love this place so deeply. I feel as much at home as in the Highlands. The view of sunset was quite lovely, all gold and opal and deep purple. It is indeed the land of Heart's delight.'

Mount Stewart in the thirties was a wonderful place to stay, welcoming, grand yet informal, with its lofty, octagonal hall, its pillars and statues. A magnificent Stubbs, *The Hambletonian*, had been brought over

* According to the accounts at Wynyard.

from Wynyard to hang on the landing at the top of the stairs; there were chairs from the Congress of Vienna and shelf upon shelf of the great Castlereagh's papers which Laura Corrigan had had bound in exquisite pinkish calf as a present to Charley. The characteristic scent of flowers mingled with the spicier smell of Edith's pot-pourri, made with whole flowerheads of delphiniums, roses and carnations dried rapidly over low heat, and the lavender that she sold (for charity) for 5s for ½ lb.

Animals were everywhere. All her life Edith was surrounded by animals and the dogs alone numbered a dozen – two or three Irish wolfhounds, the lurchers she had just begun to keep, a small pack of Pekineses that followed her everywhere, Mairi's little dachshund, Tommy, last representative of generations of wire-haired dachshunds, and Charley's bull mastiff.

The house was always full. Every summer Londonderry grandchildren came for long visits – Michael and Kathryn Stanley, Robin's two little daughters Jane and Annabel – both of whom were christened at Mount Stewart – and Dorothé and Teddy Plunket's small sons. The grandchildren, who called Edith and Charley 'Mamma' and 'Papa', found Charley kindly but remote, Edith the source of fun, enjoyment, treats but also, to a child, an awesome figure. 'Absolutely the most formidable person in the world,' remembers one. 'Even when our parents were there Mamma was the one you obeyed. I longed and longed to please her.' At Christmas there would be a play, often written by Mairi, acted by any visiting children and the house party. One constant feature of these plays was 'The Londonderry Air', sung by Mairi.

Edith's brother and sister came to stay, with their children, so did Prince Henry, asked over for Helen or Margaret, and the Spanish royal family, with Prince Juan, the two Infantas and two Bourbon cousins. Members of the Ark appeared regularly (one rode a horse up the stairs), so did writers – James Stephens, Osbert Sitwell, Harold and Vita Nicolson, Compton Mackenzie and W. B. Yeats. Ramsay MacDonald flew over from Scotland, Shane Leslie, bedecked in his saffron kilt, would turn up without warning from Castle Leslie in County Monaghan, and there would always be an elderly dependent or two over for a holiday (their fare invariably paid by Edith). There was always a piper in the house or someone who could play on the harp the old Scottish airs Edith loved.

There were bridge tournaments and *thés dansants*, or riding, tennis, golf and swimming – Edith had designed a pool between the house and the Lough shore, sheltered by trees and shrubs, and fed by salt water from the Lough. Here, on hot afternoons family, their cousins and friends would swim and picnic, brewing tea and cooking sausages on a stove in one of the cabins as the day drew into evening. Favoured guests, especially the young and pretty, might be strapped into Charley's open biplane and taken up for a spin, winding up with looping the loop above the Lough.

Flying was very much part of the family's life – Edith, who had her first flying lessons in 1933, was the only one who did not achieve a pilot's licence. At the beginning of 1932 Charley had made a landing strip from two of the fields beside Mount Stewart and from here he regularly flew himself to England, landing at Heston or, occasionally, Northolt. In 1934 he built the airfield at the nearby town of Newtownards.* All through the thirties he had two aeroplanes, one small and single-engined, the other larger and twin-engined that could take several passengers. The first small ones were Gypsy One Moths, with their three seats one behind the other – after getting out you folded up the wings and tied up the rudder – on which his daughters learned to fly; after these came Avro Cadets and finally a De Havilland Hornet Moth (which he still flew after the Second World War); the larger ones were first a four-seater Monospar and later a six-seater Percival Q6.

Most of all, though, there was sailing, which all the Stewart family adored. For Edith, sailing had something of the physical challenge and excitement of hunting, and a freedom and informality of its own. Both she and Charley had River Class boats. These, rather like smaller six-metre yachts, were eighteen feet on the water line, drew four feet and had Bermuda rig, jib and spinnaker. The original two, built on the Clyde, belonged to Lord Bangor and John Andrews (a former Prime Minister of Northern Ireland); by the thirties there were eleven of them. All summer long, on Wednesday evenings and Saturday mornings, there were River Class races on the Lough, for a points prize awarded at the end of the season. Edith, Charley, Helen, Margaret and sometimes Mairi would race the two Mount Stewart boats, lending them to friends to compete for the prize when they were away. In racing too Edith had her own idiosyncratic style: often Lord Bangor, as the Yacht Club's president, had to dispatch a firm letter. 'Dear Edith, I am afraid you have missed out on the rules again. You did something quite dreadful yesterday. . . .' But she seldom paid much attention.

Presents were a great feature in Edith's life. The Aga Khan sent her mangoes, George Robey dispatched first night tickets, Sir Austen Cham-

---

* It still belongs to Lady Mairi Bury.

berlain sent her his small book on how to make an alpine garden, urging her to create one. Laura Corrigan would arrive with some lavish present: one year, for Edith's birthday, a shooting stick, an Elizabeth Arden beauty case and a Cartier wristwatch (Edith had to have its gold bracelet strap taken in to fit her 6½ in wrist) were followed by a Christmas present of a gun. 'What a pretty bag, Aunt Edie,' remarked a young cousin another day, picking it up and then gasping at the weight. 'Yes,' said Edith, laughing. 'One of Laura's little tricks – real gold handles, you see.'

Her own presents, which she sent at Easter as well as at Christmas and on birthdays, were carefully chosen. Her cousin Alastair's ten-year-old daughter Elizabeth opened her Easter egg to find a long-desired camera; another time everyone got cashmere sweaters with specially designed collars that could be worn open or buttoned up into a polo neck. Godchildren received Bibles and prayer books at their confirmation. Every present was invariably accompanied by a letter, written during the two hours that she devoted to her correspondence every day. She regarded her family as a clan, and to many of her relations Londonderry House was like a second home.

Her kindness was always practical – the Rolls sent round to take someone to the doctor, the money 'loaned' to help someone over a sticky patch, an introduction to her friend Harold Macmillan for Sean O'Casey, with the result that Macmillan's published all his plays and other work in England.

Frank herself, she never minded plain speaking from others. One young girl she had taken out sailing listened incredulously when the boathand said: 'Yer suttin' on the main sheet! It's under yer backside, m'lady.' *My* mother would have seen him off in an instant, thought the young visitor, but Edith merely laughed and remarked: 'Oh dear, am I?' Harmless though such a remark sounds today, it was unusual in an era when servants, like children, were supposed to be seen and not heard, and when even the liberal-minded Virginia Woolf treated servants as another species ('I stepped past the dreary slut soaping the front doorstep'). But though never offended by well-meaning bluntness, she was insistent on good manners. No one could be as crushing when she wished, and few risked a second rebuke. When a debutante at one of her dances stubbed out a cigarette on the thigh of one of the Canova nymphs, Edith stopped the band, walked across to the cringing girl and said in the distinct voice that carried to every corner of the room, 'Now, my dear girl, while the music has stopped let me find you an ash tray.'

The Londonderry scale of living demanded a large staff. There was the Comptroller, the Groom of the Chambers, the butler and the under butler, three footmen, Edith's footman and piper, the nursery footman, an odd man and a night watchman. The Head Housekeeper and the Housekeeper ran the staff; in the kitchen there were cook, head kitchen-maid, two other kitchenmaids, scullery maid and stillroom maid; three housemaids, a nursery maid, a schoolroom maid and various daily women kept the house clean; the Travelling Head Housemaid went ahead of the family to prepare whatever house they were going to; and there was a telephonist and a hospital nurse. (Young or impoverished guests, glumly noting the number of servants, were relieved to find the small notices in all the Mount Stewart bedrooms saying 'No tips allowed'. What the servants thought of this ruling is not recorded.) Charley and Edith each had a secretary. Charley had a valet and Edith a lady's maid, and Margaret and Helen shared another. Mairi had a governess. There were four chauf-feurs to drive the four cars, and what would now be called a minibus to take the servants into Belfast or Stockton – Charley was worried that they might feel isolated. Charley and Edith each had a Rolls-Royce; Edith, who had first learned to drive in 1902 when she had had a Delage, liked to be driven very fast and for safety's sake designed herself a precursor of the seat belt, an idea which she had adapted from the safety straps holding a pilot in his seat.

Edith herself was never idle. Practical, active, energetic and a natural leader, she was chairman of the Red Cross, sat on the Bench and was on various local committees. Her sitting room was always piled with papers, correspondence, gardening books, diagrams of some part of the garden, an article she was writing; she filed, catalogued and planned her planting or sat in the window of the drawing room sorting seeds and bulbs; and if she had a spare moment she picked up her embroidery. She was an exquisite needlewoman, stitching tapestries, doing crewel work on pel-mets and curtains, working a bedspread for Mairi's bed or sometimes for her friends. 'Ten thousand thanks for the lovely fox cover,' wrote Sir Philip Sassoon (his Ark name was Philip the Fox). 'It will be my refuge on cold and stormy nights, my only dread that the Bitch pack may draw it some day blank, which would be a dreadful humiliation. It is additionally precious as it was worked by your own fair hands. . . .'

At the beginning of the thirties she was more occupied than ever. As the Depression bit deeper she had begun to wonder what she could do to help. Her social conscience was invariably stirred by anything she saw at first hand and, as many of the hardest-hit parts of the country were in the north, she must have seen pitiful examples of wretchedness on her visits to County Durham. For years, she had been promoting the local industries of linen and lacemaking around Mount Stewart, where she ran an embroidery school, but the depressed areas needed more direct help. With Lady Reading, Lady Peel and other friends she formed the Personal Service League, of which the chief aim was to make or give, and then distribute, the clothing that the unemployed could no longer afford to buy. Edith herself was chairman, president and moving spirit.

As she had done in the days of the Women's Legion, she used every line of influence open to her – including, this time, her unique relationship with the Prime Minister. He was off for his annual visit to Balmoral; would he ask the Queen if she would be their 'patroness'? It was a move typical of her natural tactical sense: though on extremely good terms with the Queen and perfectly capable of writing to her direct, by using MacDonald she was making it clear to the Royal Family that the scheme had the blessing of the Prime Minister – a prime minister, moreover, whom the Royal Family liked and admired.

Within a few days, MacDonald was able to reply that the Queen would indeed be patroness as long as the League was both completely dissociated from politics and prepared to work with existing agencies such as Toc H, the Salvation Army, the British Legion and the Docklands Settlement. MacDonald added that for his own part he thought the League's committee was 'over-classy' – few were without a title – and not strong enough. Edith agreed by return, tactfully suggesting that Ishbel should be one of those who lent her weight to the committee.

Edith's insistence on efficiency and commitment meant that the Personal Service League grew rapidly. Even so, as she pointed out in a memorandum sent to the Prime Minister on 19 February 1933, after touring the north of England, it merely scratched at the surface of its own limited field. 'Tyneside, Tees-side and parts of Wearside are in a really destitute condition ... the distress is on such a vast scale and clothing, especially boots, so badly needed that present measures are totally inadequate.'

She saw no prospect whatever of unemployment decreasing, she continued. 'On the contrary, in some districts it has become chronic. ... It appears to me essential to work out a carefully thought out plan for the unemployed women themselves to be taught to make the garments at the various Depots. Not only will this provide occupation but they will learn to sew and to mend which has apparently not been taught either at home or in the schools. ... I consider the time has arrived when materials will have to be provided free to all our Depots in the really distressed areas. There will of necessity have to be paid instructresses in certain Depots.' She concluded by describing an example, in Berwick, of what she had been suggesting. 'The local branch of the Women's section British Legion and the Unemployed Men's Club have combined with the PSL. The wives of the unemployed men are making their own and their families' clothes and the men are making boots with leather provided from the local PSL funds. I propose to get in touch with Captain Ellis of the National Council of Social Service immediately to discuss with him how best we can co-operate and deal with the situation.'

Captain Ellis was enthusiastic and suggested giving the Personal Service League a substantial grant. MacDonald deputed Tom Jones, the Assistant Secretary of the Cabinet, to co-ordinate the efforts of the National Council of Social Service and the Personal Service League; in his diary, Jones left an acidulous little portrait of Edith. '...I saw her Ladyship in Park Lane. The butler took me up in a narrow lift to a study or boudoir in the roof of the house and I had half an hour or 40 minutes with her Ladyship, who talked at me about starving and dying children, ordered cocktails, phoned to a servant to take the dogs out for their exercise, demanded to know what Ellis and his Council were doing about it ... all with a ceaseless volubility and an attempt to charm and hypnotise which entirely failed in its object. She is 54 and still handsome and a few years ago must have been extremely so. She is perfectly dressed and I am sure means well.'

Two days later there was a meeting at which the positions of both sides became increasingly polarised; Captain Ellis, unfortunately, was away at the time. 'Dr Jones and Miss Joan Fry of the NCSS stressed that they thought that teaching of dancing and physical exercise and shelters where the unemployed could have reading parties were really of as much importance as clothes and food,' recorded Edith. 'The cleavage of opinion between Dr Jones and Lady L is that Lady L considered that food and clothing are the really vital necessities of the moment and that the unemployed women should be employed in making the clothes and learning to cook. Dr Jones and Miss Fry hold that food and clothing is a matter for the State: it is their business to make it possible that these things should be supplied through increasing the dole or by other means.' Again, Jones jotted down his impression of Edith: 'agitated and overwrought, kept "scrambling eggs" with a pair of gloves, hiding and revealing fingers blazing with diamonds'.

After this, the attempt to meld charitable effort and State welfare failed. Edith, always quick to grasp the essentials of a situation, told the Prime

Minister that she believed 'if I gave up being President, the NCSS would be far less antagonistic. . . . I have made my effort and that's that.' But although the Personal Service League foundered, even Jones admitted during its short life that what it did 'it does with much success'.

At the same time that Edith was throwing her energies into the founding and work of the Personal Service League, Charley, as Air Minister, was busier than ever. It was a curious paradox that someone more akin to the eighteenth century in demeanour and instinct should be such a passionate advocate of the newest and most technological invention yet – except, perhaps, that the challenge to skill and courage that flying then represented was in the direct Corinthian tradition. He believed passionately in the future of the Royal Air Force, he was enthusiastic, knowledgeable about the technical aspects of flight, and appreciated the problems and potential of both military and civil aviation. It was a pity that his Under-Secretary was Sir Philip Sassoon, a great friend and Park Lane neighbour, but in the eyes of many a lightweight figure not dissimilar to Charley himself – rich, famous for his possessions, and a constant and lavish host – though this drawback might have been overcome had Charley been a professional politician and prepared to bend with the wind.

As it was, the seeds of difficulties to come were already sown. From the beginning of the Disarmament Conference irreconcilable differences of opinion had emerged, especially in that which concerned Charley: the question of bomber aircraft.

In 1923 Britain had begun a programme of aircraft building designed to result in fifty-two squadrons by 1928, but only forty-two of these had been equipped by the time the Disarmament Conference began in February 1932 – and no further squadrons were planned. Baldwin, virtually in control of the Government, was implacably opposed to expanding the Air Force. On 4 May 1932 he had spoken in Cabinet of how he 'had been impressed with the appalling consequence of a future war conducted from the air' and that he therefore believed that the building of all new military aircraft should be banned by international agreement. In November, speaking in the House of Commons, he spelt this fear out even more precisely: 'I think it is well also for the man in the street to realise that there is no power on earth that can protect him from being bombed. Whatever people may tell him, *the bomber will always get through.*'

Charley, a younger man, a pilot himself and a former professional soldier – who, unlike Baldwin, had seen active service – instinctively thought in terms of defending his country. He believed that strong armed

239

services were the best deterrent to aggression and that Britain should not disarm beyond the limits of national safety. Baldwin's disarmament policy, and Charley's spirited opposition to it, were to have a disastrous effect on Charley's future.

Baldwin, of course, was in tune with the British public's longing for peace at almost any price. In the aftermath of the Great War, there was a determination that such a catastrophe should never happen again. In February 1933 (a month after Hitler had come to power), a motion in the Oxford Union that 'this House will in no circumstances fight for its King and country' was passed overwhelmingly. Disarmament, under strictly controlled conditions, seemed a logical first step; and the reduction in public expenditure was welcome to the Treasury.

Charley, who believed fervently in the need for a strong air force capable of offensive as well as defensive action, wrote constantly from Geneva to the Prime Minister at home using every argument he could to back up his case. In June 1932, he reported a conversation he had had with the King before returning to Geneva from one of his frequent visits home. 'I found HM very indignant against any attempt to do away with the Air Force, more even than he was before. I endeavoured to give him a fair picture of the situation but found a difficulty in getting into the conversation which as you know is always very one-sided. . . . I cannot become reconciled to acquiescing in the abolition of military aircraft except under the remote possibility of an international agreement to abolish *all* weapons of war.'

In July he was pointing out that '. . . the acquiescing in the total abolition of bombardment from the air was the Foreign Office plan from the very beginning. . . . I never think the Foreign Office are particularly safe when left to themselves on questions of policy, and I feel they have taken an incorrect view throughout in connection with this Disarmament Conference. . . . The atmosphere here, as you know, is a very artificial one and I am quite convinced that, for the discussion of these matters, it would be much better if the Conference were held in some centre which is in close touch with the real life of the world, instead of at Geneva, which is full of old women and sentimental cranks. . . .'

Halfway through the Disarmament Conference came an event that was to make a total mockery of all it stood for. In January 1933 Hitler came to power in Germany. In April he repudiated the Treaty of Versailles and restored conscription; in October Germany left the League of Nations and withdrew from the Disarmament Conference and, almost simultaneously, Mussolini's forces invaded Abyssinia. By the end of 1933 the Conference was doomed, although it tottered on until June 1934.

In London, a constant stream of visitors came to Londonderry House. 'Yesterday Mr Baldwin called here at about 11.45 and stayed till luncheon, having nothing else to do. He was very nice and most interesting about everything,' wrote Edith in February 1932, just after Charley had left for the start of the Conference. The Prime Minister would appear for a brisk and early luncheon before dashing off to Question Time. There were music recitals for Edith's various charities, there were luncheons and house parties, there were Ark evenings that included dancing – Edith called these sausage parties. 'They all came here to the Ark, some from the House, others from dinner. Baldwin said as they were the Bears they came to tear a sausage. Horne, Hailsham, all the nice young men from the House, the Swedish Minister, James Stephens, the Ian Malcolms and the rest. A real salon, stage and stars and they started bridge at 12.30. Ruby, Lenda, Zina and girls, backgammon and a gramophone. The girls had a real evening with the sparks and it went on till after 11 p.m. and they ate sausages all the time. I gave the Cabinet a little champagne and old brandy – the old and knowing ones – otherwise they had beer and wine.'

Londonderry House dinner parties, forty to sixty strong, were famous. 'In the evening to Londonderry House where we found half political and social London,' Chips Channon wrote (in 1935). 'We supped with Mrs Keppel, Lady Oxford and poor Sir John Lavery, nearly 80 and a widower. Circe L took in Corbin, the French Ambassador.' The sixty-piece set of ambassadorial gold plate, dating from Charley's great-grandfather's days as Ambassador in Vienna, would be brought out; always flowers were everywhere, sent up from the Wynyard greenhouses, trailing orchids, pink and purple foxgloves in stone containers in the hall, smilax between the candles on the dining table. Kilted footmen, so handsome it was rumoured they were chosen for their good looks, stood behind the chairs, and often after dinner a piper marched round the table playing. Dinner was always excellent – Edith was fond of her food and her chef, Mrs Harris, inherited from Theresa, was the equal of any in London.

At these dinners Edith herself was always *en grande tenue*. She had a profound, almost Elizabethan, consciousness of image, in which she was encouraged by Charley, and a certain natural flamboyance, which expressed itself in a theatrical magnificence on public occasions. When, at her Eve-of-Parliament reception in 1934, she stood at the head of the Londonderry House staircase flanked by MacDonald and the Baldwins, she wore a black and silver sequined sheath dress like a dazzling coat of mail, against which flashed tiara, pendant earrings and a wristful of diamond bracelets. She loved teagowns: in pale blue and green hand-woven Sutherland tartan for cold Scottish country houses, or something more exotic, like the 'gold trouser teagown' (later sold for £1 10s at a Mayfair second-hand dress shop). Most of her clothes, from dresses to silk lingerie, chiffon nightdresses and even curlers, came from Paris, her shoes were handmade from Fortnums, her hats dramatic in fur, velvet or feathers. Her tattooed legs – the left with the famous snake, the right with scattered motifs – first noted publicly in May 1933 when they were mistaken for a new fashion in stockings, only added to the legend she had now become with their titillating hint of an adventurous past.

Much of the Londonderrys' entertaining was for the benefit of Helen and Margaret. Edith and Charley both hoped their daughters would marry well, or even brilliantly – Prince Henry and Prince George were still bachelors – at least an eldest son with a place. So far, though, they had turned up their noses at all the suitable young men provided for them, and it was to Mairi that Prince Henry sent messages after staying at Mount Stewart ('owing to the amount of laughing we did it still hurts me to laugh') or stalking at Loch Choire. Helen and Margaret were pretty, lively and talented, their allowance of £100 a year each was not quite enough to run a car (at Mount Stewart they shared one) and in many ways they longed for freedom. Edith and Charley, who had grown up in a different era and who had firm views on the behaviour of young girls, found themselves facing a younger generation who looked at life from a different standpoint.

Margaret was the first to run counter to her parents' ideas. One day the Ward girls, who often came over to Mount Stewart for tennis or swimming, were invited for a pageant. They brought with them a friend who was staying, a good-looking, attractive young man called 'Bunny' Phillips (his name was Harold but he was universally known by this childhood nickname). He was the younger of two attractive brothers whose uncle, Gray Phillips, was private secretary to Edith's cousin Geordie and was later to be Comptroller to the Duke of Windsor in exile. Bunny was immediately taken with Margaret.

Miggy, as she was usually known in the family, was warm-hearted, very pretty, great fun, mildly eccentric, and a dazzling sight on her bright chestnut thoroughbred, its glossy coat and silky mane the exact colour of her own long tresses. She was a talented painter, a good tennis player, a good rifle shot, a natural pilot who flew solo after only 6½ hours' instruction and the first of her family to achieve a pilot's licence, beating her father by three days and her sister Helen by three weeks.

At first, Charley and Edith were inclined to view their daughter's attachment as nothing more than another mild flirtation. It soon became apparent, though, that it was more. 'My Most Beloved, I am sorry about "Bunny",' Charley wrote from Geneva. 'It really is very tiresome.' But by September 1932, this mild disfavour had given way to a stronger emotion and he fretted angrily: 'About this young man: if he is to be spoken to and given the facts in plain English, as he does not seem to understand being treated like a gentleman, you had best let me know when and where he is to be found. I think there is a danger in his going off and saying that we said that after a year we would consent to the arrangement; and all we shall be able to do is to submit.' Two days later, he was complaining: 'I cannot find out how to get hold of this dreadful "Bunny" (fancy a "Bunny" son-in-law). I don't want to write but I shall have to do so if I cannot get hold of him.'

The reason for Charley's disapproval was simple: he thought Bunny was a fortune-hunter. 'These two Phillips boys are nothing but hangers-on,' he wrote in January 1933. 'Their whole plan is to get attached to houses like Grimsthorpe or Londonderry House, where they look for a certain amount of their keep and hope to pick up one of the girls and whatever fortune they may get.'

As Margaret and Bunny grew closer, Charley's feelings varied between distaste for the continual battles ('Margaret is 23 and I really feel inclined to wash my hands of the whole business and let her marry this dreadful man'), sympathy for his daughter's feelings, determination not to let her fall into Bunny's arms and the gloomy realism of the disgruntled father. 'Women certainly fancy the most hopeless men, and if you can steer them off it usually is to their good. But there comes a time when you can't go on stopping it.'

Charley did, however, have one last weapon in reserve. He sent for Bunny and told him that if he married Margaret she would be disinherited.

Bunny was off. Within a few months he had become the accredited lover of Edwina Mountbatten (a position previously held by his brother Ted), an affair that was to end ten years later when he left Edwina to marry Sir Harold and Lady Zia Wernher's elder daughter Georgina (Gina), who eventually inherited Luton Hoo.

Margaret's misery, disillusionment and humiliation were painful for her family to see. 'I am very sorry for her heartaches and while it is a mistake to be too sympathetic because she would misunderstand, she obviously has been badly struck,' wrote Charley, though for both him and Edith there was a distinct sense of relief at a danger averted. Brought up in an age when young girls were carefully chaperoned almost up to marriage and unquestioningly obedient to their parents, and a rigid formality prevailed between unmarried members of the opposite sex, it was difficult for either of them to come to terms with what Charley called 'this present-day freedom of behaviour'. What neither of them seem to have considered was how much their children's behaviour was the result of their father's example.

XXIII

CHARLEY IN his fifties was as unfaithful as ever. His handsome face and thin, elegant body had hardly changed. 'This morning you looked just 18 years of age, fresh, slim and beautiful. No one could have such an attractive man for a mate,' Edith had written adoringly on his fifty-fourth birthday and contemporary photographs and accounts all confirm his youthful appearance.

His clothes were always beautifully cut, with a few individual touches – the brown cane stick he always carried, its cork top embossed with his 'L' cypher in gold, the cravat he often wore instead of a tie. His air was that of an eighteenth-century *grand seigneur* – 'a nice man who looked more like Lord Londonderry than any Lord Londonderry has before', said Harold Nicolson – and, though always amiable and courteous, his natural reserve gave him an air of aloofness. The few who managed to penetrate this somewhat intimidating façade found warmth and affection. To Ettie Desborough, connoisseur of friendships, he was her 'Beloved Charley, infinitely dear', with whom she felt completely in tune. 'Our friendship is the one most wholly independent of words that I have ever known. Yet there are sometimes very simple ones that I want to say, that I love you, thank you, trust you, need you.'

He was a perfectionist, brought up in the belief that the aristocrat was both innately superior and had a duty to be so, and he became cross and irritable whenever he fell below these self-imposed standards in even trivial things. He was a bad loser: the defeat of one of his horses or a partner's failure to lead the right card at bridge, upset him out of all proportion. When Olive Murray-Smith, his bridge partner, played badly one evening he was so biting that she rushed up the stairs in tears. Characteristically, it was Edith who went after her and comforted her.

Olive Murray-Smith, a pretty widow with a cloud of fluffy blonde hair, was Charley's chief mistress in the thirties and established closer links with his family than any of her predecessors. She was the daughter of the third Baron Burnham and her great-grandfather was a printer called Levy who had founded the *Cheap Press*, the forerunner of the *Daily Telegraph*. In 1875 he assumed the additional surname of Lawson by royal licence. Olive's father, managing director of the *Telegraph*, used the name of Lawson only. Olive, who had married Major John Edward Murray-Smith in 1916, was widowed in 1928. She lived in Market Overton, near Oakham, so was a neighbour of the Londonderrys during the hunting season, and she had a London house in Kensington Gate. She used to play both bridge and golf with Charley, who liked his girlfriends to enjoy at least one of his favourite pastimes – so much so that Edith would often categorise them as 'Your bridge girl', 'your hunting girl' – and was frequently invited to stay by Edith.

For by now Edith knew that, unlike Consuelo or Eloise, these later mistresses posed no threat to her marriage; indeed, if Charley found he had got himself too involved with one, it was to Edith he turned for help in extricating himself. 'You've got to get me out of this,' he would cry – and she always did. Sometimes she would tease him. 'Kitty R [Rothschild] on finding me here, is hurrying to London to see you,' she wrote from the Paris Ritz. 'So I told her you were most probably going to Geneva. Her face dropped at least three inches. Aren't I naughty? I know she has wired you, so Olive will be furious.'

This tolerance was neither cynical complaisance nor the sign of a nature so altruistic as to verge on the saintly. Edith was a pragmatist and Charley, as he had amply proved throughout their marriage, would never change. The belief that these affairs could not, and would not, affect what was between him and her was what she had clung to during the bleakest days of her marriage; how much less, then, did they matter now. Cloaking Charley's later and lesser amours with her own friendship removed from them not only the thrill of the illicit and the spice of danger but also the element of humiliation to herself. She may also have reflected that to be in her house, under her eye, must have been extremely inhibiting – most mistresses would find it difficult to disport themselves seductively under the gaze of a wife who was clearly under no illusions – and who could still write, as Edith did: 'You are such a darling and you don't realise how wonderful you are. Perhaps it is as well as you would not survive it if you did.'

In any case, Olive was no Eloise – bold, determined, confident, piratical – but someone altogether more diffident, anxious only to catch a glimpse of Charley on his visits home from Geneva and, in his absence, to haunt the place where her beloved lived. Possibly, too, a guilty conscience made her more subservient and eager to please than she might otherwise have been. 'Olive is very pathetic,' wrote Edith, who treated her as a mixture of child and unpaid aide, taking her to concerts to cheer her up, bossing her about and fagging her shamelessly. 'Olive came round and I got her to take Mairi to the circus.' 'Olive is at Ranksborough, chaperoning the girls to a good party that I would not let them go to alone.' 'I told Olive I would not allow "Bunnying" at Melton.' She even bought Charley presents to give Olive – perhaps she could not bear the thought of a weeping Olive after a forgotten birthday. 'I have bought you a small bottle of scent to give to Olive called Ce Soir ou jamais.' Alas, *ce soir* was the alternative Charley usually preferred.

Charley had more than Olive to think about. He was becoming increasingly isolated in his views on the future of the Air Force and the whole question of disarmament. The Prime Minister had, of course, been strongly pacifist throughout the 1914–18 war and the Chancellor, Neville Chamberlain, said that economic risks were the greatest ones the country had to face and that other priorities would have to wait until financial stability was re-established. Charley set out his own position in a long letter to the Prime Minister dated 24 February 1933.

'. . . I am beginning to feel very acutely that I am in total disagreement with the articulate section of the Cabinet in relation to disarmament and the League of Nations and that is why you find me comparatively silent on these matters. . . . JS [Sir John Simon] and the Foreign Office are very anxious that a spectacular resolution should be put forward by Great Britain at the Disarmament Conference, which in my judgement would be highly dangerous. We have stated our positions and it is for other countries who have previously urged total abolition coupled with safeguards to put forward plans for examination.

'The function of Great Britain is to keep order in the world and in addition to the moral influence we exercise we do it by the threat implied in the strength of our right arm. Our right arm is desperately weak at the present moment and the object of the great majority of our colleagues in the Disarmament Conference is to weaken that right arm still further. I look with the gravest apprehension on this determined attempt to destroy the Air Force, the potency of which depends, as you and I know quite well, on the existence of the independent Air Force. The Air Force is a modern development of our fighting forces and if it is eliminated from the picture it means that we return to 1914 for our weapons of aggression and defence. The more old-fashioned the weapon, the more likely the world is to fight and the more old-fashioned our ideas become the more certain we are to be defeated if ever we are called upon to defend ourselves.'

In March, Ramsay MacDonald went to Geneva, where he was to put forward the British proposals. His craving for Edith's company was as great as ever ('I just long to see you') but his earlier gaiety had evaporated. His insomnia had worsened, his health was deteriorating and his protestations of affection were more depressing than warming. 'Why did Providence wait until youth had gone & the bleak winds had come?' Edith, though deeply fond of him, had begun to find this incessant, gloomy longing emotionally draining. 'He is a vampire and tires me out.' Nevertheless, she joined Charley at his hotel in Geneva for the Prime Minister's important speech on 16 March (in French eyes, this confirmed speculation which had appeared in an article headed *L'Influence du Jupon*).

MacDonald made the most of her presence. 'Ramsay used to go into Lady Londonderry's bedroom every night and talk to her from 11.30 until two,' noted Robert Bruce Lockhart in his diary, adding that 'the visits ... were quite innocent. Ramsay calls her his fairy godmother.'

In many ways she preferred the more light-hearted company of Fono Pallavicini, still gallantly attentive. He accompanied her to Geneva, carrying coats and bags, organising the baggage and generally making himself agreeable and useful. He was, she said, the most perfect travelling companion, happy with her or on his own ('but as no sound comes from his room until a late hour in the morning I conclude he is not wasting his time'). Nor did Charley have to worry about the possibility of scandal. 'No one notices poor Fono. They all think my flirtation is with "Monsieur Mac-Don-ald".'

Her 'wee Hungarian' had a further, invaluable asset; he was a great gossip. 'Did you hear that Prince Arthur of Connaught shot Wigram badly this year? He just missed the King, too. Fono had it direct from Shaftesbury, when he came from Alloa to Balmoral.' 'Fono had a long talk with him [the Prince of Wales] at a party at Emerald's. He says the Prince likes us both very much but is frightened of me.'

The proposals put forward by MacDonald in his 16 March speech included a limit of 500 military aircraft for Britain, France, Japan, Italy, Russia and the United States (the German figure was left open), none to exceed three tons in weight, with any that did to be disposed of, half by June 1936, the rest by 1939. This meant, of course, the virtual abolition of the bomber. A week later, Hitler, elected Chancellor two months earlier, achieved full dictatorial powers.

The MacDonald Plan, as the British proposals came to be known, was the Prime Minister's last great public effort. He was failing rapidly – at one point during his speech he momentarily lost consciousness, reeled back, and recovered to ask the mystified delegates: 'Are you men or mannequins?' At home his speeches in Parliament had become more muddled and jumbled than ever and his diary entries are pathetic. 'Tomorrow there will be another "vague" speech impossible to follow & as usual with these attacks of head and eyes no sleep tonight.' 'The Creator might have devised a more humane means for punishing me for overdrive & reckless use of body.' He still suffered deeply from the loss of his friends in the Labour Party and his children begged him to resign so that he could leave politics on a note of success. To Edith, unable to see him as often as he wished, he wrote wretchedly: 'I am just tired in mind and body and am feeling the strain. For years I have had nothing but trouble after trouble and anxiety after anxiety and the ... heartbreaking deterioration which has taken place in the party in which my whole being has been wrapped up has struck me right into my soul.... Joy and zest have gone out of work. I am tired; I grow old and I need rest.... You certainly must remain in Paris till you get well and then return fit and flourishing to shed life and sunshine about you. You really must not worry about me.'

In the House of Commons, opinion was slowly moving towards the idea of restoring to the armed services some of the strength lost since the end of the war. In Cabinet on 29 November 1933, Charley told his colleagues: 'We should admit that we had disarmed to the edge of risk and had done it deliberately in pursuit of a policy of disarmament.' Baldwin retorted that if Germany saw the House of Commons pass an air rearmament motion the effect on her would be 'serious', and the Chancellor pointed out yet again that Britain could not afford to rearm in even a modest way.

By the spring of 1934 Baldwin had begun to show interest in air defence. 'This Government ... will see to it that in air strength and air power this country will no longer be in a position inferior to any country within striking distance of our shores,' he promised the House of Commons on 8 March. But the vindication of Charley's belief that a strong Air Force was essential did him no good with the most powerful man in Parliament. Stanley Baldwin had already decided that Charley did not have the political clout to stand up to the Treasury nor the necessary adroitness to handle public opinion – the general populace being still unaware of the incipient danger and largely in favour of disarmament, as by-elections favouring pacifist candidates showed. In May, Charley spoke of the value of bombers in policing operations in Iraq and on the Indian Northwest Frontier. When a tribe misbehaved, warning was given that their village would be bombed on a certain date, allowing ample time for its evacuation, and the village was then bombed. The Opposition pounced on this, claiming that it showed that the Government was in favour of bombing and its attendant horrors. In short, Charley would be a liability in the General Election due in 1935 and Baldwin was determined to move him.

Baldwin installed his own nominee in the Air Ministry, Philip Cunliffe-Lister (later Lord Swinton), with whom he discussed matters and took decisions, with the result that Charley was largely bypassed. In July Charley wrote privately to Baldwin, expressing yet again his fears for the country if the Air Force remained weak – 'there would be nothing to stop the enemy concentrating his maximum bombing force against London and continuing to bombard it until he achieved his aim'. In November Winston Churchill predicted that by 1935 the Germans would reach parity in the air and, at the end of the year, the Government decided it was time to reverse its previous policy. The slow process of re-equipping the Air Force began – but it was Cunliffe-Lister, not Charley, who was appointed Chairman of the vital Cabinet Committee on Air Armament.

There were family preoccupations too. Margaret had fallen in love again. It may have been on the rebound after her heartbreak over Bunny, it may have been because Alan Muntz was too glamorous to resist: as well as being that dashing figure, the pioneer aviator, he was highly intelligent and imbued with immense energy.

Muntz, born in 1899, had been educated at Winchester and then read the Mechanical Sciences Tripos at Trinity College, Cambridge, with his great friend and schoolfellow Nigel Norman. They were both commissioned into the Royal Engineers, saw service in France and then, after Muntz had learned to fly at the age of twenty-eight, teamed up again to form a company, Airwork, and founded Heston Air Park on agricultural land just off the Great West Road (near London Airport).

Heston quickly became a success. As well as the buying, selling and servicing of aircraft, it offered expert tuition and such good overnight accommodation and food that it attracted many of the young, smart and rich for whom flying was the latest thrill. But Muntz was no simple pilot turning his skill to account; he was a brilliant and vigorous businessman. In 1932 he had founded a sister company in Canada, by 1933 he had helped set up Air India. He was to go on to run half a dozen airfields after the 1939 war, among them Gatwick and Blackbushe, before forming British United Airways (which, in 1970, became part of British Caledonian).

It was at Heston that the Londonderrys learned to fly and Charley, always fascinated by anything to do with the air, quickly formed a friendship with Muntz – thanks to which Airwork was able to establish an airport and flying school just outside Belfast – asking him to stay several times at Mount Stewart. What Charley had not bargained for was that his protégé would fall in love with his daughter, and she with him.

This time, Margaret held firm. She was a year older than when she had broken her heart over Bunny, she did not want to suffer again, and she was more independent – Charley and Edith had given her a small studio flat where, surrounded by pictures and gramophone records stacked on tables, she painted busily. Arguments and discussions raged but to no avail.

It was Edith rather than Charley who reacted the most strongly to Margaret's proposed marriage. It made her bitterly unhappy. Quite apart from any worldly consideration – and she would undoubtedly have liked her beautiful daughter to make what she and Charley would have called a good match – there was, to her, one insuperable barrier. Muntz had been married and his former wife was still alive.

Edith's religion was a real and living thing to her. She was a regular communicant, she maintained the custom of family prayers at Wynyard, she taught her grandchildren their catechism, she tried constantly to help others (her kindness was the first thing anyone who knew her mentioned), she thought hard about her prayers. 'I have been to church as I said and remembered what you said about being peremptory, and will try to do better,' she wrote humbly to Charley during those difficult weeks.

To her, the doctrines of the Church were sacrosanct – and one of them was that marriage lasted for life. She had passed through fire to preserve her own marriage, through her unwearying determination, love and acceptance she and Charley were now indissolubly bonded; and she believed this was largely owing to her faith. The year before, when the Duke of Sutherland, the cousin whom she always thought of as her younger brother, was toying with the idea of leaving his wife for another woman, she had written to Charley: 'There was a time when it crossed your mind, and once I too wanted to go away and leave you. Not because I did not always love you better than anyone else but I was so enraged I wanted to run somewhere, just, in fact, to leave you. Had I . . . not been brought up to know what religion teaches, I should have done this, I think, but I was saved from it, I really think, because I have always been to Holy Communion, which gives one strength.' And now her own daughter wanted to marry a divorced man.

'He offers her a soiled life,' she wrote furiously and miserably to Charley, 'a man who has made a failure of married life and has no very great prospects either and such as he has he owes a great deal to your influence.'

Matters came to a head at the end of the year. On 6 November 1934, Margaret and Alan Muntz announced their engagement, and the same evening Charley denied that he had given his consent. Next day Margaret said that she and her fiancé would be married shortly ('My father's attitude makes no difference to my plans'), and a few days later Edith took Margaret and Helen over to Mount Stewart, buying them both single tickets but a return for herself, and describing talk of an engagement as 'Rubbish' to the photographers and reporters who besieged them at Croydon airfield.

All the younger generation rallied round Margaret ('They are all stuffed up with A. P. Herbert's book,' groaned Edith). Maureen, dashing, established, thoroughly 'modern' in her outlook – and determined not to be dominated by the powerful mother whom in many ways she was so like – gave help and encouragement, while her husband Oliver Stanley made the wedding arrangements, Helen was a constant support and Dorothé had Margaret to stay in Wilton Crescent. Edith had to give in. 'I have left her severely alone all day. She is so determined that I would not even ask her to postpone it. It feels exactly as if she was going away to die, making all these final arrangements. But there it is, I don't see we can do anything more.'

Her friend Hugh Cecil, to whom she had again turned for spiritual counsel, concurred. 'It is very sad and distressing but I am sure it would be wrong to be unkind. Of course it is right for your opinion that such a union is really adultery to be made clear. That doubtless is done; and there being no misunderstanding I should be as kind as possible to Margaret. It is only too likely that the thing will go smash in a few years and then she ought to feel she has got you to turn to.'

At the wedding, which took place on 22 November at Kensington Register Office, Helen was the only family member present, though afterwards their cousin Lady Mary Herbert gave a luncheon party for Margaret and her new husband. Almost at once, they set off for a flying honeymoon: Muntz made an annual trip to Egypt, India and Iraq and this year they would go to Persia, Kashmir and Burma as well. By the time they came back, Charley had settled £1,000 a year on Margaret – and both he and Edith were now occupied with Helen's affairs.

For Helen, generally considered the most beautiful of the sisters, had declared that she too wanted to get married. Not, as had been widely believed, to Prince Juan, the third son of King Alfonso of Spain (a rumour that Helen discounted as 'absurd and embarrassing'), but to the Hon. Edward Jessel. Though rich, good-looking, charming, single and an eldest son – his father was the first Baron Jessel – he possessed one major disadvantage in the eyes of Charley and, particularly, Edith. He belonged to the Jewish faith, which meant that he and Helen would not be married in church. In Edith's eyes, this meant it would not be a true marriage, and that her 'lovely child' would be living in sin. She told her daughter that she and Charley disapproved, but that they would make the best of it; Helen wept bitterly at this, but remained determined.

She was the most reserved of the sisters, with none of Margaret's open warmth or Maureen's dazzling confidence and *élan*. As her future husband put it: 'Helen needed encouraging.' Fortunately, her older sister's victory had quashed most of the opposition Edith might otherwise have put up and both Londonderrys bit the bullet and pronounced themselves delighted. In December Charley formally announced his third daughter's engagement. Edith must have agreed with the comment of her old friend Herbert Maxwell: 'In any hitch in family matters my mother used to exclaim "Wha' wad hae bairns!"'

Teddy Jessel and Helen were married at Caxton Hall in February 1935. Robin was best man and though Edith suffered a diplomatic chill, Charley, Robin, Margaret and the children's old nanny, Mrs Stevenson, were all there. It was a grand wedding in everything except what mattered most to Edith, the religious service: police were needed to control the crowd and Helen's wedding presents were put on show at Londonderry House – they included a green leather dressing case fitted with bottles in green enamel and silver from the King and Queen, a round mahogany table from Princess Alice and a large yellow vase from Edith's great friend Princess Helena Victoria.

Edith soon took a more philosophical view of her third daughter's marriage. 'What a trial these girls are and what chances they have had and what a mess they seem to be making of everything,' she wrote soon afterwards. 'But who knows, they may have found the pathway to happiness. . . .'

XXIV

B
Y THE beginning of 1935 Ramsay MacDonald's health was causing serious concern to all his colleagues. Almost a year earlier his
friend John Buchan, who saw him constantly, had told Edith that
he was 'very clear that unless he gets some real assistance there will be
a smash'. Buchan's suggestion of a Minister without portfolio to act as
an aide-de-camp was, not surprisingly, vetoed by MacDonald as likely to
cause difficulties within the Cabinet. Frances Stevenson, Lloyd George's
mistress (and later wife) thought the Prime Minister had hardening of
the arteries of the brain. Seely thought he was 'physically fit but spiri-
tually sick'. Lloyd George described a speech made by MacDonald in
April 1935 as 'the speech of a man nine-tenths gaga'. His doctor, Horder,
said he could not and ought not to carry on. As for his family, they had
been imploring him to resign for almost two years.

MacDonald himself was slowly coming to the same conclusion. 'My
health compels me to ease myself of the weight of my burdens,' he wrote
to Edith. '. . . For weeks I have been struggling to keep going against
heavy odds and great depression and the limit is passed.' For John Buchan
the knowledge that his old friend was at last going to lead a less wearing
life must have been an enormous relief as he, Buchan, would no longer
be there to act as buffer to the outside world. Buchan had just accepted
the Governor-Generalship of Canada; one measure of Edith's effect on
those she set herself out to charm lay in the fact that his somewhat
disapproving submission to her allure and position had given way to
wholehearted affection. 'I feel I must tell *you* first about the Canadian
thing,' he wrote on 25 March 1935, 'for you are my dearest friend.'

For Edith, and especially for Charley, MacDonald's resignation meant
the beginning of a period of unhappiness and change.

Baldwin was now attempting the difficult political manoeuvre of appearing outwardly in favour of disarmament while simultaneously moving towards rearmament as unobtrusively as possible. 'Supposing that I had gone to the country and said that we must rearm, does anybody think that this pacific democracy would have rallied to the cry?' he was to say to the House of Commons eighteen months later, adding, 'I cannot think of anything that would have made the loss of the election from my point of view more certain.' In this climate, Charley's blunt outspokenness had no place; not only Baldwin but senior members of the Cabinet, including the Chancellor of the Exchequer, Neville Chamberlain, considered that Charley would be an electoral liability.

MacDonald, who had discussed possible Cabinet changes with Baldwin, knew that once he himself was out of the way Baldwin intended to get rid of Charley, replacing him as Air Minister with Philip Cunliffe-Lister, and he found it difficult to hide this from Charley. 'He [Mac-Donald] is very sensitive about my appointment, I think, and flinches whenever some criticism is made,' wrote Charley to Edith on 27 April. 'It does not matter if the attack comes from an enemy or a visionary, he becomes terribly scared and warns me for my own good. . . . If I survive I think it will be on your merits. I am sure the PM would never sponsor me again and SB has always resented (I think) our support of the PM.'

Though Baldwin, slow-moving, shrewd and with a marked predilection for the conciliatory approach, was unlikely to strike out of the blue, MacDonald knew that his protection of Charley could only continue while he was Prime Minister. After he had stepped down, as he pointed out, his influence would be slight. 'If a National Government (not only in name) remains, I remain as a member; if it be a Tory Government, I do not remain.' He did his best to alert his beloved Circe to the difficulties ahead.

For some time, Winston Churchill had told his cousin he should resign rather than be sacked and by now Edith too was urging this course. Early risers both, Edith and Charley invariably breakfasted together in her bedroom at 8.00 when in Londonderry House, often joined by Mairi. She recalls: 'One morning when I was having breakfast with my parents, Mother finally persuaded my father that he must resign and he went off to see Stanley Baldwin to tender his resignation. But on the way he met Lord Hailsham [now Secretary of State for War], a great friend, and told him what he was going to do. Lord Hailsham said: "You can't let Stanley down!" So he stayed.'

MacDonald was under no illusions as to what would happen. 'I warned you some time ago that within your flock were gathering caves and cliques now that things were going well and that a Socialist at the head of a Government where Tories predominate was an offence,' he wrote to Edith in mid-May. And again: 'When the reorganisation comes I shall be pretty well out of it and decisions will be more in Conservative hands than ever.' He was sorry, he said, that Charley had not been more on the offensive. 'There were also offices which were coveted, and circumstances laid the air specially open to attack. The announcement of a great air programme not by the Ministry was settled when I was still away.'

He referred to the expansion plan based on the report of the Air Parity Committee. This small Cabinet sub-Committee had been set up on 30 April to decide what should be done to implement Baldwin's pledge of 'air parity with our nearest neighbour within striking distance' – the true numbers and strength of the German air force had begun to filter out and it was becoming ever clearer that Germany was now the greatest armed power in Europe. The arms race was on, with the air a paramount feature; and the Air Parity Committee was a first, vital step. The Committee, which produced its report within ten days, consisted of Walter (later Lord) Runciman, William Ormsby-Gore (later the fourth Baron Harlech) and Philip Cunliffe-Lister – but not the Air Minister. It is difficult to imagine a greater snub to Charley.

Only days later, on 21 May, Charley gave Baldwin the pretext for which he had been waiting. On 22 May Baldwin was due to announce to the House of Commons the expansion of the Royal Air Force, and the day before Charley replied to a defence debate in the House of Lords. After justifying his ministerial record he moved on to speak of the Disarmament Conference and of how he had 'kept impressing on my colleagues and the country generally the vital nature and the place of the Royal Air Force in the scheme of our defence'. Then he added an impromptu. 'I had the utmost difficulty at that time, amid the public outcry, in preserving the use of the bombing aeroplane, even on the frontier of the Middle East and India, where it was only owing to the presence of the Air Force that we have controlled these territories, without the old and heavy cost of blood and treasure.' It was a sentence that was to dog him for the rest of his life. 'My name became forthwith associated with air bombing and its attendant horrors.'

The Labour Opposition seized on Charley's impromptu sentence with a howl of triumph. With change in the air – MacDonald's decision to retire had become generally known by the end of May – it was electoral dynamite. As Baldwin later told Robin: 'The Opposition . . . made it the spearhead of their election and pre-election campaign, but a far bigger outcry came from the Conservative Party. Members were beginning to look to their seats and here was a Cabinet Minister giving the enemy ammunition free and for nothing.'

As Charley himself later ruefully admitted: 'From a purely political point of view my statement of fact had made me an embarrassment.' He had been strongly against disarming when all around were crying for the abandonment of arms, he had fought for the retention of the bomber and the expansion of the Air Force in the teeth of popular opinion and had now been proved right – but he had to go. His successor, Cunliffe-Lister, was to describe Charley as having had 'a thankless and impossible task, with no opportunity to give the [aircraft] industry either orders or encouragement. He and his professional colleagues deserve credit having maintained the spirit, the tradition and the training of our small Air Force in those disappointing days.'

Ramsay MacDonald resigned as Prime Minister during the Whitsun recess, on 7 June 1935, and Stanley Baldwin succeeded him. MacDonald's diary entry for that day reads dolefully: 'First thing of which awakening made me conscious was "I die today . . ." 3.50 audience with King which in end lasted 50 minutes and he was a ¼ hour late in seeing Baldwin. He was most friendly. He said again, looking sadly down to the floor, with his right elbow on the arm of his chair, "I hoped you might have seen me through, but I know it is impossible. But I do not think it will be very long. I wonder how you have stood it – especially the loss of your friends and their beastly behaviour." Again: "You have been the Prime Minister I have liked best; you have so many qualities, you have kept up the dignity of the office without using it to give you dignity." . . . He made me doubly and trebly sorry to lay down my office. My first duty as Lord President was to call up Malcolm to be sworn in (note: his coat fitted badly). New Government sworn and left to catch the 7.30 train for Lossiemouth – I left with feelings which mingled regret with relief, a sense of freedom with one of impotence. I might have been a memory disembodied. . . .' MacDonald remained in the Cabinet as Lord President of the Council.

To Edith he wrote the next day: ". . . The last days were not pleasant. They came hustling me along as though I were to be hung at the end of them. Well, it is over and I feel like one strange in heaven after a rough passage through life.'

Charley remained in the Government by the skin of his teeth. Lord Hailsham, who had heard the rumours that Charley was to be dropped, interceded for him with Baldwin, pointing out how hard, loyally and on the whole successfully Charley had worked. 'I know my many weaknesses as a PM,' Baldwin had written a few months earlier, 'not the least of them is my inability to be a butcher.' Nevertheless, he appointed Cunliffe-Lister Secretary of State for Air, offering Charley the position of Lord Privy Seal and, additionally, the Leadership of the House of Lords, which Baldwin thought would be 'a very appropriate wind-up to an honourable career'.

Edith, who felt this was simply part of the process of squeezing her husband out, wanted Charley to refuse. Hailsham, who had been instrumental in securing these posts for his friend, naturally wanted him to accept and Charley himself did not relish the prospect of leaving the Government. He asked Baldwin for twenty-four hours in which to think over his offer, in particular asking for clarification on the point that meant most to him: whether the appointment as Leader of the House of Lords carried Cabinet rank. 'Of course you continue in the Cabinet: it was, as I told you, my desire and that of our colleagues that you should remain with us,' wrote Baldwin on 6 June.

Charley took these words to mean that his position was secure. They were to lay the foundation of the bitterness he later felt towards Baldwin, when, after only five months, he was removed from both positions. But at the time, reassured, he accepted the offer.

Edith, convinced that her instinct was correct, felt that her husband should not allow himself to be pushed, or to drift, away from the centre of the political scene. To her, personal contact had always been all-important. An approach to Neville Chamberlain, she felt, might pay especial dividends. 'You can gain his friendship, I am sure, and, if it is possible, float the idea of the Air in the House of Lords.' Ettie Desborough, whose admiration and affection for Charley never faltered, felt sure that he could win Baldwin over. As Charley told Edith: 'She suggested I saw Baldwin promptly and got him to lunch. "Remember, he is deaf, lazy and inattentive," she said. I thought this was a strange recommendation for a Prime Minister.'

In October the suggested interview duly took place, it was, as always with Baldwin, friendly, but the Prime Minister threw out various remarks and questions – such as: 'Would you be happy in a different kind of life?' – that left Charley with the impression that 'our friend SB will not be at all sorry to get the disposal of my place'. It was not to be long before the truth of this became apparent.

Towards the end of October Baldwin asked for the dissolution of Parliament, and the General Election took place on 14 November 1935.

MacDonald, newly vigorous since his retirement as Premier ('How sweet life is when we know how to live,' he wrote to his 'dearest, not only of those called Circe, or E., or anything else, but of everybody'), now threw himself into the campaign. In the result, the Conservatives lost 67 seats, leaving them with 387 members, and the Labour Party, which went into the election with 46 seats, came out with 154.

MacDonald's was not one of them. He had first won Seaham as Leader of the Labour party in 1929 with a majority of 28,794, and held on to it – standing as National Labour – with a 5,951 majority against a Labour candidate in 1931. But that had been only months after the 'great betrayal', when many of the rank and file of the Party had not yet turned against him. Now, again standing as National Labour, he was trounced by the Labour candidate, Emanuel Shinwell, standing at Seaham for the first time, who gained a majority of 20,498.

Much more than his own defeat at Seaham, MacDonald minded that the loathing felt for him by the Labour Party had caused his son Malcolm to lose his seat. This double misfortune prompted Baldwin (whose own son, Oliver, was a Labour MP) to write to MacDonald the day after the election:

'My dear Friend, You have shared the fate of the prophets and my heart is heavy for you. I know your own defeat will not cause you the sharp, piercing disappointment that Malcolm's will. It is something to have a son who stands by his father's side at all times, good and bad and, if I know him, he would rather fall in battle with his father than win a score on the other side. We will both have a day or two of rest and quiet before we have a talk. I shall be at Chequers on Saturday and Sunday (I go down at 5 today) and at your service any time after lunch on Monday or indeed if you want to see me before when you like. But I do know much of what you are feeling if not all. I give you my hand in enduring friendship. Yours ever, S.B.' In the event, MacDonald was quickly found another seat, winning a by-election two months later to become Member for the Scottish Universities.

For Charley the new Government spelt the end of his political life. A week after the election, a letter in Baldwin's small, neat handwriting arrived from Downing Street.

My dear Charley,

I have been working for three days on one of the most difficult problems with which I have ever had to contend, and I am profoundly distressed that I find myself unable to offer you a place in the new Government.

The refusal of Ramsay to serve unless accompanied by Malcolm and Thomas, and the desire of Halifax to continue, have upset my calculations and I have more men than places.

You remember our talk in the House: you know what I feel. You have ever been a loyal and trusted friend: I think I know what you will feel.

Yet I have faith to believe that our friendship is too firmly based to be broken by a cruel political necessity that obliges a Prime Minister – and none have escaped it – to inflict pain on those he holds not only in regard but in affection.

I am, Yours very sincerely,
Stanley Baldwin

It cannot have been altogether a surprise – this was the first election in which Charley had not been invited to speak or otherwise take part in the campaign – but it was a dreadful shock. When Robin, who had heard the news the night before from his brother-in-law Oliver Stanley, went round with Maureen to Londonderry House to see Charley, they were shattered by his pitiful state. Their father, so elegant, so reserved, so impeccable in public, was slumped sideways in his chair, legs dangling over the side, with Baldwin's letter in his hand and tears trickling uncontrollably down his cheeks. 'I've been sacked – kicked out – sacked,' he kept muttering. He was, said Robin later, 'a broken man'.

Charley managed to pull himself together sufficiently to reply to the Prime Minister that evening. Though he accepted the inevitable, he did draw attention to the assurance he thought he had been given only a few months earlier. 'I have received your letter ... with some surprise because I recollect that you very expressly said that if I joined your Government in June I might retain the leadership of the House of Lords as long as I wished to do so.' Later, Baldwin was to deny that he had ever given such a promise: 'No PM is in a position to do so. He must have misunderstood something I said.'

Charley's place as Lord Privy Seal and Leader of the House of Lords was taken by the man who had once been his fag at Eton, Lord Halifax, former Viceroy and for the past five months Secretary of State for War – Edward the Woodpecker.

Charley's going did not meet with universal approval. Among those who felt he had been shabbily treated was Rudyard Kipling, Baldwin's first cousin. Kipling, though in constant, terrible pain from an ulcer (he died two months later after an operation), felt strongly enough to write and say how sorry he was 'that after your courageous stand and speech on rearmament you are not to lead the debates in the Upper House on this vital matter.... With very many others, I am disappointed and disheartened: but at any rate *you* have put yourself on record and we shall not forget it.' Ettie sent messages of love and sympathy. '... *never* have I admired you more. No one can have met a difficult situation with greater serenity and dignity. I feel so proud to be your friend. My dear and true love to Edie. I know that we are thinking in exactly the same vein.' Lord Beaverbrook, whose papers had avidly pursued the Londonderry family through their gossip columns, told Charley that the public understood perfectly that the Cabinet had refused him money for the air but were now pouring it out recklessly and that it was his duty to go back to public life. 'And if you will allow me to say so, you should go without the slightest feeling against Baldwin. In any case, he will pretend that you have a vendetta against him.'

It was wise advice but difficult to take. It was humiliating enough to be the only colleague of the Prime Minister's dropped from the new Government but worse was to follow. One of the reasons Baldwin had given Charley for shifting him from the Air Ministry was the increasing need, with the German threat and consequent emphasis on the Air Force, for any Air Minister to be in the House of Commons, yet he now sent Cunliffe-Lister to the House of Lords (as Lord Swinton of Masham). Though Baldwin, breaking with custom, had written Edith a consolatory letter when he dispatched her husband, that year there was to be no Eve-of-Parliament reception at Londonderry House.

At the same time as Charley was suffering the shocks and miseries of the successive loss of his various political offices, Edith's customary vigour deserted her. She had felt 'seedy' all year, she was recovering from shingles, the trouble with her antrum to which she was always liable had erupted, she was finally passing through the menopause and she had suddenly put on weight. 'I have been feeling so unwell and I have got such a size that I cannot fit into any of my clothes,' she wailed just before Baldwin disposed of Charley. 'I am so ashamed of myself. I am touching nothing but water and eating as little as I can. Even if I felt fit, I should be much too ashamed to go to Eric Dudley as all my clothes look dreadful. I wrote to him and said I still felt such a worm I would be no good at a party and that I would stay here [Mount Stewart] quietly until I had to go to London. I really am very sorry as I wanted to be with you and see you shoot but I felt miserable and wretched and am best alone until I pick up.' Eventually, she was found to be suffering from gallstones, and an effective treatment was begun.

Before this diagnosis, Edith's ill health and distress at Charley's misery combined with his own wretchedness made this an intensely unhappy time for both of them. Her letters reflect the quarrels, recriminations and misunderstandings of this time, though characteristically she always sought to take the blame. After all the years they had been married she was still intensely vulnerable to any hint of his displeasure. 'I was very unhappy at what you said to me, darling, and I feel sure you are right, and I have been no help to you in your public life. But it is not because I do not wish to. There you are quite wrong but I am very proud and I feel often that you do not want to take me into your confidence ... in the old regimental days, I always felt that you deprecated my presence in a way. In the colliery work it was the same. I feel sure it was difficult and it was my fault. I know I could not have behaved worse at the first election but I was frankly wicked then. . . . I want you to know, darling one, that I honestly feel I must be to blame, or perhaps we are both difficult natures to work together, but you do know how much I adore and admire you, even more now than ever before.'

Gradually, the bad patch passed, their mutual understanding reasserted itself and recrimination gave way to loving reconciliation. Just before Christmas 1935, Edith wrote: 'After we had had that argument and you said all sorts of things from your sad heart and no doubt feeling some bitterness, I felt very upset and ill. Then a sort of numb feeling inside, then tears, inward tears. I know I was not well so I waited two days before writing. Meanwhile all you said came home to me and I knew that a great deal of what you complained of was true ... but it is wonderful for me to read a letter like this one you have written, and to know how much we mean to each other. You do know, beloved one, don't you, how much I love you? It is no dream, nor pack of cards, and you have never failed me, you could not begin to do so. I would not have you different from what you are. You wouldn't be the man I have always loved all these years. I feel almost glad we have had this upset; it has shown us both how much we have and how we can help each other. I just long to see you again and hug and kiss you and lie in your arms and ask you to forgive me for making you so unhappy and all for no reason. . . . Please, darling, forget all this and let us be happy together.'

A month later, at midnight on 20 January 1936, the King died. He was seventy-one, but his death had not been expected – his last illness had begun only four days earlier. His heart was weak and when he developed an attack of the bronchial catarrh to which he was subject its effects quickly dragged him down. By Sunday 19 January it was apparent that he had, at most, only days to live and the Prince of Wales drove to London so to inform the Prime Minister. As the King's life ebbed away, it was necessary for the Privy Council to appoint a Council of State, and Ramsay MacDonald, as Lord President, was summoned to Sandringham. He wrote to Edith on his return to Upper Frognal Lodge that night. 'I was at Sandringham today. There the sands of time are sinking fast, and I bade my King and friend farewell. I was profoundly moved as I looked upon him and saw his pathetic struggle with the numbing finger of death. I sat next to the Queen at lunch and had an interesting talk with her. She has the fortitude of a Roman and made me almost believe that her chief interests for the moment are Malcolm and Ishbel. . . .'

The story of King Edward VIII and Mrs Simpson is too familiar to need recounting again. It is only necessary to say here that his accession brought their love affair into more prominence, though it was still disregarded by the press and unknown to the public at large. In the inner circle of London society, however, *bons mots* like 'Honi soit qui Wally pense' referred to her complete domination over the new King, and new groupings began to form – those who took the late King George's disapproving line over his son's liaison, those who formed an Edward-and-Wallis 'court' and those who attempted to steer a middle course.

Some hostesses attempted to foster the affair, notably Lady Cunard. Not well looked on in Court circles, Emerald Cunard was prepared to do anything she could to strengthen her links with the Prince of Wales. She cultivated a friendship with Mrs Simpson and her small suppers of half a dozen close friends, where the Prince could meet Wallis in comparative privacy, were exactly tailored to his wishes. Later Emerald Cunard's open partisanship was to rebound on her. When George VI became King, Queen Mary recorded that he told his brother and sister-in-law the Duke and Duchess of Kent that he never wished them to see Lady Cunard again; and when the King and Queen accepted an invitation to a ball at Londonderry House to celebrate their coronation, the Queen wrote sweetly to say that the only person on the list of guests Edith had submitted that she did not wish to meet was Lady Cunard. 'The bitter months of last autumn and winter are still so fresh in our minds and her presence will inevitably bring so many sad thoughts that we would prefer not to.'

At first Edith, like many others, had ignored the gossip, behaving as if there were no particular connection between the Prince of Wales and the Ernest Simpsons. She continued to abide by the social rule that, if a man was neither married nor engaged, he was treated as single. She herself knew all the Royal Family well, and she naturally asked the Prince of Wales to her own receptions and parties – but as the bachelor he was.

This did not go down well with the Prince. John Buchan's daughter Alice, the Hon. Lady Fairfax Lucy, remembers going to 'an absolutely dreadful party at Londonderry House. We wore our most splendid clothes, and were taken into a private room. There were the Duke and Duchess of York, he shy but agreeable, she very pretty and charming, and the Prince of Wales, absolutely *furious* because Mrs Simpson hadn't been asked.'

The Prince got his own back with a public snub. At one of Edith's Wednesday evening dances, the music began but the Prince, who enjoyed dancing and was normally the first on the floor – nobody could dance before he did – remained chatting and drinking. Feet had begun to tap longingly when finally the Prince turned and crossed the floor. Everyone waited expectantly for him to ask Edith, his hostess, for the first dance in the customary fashion. But he ignored her, walking straight past her to the daughter of the Brazilian Ambassador (the senior diplomat present), over whose hand he bowed low before asking her to dance.

Edith's own views as well as her closeness to the King and Queen meant that she shared the growing disapproval and dismay at Mrs Simpson's influence over the Prince. She never willingly asked Mrs Simpson to Londonderry House and although she could not, of course, refuse a direct request from the Prince her attitude was always perfectly clear. This pattern continued sporadically up to and after the Prince's accession to the throne.

Edith, now restored to health again and on terms with Baldwin, gave her customary Eve-of-Parliament reception in November 1936. Montgomery Hyde records that, on the morning of the reception, a message was received from Buckingham Palace asking if the King could come, and bring Mrs Simpson. This time, the situation was dramatically different: Mrs Simpson had just been granted a decree nisi. So far, the British press had remained silent about the affair though American and Continental newspapers were full of it.

Three days later, on 6 November, Edith and Wallis Simpson met again, at one of Emerald Cunard's evening parties. Edith, now *au fait* with the seriousness of the situation and never one to shirk speaking her mind in what she deemed was the cause of duty, tackled Mrs Simpson at once. Speaking with her usual forceful blend of charm, frankness and moral conviction, she launched straightaway into her views on Mrs Simpson's relationship with the King. She spoke of the harm being done by American newspapers (the British Press were still silent) and she said roundly that if the King had any notion of marrying Mrs Simpson he should be disabused of this forthwith – the English people would never stand for a consort who had been twice divorced and whose previous husbands were both still living. Such was the power of Edith's personality that Mrs Simpson listened meekly to this almost complete stranger discussing her love affair and telling her where her duty lay. Next day Mrs Simpson, who did not know that Edith had just left for Wynyard, wrote to her at Londonderry House.

'I have been thinking over all you told me last night. I have come to the conclusion that perhaps no one has been *really* frank with a certain person in telling him how the country feels about his friendship with me; perhaps nothing has been said to him at all. I feel he should know however and therefore I am going to tell him the things you told me.

'I was sorry we had so many interruptions for it made one express oneself badly last night. I wanted to say a word about the American press. As you know, America is a country that lives on sensations, so to sell their papers, the more sensational they are the better the circulation. One is a victim of that form of journalism because your King has always been to the Americans more news than anyone in their own country – and so they have taken a very nice friendship and made it something more spectacular, and are growing rich on it. No one is spared, the truth is not sensational enough, misstatements attract more.

'I am *afraid* I am the innocent victim – put "on the spot" by my own country. I have never been in the press, my family having always fought against it, even when I made my debut.

'I appreciated your talk to me so much . . . I hope I shall see you when you return and again with thanks for telling me what you told me.'

So much did Edith want to stress the importance of their conversation that, unaware that Mrs Simpson had already written to her, she wrote to her from Wynyard on 8 November.

'I was very pleased to have been able to have a word with you at Emerald's. My husband and myself only returned from our trip abroad a few days ago and we are both horrified and shocked at the things that are being bandied about on all sides. The only thing is to remain calm and pay no attention yourself to these attacks. If your own friends exercise tact and discretion, they can do a great deal to help.

'Personally I cannot but feel the whole thing has been organised from America, with the set purpose of doing "him" harm – I could not say that to you on Friday, because everything is impossible in a milieu like that with servants and busybodies looking on and listening but I am quite sure that if his real friends all help, much can be done to silence all this wicked conspiracy and you yourself know best how to steer a judicious and wise course.

'I am so sorry for you and only write now to tell you that any indirect help I can give to help "him", I will do, & do all I can quietly.'

Less than a month afterwards, on 10 December 1936, Edward VIII abdicated, and a few hours later left the country. Edith and Charley both wrote to him. The letters are worthy of remark in that both of them referred to him throughout as 'Your Majesty' and – according to Montgomery Hyde – the Duke transcribed their text in his own hand, and kept these copies with the rest of his private papers.

Charley's letter, which began '...I venture to send my humble sympathy to Your Majesty at this very sad moment', recalled the fact that he had known the Duke since his cradle days. 'I was one of those who has known Your Majesty from my early days as I was one of the first to see Your Majesty at White Lodge in the summer of 1894 [the Duke was born in June 1894]. I have always regretted that it was never my good fortune except on rare occasions to cooperate with Your Majesty in activities connected with Social Reform for which you have done so much, and which has been a part of my life's work....

'I would say, if I may, that should Your Majesty require any service from me in the future I will gladly do what lies within my power.'

Edith's letter expressed warmth, regret and a tribute to the former monarch's most salient trait: his humanness. 'I feel I must write you a line to tell you that you are very much in our thoughts & that we all feel that in losing you we are parting with a great King. You have my deepest sympathy in the great struggle. Although I did not have the privilege of knowing you very well, I have always admired the manner in which you took a vy human interest in the big problems confronting the nation and in many spots in which I too in my humble way was interested. I wanted to tell Your Majesty that, wherever you are, we shall never forget all the hard & good work that you have done & that I shall always remember you as a vy human personality. May God Bless you & give you happiness.' Neither of them mentioned Mrs Simpson.

XXV

Lord Londonderry, a much-abused Air Minister in Mr Baldwin's Cabinet, once said to me with simple but irrefutable logic: 'There were really only two things I could do. Build an Air Force, or try to make friends with the Germans.'

Robert Boothby, in *I Fight To Live*.

AS AIR MINISTER, Charley had never ceased to advocate that all dealings with Germany, which was growing increasingly powerful under Hitler, should be from a position of strength. But all his efforts to persuade the Government to build up a strong, balanced Air Force capable of attack as well as defence had failed and he did not believe that the rearmament which was now taking place could catch up with that of Germany. 'I told the Government in 1933 that it was necessary to expand the Air Force and that they should begin that expansion then, as it was quite certain public opinion would change and would demand a strong Air Force,' he wrote to the Earl of Clanwilliam in June 1936. With the authority and conviction of one who was a pilot himself, he continued: 'I wanted at least four years for the training of pilots. Instead of that, when the Government were pushed into rearmament in 1935, the scheme which I had planned is to be compressed into two years instead of four and the result has been that 45 pilots have already lost their lives in the first six months of this year and to anyone with any expert knowledge, the loss of these lives is due to lack of training.'

As he saw it, if Britain could not afford sufficient armaments to deter German expansionism, the only alternative was *détente* and he now turned his energies to the cause of Anglo-German friendship. As he later put it in his book *Ourselves and Germany**: 'The time may well be not far off,

* Published in 1938 by Robert Hale Ltd.

should the present unsatisfactory and uncertain state of Anglo-German relations be allowed to continue, when the Germans will be able to dispense with the hope of any understanding with us and to strike out along a course of Weltpolitik frankly antagonistic to Great Britain and her many imperial and commercial interests.' His intentions were honourable but the course he followed was to blemish his reputation and earn him the description of 'Nazi sympathiser' and, later, 'appeaser'. Edith, always unquestioningly loyal, backed him wholeheartedly.

Charley's attempt at rapprochement began, appropriately enough, with a visit to the Commander in Chief of the Luftwaffe, and President of the Reichstag, Hermann Goering. Charley, Edith and Mairi flew to Germany on 29 January 1936, the day after George V's funeral, in a Lufthansa machine ('very comfortable and surprisingly quiet'). Once in Germany, Goering put his private aeroplane, a JU52, at Charley's disposal.

Goering, stocky, smiling, cheerful, a former pilot who held the highest German decoration for gallantry – in 1918 he had risen to be the Commander of the famed Richthofen Squadron – appealed to the Londonderrys. They always admired physical courage, they found his jollity and gusto engaging, they enjoyed the superb pictures, tapestries and sculptures in his enormous house, innocently thinking of him as an art-lover who had been fortunate in his purchases.

They were made welcome like royalty. They looked at airfields, colleges, lecture halls, watched a fly-past by the Richthofen Squadron in honour of the third anniversary of Hitler's accession to power, and dined that evening with the Goerings, where they met many senior Party members, including the one they were to grow to know the best, Ribbentrop. After dinner the forty guests listened to a Wagner concert before seeing a film featuring Germany's military strength and a stirring speech by the Fuehrer.

Next day there was a visit to the Karinhall, Goering's hunting lodge, in his country estate forty miles north of Berlin in the middle of the Schorfeide forest. The Karinhall, set on the banks of a lake, was a long, low Scandinavian-style log cabin but with comforts not found in the usual wooden forest hut – electric light, piping-hot water, and the most up-to-date heating. Its furnishings carried out the theme of an owner devoted to the simple life, with a large, rustic dining table in the long central room, and massive wooden chairs. It was a room designed for feasting, recounting the day's exploits and drinking deep after hours in the open air. (By the time the Duke and Duchess of Windsor visited it late the following year it had been greatly enlarged, with a gymnasium in the basement and a model railway laid out in the attic for one of the Goering nephews, to which the *Reichsmarschal* had added his own individual touch: a toy aeroplane which could be sent flying over the railway, dropping some small wooden bombs as it did so.)

At the Karinhall Goering gave full rein to his passion for dressing up – be the part that of air supremo or intrepid hunter – striding through the forest in leather jerkin and huge hunter's hat, wielding an old Germanic spear in Wagnerian fashion and blowing his circular hunting horn at the bison enclosure until the great beasts lumbered up. There were family meals, there were long walks, there were discussions about shooting and stalking – aurochs, elk and deer – as well as about the Air Force and the Luftwaffe. A recurring theme in Goering's conversation was the close kinship between the British and German nations and the common characteristics they shared.

Charley's German was reasonable ('I could understand most of the German spoken by Ribbentrop but I had to rely on the interpreter for Hess') but Edith and Mairi could not speak a word. This may have been why Dr Paul Schmidt, Hitler's interpreter, who had been seconded to Goering for the Londonderrys' visit, recorded of Charley: 'One knew at once that this man sincerely desired an understanding with Germany. Goering must also have had this impression for I have seldom heard him speak with less reserve than in his conversations with Lord Londonderry.'

Edith was not taken in. 'To live in the upper levels of National Socialism may be quite pleasant, but woe to the poor folk who do not belong to the upper orders,' she said to Dr Schmidt. She also had her first brush with Ribbentrop: when, after they had lunched at his country house, he held forth with loudmouthed certainty on some aspect of the Nazi credo, Edith became so infuriated she grabbed him by the arm and began to shake him.

The following days were spent flying to various aerodromes, often in bumpy conditions ('our unfortunate interpreter was sick'), and the visit culminated in a two-hour talk with Hitler on the afternoon of 4 February. The Fuehrer declared that what disturbed him most was the growing menace to the world from Bolshevism; it was an argument exactly designed to appeal to a large body of opinion in England. When Charley brought up the subject of German colonial aims, the Fuehrer responded by saying that Germany's colonies (then mandated territories under the League of Nations) had been unjustly taken from her. 'Germany wants to live in close friendly alliance with England,' he concluded, 'and for England perhaps the time will come when she will have to consider the question whether an active friendship with Germany, or whether the possession of a couple of colonies which for the British Empire are not of very great value, is the more important.' The interview was over.

The visit continued with more inspections of efficient, smiling air squadrons, more entertaining, and a week at the Olympic Games that brought further encounters with Hitler and Goering. Finally, the Londonderrys departed, heaped with compliments, smiling photographs of the Nazi leaders in silver frames and, for Mairi, a silver model of Goering's aeroplane.

On his return, Charley attempted to report all that he had seen, learned and spoken of to those in power. But the Prime Minister was too busy to see him and none of his former Cabinet colleagues – with the exception of his son-in-law, Oliver Stanley, who could hardly refuse – was prepared to listen. In the eyes of most people, a private visit by an ex-Cabinet minister to Hitler was at the least injudicious ('Londonderry just back from hobnobbing with Hitler', was how Harold Nicolson put it), at the worst smacked of secret negotiations. Even Ramsay MacDonald noted in his diary after a lunch party given by one of Edith's American friends: 'Rather spiteful talk on the Londonderrys' visit to Hitler but they have certainly laid themselves out for it.'

Correspondence with the faces in the silver frames ensued. There were letters from Hitler, written on thick, yellowish-cream paper, crested in gold with a German eagle over a globe, emblazoned with a swastika, and bearing the solitary word 'Berlin', as its sender's address, with the Fuehrer's extraordinary signature, black, cramped and sinister, written as if up and down an inverted V. 'Please accept my warmest thanks for sending me the picture and the charming collection of songs with the beautiful old melodies,' wrote the Fuehrer. 'I was particularly overjoyed to learn from your accompanying letter how much you and your husband sympathised with my efforts to bring about a genuine peace. I would like also, with all my heart, to wish you success in the noble and beneficent task that you have set yourself.'

Letters to and from Goering were more explicit. After their return Edith wrote to Frau Goering to thank her for her hospitality, and said that she would be dispatching a present of linen sheets and tablecloths 'in air force blue'. On the same day, 21 February, she also wrote to Goering; the opening of her letter, couched as it was in terms of the most grovelling flattery ('Dear General der Flieger and Minister President – although I would prefer to call you "Siegfried" as you are my conception of a Siegfried of modern times!'), must have been deeply satisfying to the Reichsmarschal.

'. . . You may rest assured we shall do all that is possible to help forward the cause of peace between our two countries, coupled with France. The difficulties are very great, especially at the present moment, fear and an ingrained dislike of certain things in your country on the part of many very nice people here, who have been led by the Government in the past to pin their entire faith on the Geneva policy in order, as they imagine, to create a more human world. The Press too, as you know, is largely hostile and controlled to a great extent by Jews. Beside this large body of opinion in England is another and smaller section, though vociferous and strong, whose sympathies are secretly with Russia to some extent – and all the Trade Unionists quite openly. Together all these parties combine to make a situation which will be difficult for the present Prime Minister to steer another course.

'No one in this country wants War – on the contrary, they are almost hostile in the cause of peace!! except of course the Communists, who are the same in all countries, but they are negligible here. Your help will be of great assistance to us. You are a pillar of strength in your country. If you will make your people realise that our difficulties are not that "we will not" but that "we cannot" without a good deal of preparation. Public opinion has not only to be led but swayed. You are fortunately in a strong position, where you can command, so you must have patience with those whose task is to guide and steer the boat through unruly currents. If an understanding can be achieved between the three countries, much will have been gained. My husband has already seen several people, and I have seen many MPs before I came here.

'I am so very glad to have had the opportunity to have seen Germany under present conditions. It is nothing less than a miracle what has been accomplished in three years.'

The disparaging reference to Jews in this letter strikes an unhappy note but it should be remembered that many people were prejudiced against Jews to a greater or lesser extent, a widespread, almost unthinking bigotry reflected in popular novels like those of Sapper, Dornford Yates and John Buchan – who was in fact a supporter of Zionism. Although Nazi persecution of Jews had already begun, attitudes did not really change until the full horror of the Holocaust started to emerge. Charley and Edith had opposed Teddy Jessel's marriage to their daughter Helen because he was of the Jewish faith; once they were married, Lord Jessel told the writer, they accepted him as part of the family and treated him with great kindness, though Edith did try at intervals throughout the marriage to convert him to Christianity.

At the end of February Charley and Edith went up to fish on the Brora, in Sutherland. They were still there when the German army, in breach of the Treaty of Versailles, crossed the Rhine and reoccupied the demilitarised Rhineland on 7 March. Soon afterwards Edith had to return south. Charley, alone on the river, spent many of the undisturbed hours thinking over the events of the past months and trying to decide a future course. On 30 March, he set down what he had finally come to feel in a long and revelatory letter to Edith.

'I am afraid my seeming discomfiture and setback has worried you a great deal. Probably we mind it much more for each other than for ourselves. I feel I have let you down, that I have not justified the faith you have had in me and it is for these feelings really that I feel irritated with Baldwin and those who brought about my downfall. On reflection I do not believe I ever was a good Cabinet Minister or colleague, because I like to keep in control and I detest supporting or playing a minor role. . . . I have noted your scathing criticism and condemnations of those who have bested me lately [Edith was apt to call Lord Swinton Lord Swineton] but I think you are doing them an injustice owing to your intense loyalty to me. . . . I got the Air Ministry through Ramsay and I shall be eternally grateful . . . but I think we built up a lot of jealousy and animosity and our detractors – and I have a great many more than you – are revelling in all this. So the stiff upper lip and a laugh and a smile is the proper line.

'I hope I have not wearied you with all this. I am glad I can see much more of you now, as I didn't bring you into my work. It is a failing of mine which I have become conscious of that I am a bad co-operator and must have my own show. And I do want to make you happy and contented and I felt it like a lash when I said I should like to go back all over again and you said you wouldn't, and you explained to me why. I can't think how I have been so thoughtless because you have always been on the pinnacle, no matter where anybody else was, and I have always thought you understood that. I know everybody else does but I hate the thought of ever having made you unhappy and I should destroy everything to make you happy. . . . We shall have to accept a lot of boring things, I know, we shall be left out of everything and it will be a trifle galling but if we understand it and are ready for it, and I have got you, I feel I don't mind.'

His bitterness towards Baldwin, and his resentment at the loss of office, continued. An added humiliation was that he had been left off the Coronation Committee, though socially the Londonderrys were still as eminent as ever – when the new King and Queen dined at Londonderry House, no one else was likely to refuse an invitation. Ramsay Mac-Donald's attempts to soothe his feelings provoked only a reproach. 'I don't as a rule blow my own trumpet but as Air Minister my position was absolutely unassailable, as I think you have all found out by now. I held the Air Force together, raised their morale and their self-respect, and I know I had the support of all those who counted. But when I turned to you to get the support I expected, you remained silent, and it was left to Baldwin to say: "Of course the PM has confidence in all his Ministers." Baldwin then left, and you would have witnessed an explosion which really might have alarmed you but you produced Horder's letter out of your pocket and I just subsided with a few words of sympathy.'

Edith was determined to do everything she could to assist Charley in his aim of improving Anglo-German relations. This meant trying to obliterate the scepticism she had shown during the German visit. A long letter from Goering, dated 16 May 1936, makes it clear he knew the importance of gaining Edith's goodwill as well as Charley's. After hoping that the Londonderrys would come and stay again in the autumn 'to shoot a capital stag', he continued in the familiar vein of veiled threat and propaganda.

'Politically, things look somewhat unpromising, to put it frankly, especially for England. The quick Italian victory and the complete annexation of Abyssinia may mean a great danger for England in the long run. Mussolini will make the brave Abyssinians within a few years into an army of millions trained and equipped on up-to-date lines. Abyssinia will also become a very strong naval and aviation base. On the other hand he will threaten the Sudanese frontier from Libya. Moreover, I happen to know that Italy is now beginning to develop her fleet and submarines. All this is extremely serious for England's position in the Mediterranean and particularly for navigation through the Suez Canal.

'I must confess that I have seldom seen in history a combination of circumstances which so directly affects England's vital nerve as the present situation in Abyssinia. I am rather curious to see how English politics will size up the situation and how it will react. Italy makes extraordinary efforts to secure German friendship. You know however that the Fuehrer has provided for co-operation with England in his political programme. As this is also my sincere desire I trust that England will at last make English politics and not be dependent on French politics.

'A great deal will now depend on England's attitude in the Locarno and Rhine question. This will be the test question for our people in our relations with England. The League of Nations at the moment does not stand very high in world opinion. I think Italy will leave the League and will certainly induce a few other countries to leave. In any case, these are very uncertain times. In addition to all this the Bolsheviks are beginning to agitate more than ever everywhere; Spain is almost a Soviet State, France is tending towards the left under strongly Communistic influences. In Germany we are quiet and working hard. The people are happy and full of confidence in the Fuehrer who has freed them from all internal agitation and trouble, and who has made Germany so strong that she is absolutely firmly established also in the international commonwealth of nations. She is a bulwark against Bolshevism and for peace and quiet. God grant that the two great Germanic nations, England and Germany, may come together in the future to guarantee world peace, or at least peace for our own countries. I know, my dear Lady Londonderry, that you are also looking towards this end and this is the reason I am writing to you as I do, and hope that we can discuss it frequently and fully.'

The representative of Nazi Germany with whom the Londonderrys had most to do, however, was Joachim Ribbentrop.

Born in 1893, Ribbentrop had had a varied career, much of it devoted to social climbing. The first upward step was taken in the unlikely setting of Canada, whither he had gone in 1910 after being educated in Grenoble and London. Neither his youth nor the fact that he was only a junior clerk in the offices of the Canadian Pacific Railway deterred him from signing his name in the visitors' book kept by the Governor-General and, in consequence, he received the customary invitation to Rideau Hall. He could not have fallen into a milieu more ready to welcome a young German far from home: the Governor-General, the Duke of Connaught*, was married to the Prussian Princess Louise-Margaret, most of the staff spoke German and all entertained strong German sympathies. Ribbentrop, young and good-looking, with grey eyes in a square-jawed face, was out to charm; his manners, of the excessively formal, heel-clicking German school, were impeccable. He was soon taken up by the Governor-General's circle – which was, later, to provide him with many useful contacts.

Ambitious and shrewd, Ribbentrop, by the time Edith and Charley

* Queen Victoria's third son, Prince Arthur.

met him, had acquired numerous social skills. He had been a cavalryman in the 1914–18 war. He was always beautifully dressed, he could play the violin, he spoke French and English almost perfectly – ironically, his German always had an English accent – he was a good tennis player and an excellent dancer. He had married a pretty woman from a well-off family: Anneliese Henkell was the daughter of a rich German wine grower and from his father-in-law Ribbentrop quickly learned everything he could about wine.

Soon there was only one thing missing to complete this upward mobility: the prefix 'von' that indicated he was on the right side of the divide between those of noble birth and the rest; and in 1925 he acquired it. Two or three branches of Ribbentrops had the 'von', and when Joachim met Gertrude von Ribbentrop, an elderly woman who may have been a distant relative, he saw his chance. It was not long before he was calling her 'Aunt' and she had agreed to adopt him. He affirmed on oath that he was her nephew and, as it was possible in the Weimar Republic to acquire a patent of nobility through adoption by a blood relation, he now began to call himself von Ribbentrop.

The Nazi movement offered an obvious channel for self-advancement. Soon his speeches against Bolshevism were well known and many of the early meetings of the Nazi inner circle took place in the Ribbentrops' home. Anneliese was a particular favourite of Hitler's, fitting to perfection the Fuehrer's ideal of German womanhood – a blonde Aryan beauty with a face free of cosmetics who was an excellent cook and a prolific mother (the Ribbentrops had five children).

With more social polish than any other Party member, and a charming wife, Ribbentrop was a natural choice as Ambassador to Britain. Both Hitler and Ribbentrop attached disproportionate importance to lulling the suspicions of the British upper classes as to German aims; both felt that securing their goodwill was a vital step in the master plan. Though the abdication of Edward VIII, known to be sympathetic to Germany, was a blow, there was much pro-German sentiment in the upper echelons of English society. Many people in Great Britain – including the Royal Family – had German blood. The German president of the Anglo-German Fellowship, the aim of which was to foster friendship through various cultural activities, was the Duke of Saxe-Coburg-Gotha, Queen Victoria's grandson, who had been born and brought up in England as the Duke of Albany. Its English president was Lord Mount Temple, and among its members were Charley, the Marquis of Lothian, Lord Redesdale and Lord Rennell.

Ribbentrop was given a huge budget to help him storm London society. The Embassy staff, chosen in part for looks and agreeableness, were all given new evening clothes, the German Embassy was expanded to take in numbers 7, 8 and 9 Carlton House Terrace, and the interior remodelled to allow entertaining on a grand scale. There were lavish receptions at which Ribbentrop's undoubted ability to choose excellent wines came into its own. There were marquees, footmen, celebrities, marvellous dance bands, suppers of lobsters, truffles and game cooked by the most famous chef in Germany, amidst which Ribbentrop, as Lady Diana Cooper recorded, 'would kiss the shrinking hands of the ladies'. For at the level of society which he sought to penetrate, most of the English were impressed neither by his aristocratic pretensions nor his ersatz charm: they found him a risible if slightly sinister figure. Young women in particular disliked him, with his hooded, assessing eyes and his wandering hands. Behind his back he was called Brickendrop, Ribbensnob and soon – according to Chips Channon – the Londonderry Herr.

Neither Edith nor Charley liked Ribbentrop, finding him simultaneously arrogant and ingratiating. But in pursuance of their policy of cultivating Anglo-German friendship, they were assiduously cordial to him. In May 1936 they asked him to stay at Mount Stewart for Whitsun. They also asked Sir Edward Ellington, Chief of the Air Staff, and several senior Air Force officers. The Ribbentrops arrived in one of Goering's larger aeroplanes, accompanied by some of the Embassy staff and a noisy gang of SS men. Charley had arranged for three air squadrons – the City of Glasgow, City of Edinburgh and City of Durham – to fly over to Belfast airfield to impress Ribbentrop, and Edith gave a huge luncheon party for the occasion.

It was not altogether a happy visit. Edith and Charley took their guest out sailing, Charley taking Ribbentrop in his boat, Edith sailing her own, for the regular River Class races. Edith ran into Charley's boat and Ribbentrop fell overboard; for the Londonderrys, the collision was nothing out of the way but Ribbentrop was terrified. All the young women who were staying or visiting knew of Ribbentrop's reputation and would not let him get near them; and finally he was overshadowed by a young secretary at the Embassy who endeared himself to everyone with his easy, unaffected niceness. Afterwards, several of the house party tried to invite the young man to luncheon or dinner – only to find that he had been packed off back to Berlin. Ribbentrop was also invited for a three-day shoot at Wynyard, in November. There were eight guns – including

Charley and Robin – and on the first day they shot 211 pheasants, a hare, eight rabbits, three woodcock and twenty-eight duck.

The correspondence with Goering continued ('I am convinced that you know how much the Leader and all of us desire and love Peace'). In July there was a further long letter to Edith, this time complaining of the attitude of English statesmen and the Press. 'Now, as ever, all responsible statesmen here are concerned to promote a rapprochement with the English people, and we are therefore genuinely sorry when we read such pronouncements and speeches as the English Minister for War has recently made. Lord Halifax's observations in the House of Lords on Duff Cooper's speech also were in part very distressing, especially when he says that France and England are natural allies in the defence of the ideals of freedom and democracy. I hope that you have satisfied yourself that the German people prizes and cherishes nothing more highly than its freedom, that internally too it feels itself absolutely free and that, above all, it is ready to defend its honour and its freedom to the last breath against any that may venture to encroach thereon. . . . England must understand that Germany cannot for ever go on making offers to England but that she is forced, in case England rejects the proffered hand, to seek her friends where she finds them. . . . It is my constant concern to advocate the creation at the earliest possible moment of an atmosphere of confidence and co-operation between our two peoples before Germany finds it necessary to make enquiries elsewhere. When I read today that there are still English politicians like Churchill and Austen Chamberlain who speak of a German danger to England, I can only say that those people do not know Germany, or are determined to thwart any understanding.'

So hospitable was Goering to distinguished English visitors that on 10 November Ramsay MacDonald wrote privately to Anthony Eden on a dilemma that was beginning to exercise some of the Government. 'Goering as you know entertains his English guests in a lavish and generous manner but so far they have been unable to give him anything in return (not even a colony). I fear the result of all this one-sided hospitality may well be an attempt on Goering's part, which will be difficult to resist, and perhaps still more difficult to satisfy, to come to England (possibly as Hitler's representative at the Coronation). If we resist we may incur Goering's undying hostility and if we let him come we run quite a good risk of his being shot in England. Neither of these alternatives would be likely permanently to improve Anglo-German relations.'

Fortunately, Goering was not anxious to represent Germany at the Coronation, which took place on 12 May 1937, and wrote to Charley: 'You will appreciate that after all the agitation against my coming to England, which was carried to the extent of holding meetings at which I was called all kinds of insulting names, it is quite impossible for me to attend the Coronation.' Ribbentrop had already made an unfortunate impression on the new King. By now Germany was pressing Britain hard on the question of her former colonies, and Ribbentrop had left Germany on 3 February 1937 with a memorandum setting out in detail Hitler's arguments for their return. Britain's response to this was, predictably, an unqualified 'No'; when Ribbentrop was presented to the King at a levee on 4 February he made the usual three bows, then stepped forward raising his arm stiffly in a 'Heil Hitler!' salute. The King drew back slightly, no one said a thing, but London society was infuriated at the insult to the Sovereign.

Coronation Year was busy for both Charley and Edith. Charley held a number of public offices. He was Mayor of Durham – as his father had been for the Coronation Year of George V – and he was Chancellor of Durham University (1937 was its centenary year). He was Honorary Air Commodore of 607 Auxiliary Fighter Squadron and of 502 Auxiliary Bomber Squadron; he was Lord Lieutenant of County Down and Chancellor of Queen's University, Belfast. Edith's time was occupied with organising a fête for the Queen's nurses at Mount Stewart (£400 was raised), yachting in the Western Isles, visiting Doncaster and Sunderland with Charley, going to stay with Marthe Bibesco in Romania, visiting Hungary, slipping over to Paris for a few days every now and then, as well as the usual movements between the various Londonderry houses.

She had hardly seen Ramsay MacDonald, who now spent much more of his time in Lossiemouth. The ardent sentiments and vivid fantasies of a few years earlier had disappeared; his letters had become depressed, short and infrequent. Many of them are simply attempts to arrange meetings – somehow, one or other always seemed to have an engagement – and by 1937 there is a note of plaintive admonishment. 'I am not sure where you were when you were slipping out of the arms of 1936 into those of 1937, so I could not first-foot you by telephone as usual. I hope however, the New Year has come to you with happiness as a gift. I am still feeling the effects of prolonged overwork and dwell near the bottom of a well. . . .' 'All I can say is that I had convinced myself that I had booked the day and believed you were to tell me what you proposed to do with it. But my memory has now become so faulty that you probably have good grounds for your view.'

The truth was that the peak of their friendship had passed. Edith, though still fond of the old man – he was now seventy – had become increasingly bored by his complaints. She was still extremely solicitous of his welfare, she wrote to him and she sent him presents, but she no longer saw so much of him.

MacDonald's physical condition was steadily deteriorating. Over the last year or so his handwriting, a sure indicator of health, had got worse; there were errors of grammar and spelling mistakes. He had begun to forget words in conversation as well as people's names. At the beginning of the year he had decided it was time to withdraw from all public activities and on 28 May resigned as Lord President of the Council. Once again, he was offered a marquisate – which he had always refused before on the grounds that 'I was born Mr, I made my way as Mr, and I will die as Mr' – but now he felt he was not up even to the more leisurely pace of the House of Lords. However, he had read a book called *The Marquis of Lossie* by a Scottish writer also named MacDonald. He called a family conference in his study at Lossiemouth and admitted to being 'a wee bit tempted' by this coincidence. Turning to his daughters, he said: 'I thought I would not refuse before I asked you. I thought I should give you the opportunity of at last becoming ladies.' But his children were agreed: enoblement would betray the Socialist principles in which they all believed.

He was too exhausted even to attend the Eve-of-Parliament reception for the National Government on 25 October that Edith gave – now that Charley would no longer have to stand next to the man who had brought about his downfall. For Baldwin, seventy in August, had resigned on 28 May, just after the Coronation, to be succeeded by Neville Chamberlain, the unanimous choice of his colleagues. Chamberlain, sixty-eight and himself suffering from gout – while waiting beside Edith at the head of the stairs for the 2,000-odd guests to arrive he had to sit and rest – also realised how valuable to the Conservative Party his hostess was. He wrote to Edith: 'It is difficult to realise what a party at Londonderry House means to the provincial Conservative. I had a letter from a Birmingham man who has given a great deal of money and time to the cause there and had received his invitation for himself and his wife and daughter. He is a wealthy man and chairman of various important companies but he wrote a letter of thanks that was quite touching in its simple gratitude.' The party was once again in the evening and consequently more colourful.

To try and restore his health, MacDonald planned a sea voyage to South America, which he had always wanted to see. Everyone in the Lossiemouth house knew that he was not well. When he said goodbye to Meta, the local girl who was the MacDonalds' maid and friend (she had been head housemaid at No. 10), she was so upset that she ran to Ishbel's bedroom to hide her tears. Convinced that she had seen him for the last time, she was sitting on the bed weeping when there was a knock at the door and in walked MacDonald. 'But Mr MacDonald, we've already said goodbye,' she said, between her sobs. He took her hand, smiled, and said gently: 'There's no harm in an extra handshake between friends.' The last thing he did before leaving was to take his large diary from his desk, where it always rested, open it, and lay it on the floor, as if, said Meta, 'he knew it was all finished'. The final entry in it read: 'Sorry shall not see Malcolm till I return.'

His last letter to Edith seems to show that he thought he would never see her again; though sweet and loving, there is an underlying note of sadness, and regret that they are no longer so close. 'You were charming yesterday and I was so sorry to have to leave without a real goodbye. . . . I shall have to take your memory away with me. The result of the journey will remain uncertain, though I shall face it whatever it may be and make the best of it. So let us "greet the unseen with a cheer", whatever it may be. I shall think much of you as I go along from pagan to saint and pray do not altogether forget me. . . .'

On 5 November 1937 he set off from Liverpool on the *Reina del Pacifico*, with his youngest daughter Sheila, bound for South America. He had no plans, he said, adding the typical MacDonald coda: 'I am in search of that most elusive of all forms of happiness – rest.' It was a journey to which Sheila had been looking forward immensely. 'Father was so reserved, so busy, and I thought "At last I have got him to myself, at sea, free of politics, and we can really talk".'

They had scarcely two days together. On the morning of 8 November, after playing a game of deck quoits, he said to Sheila: 'I think I will go and lie down. I don't feel up to much.' The doctor was summoned, and by the afternoon MacDonald felt so much better he had tea with the Bishop of Nassau. But at 6.30 he sent for the doctor again, and at 7.45 he died of heart failure, with Sheila beside him. The *Reina del Pacifico*, which had just passed the Azores, went on to Bermuda, whence Mac-Donald's body was taken back to England on the cruiser HMS *Apollo*. It was a death that would have appealed to MacDonald, with its romantic overtones – freedom from the constraints of the land; solitude; the old leader borne back to his country on a warship.

'He loved beautiful things – books, pictures, beautiful women, and lovely jewels and colours,' wrote Edith. 'And why shouldn't he? He was, for these days, an old-fashioned Socialist. His aim was to improve, not destroy. He fought against privilege and inequality of opportunity. . . .' It was not a bad epitaph to receive from his 'Dearest Ladye'.

XXVI

I N FEBRUARY 1938, tragedy struck the Londonderry family. All through the thirties, the Plunkets were two of the most familiar and popular figures on the social scene. Dorothé was sophisticated and chic in the idiom of the day though her nature had remained as sweet, affectionate and unspoiled as when she was an ingenuous seventeen-year-old bride. Her dancing was famous: she danced at home with friends to the gramophone, she danced for Edith's favourite charities, in 1935 she partnered Robert Helpmann. Diana Barnato Walker, her goddaughter and niece by marriage who came out in 1936, remembers her tangoing in a green and blue spangled sheath dress 'that made her look like a languorous mermaid' in a charity cabaret at the Dorchester. Dorothé was one of the Queen's closest friends – there was only six months' difference in their ages – and the King was godfather to the youngest Plunket son, Sean. And like Charley's other daughters, she was an experienced and accomplished pilot.

She and Teddy were constantly at Londonderry House and often stayed at Mount Stewart. Edith was devoted to her, and Charley, though not particularly adept with small children, was encouraging to his little grandsons. Robin (now Lord) Plunket remembers his grandfather promising him a shilling a run and a pound a wicket when he played as a schoolboy in a match near Belfast.

Dorothé saw her mother whenever possible. Fannie, now living mainly in the South of France, had kept on the Cleveland Square house until the end of 1936. Here her grandsons would visit 'Fannie the grannie' and her husband Jack Dean, known to the little boys as The Bean. The house was in The Bean's name, but his room was the worst, a small windowless cell with damp oozing from the walls. 'Running water in every room,' he would joke to the boys.

Through Fannie, Dorothé knew many of the aristocracy of Hollywood – Douglas Fairbanks in particular was a close friend. Every summer Dorothé and Teddy would take a large house in the country, in part for the children's holidays, in part so that they could entertain house parties. One year they took Bibury Court, another Albury, near Guildford, another the Dashwoods' house at West Wycombe, but their favourite was Hackwood, near Basingstoke, owned by Lord Camrose. Here Douglas Fairbanks would bring his film-star friends, set up a screen in the ballroom and show one of his own films in the evening.

In late 1937, Dorothé, Teddy and their friend Jim Lawrence, Dorothé's partner in most of her exhibition dances, set off to spend some months in California. After staying with Douglas Fairbanks in Los Angeles, they moved to a house they had rented for six weeks. Marion Davies, the mistress of William Randolph Hearst, telephoned to ask the three of them to spend the weekend of 23 February at the Hearst ranch, San Simeon, 160 miles to the south. They accepted, and Marion handed the telephone to Hearst, who gave them directions to the airfield at Burbank where his private plane would be waiting to fly them to San Luis Obispo, the nearest airfield to San Simeon. The ranch itself, on high ground, was reached by a winding six-mile drive uphill. Hearst warned them that every afternoon at three o'clock fog rolled in from the sea and blanketed San Luis Obispo, making landing impossible – to be absolutely safe, they should leave Burbank before noon.

The Plunket party arrived late at Burbank and Hearst's regular pilot refused to fly them. But the sky was clear and brilliant and the Plunkets, used to crossing America by plane, were convinced that Hearst and his pilot were fussing unnecessarily. They found another plane and persuaded the pilot to take them.

All went well until they neared San Luis Obispo. At three precisely the fog rolled in; an hour later, Hearst, sitting in his tower study high above the fog, saw to his horror their aeroplane coming in to land. So bad was the visibility that the pilot had almost touched down before he realised he had overshot the airfield by a mile or so. As he banked to return one wingtip touched the ground and the plane cartwheeled over and burst into flames. Teddy, Dorothé and the pilot were killed; Jim Lawrence survived, badly injured. To Marion Davies fell the task of telephoning Fannie before she saw it in the newspapers. 'As long as I live,' said Marion later, 'I will never forget the silence at the other end of the line.'

The bodies of Teddy and Dorothé were cremated and on 14 March the Fairbanks, accompanied by Sam Goldwyn, left Los Angeles to bring the ashes of their friends back for burial at home. They picked up Fannie and her husband in New York, and boarded the *Queen Mary*, where the caskets were placed in a flower-filled cabin on a pedestal draped with the Union Jack. The funeral, in late March, was at Denham, in the church where they had been married sixteen years earlier. Both Fannie and the Londonderrys were there.

'I know you and he [Charley] will feel it very much,' wrote Hugh Cecil, one of those who knew the true facts of Dorothé's birth. 'It is to be sure a beautiful thing for husband and wife to die together with unbroken companionship beyond the grave but it leaves the children terribly friendless.' The Queen's sentiments were less Victorian. '... We both felt so sad over the ghastly tragedy of Dorothé and Teddy, as you know what intimate friends of ours they had been for many years. They both gave so much happiness to so many people of all kinds and sorts. Their going does leave a terrible blank indeed. Those dear little boys make one's heart ache....' A few days later, a discreet notice in *The Times* announced that Lord Londonderry and Mr Denis Kiwa Plunket (Teddy's 29-year-old younger brother) would be the boys' guardians. The children would not be poor: their father, who died intestate, left £66,880, their mother, in possession of most of the Barnato fortune, £362,000.

Charley was still suffering from the depression and apathy that had engulfed him after the sudden loss of office. Only two months earlier he had written to Edith: '... I have relapsed into a sort of ineffectiveness, and Robin's words keep ringing in my ears. "There are you, having slaved all your life, bitterly disappointed at the end." I feel I no longer do you any credit. This isn't self depreciation but I seem to be unable to get going in any direction. I feel a sort of laziness coming over me and I find myself continually saying "What's the use?"' Robin's own success – he had been re-elected as MP for County Down with the huge majority of 45,593 – must have been small consolation.

Charley overcame the inertia of unemployment chiefly by writing a justification of his position, entitled *Ourselves and Germany*. It was dedicated to Edith and he sent copies to the King, Queen Mary, the Duke of Windsor and his former Cabinet colleagues. It was his apologia for a course of conduct that was increasingly bringing him into conflict with many of his former colleagues, and had already earned him odium as a Nazi sympathiser. Though much that he wrote was undoubtedly true – the effect on Germany of the harshness of the Versailles Treaty, for instance – it betrayed a lack of understanding of the methods used by Hitler and his followers. 'Herr Hitler had had the satisfaction of seeing 99 per cent of the German people endorse his policy by voting for the Nazi Party candidates at the election which had been purposely called.'

Just before the book's proposed date of publication Austria was absorbed into the German Reich. Publication was delayed and a post-script added. Charley was prepared to defend the *Anschluss*, on the ground that a large proportion of the Austrian population was heartily in favour of it. He argued that any international protests should be directed against the method of accomplishment rather than the fact. But he went on to say: '. . . If it is possible to say that the incorporation of Austria in the German Reich, in a peaceful manner and by the evolution of time, was a legitimate German aspiration, the same can in no way be said in relation to Czechoslovakia; and whereas no international action could with propriety be taken to oppose Herr Hitler in his policy in regard to Austria, a totally different situation arises should the German policy of expansion extend to the incorporation or forcible acquisition of Czechoslovakia.'

Despite the need – as Charley saw it – to keep in touch with leading Nazis, Edith wrote furiously to both Ribbentrop and Goering when two Austrian guides she knew were arrested on suspicion of being anti-Nazi. Her anger was increased by the fact that the men were training for an international ski race – the Londonderry Snow Eagle Race – for which she had given a silver cup. Ribbentrop, who had left London in March to become German Foreign Minister, did not reply but Goering responded with three pages of propaganda ('the overwhelming mass of the [Tyrolese] people stand like a wall behind Germany') and a non-committal promise to release the guides if they had been wrongly arrested. They were released.

As the summer passed, relations between England and Germany worsened rapidly. Germany was poised to invade Czechoslovakia, to whose aid France was pledged to come. War seemed imminent.

The meetings that led up to the Munich Agreement began with Chamberlain's flight to Berchtesgaden on Thursday 15 September. After seeing Hitler, he returned to London the following day; on Saturday there were lengthy Cabinet discussions; and on Sunday meetings with representatives of the French government. On Thursday 22 September Chamberlain flew back to Germany, this time to Godesberg. In those frantic days, when it seemed European war could break out at any moment, this proud, idealistic, almost painfully reserved man somehow found the time – on 20 September – to write Edith a note.

'Just a line to thank you for your kind and generous letter. I shall want all your good wishes for I have never been under any delusions that [sic] the hostility I should have to face as soon as the fear of war began to recede. But as long as I keep the approval of my own conscience I care very little about the criticisms of those who don't carry my responsibilities. I saw yesterday a very interesting letter from Goering to Charley. It was interesting because it repeated in almost identical terms what Hitler said to me.'

Hitler's response to Chamberlain's second visit was to order the Czech government to evacuate the Sudetenland within forty-eight hours, a *démarche* unacceptable to Chamberlain, who returned to London on 24 September. The Czech government rejected Hitler's ultimatum. War appeared certain. But Chamberlain refused to give up hope, and continued his efforts, now drawing in Mussolini. Then, at twenty-four hours' notice, Hitler invited him to a four-power conference, with Daladier and Mussolini, in Munich on 29 September.

Charley, who was still pursuing his private discussions with the German leaders, was also in Munich, having flown out on the 28th (the day before Chamberlain). When he told Ribbentrop of his disappointment at the changed climate of Anglo-German relations, the former Ambassador was testy and impatient, and the interview ended abruptly. It was the last time they saw each other. The next day, Friday 30 September, the Munich Agreement was signed. Chamberlain was cheered in the streets of Munich and on his arrival home, waving the piece of paper with Hitler's signature on it. Goering, whom Charley saw soon afterwards, was 'very jubilant and said that he was quite sure that this was the way to establish peace for all time', though he added, 'Chamberlain is always making difficulties.'

Charley's visit brought him sharp criticism. It was embarrassing to the Government to have an ex-Cabinet minister meeting several of the German leaders in the same city in which the Prime Minister was simultaneously negotiating with Hitler. The accusations that he was pro-Nazi were renewed. In a speech at Sunderland on 10 October, he vehemently rejected both charges.

'I went with one object in mind – to see the reactions of the people to something for which I have been striving for years. I went as a tourist and onlooker. I tried to keep clear of everyone I knew. I deliberately kept clear of the British delegation because I was afraid of the Press. I knew exactly what they would say if I had any contact.

'I wanted to see the people. I walked the streets and talked to the people, and I was struck by the expressions on the faces of everyone I saw when they knew that these delegations which they looked on as harbingers of peace were arriving. I was astonished at their acclamation and their relief that there was to be no war. I was an onlooker only, but it happened that the German and French delegations came to the hotel at which I was staying, and I could not avoid meeting them with some of the Germans whom I knew personally. I did not go over to see any of them. It was merely for the sake of the contact with the common people. It is only by such contacts as these, however they may be misrepresented, that one can learn the truth in these days.'

He had not learned all of it. In November a member of the German Embassy staff in Paris was assassinated by a young Jewish man, half-crazed with grief because his father had been taken away by the Gestapo, and immediately 20,000 Jews in the Reich were arrested, 191 synagogues and 171 communal dwellings burned down and 7,500 shops smashed and looted. Charley wrote at once to Goering.

'I am completely at a loss to understand your policy towards the Jews. While deploring the terrible tragedy on the part of a demented young man which took place at your Embassy in Paris, I cannot feel that it is possible to justify the imposing of penalties on that account on a whole community.... I profoundly disagree with your claim that this is a matter of internal politics. When individuals and sections of individuals are driven out of one country, they must find a refuge in some other country, and in these days, when we are hoping that civilisation is advancing, that becomes an international matter at once, and I am entirely at a loss to understand how you can suggest that it can be otherwise. I do not want to dwell on the grievous disappointment which I have had to undergo. I was able for so long to reply to any arguments put forward by those who have never had any belief that Germany had any desire to become a helpful partner in the comity of nations, but in relation to your treatment of the Jews I have no reply whatsoever, and all I can do is remain silent and take no further part in these matters, in which most people in this country are thinking my opinions have been wrong from the beginning.'

Goering did not reply. This letter marked the end of Charley's correspondence with the German leaders.

Ourselves and Germany was reissued in a Penguin paperback just before Christmas. Charley sent a copy to Baldwin, who thanked him with one of his charming little handwritten notes: 'You are a faithful friend. The little book arrived last night and I shall read it with care. It is tragic how the Germans seem to do everything to neutralise all the efforts of men like yourself who have done everything in your power and risking all kinds of misunderstandings to obtain understanding, and through understanding, Peace. . . . You are the last man I would wittingly offend and I have always regarded you as a true friend in good times and bad. . . .'

But, for Charley, the bad times were entirely Baldwin's fault. He responded with a fourteen-page typed letter reiterating his grievances which concluded: 'I could not refrain from smiling when you associated me with your ups and downs. I had never experienced any downs that I could complain of . . . until with one stroke you wiped me off the political map, whereas notwithstanding the downs which you may have experienced, you retired from an active part in public life in a blaze of glory.'

Edith's approach towards restoring Charley's position was quite different. She thought reproaches only caused bad blood and she did not believe in making enemies. Warmth and friendship were not only natural to her, they were, she felt, much more effective.

She had already advised Charley to keep on good terms with Churchill. 'Must keep on friendly terms with him at all costs, I think', she had written on 27 January 1938, aware that disagreement had been building up for some time. As early as October 1937, after Charley's third German visit, Churchill had warned Charley that when the German government spoke of friendship with England, 'what they mean is that we shall give them back their former colonies, and also agree to their having a free hand so far as we are concerned in Central and Southern Europe. This means they would devour Austria and Czechoslovakia as a preliminary to making a gigantic mid-Europe block. It would certainly not be in our interests to connive at such policies of aggression.' But Charley always took his own line: as he himself had said, he was a bad member of a team.

Edith remained a close friend of Lucy Baldwin. Only months after Baldwin's dismissal of Charley, when Baldwin's doctor, Lord Dawson, had prescribed three months' complete rest, she had invited the Baldwins to stay at Mount Stewart for the summer. 'Circe, you are a darling . . . I will keep it up my sleeve and courageously write to offer ourselves if I find a hiatus in our plans . . . we love you more than ever,' wrote Lucy gratefully. Edith sent Baldwin himself her book of Disraeli's letters to Frances Anne for Christmas – she had also published an autobiographical memoir called *Retrospect* in the same year. She got Charley to ask Neville Chamberlain to fish on the Brora ('I said I was half committed already to the Forbeses and the Barnetts,' wrote the Prime Minister, 'but I have been thinking further about it and if Charley really means me to take his invitation seriously I should very much like to accept and would put off the others'). She asked Leslie Hore Belisha, the Secretary of State for War, to join the Ark, suggesting the flattering 'Lion' as his Ark name, and received an ecstatic reply.

Old friends were not neglected, though Hugh Cecil, now Provost of Eton, refused an invitation to dine and sleep at Londonderry House in characteristic fashion. 'The [Eton] statutes require that I shall always reside, which is understood to mean sleep, in Eton during the school term, except for grave cause and business of the College. "Grave cause" includes the Church Assembly and Lords Cricket Match is the business of the College; but I am afraid Londonderry House is neither.' When Bernard Shaw, asked to luncheon at Londonderry House, fainted in the hall on arrival, Edith sent him and his wife Charlotte back in the car accompanied by a trained nurse to look after GBS until he was well again, and a footman to run any commissions for them. Next day she sent three boxes of wonderful flowers, prompting Charlotte to exclaim (as GBS reported in his letter of thanks): 'They are so well grown and healthy and beautiful – like herself!'

As the likelihood of war increased, editors began to request articles from Edith. As the founder of the Women's Legion, the greatest organisation to utilise female talent and labour known until then, her views were in demand. A typical article, in the *Sunday Dispatch* of 15 May 1938, entitled Girls in Khaki, stated Edith's welcome for the 'move to enlist women for emergency service, should a general military mobilisation unfortunately become necessary', described in clear detail the work of the Women's Legion and echoed the War Secretary's appeal to women to train as military auxiliaries. There were letters to *The Times* and the *Telegraph*, there were three military articles for a publication called *Searchlight*.

When Hitler occupied Prague on 16 March 1939, Charley's disillusionment was complete. As he had said in *Ourselves and Germany*, the conquest of Czechoslovakia could not be defended. Those who, like him, had pinned their hopes on an Anglo-German understanding now realised that this had never been anything but a mirage. Henceforth he devoted his energies to running the Civil Air Guard, an organisation designed to produce men and women who could fly and who understood aeroplanes to aid the Royal Air Force in case of war. For this he mobilised the facilities of the numerous small flying clubs dotted round the country, a field with which he was thoroughly familiar (the civil flying schools were already fully occupied training young men for the RAFVR). It was unfortunate that just at this moment he should quarrel violently with his cousin Winston Churchill, at Lady Cunard's dinner table. The subject of the row was not their familiar disagreement over German trustworthiness and intentions – on which Charley had now shed his illusions – but the reliability of France, which Churchill believed in but which Charley questioned. Sadly, on this issue, Charley's judgement was better than Churchill's.

Like most marriages, that of Edith and Charley had periods of growth and evolution. The last painful years of peace and the beginning of the war were to bring one, its chief fruit a greater frankness between them. 'I have always been so reticent and it is silly,' wrote Edith. 'We will talk of love too, real love, which we both know is eternal: how, we can't know, but it is. . . . Beloved, you must strengthen your faith – we all must. By faith we live. We need not bother about details but believe we shall be together and we shall be, as God intended from the very first that marriage should be, two entities to make one whole (now don't laugh).'

To Edith, Charley was still everything he had always been: glamorous, attractive and beloved. Three months after war had been declared, she wrote him a letter of the kind she sent to him or slipped into his hand every year on their wedding anniversary, 28 November. 'My own beloved, I do hope this will arrive on our wedding day. It is the fortieth. Think of that! and how very lucky I was. The time seems to have gone so quickly and here we are, in the middle of a war, when we might have expected a totally different state of affairs.'

XXVII

EDITH WAS sixty when war broke out. She was active, healthy and an expert organiser. But a new generation was now running affairs, and her services were not wanted. 'I am inundated with letters from women all thinking I am the head of the WAAFs. I wish I was,' she wrote plaintively in the third week of the war. She kept up her friendships as best she could in her visits to London from Mount Stewart and her gaiety and wit were as vivid as ever. 'Circe Londonderry made me laugh when she repeated Mrs Greville's crack about Mrs Keppel. "To hear Alice talk about her escape from France, one would think she had swum the Channel with her maid between her teeth",' wrote Chips Channon in 1940.

The war was harder for Charley. He felt powerless and frustrated and he still harboured grudges against those he felt had encompassed his downfall. With little to do, his normally sweet nature soured, and he began to see malevolent intention and slights everywhere, and his resentment now extended to Chamberlain. By contrast, Edith's attitude did not change. She had always been on excellent terms with the Prime Minister: he was on her "present" list and they exchanged letters – in April 1939, for instance, he was writing to her in jokey fashion to thank her for her Easter present of a fishing knife. 'Nothing has frightened me so much for a long time but I have now found out how to shut it safely.

'What do I do with it? Do I ward off the attacks of furious salmon? or suddenly draw it on the two importunate photographers? And does the lump of cork, in which the knife is embedded, save me from drowning if I fall in? You see you have given me a wealth of problems to solve. . . .'

Chamberlain, busy though he was, could not help noticing Charley's changed attitude. In his letter thanking Edith for her present of a book for Christmas 1939, he said: 'Charley writes to his friends so bitterly that

I thought you must have given me up as a bad job, though I am totally unaware of having ever done him an injury.'

Edith flew to Charley's defence at once. 'I am quite sure you have not realised why Charley has felt resentful about affairs – I will not even say bitter – otherwise you would have said to yourself: Charley was the only independent link in the years 1936–8 between this country and Germany. You never once mentioned the matter to him, either in Scotland or elsewhere. It would have been so easy for you and would have appealed to him had you ever asked him to go and see you. I shall always believe that in those days much might have been done, but he has always been studiously ignored and he could have given you very useful help. This at least is what we both feel.'

But Chamberlain had more to think about than an ex-minister's ruffled feelings and Edith never bore a grudge. Their friendship continued.

Edith and Charley spent most of the war years at Mount Stewart. They toyed with the idea of selling Wynyard. It was increasingly expensive and they did not know if Robin would want to live there after the war; alternatively, they thought of pulling it down and building him a smaller house there. Though Charley loved Wynyard, he was quite prepared to admit that it was 'no use labouring sentiment, and moreover Wynyard is 98 years old, no more'.

Charley was still a rich man – in 1940 he paid, in income tax, surtax and mineral rights duty, a total of £62,384 – but his expenditure had begun to exceed his income; in 1939 by £106,394. (Subscriptions for the same year to the half-dozen hunts and nineteen clubs, from the Durham County Cricket Club to the Jockey Club Rooms, Household Brigade Boat Club, the Travellers in Paris and the Turf Club, cost him in all under £250.) Just before the war Edith had started driving again – though only round the Mount Stewart estate – in a small van she had designed herself; it had a Baby Austin engine and was always crammed with dogs – the mixed pack of pekineses, chihuahuas and lurchers that followed her everywhere. Now she told Charley: 'We can manage here perfectly now with one chauffeur, as I can drive too, and so does Mairi.' Several grand-children were with her: Robin's three children, and Kathryn Stanley ('so like Maureen was at that age it makes me laugh'), and all of them were snowed up until the end of January 1940.

Charley's unhappiness made him irritable and angry. Edith, as the person nearest to him, bore the brunt of this. He accused her of being self-centred, wrapped up in her own concerns and having little time for him, a charge that was, up to a point, true. For Edith, Mount Stewart had long been home, and she was always happy and absorbed when there – the garden alone took up much of her time. Over and above this, though, a husband whose absences from her side had begun from the moment they were married had forced her to develop an independent life of her own. At first it had been horribly painful, now it was second nature. But his accusations that she had no time for him hurt her sorely.

'If you only knew how I feel when you are away,' she wrote to him in October 1940; 'there's always a gnawing feeling, and when you are here, I suppose, it is because I feel so relieved, I go on with my idiotic tasks. But I do adore you only and you know this. . . . I do try to become less self-centred and engrossed in all my foolish things. I get so self-absorbed in this war – I find it so hard not to be doing something active but this never means I forget you. When I go into your room and find you reading I think "well, he is occupied and happy", and lots of times I go in and you are not there. But you don't believe this. And off I go to do something foolish in the garden.

'I am going to tell you what I think. I knew your Father so well, in fact intimately, all the War, and he suffered as you are doing from not enough to do. He was gregarious, as you are, and loved seeing and talking to his friends. He did not like the country or country pursuits at all really, and they do not satisfy you. What you want is a real job that interests you, and although you are too old to be in the active services, if you resolved yourself – and only you can do it – I am sure Archie Sinclair could find you something to do with the air, administration . . . you must have something to occupy yourself as you are so young and active in yourself and the only times you are really happy are when you are working at something definite. Anything else drives you frantic. I know this is the correct diagnosis, and you can find a job if you really think of what you would like to do. But it must be something younger men should not be doing. This I know does not appeal to you but I know it is right.'

The enforced exile at Mount Stewart increased Charley's sense of being on the sidelines. Edith, better at turning her hand to what lay nearest, quickly found plenty of war work to do. She put her gardening knowledge to good use with a scheme to train allotment holders at Mount Stewart, she was president of the County Down and Durham branches of the Red Cross, she resuscitated the Women's Legion, forming a special flying section which supplied ferry pilots. In a curious echo of the opposition she had encountered in the 1914 war, when much male opinion was outraged at the idea of the Women's Legion doing 'men's work', the National Men's Defence League now objected to women pilots being used in preference to men to ferry planes from factories to RAF bases. In the early months of 1940, Edith once more found herself writing to the Press to defend the Legion's right to do this work. The Legion also fed people in shelters and ran mobile canteens which, during the intensive bombing of the docklands, brought a steady stream of hot meals to dockers and their families whose houses had been destroyed. They continued to bring meals to dockers who were working round the clock during the run-up to D-Day loading the invasion vessels and at one point were providing a million meals a month. A few weeks after D-Day she received a letter of thanks for the Legion's work from General Eisenhower.

Charley, used to a more structured life, more conscious of the dignity of his position, less flexible in outlook and never keen on second-best, found it difficult to readjust to what was available. He became Northern Ireland Regional Commandant of the Air Training Corps but, though he enjoyed this – especially the flying with the boys – it was nothing to what he felt he *could* be doing. He was Chancellor of Queen's University, Belfast, and he went to London sometimes to attend the House of Lords, where he spoke from time to time. Edith, who was doing her best to raise his morale, teased him about being an *homme fatal* – one of the secretaries, she said, was in love with him ('Now the only thing is to find her a really good job') – told him he was wonderful and wired in one of the loving birthday messages she had now been sending for over forty years: 'To my beloved wishing him his heart's desire and love always.'

Changes within the family had also caused unhappiness. Just as her parents had feared, Margaret's marriage did not last. After four years, her marriage to Alan Muntz had ended in divorce. For Edith especially, it was a hard blow. When Mairi married Flight Lieutenant Viscount Bury, the eldest son of Lord Albemarle, in December 1941, Edith and Charley were both delighted, but they missed her very much. As Charley wrote to Ettie: 'For over 20 years she has been the star in our little universe and this is the end of a chapter.'

What followed was far worse. Maureen was found to be suffering from tuberculosis. She faced her illness with the same bravery and insouciance she had always shown. Her life was full, she lectured for the British Council, she had been one of the first people to appear on television, she was a brilliant speaker and spoke often in her husband's constituency, she encouraged, exhorted and comforted the politicians who came to the

Stanleys' house in Smith Square. She continued to do these things but by the spring of 1942 she was clearly very ill.

Maureen was enormously popular and her looks and powerful personality were still at their peak. Friends streamed down to see her at Folly Farm, near Reading, where the Stanleys were living. Among them were the King and Queen, whose affection had never faltered since those distant days when she had enchanted the young Prince Albert; they visited her constantly as she went rapidly downhill. Charley was badly upset; after Mairi, Maureen was his favourite child and in many ways the most like him. Writing to Ettie, whom he now seldom saw – at the beginning of the war she had handed over both her country houses, Taplow and Panshanger, for use by the authorities – he poured out not only his anxiety over his daughter but his frustration, his gloom over the coal industry and his general feeling of wretchedness.

'Poor Maureen has had a dreadful time and it is only her courage and her marvellous powers of resistance which have kept her going. It is still touch and go but the enemy for the moment is localised in the sense that we know what the germ is. At the best it must be a long business with varying fortunes. A few hours ahead is all that we can count on. We were inclined to allow our hopes to be raised on small improvements and the setbacks were inevitable. We now hope that the violent changes may give place to small oscillations. We have had a close insight into the medical profession. Of some one cannot speak too highly but in a case of this sort, influence has been vital. I think E. has been instrumental in saving her life. I think the doctors actually failed and would have said it was a hopeless case but I can tell you all about this. I am making no plans and letting things slide. It is fortunate sometimes not to be important. I think the future is terribly grim and I feel quite impotent. So many good influences are being smothered in the country owing to a lack of leadership. The best people are loyal and play up to the war effort. The socialists are disloyal and are just seeking their own political ends. The coal controversy is only a symptom. The miners, the spearhead of the Socialist advance, must be placated at all costs and the other side of the industry is ignored or held up to opprobrium. I think Cripps' speech was a scandal. The miners through their leaders refused to help the industry although the full machinery which they refuse to use in is in existence. Their sole policy is to increase wages until there is nothing left.'

Five days later, on the morning of 20 June, Maureen Stanley died. Robin Castlereagh, arriving back from North Africa, was just too late to say goodbye to her. On rushing to the nursing home, he learned to his

296

distress that she had died as his ship was docking. A few hours later, at midnight, Charley pencilled a few lines to Ettie. 'She has gone. And I held her hand and kissed her as she went. She just floated away on perfect peace. You know the sadness of it all and your courage is and has been always a help to me.'

It was a crushing blow for Charley. When Margaret – like all the Stewarts, physically intrepid – became a war correspondent he worried about her too. The dangers of her job, and her steadier, professional approach to it, combined to draw them closer: her letters are full of warmth – and many expressions of thanks for presents of money from her father. Muntz was forgotten, and even the fact that she was living with a lover, an attractive Australian newspaperman called Eric Baum, at the Savoy, seemed to be something her parents could now take in their stride. Later in the war she fell in love with the famous French pilot and writer Antoine de Saint-Exupéry, about whom she subsequently wrote a radio play.

Charley had quarrelled so violently with Winston Churchill that there could be no hope of the humblest ministerial job. This did not stop Edith writing to the Prime Minister with recommendations for honours for some of the Women's Legion whose hard work and bravery during the Blitz had been outstanding. Edith herself, often in London during the bombing, piled mattresses in the basement of Londonderry House and handed out sleeping pills in case anyone was kept awake by bombing. Her young cousin Elizabeth, who had a flat nearby, would often join them, crawling in the pitch darkness between the mattresses after an evening out or a shift at the hospital where she worked. Elizabeth's old nanny, who looked after her at the flat, had another alcove, and the daily, Elsie, was put at the end of a long passage because she snored so much.

Edith's activity contrasted with what Charley saw as his own passivity. His feelings of misery festered for the rest of the war. One day in February 1945, alone in the Royal Station Hotel, Newcastle-upon-Tyne, as he waited for a train to take him to an engagement in Durham, he set out his feelings of failure and self-reproach in a long letter to Ettie. Now old and frail ('an awful old crock of a cab-horse'), she was still 'Dear Lady S' – though she was his dearest and oldest friend.

'... You have given me a clue in your last letter which I am going to take up, really for the purpose of giving you a glimpse into my heart because that is the cross I feel I have to bear and it is a tremendous effort to me to be self-controlled, pleasant to those I continually meet and as helpful as I can be in these terrible days.

'When Baldwin removed me I instinctively knew that I was finished, that my active life was over, and that I had to fall back on resources which it is difficult to cultivate when you have been in the middle of politics which I had been since the end of the last war. In your letter you say so kindly "The swing of the pendulum will come". But of course I know it won't for me and I confess that knowing this as I have known it I have touched almost the lowest depths of despair and it has been the example of courage like yours and others which has kept me going. I was so fortunate in so many ways, whatever I touched seemed to turn to gold. I wanted to succeed in everything, everything went well, every-one helped me and I seemed to have so many friends and well-wishers. Then suddenly it all came to an end.

'I tried loyally to carry on outside, then I dabbled in diplomacy with an idea which I know was correct but I could not somehow work it with anyone who counted. I made speeches which people seemed to want to hear; we went on entertaining and everyone seemed to want to come. Then I had some bitter exchanges with Baldwin and Chamberlain who I knew were wrong although I commended Chamberlain for Munich but regretted everything he subsequently did, then I fell out with Winston because I wanted to achieve by what I thought was statesmanship what he wanted to achieve by war. That quarrel I think originated some time before because I never really was fond of FE who completely absorbed Winston to the exclusion of W's allies like myself and I disagreed with both and rightly disagreed over their Irish policy which has had such fatal results. So I really planned a bad crash and was not strong enough or clever enough to strike out on my own. So the war, the crisis of our lives, finds me completely isolated and under a sort of shadow which I cannot get away from. . . . I want you to know that I have no illusions about it and that I am bitterly disappointed. I had great chances and I have missed them by not being good enough and that really sums up the whole thing.

'. . . It has all worked out badly and I know it is some inherent fault in myself. However I know I have got to carry on and am doing my best. You may wonder why I have written this to you. The reason is that I feel you are omniscient and that I do not want you to think that I am so conceited as not to realise that with all the advantages I had and with your constant and affectionate help I have been a miserable failure. I think poor Edie realises this and know Robin does too. But E. is constant in her support and her care for me and I never would know from anything she says or does that I have failed to give her the position she should have had.'

When the war in Europe ended, Edith was lying ill. That spring she had had first influenza and then measles. Her sinus trouble, which always flared up when she was below par, returned, and the whole of the summer her health was up and down. In July Lucy Baldwin died. Stanley Baldwin had spent a miserable war at his home at Bewdley, in Worcestershire. He had been totally discredited, and even the ornamental gates presented to him on his retirement had been melted down for scrap. Charley had not forgiven him but Edith, always loyal to her friends, wrote to him immediately. He replied: 'I work like an automaton daily, trying to get through about 500 letters and telegrams. What you say about her touches me deeply and indeed all that you say is a real help and comfort for which I thank you from my heart.'

A fortnight later, in the first General Election since 1935, there was a Labour landslide and Winston Churchill was thrown out of office. Edith, at Mount Stewart, wrote to Charley at Londonderry House. 'I can only think that the electors thought Winston was safe and were thoroughly irresponsible. I have written to W to tell him how indignant I am at the way he has been treated. What the Nazis failed to do, the British Bolshies have done, namely, got rid of him. However the policy all these war years had to be really socialism. They can't do more controlling than they have done and if they try to redeem their promises the fat will be in the fire. Also if the demands for more pay and no work are not fulfilled immediately, there will be more strikes and rowdiness. I feel it won't last long because they are a house divided among themselves. What a country, and what times we have lived through.'

By 18 September, after a visit to Wynyard ('I picked a large bunch of jasmine from the terrace, just opposite the spot I always cherish!'), she was back at Mount Stewart and ill again. She was still in bed on the 26th, and taking the drug M & B, cross and unhappy because the doctor had told her there was no hope of getting up or leaving Mount Stewart for some time and the first State Opening of Parliament after the war was to take place in a month, on 26 October. But despite medical advice, she managed to attend, looking magnificent enough even in that brilliant scene to provoke a comment from Chips Channon. 'One had forgotten such splendour still existed. The long Royal Gallery was gay and red with peers in their robes moving about, and bejewelled peeresses ... Circe Londonderry, as always, was the most splendid: she was literally dressed in diamonds.'

Though Charley was still extremely rich the expansive quality of the Londonderrys' pre-war life had gone for good. The enormous houses of the aristocracy had depended on an endless supply of servants – before the war, Londonderry House had had twenty-eight in the kitchen and sixteen in the steward's room – but the men and women returning from the armed services or factory work had no wish to enter or return to domestic service. Charley gave his Welsh house Plas Machynlleth, home to a girls' boarding school during the war, to the people of the town, Seaham Hall remained as a general hospital and (in 1946) a nominal 21-year lease of most of Londonderry House was granted to the Royal Aero Club. Charley and Edith kept the top floor, which became a vast, 22-room apartment.

Much else had also changed. Robin, who, although an excellent speaker, had no political ambition and disliked the House of Commons, had seized the opportunity offered by the General Election of 1945 to give up his seat. His real interest had always lain in the mines and his feelings for the miners themselves were warmly sympathetic. In February 1946, a few months before the Bill to nationalise the coal mines passed through the House of Commons (the mines were nationalised on 1 January 1947), he wrote in the *Spectator* that if he were still an MP he would, in contradiction to his Party, support it because '. . . I am convinced the existing system has broken down beyond repair . . . between the wars the mineowners have allowed the relationship between themselves and the men to deteriorate to such an extent that the latter will not give of their best in existing conditions. . . . Before the last war, over half of all industrial disputes were to do with coalmining. The average owner is rarely seen by his men; in fact, the only times they see him are when there are differences of opinion which call for strikes. The miner can hardly be blamed for regarding his employer as a man who is more interested in profits than welfare.'

After describing the bitterness and privations of 1926, exacerbated by the depression that followed, he went on: 'I am not a mineowner. If I had been I should have concentrated my energies on the human aspect. I should have gone down the pit regularly and talked to as many men as possible so as to learn their views. My wife would have visited their houses and heard about the problems confronting their wives and children. If a man employed by me was killed, I should have made it my special duty to visit the widow and to have taken a personal interest, apart from any legal obligation, in the future of her and her family. . . . I should have appointed wholetime welfare officers to keep an eye on those injured in hospital and to see the wives were provided for. As the miner is a keen sportsman, these men would have assisted in all activities of this nature, while every year I should have organised a picnic or gala especially for the miners' children. I cannot help feeling that if more attention had been paid to the human, as opposed to the purely economic, element, there would have been a happier atmosphere prevailing in the mines today.' He concluded that the changes about to take place would, it was to be hoped, remove for ever the long-standing grievances of the miner, and restore his confidence in his industry. 'That is why the nation should support Mr Shinwell in his effort to give the miner pride of place in the industrial world, while the miner in return gives his maximum output.' As a statement of attitude his article was admirable; as a wholesale condemnation of his father's conduct as a coalowner it could hardly have been more outspoken.

Charley's true interest lay above rather than below the ground. The glamour of the air, the emotional experience of flying, with its limitless horizons and almost spiritual sense of exhilaration, had never ceased to hold him. During the war he had flown gliders with his air cadets and enjoyed this silent, soaring, eagle-like form of flight so much that he went on practising regularly at Ards airport. It was, indirectly, to hasten his death.

At the beginning of November 1945, as his glider was being winched into the air, the towing cable snapped. Though he did not actually break any bones he was severely jolted, cracked some vertebrae and was immobilised for several weeks. When, at last, he was on his feet again, he resumed visiting London as before, but he gradually became conscious that, as he put it, some vital force had gone. With this knowledge came a greater dependence on Edith. He now hated being away from her and, when they were together, complained that she did not pay him enough attention – but the habit of independence, once learned, is not easy to forget. 'You are not correct in thinking you miss me more than I do you,' she wrote in May 1946. 'I may appear to be engrossed in things but my inner kernel is quite centred on you. All I do is with the object of relating it to you. You are the mainspring of my existence, whatever you may think. But we need not worry about our departures from this sphere. It so happens that when two people are closely linked together one follows the other very quickly because one without the other is not complete.'

At first Charley seemed to recover from his accident. In July 1947 he had the thrilling experience of flying in a Mosquito ('I did not take much part but sat there and so enjoyed myself with a first-class pilot'); Edith's sister Florence came to stay 'and was particularly nice', his own sister Birdie followed soon afterwards; and he continued going to London occasionally. 'You looked wonderful that evening, lying on your sofa in white shirtsleeves like the Duc of Reichstadt in L'Aiglon – don't show this to your harem!' wrote Ettie in September 1947 after one of their now rare meetings. 'There never was such a friend,' she wrote to him shortly afterwards. 'There is no one in the whole world I turn to with such *confidence* at every angle of life. I thought with such comfort and happiness last night of all that you have done for me and been to me through many years now and all your spoiling magic of delicate intuition and understanding.' He looked ridiculously young, she added, 'about 17'.

While Edith's physical stamina was still superb Charley was becoming frailer. In September he had the first of a series of small strokes. He faced his illness, and the realisation of what it entailed, with unflinching courage, writing to Ettie, on 21 September 1947:

'I have not written for ages for the reason that I have not known what to say or how to say it. Well, I have been ill. I am all right now, in the sense that I have had a light warning and that I have got to go slow and realise that my active life is really over. I have only just realised that I have never stood still and that in these forties – the war years and after – I have had endless worries and sorrows with you and Edie my only real friends and supports. That is the whole story really. I was trying to do crazy little jobs because I have had to realise that I do not come into the bigger ones. . . .

'I left London in the morning perfectly well. The sun seemed to be hitting the front of the aeroplane and making it all very bright and hot. To cut a long story short I arrived here not feeling at all well and got straight into bed where I remained for a fortnight. I then felt quite well and did a little more than a wise person would have done and got another warning in the form of my speech not being clear and my right hand not being as efficient as it should be and told by the doctor to rest completely for three weeks and I should be perfectly well. I am nearing the end of a fortnight and feel perfectly well but I have got to remember that as regards activities and rushing about, I am 70. That is the whole story for my best friend to know all the facts. . . . I am doing nothing and have cancelled endless small jobs so as to concentrate on Princess Elizabeth who comes to Wynyard on the 22nd to lay a University foundation stone. After that I am going to lead a much easier life and a more pleasant one. . . .'

For the last time, he set out his regrets. 'I am sorry I failed to handle Winston because he really could have saved the war instead of gaining the credit, which he fully deserves, for winning it, and we are now paying the price. . . . If only someone had been powerful enough to combine Chamberlain, with his passion for peace, with Winston, as late as 1937, we need never have had the war, with its ghastly results, as the price for Winston gaining an everlasting historical name as a war-leader. That is all that has been achieved on our account and I do not believe the price has been anything like paid yet, if it ever will be.'

He was never able to write to Ettie again and his condition quickly deteriorated. As Hugh Cecil, in his affectionate but typically rather arid words of comfort wrote to Edith at Christmas: 'I am so sorry for Charley, it must be very trying for him. No doubt he hears, and probably understands quite well, but cannot answer properly.'

Charley never recovered his speech. Edith, whose instinctive attitude to illness was to fight it, was determined that his life should be as normal as possible in the circumstances. Visitors, in the main, family, including his wards, the Plunket boys, came as usual to stay; and Charley, urged on by Edith, made valiant efforts to fight against his growing disabilities.

The end came quickly. He died at Mount Stewart late on the night of 10 February 1949. The next day Chips Channon wrote: 'Charlie Londonderry died in the night at Mount Stewart and I am very sorry; he was a good friend and a grand seigneur of the old school; even his appearance was almost theatrically 18th century. Slim, with an elegant figure and pointed features, he was red in the face and dressed with distinction. He was always gay and amiable and completely sure of himself. In the long run, he will be proved right politically; he always maintained that there were only two possible courses for us: either to make friends with Germany, or, if this was impossible, to re-arm. We did neither, and war was the result.' It was the political obituary Charley would have wished for.

Edith, who had always maintained an iron self-control, even through the miseries of Charley's worst unfaithfulnesses, now gave way and for the first time Mairi saw her mother weep. Charley's body lay for three days in the flower-filled private chapel. He was buried on 14 February, in Tir-N'an Og, the sweetly planted burial ground designed by Edith so many years before. As his coffin was lowered into the ground his piper played 'The Flowers of the Forest'. Each letter that arrived reduced Edith to fresh tears until suddenly, opening one, Mairi saw her mother begin to laugh. It was from Edith's little grandson, Alastair Vane-Tempest-Stewart, who wrote from his private school: 'Dear Mamma, I am so sorry to hear about Papa . . . but as Mr Barbour [his headmaster] said, he had a long innings and death'll do him a power of good.'

Two days later there was a memorial service for The Most Honourable Sir Charles Stewart Henry Vane-Tempest-Stewart, seventh Marquess of Londonderry in the Peerage of Ireland, Earl Vane, Viscount Seaham and Wynyard, County Durham, and Baron Stewart, of Stewart's Court and Ballylawn in the Peerage of the United Kingdom, KG, PC, MVO, in St Anne's Cathedral, Belfast, and the day after another in Westminster Abbey.

Charley left Mount Stewart to Edith for her lifetime (after which it would go to Mairi), a substantial income and everything she wanted of his possessions, from cars, carriages, horses and pictures to silver and gold plate. Robin inherited Wynyard, which he loved – he was not fond of Mount Stewart. The family jewellery was left to Edith for life, and then to Robin.

'How many years is it now?' she had written to him a decade earlier in one of their anniversary letters. 'I hardly like to think but you don't look it and I certainly don't feel it.' She had, as he had once told her, 'carried the whole family on your lovely shoulders all these years', she had loved him as romantically and wholeheartedly after fifty years as when he had proposed to her on the jasmine-scented terrace at Wynyard, looking down at the lake and across to the woods beyond. Now there was the short letter, marked 'To be opened in the event of my death'. He had written it when alone in London during the Blitz, while she was at Mount Stewart. Its first lines must have comforted her a little:

'Thank you a million times for your love and support. I have been difficult – very difficult – but I know you have always realised my entire devotion to yourself.'

XXVIII

EDITH lived for ten years after Charley's death. She was as active and fit as ever, gardening, walking, swimming, riding and shooting. At the age of seventy, riding competitively for the first time, she won a lightweight hunter class in Dublin Horse Show. On 8 October 1951, two months before her seventy-third birthday, she shot a stag, an eleven-pointer, on Dooish Mountain, in Donegal. Unlike Charley, she had no difficulty in adapting to post-war conditions, so different from the stylised grandeur she had known for most of her life. Visiting Mairi's small farm in the south of Ireland, she became adept at helping in the kitchen, peeling potatoes and chopping beans – though she never learned to cook – and at Mount Stewart, wearing trousers most of the time, she worked harder than ever in the garden.

She is best remembered as the greatest political hostess of her day, a *grande dame* covered in a mass of jewels who inspired as much awe as she did affection. But she was much more: a woman many of whose achievements benefited her country, a woman who was her own person at a time when dependency was just as much a part of being female as a soft skin. When most women's opinions and attitudes were influenced by the views of the men nearest to them, she thought for herself and was quite prepared to stand by her conclusions in the face of opposition.

Her most original and far-reaching efforts were devoted to helping other women at a time when the idea of male supremacy was inculcated from the cradle. Edith herself always stressed that women were extraordinarily responsible and hardworking and her views on their capabilities were farsighted and imaginative. She was never afraid to pick up her pen, writing books, articles and numerous letters to the press. The early ones, like her long letters to *The Times*, were generally to express forcibly and often passionately her belief that the lot of women should be improved, and that the vote was the necessary first step. For the vote, she always declared, was not just a way of supporting this political party instead of that, but a voice – without it, what hope was there of getting *any* M.P. to take cognisance of the injustices under which so many women suffered?

The creation of the Women's Legion at the beginning of the 1914 war and its expansion and organisation was an immense achievement by any standards, especially when contemporary opinion held that women were neither competent to do most male jobs nor capable of working with each other. The Legion's work in the war, by the end of which 80 per cent of the jobs formerly done by men had been taken over by women must have had much to do with the realisation that it was impossible to deny women the franchise any longer.

Her public work did not stop with the end of the war. She found work for disabled ex-Servicemen, she became one of the first women magistrates, during the Depression she helped to found and was the moving spirit of the Personal Service League, and she revivified the Women's Legion as the Second World War loomed. Her books include a life of her father, Henry Chaplin, a collection of fairy stories, the edited correspondence of her predecessor the third Marchioness (Frances Anne) and Disraeli, and her own memoirs, *Retrospect*.

As a gardener alone her life would have been worth recording. Few people with her limited experience – until she took over Mount Stewart, there had only been the garden at the Londonderry hunting box, Springfield – would have dared to embark on such wholesale re-landscaping, such bold uprootings and grand designs, or would have been able to transform themselves into experts in the midst of a busy life. Today the Mount Stewart gardens (now owned by the National Trust), with their luxuriant, stylish and original planting, are deservedly famous and a place of pilgrimage for gardeners in Northern Ireland.

Edith was one of those people whose impact and charm are immediate. Her circle of friends was enormous, she was the confidante of many at the heart of politics, and her judgement was shrewd. Everyone who talked of her to me invariably mentioned three things: the force of her personality, her kindness, and her gaiety. 'What lovely fun!' was one of her most characteristic remarks. She could terrify, she was conscious of her social position and ambitious for her husband and daughters, and on occasion she could be outspoken almost to the point of rudeness – 'disconcertingly frank' said *The Times* in her obituary – but there was nothing petty or mean about her. She was incapable of bearing a grudge and anyway infinitely preferred liking people. Perhaps her greatest quality was that she was never afraid – of people, of things, of doing what she wanted, of taking control of her own life. Most of all, she was not afraid of loving. Ultimately, her greatest creation of all was her marriage and it was here that her courage, faith and will show most clearly.

She believed in the Christian ideal of marriage. She believed also that a marriage should be deeply loving, and she was determined that there would be great love in her own. Many another Edwardian society beauty who found herself married to a philanderer might have become soured, unhappy, suffered a demoralising loss of self-esteem or slipped gradually into discreet affairs of her own. Indeed, Edith must have seen plenty of examples of all these around her.

She was determined to preserve not just the facade of her marriage but its reality, which to her meant the continuing mutual and profound love of herself and her husband. If this involved overlooking his transgressions, so be it: she was never afraid to forgive him and she poured out love upon him with the same wholeheartedness with which she showered her family and friends with presents. Essentially affectionate and sweet-natured, conscious always of what he owed her, he responded; all their lives, even at their worst moments, their marriage was living tissue and in the hundreds upon hundreds of letters that each wrote to the other, there is no mistaking the true voice of love – sometimes loud and clear, sometimes distant or anguished, but always there. As she told him after almost forty years: 'I have never loved anyone but your darling self'.

The last years of her life were characterised by the same courage and generosity of spirit she had always shown. To Winston Churchill, with whom Charley had had such political differences, she made a reconciliatory and affectionate gesture, offering to lend him Charley's ancestral Star and Garter for the Coronation. 'I shall feel it an honour to wear the insignia which belonged to Castlereagh and to all his successors including Charley himself,' responded Churchill.

In 1957 she was found to have cancer. She had been travelling backwards and forwards to London regularly, chiefly to see friends; now, she combined these visits with radiotherapy. It was painful and nauseating, but complaints and illness, she thought, were not fit subjects for conversation, still less was self-pity, and she never mentioned her illness even when she was clearly suffering. She held her eightieth birthday party at Londonderry House on December 3, 1958; Harold Macmillan – the seventh Prime Minister to be one of her close friends – was guest of honour. The cancer had by now attacked her spine and she had to take cortisone, but the pain and unpleasantness of the disease were treated with the same bravery and insouciance with which, as a small girl, she had set her pony at the highest obstacles. She went on working for the Red Cross until, finally, she was confined to bed, when daughters, grandchildren and friends came to tea or supper in her bedroom. The presents and the letters continued to flow. 'I was so delighted to get your letter and your card and your lovely [birthday] present,' wrote Macmillan on February 14, adding, in words that any one of her innumerable friends could have echoed: 'I am most grateful for all these and indeed for the many kindnesses and affection you have shown me for so many years . . .'

She died where she would have wanted to, in the house she loved, Mount Stewart, on April 23, 1959. She is buried beside Charley, her beloved, in Tir N'an Og – the Land of the Ever Young.

Bibliography

Memoirs, Sir Almeric Fitzroy; Hutchinson, 1925

Anthony Eden, by Robert Rhodes James; Weidenfeld and Nicolson, 1986

As We Were, by E. F. Benson, Longman 1930

Baldwin, by Roy Jenkins; Collins, 1987

Behind the Screen, by Sam Goldwyn; Grant Richards, 1924

Britain in the Nineteen Twenties, by Noreen Branson; Weidenfeld and Nicolson, 1975

The Cause, by Ray Strachey; G. Bell and Sons, 1928

Chips: The Diaries of Sir Henry Channon, edited by Robert Rhodes James; Weidenfeld and Nicolson, 1967

Clever Hearts, by Hugh and Mirabel Cecil; Victor Gollancz, 1990

The Court of St James's, by E. S. Turner; Michael Joseph, 1959

The Curragh Incident, by Sir James Ferguson of Kilkerran; Faber & Faber, 1964

Daisy, Princess of Pless, by Herself; John Murray, 1928

The Decline and Fall of the British Aristocracy, by David Cannadine; Yale University Press, 1990

The Diaries of Lady Cynthia Asquith 1915–18; Century, 1968

The Diaries of Sir Robert Bruce Lockhart, 1915–38, edited by Kenneth Young; Macmillan, 1973

The Diary of Beatrice Webb, Vol. Four 1924–43, edited by Norman and Jeanne MacKenzie; The Wheel of Life, Virago Press, 1985

A Diary With Letters, Thomas Jones; Oxford University Press, 1954

The Duchess of Devonshire's Ball, by Sophia Murphy; Sidgwick and Jackson, 1984

A Durable Fire: The Letters of Duff and Diana Cooper, 1913–50, edited by Artemis Cooper; Collins, 1983

The Dukes, by Brian Masters; Blond and Briggs, 1977

Edwardians in Love, by Anita Leslie; Hutchinson, 1972

End of an Era: Letters and Journals of Sir Alan Lascelles, 1887–1920, edited by Duff Hart-Davis; Hamish Hamilton, 1986

F. E., The Life of the First Earl of Birkenhead, by his son; Eyre and Spottiswoode, 1959

The First World Disarmament Conference 1932–33 and Why it Failed, Philip Noel-Baker, Pergamon Press, 1979

The First World War, 1914–18; by Lt Col. à Court Repington; Constable, 1920

Frederick Edwin, Earl of Birkenhead, by his son Thornton Butterworth, 1933

Freddy Lonsdale, by Frances Donaldson; Heinemann, 1957

Gladys Duchess of Marlborough, by Hugo Vickers; Weidenfeld and Nicolson, 1979

The Glitter and The Gold, by Consuelo Balsan; Heinemann, 1953

The Glittering Prizes, by William Camp; MacGibbon and Kee 1960

George VI, by Sarah Bradford; Weidenfeld and Nicolson, 1989

Göring, a biography, by David Irving; Macmillan, 1989

Gossip, by Andrew Barrow; Hamish Hamilton, 1978

Go Spin You Jade, Studies in the Emancipation of Women, by D. L. Hobman; Watts, 1957

Great Hostesses, by Brian Masters; Constable, 1982

The Great Landowners of Great Britain and Ireland, by John Bateman; Augustus M. Kelley, New York, 1973 (Fourth Edition 1883, Harrison)

Harold Nicolson, by James Lees-Milne; Chatto and Windus, 1980

Henry Chaplin, a Memoir, by Edith Londonderry; Macmillan, 1926

Hitler's Interpreter, by Dr Paul Schmidt; Heinemann, 1951

The Holy Fox: a biography of Lord Halifax, by Andrew Roberts; Weidenfeld and Nicolson, 1991

I Fight to Live, by Robert Boothby; Camelot Press, 1947

Impressions and Memories, by Lord Ribblesdale; Cassell, 1927

'In a Lifetime full . . .', by Peggy Wakehurst; privately printed, 1989

John Buchan, a Memoir, by William Buchan; Buchan and Enright, 1982

J. Ramsay MacDonald, by Austen Morgan; Manchester University Press, 1987

J. Ramsay MacDonald, by Mary Agnes Hamilton; Jonathan Cape, 1929

Julian Grenfell, by Nicholas Mosley; Weidenfeld and Nicolson, 1976

King Edward VIII, by Philip Ziegler; Collins, 1990

King George V, by Kenneth Rose; Weidenfeld and Nicolson, 1983

The Letters of Sean O'Casey, 1910–41, edited by David Krause; Cassel, 1975

The Letters of Sidney and Beatrice Webb, Vol III. Pilgrimage, 1912–47, edited by Norman Mackenzie; Cambridge University Press, published in cooperation with the London School of Economics and Political Science

The Light of Common Day, by Diana Cooper; Rupert Hart-Davis, 1958

The Life of a Painter, by Sir John Lavery; Cassell, 1940

Lloyd George, A Diary, by Frances Stevenson, edited by A. J. P. Taylor; Hutchinson, 1971

Lloyd George, Family Letters 1885–1936, edited by Kenneth D. Morgan; University of Wales Press and O.U.P., 1973

The Londonderrys, by H. Montgomery Hyde; Hamish Hamilton, 1979

Looking Back: The Duke of Sutherland (George Granville Leveson Gower, 5th Duke); Odhams Press, 1957

Lord Esher, Journals and Letters; Nicholson and Watson, 1934

Margaret Ethel MacDonald, by J. Ramsay MacDonald; Hodder and Stoughton, 1912

Memories, by the Rt Hon. Viscount Long of Wraxall, F.R.S.; Hutchinson, 1923

Men and Horses I Have Known, by the Hon. George Lambton; Thornton Butterworth, 1924

Men, Women and Things, by the Duke of Portland; Faber and Faber, 1927

Michael Collins, by Tim Pat Coogan; Hutchinson, 1990

Millicent Duchess of Sutherland 1867–1955, by Denis Stuart; Victor Gollancz, 1982

Off The Record, by Margot Asquith; Frederick Muller, 1943

Orientations, by Sir Ronald Storrs; Ivor Nicholson and Watson, 1937

Ottoline at Garsington, edited by Robert Gathorne-Hardy; Faber and Faber, 1974

Ourselves and Germany, by the 7th Lord Londonderry; Robert Hale, 1938

The Passing Years, by Lord Willoughby de Broke; Constable, 1924

Personal Letters of King Edward VII, edited by Lt. Col. J.P.C. Sewell; Hutchinson, 1931

The Pocket Venus, by Henry Blyth; Weidenfeld and Nicolson, 1966

Private Palaces, by Christopher Simon Sykes; Chatto and Windus, 1985

The Proud Tower, by Barbara Tuchman; Hamish Hamilton, 1966

A Radical Life, by Mervyn Jones; Hutchinson, 1991

Ramsay MacDonald, by David Marquand; Jonathan Cape, 1977

Recollections, by John Morley; Macmillan, 1917

Recollections of Three Reigns, by Sir Frederick Ponsonby; Eyre and Spottiswoode, 1951

Reminiscences, by Lady Randolph Churchill; Edward Arnold, 1908

Retrospect, by Edith Londonderry; Frederick Muller, 1938

Rose and Crown, by Sean O'Casey; Macmillan, 1952

A Scrap Screen, by Alice Buchan; Hamish Hamilton, 1979

She Came of Decent People, by Olga Pyne Clarke; Pelham Books, 1985

Sir Almeric Fitzroy; Hutchinson, 1925

This Man Ribbentrop, by Dr Paul Schwarz; Julian Messner Inc, New York, 1943

Vanderbilts and Their Fortunes, by E. P. Hoyt; Frederick Muller, 1963

We Danced All Night, by Barbara Cartland; Hutchinson, 1971

What I Left Unsaid, by Daisy Princess of Pless; Cassell, 1936

Winston S. Churchill, 1922–39, by Martin Gilbert; Heinemann, 1976

Winston S. Churchill, by Randolph Churchill, Vol. II; Heinemann, 1967

Women's Suffrage and Party Politics in Brtain, 1866–1914, by Constance Rover; Routledge and Kegan Paul, 1967

The World Crisis, 1911–14, by Winston S. Churchill; Thornton Butterworth, 1923

Index